The Intentional Community Movement

Kennikat Press
National University Publications
Series in American Studies

General Editor
James P. Shenton
Professor of History, Columbia University

The Intentional Community Movement

Building a New Moral World

MARGUERITE BOUVARD

National University Publications
Kennikat Press • 1975
Port Washington, N. Y. • London

Manufactured in the United States of America

Published by
KENNIKAT PRESS CORP.
Port Washington, N.Y./London

Library of Congress Cataloging in Publication Data

Bouvard, Marguerite.
    The intentional community movement.

    (National university publications)
    Includes bibliographical references and index.
    1. Collective settlements — United States —
History.
I. Title.
HX653.B6   1975   335'.9'73   74-80593
ISBN 0-8046-9100-2

TO MY HUSBAND.....
    AND OUR SMALL COMMUNITY

CONTENTS

INTRODUCTION   3

Chapter One   18
THE SEARCH FOR COMMUNITY

Chapter Two   36
RELIGIOUS COMMUNITIES

Chapter Three   87
*ANARCHISM, DECENTRALISM, AND THE
NEW RURAL COMMUNITIES*

Chapter Four   130
A MODERN UTOPIA

Chapter Five   189
CONCLUSION

NOTES   200

INDEX   205

The Intentional Community Movement

With grateful acknowledgment to the Radcliffe Institute for Independent Study, under whose auspices this study was conducted

INTRODUCTION

This book was conceived in the fall of 1969. It happened at
the end of a two-hour seminar I was directing on the topic of
Plato's *Republic*. As we were winding up our discussion, one
of my students exclaimed wistfully, "Oh, that was a beautiful
book!" This was clearly a change in attitude from students I
had known over the years. Usually Plato's *Republic* with its
vision of a well-knit community cemented by common purpose and mutuality arouses some heated opposition. I decided
to investigate this new hunger for community which was to
become the major goal of a significant number of young
adults in the late sixties and early seventies.

I was well acquainted with the intentional communities
founded in the late thirties and forties in the United States.
The urge to form small societies in order to realize a set of
purposes differing from the broader social context has constituted a continuous strand in human history. Yet, until the
present it has never expanded to include such a large number
of people and to constitute a major alternative lifestyle rather
than a marginal movement. Today intentional communities
are being formed in all parts of the United States, from the
Eastern seaboard to the West Coast. Most of the new com-

munities are rural, although urban groups such as Walden Three and the Reba Place Fellowship exist. More typical of the urban areas are the new communal, as opposed to biological, families which have sprung up in response to the loneliness and pressures of urban life in the United States.

Under the auspices of the Radcliffe Institute, I spent a year traveling around the country, living with different communities and sharing their daily lives. Although communities are not anxious for exposure to the broader society, I was received with warmth and courtesy wherever I visited. Because there are literally thousands of these small communities, I decided to focus on some of the most important types of groups rather than examine all of them. I chose this path in the hope that my study would inspire further investigations.

Among the purposes of my study are the desires to dispel the widespread misconceptions of the intentional community movement and also to render this phenomenon more visible to the broader society. When questioned, many people today define intentional communities as communes[*] where free sex and drugs are the main focus of daily life. Because of this negative image of community efforts, the casual observer is apt to regard these efforts with hostility. This is not a book about sex or hippies but about serious people in search of themselves and a new way of life.

If members of the broader society have reservations about the community movement, this caution is returned by the new communitarians. They welcome visitors as possible recruits to a new way of life, but they have taken considerable pains to protect themselves from the mass media and the intruding desire to sensationalize their life in common. Visitors must write ahead and state their purpose before receiving permission to visit an intentional community. Communitarians generally devote the majority of their time to community affairs and have few hours to answer questions and shepherd visitors

---

[*] Communes are free as opposed to blood-related families. Intentional communities as defined by the Federation of Intentional Communities must include a minimum of three families and also common economic, spiritual and cultural institutions. See p. 100.

about. Also, given the small size of the communities, the possibility that visitors might outnumber the membership is a very real one. Besides the sensation seekers, communitarians avoid social scientists. The ground for this reticence is the desire to prevent definitive descriptions of their attempts while they are still in the stage of experimentation. Also, they fear what they call the "exploitation" of their daily life.

The thousands of miniature societies which exist peacefully in the interstices of American life remain invisible to the broader society. Few people except immediate neighbors are aware of their existence or of the extent of the community movement. But the movement as a whole communicates internally in a thoroughly spontaneous manner. There are conferences and workshops, both regional and national, a few times a year, and there are newsletters which connect the members of various groups. Until recently these have been mimeographed and their circulation strictly limited. Currently there are two publications regularly scheduled for nationwide distribution. However, since their focus is strictly practical—farming, construction tips, and techniques for working out membership prob lems—they are of interest to a fairly specific audience. Over and above the rather pedestrian problems of fertilizing an orchard or erecting a communal dwelling, intentional communities have developed many worthy experiments in education at all levels, in the shelter of troubled adolescents, and in the liberation of both sexes from their limited roles. Increased communication between intentional communities and the broader society would certainly facilitate the diffusion of new practices developed in community. By their very existence intentional communities broaden the choice of values and institutions for society as a whole, a welcome addition to any democratic society which upholds pluralism.

The new intentional communities were founded as alternative societies and therefore constitute a special form of social dissent. Before setting out on my travels, I had traced the beginnings of this movement to the tide of radicalism which swept American youth in the early sixties. At that time the United States experienced a peak expansion of its colleges and universities and enjoyed an unparalleled affluence. Going to college was as predictable for the middle class youth as finishing high school had been a generation ago. The result was a generation well versed in the techniques of social analysis and exposed from childhood to the dramatization of social problems through the mass media. There were ample causes to spark their idealism and competence: the civil rights movement in the early sixties, and later the Vietnam War. Most people will remember this period as a time of mass demonstrations, sit-ins, and peace vigils. It seemed as if all the forces calling for change had taken their cause to the streets. However, while this form of dissent was cresting, a new movement for reform was developing, quietly and unnoticed: veterans of the peace movement were pulling up stakes to found communal farms from Massachusetts to California. Instead of engaging in political activities, their younger cohorts turned to community building.

One of the most astonishing characteristics of the community movement is its complete apoliticism. Who would have guessed that the tide of political radicalism which swept young adults in the sixties would become transformed into an apolitical and peaceful program for gradual social reform? There were many veterans of the antiwar movement among the older communitarians I interviewed. They had dismissed their former activities to the point of refusing to talk or even think about them. The younger communitarians were totally immersed in the tasks at hand: putting up a fence or arranging the schedule for the care of the community's children.

Communitarians are "doers," sober activists on behalf of their way of life. While their radical predecessors may have spent their energies in social analysis and communication, editing and distributing underground newspapers, today's social reformers never write or talk about reform. In building their small societies, establishing land trusts and cooperatives, they are attempting to provide living models to the broader society. They are saying, "We have something that works!"

Quietly and without fanfare the new communities are clearing and farming land which they hold in common. They market their produce through cooperatives, and the returns from their venture go directly into the communal treasury. Fruits and vegetables for the community table are preserved and stored in root cellars that the community has built. Very few of these groups own expensive appliances for the needs of their daily existence. Ecology is certainly an important goal for these groups, but it is not only the concern for the balance of nature that leads them to consume very little energy. Communitarians enjoy every minute of their life. For them harnessing solar energy, laying the foundations for a communal dwelling, or even hollowing out a root cellar is a satisfying challenge. The rewards are immediate. An enthusiastic member of a Virginia community exclaimed to me, "We like the feeling of working on the land, watching things grow, and eating our own food."

The self-sufficiency of the homesteading community, its thrift, and its simple pleasures of handicrafts and square dancing evoke the American past. Even the heroes of the rural branch of the community movement have their roots in the past. Ralph Borsodi and Mildred Loomis, pillars of the School of Living and founders of the *Green Revolution* magazine, opened their homesteading school before the Great Depression. In his eighties Dr. Borsodi is a familiar figure at communitarian conferences and a frequent contributor to the movement's periodicals and seminars. Ralph Borsodi and Mildred Loomis are advocates of the small, self-sufficient homesteading community as an antidote to some of the by-products of industrialization such as urban blight and crime. They do not oppose industrialization per se, but its concentration. In other words, like all communitarians they advocate the decentralization of society and its reordering in a federation of small, self-sufficient communities.

It is their unique blend of the past with a thrust towards the future which lends rural communities their special flavor. Farm communities are the scenes of the contemporary sexual revolution as men and women seek to broaden and redefine their goals. Housekeeping, farming, and outside jobs are shared equally by all members. In community it is a widespread practice to categorize and allocate chores on the basis of time required and job characteristics rather than along sexual lines. Thus, the metas, or nurses, of the communal offspring at Twin Oaks are not necessarily the women in the community, and the maintenance crew for farm implements are not necessarily men. The universalization of roles and skills is one of the most dramatic achievements of the community movement. The expansion of sex roles in community will help enlarge the choice of careers available to adults and benefit the contemporary search of both sexes for new identities. Women especially have a greater opportunity to explore their abilities and interests than in the broader society where they are restricted to well-defined occupations and roles. However, this does not mean that there will be a rigid recasting of roles. All communities maintain a division of labor and there will always be men who prefer their more traditional roles and women who prefer child rearing or housekeeping to the construction site.

There are two factors which render the small community an eminently appropriate setting for social reform. Sheltered from the public eye and free of traditional cultural norms, it constitutes a boost to individual experimentation. While potential employers in schools, government offices, and industry are drawing up quotas for female employees, considerable time may elapse. In community, change takes place rapidly and easily. A female member does not have to face the barriers of the local union if she wishes to become a carpenter. She simply signs up for a construction task when chores are allocated. Nor does anyone exclaim at the sight of a man tending babies or a woman laying down tiles on a roof. The communal environment is benevolent and protective. The tension and doubt which attend all persons engaged in social innovation are mitigated by the support of all members of the community.

Homesteading activities are only part of the reality of intentional community. Communities are also laboratories for social change, and a new generation is being socialized within the community culture. These youngsters experience the

excitement of the free school[*] provided for them by the community and use the community itself as their school. They are
active in the kitchen, planning menus or cleaning up, and
plunge wholeheartedly into community affairs. They are the
children of the community, not of an identifiable couple.
Perhaps even more astounding than the elimination of the
traditional nuclear family based upon biological relationships
are the attitudes of the community parents. A young woman
at the Twin Oaks community, who has just given birth to Seran,
the third communal baby, is enthusiastic about collective parent-
hood. She claims delight at sharing the joys of the new baby
and relief at sharing the responsibility. None of the children
of the new age will experience private property or the nuclear
family. The community is convinced that its children will be
both wiser and happier for being raised in their small society.

With few exceptions, the communities I visited had children of all ages. They seemed to thrive on the attention prof-
fered by so many adults and on the freedom and responsibility which are theirs in community. At Twin Oaks adulthood begins at the age of thirteen. From that time the
young adult will participate in decision making and chores
on a full-time basis. None of the communities I have studied
seems to have any problems with adolescent youngsters. This
alone would seem to indicate the success of the community
as family.

Breaking down the barriers between people and constructing intimate and enduring relationships with each and
all are what the new communities are all about. The Anabaptist communities of the Bruderhof[†] and the Reba Place
Fellowship are church communities. Their essence is the
mutual commitment of the membership, both in the existential
sense of responsibility for each other's welfare and in their
covenantal relationship as a fellowship of believers. It is the

---

[*] Free schools were established in the United States in the sixties as an outgrowth
of the counter culture. They are typically non-graded and unstructured. Practical
activities such as gardening or cooking are included in the core of the curriculum.
[†] Bruderhof, the German name of the Society of Brothers. Members use both
names when referring to their community.

focus on mutuality, the organic conception of society in which the whole is greater than its combined parts, which links the purely secular and the religious communities. Anabaptist groups, the rural anarchist communities, and the behaviorist communities have differing goals and philosophic foundations. However, they share the search for a new spirit which will enable men to live together in harmony, in a new balance of "I" and "we."

Among the most interesting community experiments are the Free Church communities. They are unique in their combination of ancient lineage and religious and social radicalism. The Reba Place Fellowship and the Society of Brothers trace their origins to the rise of Anabaptism in the sixteenth century. Yet, they are as radical today as were the early Anabaptist communities. Then, as today, when people thought of religion and religious commitment, they thought of the great denominations and of formal worship. However, in the Free Church communities daily life is worship, a life described by the Sermon on the Mount: a total commitment to Christ and the mutual responsibility of the members. Upon entering the community a member pledges his life to Christ and to each member as his brother. In practice this means that each member bears responsibility for the life of the community and participates in both governance and prophecy. The members practice the Christian communism depicted in the Sermon on the Mount; each member relinquishes all his property and earnings to the community and receives his daily needs from the group. This form of communalism is a distinguishing characteristic of Anabaptism. The true church is an intentional community, sharply demarcated from the broader society by its daily practice of Christianity and by its pacifism. Operating within a secular society and rejecting power, these groups constitute one of the oldest countercultures in American society.

Koinonia Partners in Americus, Georgia, is also a Free Church community. However, it is distinguished by its intense involvement with the problems of the broader society. It has defined its task as the reconciliation of clashing interests in the contemporary United States; black and white, rich and poor. Missionary aims are also characteristic of Free Church communities, and they devote considerable energy to outreach. Koinonia Partners includes a communications ministry which spreads the radical ideas of the Gospel to the far corners of the United States. Koinonia and Reba Place perform various services for the broader society. Reba Place has served as a half-way house and shelter for troubled persons and whole families. In contrast, the Society of Brothers has experienced a pendular swing from outreach to a focus on its inner life throughout its stormy history.

While religious communities are distinguished from other small societies by their philosophies, they have many features in common with rural communities and behaviorist groups. The most salient similarity is their belief that mutual responsibility, the cement of true community, can be achieved only on a small scale. Their visions of the broader society include a federation of small, self-sufficient communities.

With the exception of the Society of Brothers, both the religious and secular communities regard themselves as experimental communities in which the pattern of daily life is regulated by the consensus of all and by a set of flexible procedures. At the Reba Place Fellowship forms of worship, means of gaining subsistence, and governance are subject to change at all times. Some of the members have even experimented with family structure and the socialization of children. Among the bases for the fluidity of institutions and procedures arc the Free Church's abhorrence of power. The true church must live in the present and therefore cannot plan for the future. Within anarchist communities, consensus and the flexibility it entails are valued as a means of avoiding power in human relationships. Even the Skinnerians at Twin Oaks who have a blueprint for their heaven on earth, are constantly changing the organization of their daily life.

Another reason for the fluidity of life in community is the hunger of communitarians for authenticity. They are trying to permeate their daily existence with their ideals, and fear that a too rigid institutionalization of their life in common will create a gap between their values and their daily life. It is the desire to live a moral existence, to practice their ideals, which has inspired many adults today to pull up stakes and join intentional communities.

In its search for a new mutuality, the intentional community movement as a whole seeks a radical transformation of spirit in contemporary man. All communities, not only the Free Church groups, believe that the search for a better life is not a political one but revolves around the spirit that informs contemporary institutions. For Koinonia Partners, for instance, the real conflict over racism is fought in men's hearts rather than in the courts or legislatures. For many of the rural communities, the establishment of a society in which there are no rich or poor and in which everyone participates in decision making is evidence of the flowering of a new spirit. The optimism and confidence of these groups is all the more remarkable when one considers the problems of the broader social context: the winding down of a long and painful war, racial problems, and international crisis. While the optimism is philosophically grounded, it is also born of the solid achievement of these groups as they develop their life in common.

The demands of community are rigorous, and the communal lifestyle is fundamentally unappealing to many people in a modern society which places great emphasis on individualism. Many casual observers of religious communities, in particular, express concern at the possibility of losing individual identity within the collective. In a very real sense, community living requires the member to renounce both property and profession as a means of individual distinction and as an expression of personality. For the Society of Brothers the Christian lifestyle means the death of the ego and its rebirth in the community as the Kingdom of God, and work as service rather than as individual achievement. The chief incentives of communities are the welfare of the group and its membership. Certainly, life in community demands that each member be concerned with the needs of all other members as if they were his own and requires that the burdens as well as the benefits will be shared by all. The mutual commitment of the membership can be compared to that of marriage. This in itself helps keep the membership from growing more rapidly than people can be absorbed. It also limits the appeal of membership to a certain kind of individual. Only the very strong will be able to pull up stakes and adopt a wholly new way of life, renouncing possessions and worldly success. These may be persons who have experienced conversion or a sudden change in their life. Regardless of whether he was born in community or joined at a later stage in life, the typical member of the Free Church community is not the pale, colorless person one imagines as living a life of self-effacement. Communal living has many rewards for its devotees: the warm mutual support of the membership and the joy of participating in an exciting adventure. This group support seems to have given the members a feeling of peace and self-confidence. When I observed the members of the Reba Place Fellowship engaged in a vigorous group discussion or pitching in to prepare a community meal, I had a real sense that in losing self, one gains a much larger self.

The membership of the Free Church communities is extraordinarily heterogeneous. For instance, the Society of Brothers includes former Catholics, Jews, Protestants, and Hutterites. The socioeconomic backgrounds of the members are as diverse as their religious backgrounds. On the other hand, the anarchist communities which dot the rural areas of the United States have a rather homogeneous membership. Although the age span of rural communitarians is broadening to include adults in their forties and fifties, the majority are white, middle class adults in their early twenties and thirties. Some have renounced a profession in teaching or engineering and others are college dropouts, but as a whole they seem to have put their former occupations out of mind. Rural communitarians are very practical people. They are interested, above all, in the techniques of farming and construction and will spend hours discussing mulching or preparing an orchard. They are also intensely interested in child socialization and sex roles. Instead of current events or politics, the drama of interpersonal relations occupies them. As a whole, I found them slightly boring and was amused at the image their immediate neighbors had formed of them. Most towns which include intentional communities regard the latter as groups of exotic and unwashed individuals. Nothing could be farther from the truth. Rural communitarians are rather average, down-to-earth people. The manner in which they share the joys and burdens of child rearing and housekeeping is admirable, and they are pleasant people. However, one expects more than these homely qualities of persons who are pioneering social ventures.

Perhaps it is the absence of truly inspiring visions which causes one to feel that something is missing within rural communities. Even though these groups demonstrate a peaceful and equitable way of life to the rest of society, their goals do not seem to constitute a real challenge. Most people need more to capture their interest and imagination than building a pleasurable, nonpolluting, and self-sufficient existence. The combination of a lack of higher purpose and a complete inner focus which characterizes these groups leads one to suspect that groups as well as individuals can display egotism. One of the tests of a community's effectiveness lies in the nature of its communication with other groups and its relevance to the broader society. Communities which have links to the broader society, either by constantly incorporating new recruits, like the Society of Brothers, or by serving society in some way, have demonstrated the greatest vigor. The only contacts with the outside world which most rural communities maintain are with other intentional communities at their yearly conference or at workshops on community living. Although they pay taxes and abide by local regulations, for all practical purposes they live at the very fringe of contemporary society. This isolation is revealed in the narrow range of their concerns. Thus, there is a real danger that the self-imposed solitude of rural communities may degenerate into the enclavism which characterizes many exclusive middle class suburbs.

If communication with the broader society is one measure of community, the ability to accommodate several interests within the small society constitutes another test of effectiveness. Many rural communities find it either impossible or unnecessary to compromise a variety of interests. On the contrary, they seem to aim at homogeneity and to solve the problem of dissension by either fission or the departure of dissenting members. The Twin Oaks community, one of the oldest and most successful of the behaviorist groups, has recently split into two. Although this move was part of the blueprint for the future, it did not occur in response to growth, as intended. It was an adjustment to irreconcilable differences among the membership. Rural communities reason that in case of differences among the members, the opportunity is always available either to find or establish a congenial group elsewhere. However, in choosing the easier way out, they avoid one of the key problems in society, the compromise of interests in a way that satisfies man's yearning for freedom and justice. Certainly, members are free to join or to leave communities at any time, and this fact plus the small size of communities with their face-to-face relationships provides some protection for the dissenting individual. However, one questions whether this is a sufficient guarantee for persons accustomed to a democratic society with its system of courts and legislation to protect individual rights. It seems that the Free Church communities alone, with the exception of the Society of Brothers, have managed to maintain a genuine pluralism and respect for the individual within their boundaries.

In the past, many intentional communities failed, either because their small scale rendered them economically vulnerable or because their experimental nature caused a drop in membership. One of the clearest indications of the success of the movement is the ability of individual communities to endure as economic units and to increase their membership. Curiously enough, the Free Church communities, which place livelihood at the bottom of their list of priorities, are experiencing economic growth. The Society of Brothers recently decided to cut back its operations in Community Playthings because it feared the impact of material success on its spiritual life. The Reba Place Fellowship is expanding steadily and integrating new members with great ease despite their heterogeneity. The combined salaries of its membership seem more than adequate for the support of the group. Although Free Church communities regard work as service and have eliminated economic incentives, their members are nevertheless highly productive.

The religious communities have a unique record of endurance in their long history. Their goals and their mutual commitment seem to evoke unusual dedication. The Society of Brothers escaped Nazi Germany and endured the difficulties of life in Paraguay before settling down in its various American locations. Koinonia Partners continued to proclaim its message of reconciliation throughout the dark years of the economic boycott and physical attack visited on them by the surrounding town of Americus.

The viability of communities is a function of their structure as well as of their goals. Flexibility of structure combined with a firm commitment to the purposes of the group have enabled Koinonia Partners and Reba Place to survive through difficult conditions and, in the case of Koinonia, in the face of overwhelming external pressure.

In contrast, the anarchist communities in rural areas are extremely vulnerable to collapse because of the lack of clearly defined goals or structure. One indication of the weakness of these groups is the high turnover in membership. One can visit a rural community two or three times during the same year and find a completely different group of members. A member of Twin Oaks commented on his feelings when he returned from a period of work outside the community: he claimed that he felt like a stranger rather than a member. The level of commitment which fosters such a turnover leaves much to be desired. However, there are differences among the many rural communities. Springtree community was founded

by a group of adults with school-age children. They intended
to combine farming with the establishment of a free college.
There have been some changes in membership, but the core
group of founders remains, and their free college has become
a reality.

Conflicting assessments can be made of the new intentional
communities. In an age when the energy resources available to
the world are dwindling and pollution has become an international problem, rural communities are admirable models of
alternative, low-consumption, non-pollution-producing
societies. On the other hand, one can also wonder at the ease
with which these middle class adults have forgotten the needs
of the large group of poor and dispossessed in the broader
society. By cutting off all communication with the broader
society and its problems, the movement practices escapism.
However, because of the youth of the community movement
and its experimental state, it is hardly fair to pass a definitive
judgment upon it. Building a new social order which will
foster a sense of mutual responsibility among its members
is the primary goal of this movement. It is a goal we cannot
ignore.

ONE

THE SEARCH FOR COMMUNITY

Not since the heyday of the early nineteenth century, when utopian colonies like Oneida, New Harmony, Brook Farm, and Icaria Speranza established their visions of a new social order, has America experienced such a vast array of community endeavors. Twentieth-century intentional communities made their modest appearance in the thirties, as alternatives to the competition and economic insecurity characteristic of American society in the postdepression years. Communities like Celo in North Carolina, the Vale in Yellow Springs, and Koinonia in Georgia were established in search of mutuality and cooperation and in the hope of inspiring similar experiments throughout the United States.

In the late fifties there were only about a dozen intentional communities in existence. Yet, a decade later the communitarian movement burgeoned and now includes hundreds of homesteading communities, thousands of urban intentional communities, and dozens of spiritually oriented groups. Within the tiny state of Vermont, there are at least five hundred known communities, collectives, and communes. In the United States as a whole, there are well over the 100,000 discovered by a *New York Times* survey in 1966, for the community movement is a fast-growing one. Frequent conferences sponsored by established intentional communities attract a host of new recruits, and new members flock to communities like the Brotherhood of the Spirit in Massachusetts and Summertown in Tennessee, swelling their numbers to four hundred each. Older communities such as Twin Oaks in Virginia and Heathcote in Maryland have spawned sister communities like the Springtree community and Nethers, both in Virginia. Through its announcements of the formation of new communities and the achievements of established groups, the communitarian press heralds a generation in search of new personal and social commitments.

Communitarians represent a wide range of age groups: older people who have been active in homesteading since the 1930s, former professionals in their early and mid-thirties, and young couples with small children. For the most part, however, they are young adults in their early to late twenties. The majority represent a population sector which traditionally assumes active roles in politics, business, and the professions: white middle class youth with educations ranging from one year of college to the Ph.D. They enjoy the health, leisure, and resources to experiment in modes of living denied their less affluent peers. It is tempting for many to confuse them with the dropout fringe of youth who form hippy communes and dedicate themselves to pot and collective oblivion. On the contrary, communitarians have eschewed drugs and the passive life for serious attempts to develop new cultural models and values. Their goals include new roles for men, women, and children and an entirely new set of institutions which will reflect their newly discovered humanism.

The impact of intentional communities on society is not only the attraction exercised by an alternative mode of living. Communitarians may have a more far-reaching influence than their numbers would warrant by the diffusion of new roles and practices throughout society, such as communal child rearing, communal ownership of land and certain kinds of property, the reshaping of career incentives, and the redefinition of male-female roles. One must not forget that contemporary education is greatly indebted to the nineteenth-century New Harmony communities established by Robert Owen in this country, or

19

that the movement for women's suffrage found one of its most inspired leaders in Frances Wright, a member of New Harmony. Thus, intentional communities may enrich society through the diffusion of their social innovations. They may eventually create greater heterogeneity in our political culture as a new generation of communitarians emerges which has experienced a socialization through alternative institutions and free schools. A significant number of communities have young children, and as the communitarians advance in age, an entirely new generation of children inspired by values of cooperative economics and egalitarianism will mature.

The historical circumstances surrounding the development of communal experiments have always been the exceptional ones of war, civil strife, and religious or ideological upheavals. Such conditions tend to heighten awareness of current inadequacies, to encourage new ideas for a better life and unusual efforts to realize them.

In the nineteenth century utopian communities in the United States sought refuge from the insecurities of early industrialization, and sectarian communities such as Amana, founded by the Rappites, migrated from Europe in search of a tolerant environment. Utopian communities flourished on the west coast of the United States in the late nineteenth and early twentieth century. The Llano community was formed in Los Angeles during a time of labor disturbances and economic problems, and included a thousand members at its peak. In the early nineteen hundreds a surge of protest literature and a new sense of humanitarianism inspired a host of reformers to reassess society as California became the scene of countless social experiments of a communal nature.

Today the yearning for a new order of life founded on a reawakening of community is worldwide and expressed in seemingly divergent trends. However, these are animated by a common challenge, the process of modernization created by the diffusion of industrialization throughout the world. Technological advance has produced the opposing trends of recognition of the relatedness of humanity while reinforcing the techniques of coercion at the disposal of the nation states which divide humanity. Thus, the search for community is occurring at opposite ends of the world in response to the varying claims of nationhood, statehood, and modernization. In the new African and Asian states, nations must be created as the most important community at the expense of tribal and religious communities. The Ibo must become a Nigerian, and emergent states such as Bangladesh strive to eliminate all lesser loyalties in the attempt to carve out a homogeneous national community. But still another pattern in the search for community is the development of experiments in communal living in China, Peru, and Tanzania as part of a total plan for modernizing developing societies and reducing the hiatus between the rapidly modernizing towns and the isolated countryside. In the industrialized nation states of the West which achieved nationhood and modernization sequentially, there is a new awareness of ethnicity, a reawakening of religious experience, and an entirely new concern with creating viable replacements for the lost primary groups of the extended family and the small political unit.

Contemporary intentional communities in the United States constitute a response to needs experienced in a vast, highly modernized, Western political society. A reexamination of mutual obligation has inspired such extensive social experimentation, a problem which embraces both a crisis in the political order and a crisis involving the grounds of political obligation and concepts of social justice. Communitarians are not only concerned with building alternate models for social and economic relations but also with shaping the values which inform our political culture and provide legitimacy for the political order. They are addressing an eternal problem of man in society: the search for purpose and for mutual support which is the crux of community. It is a concern which lies at the very core of political philosophy and was dramatically raised by Rousseau in his quest to resolve both the need for organic ties among men and an untrammeled sense of self.

The Search for the Polis

Contemporary communitarians are fleeing from the vastness and impersonality of a highly industrialized society. In their attempts to construct what they describe as islands of peace and purpose in a turbulent society, they are drawing upon the rich heritage of Western political thought—specifically, the view of man as a social being who must participate in community in order to fulfill his nature. They have rejected the utilitarian premises of Hobbes, Locke, and the Enlightenment thinkers with their concepts of men as self-contained atoms, in favor of Plato, Aristotle, and Rousseau, philosophers of men in community. They share with these theorists the basic propositions that man is inherently sociable, a political animal, that he is basically and universally reasonable, and that there is an intimate connection between politics and ethics in society.

One of the founders of the Walden Three community was inspired to establish that community by reading Plato's *Republic*. However, his deep interest in this treatise on political philosophy was not inspired by classical philosophy as such, but rather by the poetic image of a well-integrated political community. In the *Republic* the individual is in harmony with society rather than being alienated from it, and because ethics and politics are intertwined in the polis, the whole man flourishes.

In a manner reminiscent of classical political thought, communitarians have emphasized participation, small size, and agreement on values as the essence of community. Like Plato, they believe that humaneness is possible only in a small community where men can live according to their concept of the good life. Plato argued that only in the state can man achieve the highest good, which he terms justice, a harmonious union of individuals in mutual concern. The ordering of persons for the common good through the polis has an inner dimension and refers to the possibility of man's dignity, of his living in the fullness of his moral attributes. In his paradigm of the *Republic*, Plato unfolds the intimate connection between man's spirit and the institutions he devises for his polis. Justice has an internal as well as an external dimension and is based upon the inner order of the soul, a hierarchy of values to guide our actions. In a dialogue on justice which has great relevance to contemporary society, Socrates points out to Thrasymachus that unlimited self-seeking does not bring happiness. The art of living well is the function of the soul, which must ascertain ends and determine how they are to be attained. Without the soul as guide, man will destroy himself, and even Thrasymachus, apologist of the right of the strong, is forced to conclude that life is not worth living when the principles which should order it are in disarray. Just as in ancient Athens, persons who form intentional communities today define happiness as the fulfillment of man's humanity.

While communitarians mirror Plato's concern for the congruence of social purpose and humane values, they also stress the necessity of participation for man's well-being. Aristotle defined citizenship in a functional manner, as participation in the rights of governing and judging. However, according to this definition, participation requires that the political community be small enough for citizens to know each other well. The concomitance of vast size with social conformity, and the glaring gap between the emphasis on priorities of the national interest and individual dignity, are defined by many young communitarians as primary issues in the contemporary world. Although advances in communication have facilitated the orientation of a large population to common political symbols and values, they have not satisfied the need of these youth for fulfillment through participation and a genuine communication between selves.

Intentional communities slake the thirst of their members for participation and for the management of their own destiny. The new communities devote many hours to deliberation and the resolution of great and small issues: how to select new members, whether to use chemical or organic fertilizers on their crops, how to allocate cars and other community resources, and how to rotate chores. In community both participation and responsibility are universal and visible. Members of Walden Three assert that small-scale and extensive contact among community members, with the necessity for general assent to keep the community functioning, is a more adequate guarantee of freedom than the democratic process. The new intentional communities function as voluntary organizations in which the need for coercion has been replaced by an autonomous and self-chosen discipline. They have defined the balance between self and society in a radically democratic way, as one based upon consensus, a value garnered from the anarchist revival of the sixties. Like Jean Jacques Rousseau, they have established the free identification of the self with the collectivity as the ground for political obligation. However, the problem of minority rights remains. The only recourse offered to dissenters is the benevolent immediacy of direct democracy and the possibility of relinquishing membership in community.

Building upon the tradition of Western political thought, communitarians emphasize small scale, purpose, participation, and organic relations as the essence of community and the resolution of freedom and authority. Their communities are based upon shared principles, universal participation in governance, and a communion of persons freely chosen. The latter provides a sense of fellowship, a libidinal brotherhood in the flight of communitarians from the loneliness and impersonality of modern society.

The Heritage of the Past

Contemporary intentional communities are characteristic of a certain period in the social history of the United States. Their sheer numbers are a result of the communications provided by the mass media and the great mobility of the American people today. However, they constitute a strand of the utopian tradition in the United States and as such reveal many points in common with utopian communities of the nineteenth century.

Certainly, the new communities are animated by values similar to those heralded in such communities as the Owenite

Blue Springs community in Monroe County, Indiana, or the Nashoba community in Tennessee. Much like the Twin Oaks community in Virginia, the Owenite New Harmony community of the early nineteenth century was dedicated to the realization of economic equality, the universalization of skills, and equality between the sexes. Although women's suffrage was still a distant hope in the United States at that time, the women in Owenite communities were given equal rights. In several of those communities women were given the vote in legislative assemblies, in others, the right to participate in debate, and in all, widows of deceased members succeeded to rights and privileges their husbands had previously enjoyed. These Owenites abolished all special property rights previously vested in men and established coeducational institutions, a pioneering venture which attracted much attention at the time.

Perhaps they did not use the phrases "the politics of housework," "women's liberation," or "smash monogamy"; however, the nineteenth-century utopians regarded the family as institutionalized tyranny, condemning women to domestic drudgery and endless childbearing. They did not consider either sexual satisfaction or "a natural system of interpersonal relations" possible within nuclear marriage. A variety of experiments were intended to replace the couple, from early and serial marriage at New Harmony to complex marriage in the Oneida community, an institution similar to group marriage in contemporary communities.

The security of a small society compensates for the stability of social custom prevailing in the broader society. Throughout history, the small utopian community has constituted a sheltered environment in which experimentation in modes of behavior and interpersonal relations has flourished. As a concomitant with this type of freedom, utopian communities through the ages have stressed freedom of expression as well as spontaneity and openness in interpersonal relations. Self-knowledge equaled happiness for Robert Owen, or self-awareness, as modern communitarians would say. This knowledge is made available to each person through the mirror of the group and the unreserved expression of his communitarian fellows, or by "encounter" today. Communitarians believe that this knowledge will promote behavior which is aimed at the good of all.

In utopian communities single families with separate interests are replaced by the community as family with one interest. Today, as in the past, the community is frequently viewed as a substitute for the affection and security of marriage and as the primary force in the socialization of a new generation. Although separated by a century, B. F. Skinner and Robert Owen were firmly convinced that parents were too ignorant and unqualified to raise children and that this should be the job of specialists. New Harmony broke ground in establishing "infant schools" for two-year-olds modeled on the method of Pestalozzi and combined with labor in progressive doses. Today many communities have been formed around the concept of free schools: the Heathcote School of Living, Nethers, and the Springtree community.

Early communitarians regarded a cooperative economy and communal property as the chief sources of social peace and the ideal work environment. Aside from the efficiency of pooling resources and energies, work in community was arranged to provide a variety of occupations for each member. At New Harmony and Brook Farm, intellectuals engaged in farming or animal husbandry as well as education. Today a primary concern at Twin Oaks is the assignment of personalized work schedules and the calculation of labor credits. In a single day Twin Oakers may engage in farming, construction, and child care.

Like the utopians of the nineteenth century, contemporary utopians regard the road to heaven on earth as composed of a new balance of fulfilling work and leisure, new concepts of the family, including new sex roles and communal child care, a cooperative economy, and communal property. The new order in community will abolish punishment and root out all crime, dissension, and warfare.

Confronting a society plagued with dissension, communitarians have great faith in the superior method of community as the path to social peace; [1]

Beckoning those who live under the miserable anxious individual system of opposition and counteraction when they could with ease form themselves or become members of one of these associations of union, intelligence and kind feelings.

Communitarians today are heir to the problems as well as the visions of their forebears. The members of Sunrise Hill community learned the bitter lessons occasioned by lack of organization and farming skills, much as did the people at Llano in California. An overabundance of enthusiasm untempered by knowledge has plagued many communities today and in the past, with the exception of the sectarian communities, which combine agricultural skill with piety.

If the members of Sunrise Hill chafed and finally dispersed under the burden of endless discussions and eventual dissension, the Lost Tribes of Communism spawned by New Harmony also foundered under the weight of dissension. Communities in all periods of history have found that while individualism and egoism can be easily derided, they cannot be easily exorcised. Moreover, the people who flock to communities frequently feel out of place or failures in the broader society and rashly conclude that they are fitted for the world as it "ought to be." The chronicler of Sunrise Hill sadly mused that happy people do not join communities, and Robert Owen was moved to exclaim on the demise of New Harmony:[2]

If we cannot find parents who are ready and willing to educate their children to give them qualities for a community life, then when shall we have communities of united effort?

By their very nature, communities are financially fragile. The slightest misfortune can spell the end of a community, and then inevitably the verdict of failure is applied to the entire idealistic venture. Yet the reaction of communitarians to the collapse of their communities is as important as the economic or social assessment of their failure. Invariably the communitarians retain faith in community. Instead of returning to the broader society, they join other communities. In the past ex-Icarians joined the Shakers, Shakers joined the Altruria community, and one Llano veteran participated in seven communities. Today former members of Amish or Hutterite groups settle in Koinonia, and former members of Heathcote have joined the Nethers community. As in any pioneering or idealistic venture, it is the determination and hope of the membership that keeps the movement alive even when adversity strikes.

It is a characteristic of intentional communities that their real successes are visible to the broader society only after their demise. Women's suffrage, free and universal primary education, the liberation of women, free schools, and the noninstitutionalized shelter of the troubled will remain as instances of enlightened social policy when the communities which fostered them have been long forgotten. In their search for a new mutuality, new incentives for work, and new approaches to socialization, intentional communities broaden the choice of values and institutions for society as a whole.

The Flight from Society

Although the motives inspiring intentional communities are various, the movement as a whole constitutes a form of peaceful dissent from the social and political order. The community movement today represents the last swell of the wave of youthful political radicalism which crested in the sixties and receded at the end of that decade as a result of widespread disillusionment. With a few exceptions, contemporary communitarians have turned their backs on the political order, concentrating instead on the establishment of a new social and economic order.

Much as the homesteaders of the thirties, rural communitarians today flee the complexities of a vast industrial society and the congestion, crime, and loneliness of urban life. This branch of the community movement is pervaded with strains of decentralism and the anarchism propounded by Peter Kropotkin in his support of the rural villages. Kropotkin was repeatedly charged with conservatism by his contemporaries, and indeed many rural groups appear to be focused on the past rather than on the future. They seem like new wine in old bottles as they concentrate on values cherished by past generations: self-sufficiency in the necessities of life, the small economic unit, natural childbirth, and organic farming. For these people the return to rural life is intended both as a form of passing judgment on contemporary society and as a search for purity of spirit.

Communitarians are environmentalists by definition. They trace social problems to faulty institutions rather than to individual responsibility. Much as their nineteenth-century utopian antecedents, they single out private property and marriage as the main sources of distress in the broader society. An economy based upon cooperation rather than competition, and the communal ownership of property, are their answers to the social injustice and dissension that they consider endemic in the broader society. They have rejected the goals of professional success and material comfort for the ideals of sharing, equality, and ecological balance, "living in harmony with nature," as they would describe their life. Communitarians believe that these values can be most effectively achieved in rural communities based upon farming and light industry. Moreover, farming requires a broad spectrum of skills which contrasts with the specialization of functions and competences imposed by a technological society. The new farmers echo Marx's dream of an end to the alienation of man produced by the division of labor which fragments his life. They see in the homestead community the possibility of creative self-expression in many fields of activity, a total life experience.

Like the utopian socialist Robert Owen, contemporary communitarians regard marriage and private property as inextricably related evils. They see the nuclear family, isolated and self-seeking, as the source of social dissension and also of the oppression of the marriage partners. The freedom sought by communitarians includes what they define as the right of fulfilling interpersonal relations unimpeded by the burdens and tyranny of traditional marriage. As a result of widespread criticism of the nuclear family and experimentation in personal relations, the intentional communities have developed new concepts of "free" extended families and communal child rearing. They consider that children suffer a prolonged dependence in the broader society and that their education excludes work experience. In contrast, they have developed free schools and a system of child socialization which will allow the child to profit from the interest and models of several rather than one or two adults.

Sectarian communities represent a slightly different form of dissent. The Society of Brothers had its roots in the Christian social youth movement which developed in response to the turmoil of World War I in Germany and to the social problems of that period. All the Free Church communities—the Brotherhood of the Spirit, Reba Place Fellowship, and Koinonia Partners—base their separation from the broader society on a Christian counterculture with emphasis on the values of fellowship, communal living, and dedication to Christ. In order to preserve the religious authenticity of their daily lives and to serve as models for social justice, sectarian communities seek to preserve the boundaries which separate them from the larger society.

The behaviorist communities inspired by B. F. Skinner reject what they consider the "consumerism," "sexism," and "violence" of the broader society. Most of all, these communitarians dislike the concept of competition in economic life and the inequities which they see resulting from it. Each man should be able to enjoy fulfilling work and economic security, and no one should either profit from his neighbor or enjoy more than his fellows. The egalitarianism they seek and the shaping of a peaceful, productive society can be achieved through behavioral engineering as defined in Skinner's social thought. Behaviorists believe that politics is incapable of producing the good life, because all politicians, reformers included, seek power only in order to impose their views on others rather than for the good of all. Worse still, politicians can never admit their errors and therefore cannot maintain an experimental approach to problems. For Skinnerians, experiment is the only source of improvement, and that approach is possible only in a small utopian society. Unlike the rural communities which seek the simplicity of a life close to nature in reaction to a complex, modernized society, the behaviorists do not flee technology or the skills associated with it. They chafe at inefficiencies in the broader society as much as they do at crime or poverty and wish to carry the techniques of industrialization to perfection in their small society.

As a method of social reform, communitarianism is heralded by its proponents as an alternative to politics and to revolution. Because communitarians are in a state of total rebellion against society, they regard legislative reform as a mere palliative applied to a diseased social order. All intentional communities oppose violence as well as politics and therefore shun revolution. The sectarian groups in particular believe that the battle for social justice is not a political one but revolves around the spirit informing contemporary institutions, and that patterns of mutual obligation are moral issues which should be confronted in a community. By educating all men in new roads to perfection, the small community is intended to serve as a model for peaceful social change.

Paths to Perfection

By their experiments intentional communities are establishing models of perfection, a purely utopian goal. Utopian experiments are distinguished by the scope of their endeavors and by the relationship between norm and practice. They aim to actualize their theories of perfection in community life, to mold social reality to the demands of their ideas. Although contemporary intentional communities have been influenced by a greater diversity of social philosophies than their predecessors, one can distinguish three main philosophic currents which animate these small societies. Most intentional communities today are inspired by either a radical Christianity, a form of anarchism, behaviorism, or some combination of these.

Radical Christian thought has inspired community experiments since the rise of Anabaptism in Europe almost five hundred years ago. That movement was introduced in the

United States by the Hutterite communities which migrated to America in 1874 in search of freedom from state control and also by the scholarship of church historians at Goshen College.

The Free Church communities in the United States embody the distinguishing principles of the Anabaptist faith: the concept of the church as an intentional association of believing adults, freedom from governmental authority in matters of faith, pacifism, and the maintenance of a certain tension or distinction between the community and the world. In seeking to revive the apostolic pattern of the early church, these communities practice a communism of consumption and function on the basis of a consensus in which each believer has a direct role and responsibility for reaching a decision.

It is in their interpretation of the Christian witness that the Free Church communities differ from each other. The Society of Brothers has developed a Christian communist economy and a self-sufficient social order. Currently it associates only with other church communities and maintains a strict separation from the broader society. The basic goal of this community is that of its Anabaptist forebears, to bear witness to the Kingdom of God by living the life prescribed by the Sermon on the Mount. The values embraced by this small society include the unity which is symbolized by the Last Supper, brotherly love, peace, and purity; the pattern of community life revolves around these values. For the Society of Brothers breaking down the barriers between men is the primary manifestation of a life in common. It means holding property in common, for the members believe that private property erects walls between men. It means the death of the ego and its rebirth in community as in the Kingdom of God, and work as service rather than as individual achievement.

Koinonia Partners in Americus, Georgia, is also heir to the Anabaptist tradition with its reliance on the Scriptures, congregational sovereignty, and its commitment to a life patterned on the early church. However, while the Bruderhof defines the Christian witness as the loss of self and its rebirth in community as the Kingdom of God on earth, Koinonia defines its loyalty to Christ and acquires its identity through an intense involvement with a changing world. It has defined its commitment as one of reconciliation and acts as a model of fellowship in a competitive society. The true significance of the Koinonia community lies in its unique blend of pietism with its concern for perfection or authentic existence, and in its focus on current social problems in the broader society.

The Anabaptist vision includes the formation of an entire Christian culture, a society formed by the free association of church communities. While these communities have a missionary aim and hope to multiply, they form a unity in diversity, for each community has a distinctive character. The Reba Place Fellowship is the oldest urban intentional community in the United States. While Koinonia achieves its identity through its concern for social justice, Reba Place has more of a pietist orientation and places a greater emphasis on the convenantal relationship to the members. While it serves as a halfway house for the troubled and includes many social psychologists who work on the outside, its involvement with the world is less dramatic than that of Koinonia.

The new anarchists who form the core of the rural intentional communities today share with the sectarian communities their passion for egalitarianism, decision making by consensus, and the desire for a loose federation of communities as the basis for a new social order. However, anarchists have no blueprint for the perfect society. Since social cooperation and mutual obligation are both the natural and best state of society, and since society is held in check by the artificial restraints of governmental authority, the removal of these restraints will immediately result in perfection. Social progress is incompatible with authority of any kind, religious or governmental. Therefore, the new order of anarchism will be ushered in by everyone making it and living it. Anarchist perfection has a purely existential flavor and is born of self-regulation and cooperation. It takes flesh when each person grasps his destiny and attains self-sufficiency through his own efforts and a purely voluntary and spontaneous cooperation with others.

Anarchist communities thrive in the rural areas of Maryland,

Virginia, Pennsylvania, and the New England states, and are generally based upon farming activities. They hope to serve as models of peace and cooperation, free from the problems assailing the urban centers of the United States. At Heathcote in Freeland, Maryland, communitarians maintain their crops, buildings, and even their newspaper the *Green Revolution* in a thoroughly spontaneous manner. Heathcote functions as a self-contained miniature society with no authority and no organization or division of labor. Problems are solved during frequent and lengthy meetings of the entire membership, and when decisions are called for, they are reached by consensus.

Springtree, Full Circle Farm, and the Sunrise Hill community all regulate common life in a similar manner. However, newer groups such as the Springtree community enjoy the benefit of a fairly homogeneous membership and the chronicled experience of a decade of communal experiments to buttress their self-regulation.

The highly structured behaviorist communities present a striking contrast to the anarchist groups with their vague prescriptions for self-regulation and the spontaneous realization of perfection. Armed with the laws of psychology and the tools of operant conditioning, they march towards a well-defined heaven populated by a peaceful, productive, and harmonious society. Indeed, the visitor to Twin Oaks is handed an explanation of this perfection as soon as he arrives on the premises. An attractive prospectus explains the community as engaged in the creation of a culture which produces happy, peaceful, and useful people who cooperate with each other for the general good.

The key to such bliss lies in the behavior of the membership. For B. F. Skinner as for Robert Owen, individual responsibility and the idea of morality applying to individual men are evil myths. There are no moral or immoral men, only better or worse environments. Improve the environment, they enjoin, and the man will be improved. The method of operant conditioning can be applied to structure a social environment that will elicit the support of its members, the measure of perfection for Skinnerians. Skinnerians at Twin Oaks and

Walden Three believe that behavior in support of the perfect culture can be elicited by a system of positive reinforcers (rewards), rather than by relying on the tools of government which are negative reinforcers (punishments). They therefore arrange "contingencies" in the communal environment to "extinguish" negative behavior, such as jealousy for instance, or to encourage the type of behavior desired by the group, such as generosity.

As one of the oldest Skinnerian communities, Twin Oaks has just begun the task of socializing a new generation of perfect men with one communal offspring and another on the way this very year. Two-month-old Maya of Twin Oaks is not merely a charming infant, he is the first reflection of a new culture, one in which people are controlled by the consequences of their behavior rather than by governments or the nonscientific prescriptions of religion.

TWO

RELIGIOUS COMMUNITIES

Although men are tempted to consider the decline of their own age as the end of history and their own experience as unique, today's kaleidoscopic battles of ideas and political orders can be viewed in the perspective of sixteenth-century precedents. There are many parallels which can be drawn between the age of the Reformation and the contemporary age: the bitter clash of ideologies, the pervasive social and economic unrest, and the sense of deep malaise at the state of civilization. Today's clashes have bred a similar pessimism and bared a social turmoil with a renewal of religious spirit picking up from the flowering of social hope.

In sixteenth-century Europe attempts at the renewal of spirit in society took the form of the glorification of primitive cultures recently discovered in the New World. The sixteenth-century man brooded on the decadence of his age evident in the corruption of portions of the church and government. The tales of simple living and savage nobility spread by travelers from the New World sparked the hope that civilized people could become regenerated by a natural life. The rise of Anabaptism among peasants and artisans in Switzerland and Germany launched a great movement to revive the first Christian community described in the Acts of the Apostles.

Both the coupling of a return to the soil with a receptive spirit and the use of primitivism as a device for passing judgment on contemporary society are recurrent themes in history. In the past these themes have anticipated a renewal, a birth of spiritual vigor after a long decline. Today the appeal of the primitive, in which purity is nurtured by harmony with nature, has been transmitted through the anthropological studies of Claude Lévi-Strauss. It is also manifested in the United States by a widespread interest in the culture of American Indians on the one hand and a massive migration of youth to rural life on the other. And just as in the storm of the Reformation period, today there is widespread disaffection from the functioning of governmental and religious institutions and a corresponding search for purity of spirit.

What is distinctive in the modern age, however, is the coincidence of the loss of purpose and the dominance of technique which is peculiar to the modern polity of all types and which has deep roots in the culture of modernity. The loss of purpose does not refer to the absence of national goals or the weakening of national resolve, but rather to a lack of moral direction. Democracy, the main legitimizing principle of modern government, is at best neutral if not hostile towards the selection of purpose. Modernity liberated men from the constraints of monarchy, aristocracy, and a monopolistic church, freeing group after group from the coercion of premodern systems. However, the liberating ethos of modern political culture is animated by a great negative thrust. It does not generate visions for people to pursue. Rather, it allows men the freedom to seek them where they do have a conception of common purpose. Where such positive goals are lacking, democracy will not provide them. Thus, while the modern polity has released the energies of men and enabled them to work towards their freely chosen ends. democracy, its legitimizing principle, is based upon a powerful negation of premodern established authority and the ethical systems associated with them.

Yet men do seek a purpose in life and a communion with

something larger than themselves: a meaning and a place for themselves within that meaning. The search for a new morality and for a reinvigoration of ethical systems is strikingly evident in contemporary American society. It has assumed a variety of forms and is apparent both within established religions, in the proliferation of a host of fundamentalist communities, and in the revival of Anabaptism, a branch of Christianity which stresses community life.

Among the established religions the charismatic renewal of Roman Catholicism, known as the Pentecostal Spirit movement, has burgeoned since its origins in 1966. In the early seventies it includes over 1200 prayer communities, and increasing numbers of Presbyterian, Lutheran, Episcopal, and Methodist churches have joined this movement. Besides its stress on spontaneous prayer and study of the Scriptures, this movement is characterized by "gifts of the spirit," such as healing, teaching, and speaking in unknown tongues to praise God.

On the other hand, an increasing number of young adults are establishing fundamentalist communities such as the New Testament Missionary Fellowship groups or the Children of God. These communities are fed by a variety of streams. The sense of powerlessness which has resulted from the futile marches, sit-ins, and peace rallies devoted to social issues and the Vietnam War has bred a compensating search for spirit. The great surge toward social reform which burgeoned in the tumultuous sixties brought youthful reformers squarely in face of the need for ultimate value. While some youth have turned to extremes of radicalism as an antidote to social problems, others have rediscovered purpose in the fellowship of small communities and have sought to exchange power for spirit in their dealings with the world. There is also the realization on the part of groups formerly engaged in a variety of drug-induced illuminations that the pilgrimage to retrieve the lost self may easily end in the swamp of introspection or, worse yet, in self-destruction. Part of the lost self which needs rescuing has been defined by the young as man within a moral system rather than the sentient being adrift within a hostile universe.

In addition, the Jesus movement offers a safe harbor for many youth confronted by a bewildering array of choices and behavior patterns in their daily lives. For some the sheer array of choice and the concomitant dearth of moral standards to guide them is terrifying. Adulthood borders a precipice in which they may experiment with anything from drugs to sex and lifestyles. Thus, in turning towards fundamentalism, they are exchanging the fear and uncertainty generated by turbulent times for a harsh but simple set of moral precepts.

Many of these groups display puritanical attitudes which have long been rejected by contemporary society. The Children of God, an ultraconservative branch of the Jesus movement which includes more than fifty communities throughout the United States, forbids the use of drugs and alcohol and maintains very strict sexual mores. Married couples in these communities live as chaperons in the separate housing for men and women.

Young people joining these communities are especially attracted by their view of a group actually living according to Christ's teaching, rather than merely preaching. Like the itinerant lay preachers of the Middle Ages, Jesus communes answer the desire of many to see in their midst men living and preaching like the original Apostles. They experience a similar hunger for evangelism, a longing to hear the Gospel preached simply and in a manner which relates to their own experience. In addition, the simple life practiced in fundamentalist communities offers a haven from servitude to drugs and a perplexing social environment. Many communities are devoted entirely to worship. Rather than taking jobs, the membership depends upon donations from sympathetic persons and the savings of individuals who turn over all their possessions before joining the community.

Some of the more conservative Jesus communities are theocracies. In the Jesus People, Incorporated, also known as the Love Inn, two elders make all the major decisions for the community. Members of this particular group do not like to be identified with the moral absolutism of the Children of God. However, they share with the latter group the belief in the healing of disease by prayer and await the second coming of Christ.

There are several new religious communities absorbed in the search for a type of mysticism which borders on superstition and cultism. Steven Gaskin's Summertown in Tennessee and Michael Metelica's Brotherhood of the Spirit are both characterized by authoritarian leadership and flavored with cultist fervor. The associate dean of student affairs at Boston University attributes the trend towards mysticism to the neglect of mystery in worship in favor of social action on the part of ministries.[1] However, this phenomenon is paralleled by a growing concern on the part of young adults with ethics. They hunger for authenticity and for the chance to realize ethical values in their daily lives.

Parallel to the renewal of established religion and the burgeoning of fundamentalist communities is one of the most striking features of the contemporary age, the emergence of a Christian subculture based upon the mutual fellowship of intentional community. The revival of Anabaptism has resulted in the formation of various types of Free Church communities in the United States. For these proliferating Free Church communities, the battle against evil is immanent and takes place between the intentional community and the greater society.

The Anabaptist vision of a Christian society formed by the free association of church communities constitutes the core belief animating such diverse communities as the Society of Brothers, the urban community of the Reba Place Fellowship, and Koinonia Partners.

The Concept of the Free Church

One of the most challenging responses to the spiritual turmoil of the sixteenth century was Anabaptism, a movement which has surfaced with renewed vigor in the United States. Under the impact of the sociology of religion and the rediscovery of primary materials, contemporary church historians have rescued Anabaptism from the polemical treatment of both Protestant and Roman Catholic historiography. As a result, the Anabaptist vision has emerged from the status of a marginal and misunderstood strand of reformers to its rightful position as a third form of Christianity distinguished from Roman Catholicism and Protestantism by its view of the true church.

Unlike the reformers, the Anabaptists did not regard themselves as a corrective to the errors of an intact Christendom, but as founders of an entirely new movement, based upon the restitution of the apostolic pattern of the early church. In their eyes, the existing church had decayed as an institution, necessitating the renewal of Christianity as pure faith. The Anabaptists dated the fall of the church from the reign of Constantine when it took in large groups of adults who had no understanding of the Gospel and generations of children who had not yet reached the age of understanding.[2] The special mark of the fall was the union of church and state and the use of secular authority in matters of religion. Political compulsion in religion is contrary to several of the distinguishing principles of the Anabaptist faith: the concept of the church as an intentional association of believing adults, the complementarity of limited secular government with the concept of the believer's church, and the maintenance of a certain tension or distinction between the Free Church and the world.[3] This tension does not involve a mere separation of function, but of attitudes towards history and social crisis. According to the Anabaptists, the true Christian is distinguished not by his apoliticism, but by his life of hope in the coming kingdom and by his distance from the spirit of the times and its accompanying ills which will pass away. As Clarence Jordan of Koinonia pointed out, Christians must always be distinct in the social order. Closely related to the affirmation of tension with the world is the Anabaptist opposition to war. The pacifism of the Free

Church is biblical and not cultural. It refers to the separation of the true church from power and political interest as well as to the opposition to violence among Christian brothers.[4] However, the concept that Christians should stand apart from society through their practices does not mean that the church should be indifferent to society, but that it should be co-creator with God in seeking to realize His will in the world. Freedom from governmental control in matters of faith does not exempt the church from obedience.

In shaping the Free Church, Anabaptists eliminated religious hierarchy, power consciousness, any trace of accommodation to society or externalization of faith. They sought to restore the congregational life of apostolic times: an intentional association of believers, fully committed to God and renouncing the world and sin. However, although outwardly composed of volunteers, the community of believers of the Free Church belongs to Christ and therefore cannot compromise with ethnicity.* Like the apostolic church of early Christianity, the believing community is organized around a missionary purpose, a voluntary association of pilgrims who consider evangelism a clear command of Christ.[5]

Because the Free Church has repudiated formalism and hierarchy, the status of the laity in spiritual government and in the interpretation of biblical teaching is exceedingly important. In fact, the very term "laity" can be eliminated, for Anabaptists allow no special group of professionals to reduce the sovereignty of the community of believers in matters of faith and order. As an apostolic church, the Free Church is bound by a consensus in which each believer has a direct role and responsibility in reaching a decision. Within the community, each member is immediately accountable for his brother, and the fellowship is maintained by mutual admonition. The sanction of last resort in spiritual government is the threat of expulsion from the congregation of believers. Thus, the idea of a covenantal relationship to

---

*Associated with any particular national culture.

Christ and among believing brothers constitutes the very foundation of Anabaptism.

Some of the basic concepts of the Free Church are apparent to some extent among the Quakers, the Church of the Brethren, and the Mennonites in America today. However, the lineal descendants of the Anabaptists in the United States are the Hutterites.

Founded by Jacob Wideman and a band of Swiss Brethren in 1529, the Hutterites were the only group of Anabaptists who developed the concept of the true church through the creation of total Christian communities.[6] The Anabaptist movement as a whole—the Swiss Brethren, South German Brethren, and the Dutch Mennonites—were all dedicated to sharing, a communism of consumption on the model of the early Christian heroes. However, the Hutterites alone developed a Christian communist economy and a self-sufficient social order as a means of revitalizing the pure faith of the church.

To all appearances, the Hutterite communities in America have persisted relatively unchanged by their wanderings throughout widely scattered countries in search of freedom from state control. However, the concept of tension between church and world to be bridged by a missionary outreach has become a tension between centuries as the Hutterites have retreated into cultural enclaves. The development of highly disciplined self-sufficient communities to preserve the faith amid hostile conditions has led to the isolation of a group settled into antiquated social patterns and sealed off from contemporary society. In the Hutterite communities which flourish in the Dakotas and in Canada, the religious primitivism of the Anabaptists based on the restitution of the early church and the Christian ideal of the communism of the Golden Age, has slipped into a cultural primitivism. Moreover, as we shall see in the discussion of the Society of Brothers, a group of communities related to the Hutterites, the concept of a consenting, egalitarian brotherhood has been transformed into new forms of hierarchy and authoritarian control.

The Society of Brothers

The Society of Brothers was founded by Dr. Eberhard Arnold amid the troubled times of post-World War I Germany. Dr. Arnold played an important role in the Christian social youth movement which developed in response to the turmoil of war and the revelation of social decadence. Like contemporary American youth, the German youth of the twenties rejected the values and lifestyles of their parents in favor of social experimentation and religious revival. The crowded meetings in the Arnolds' Berlin home focused on the desire to foster a new world in the spirit of reconciliation and brotherhood and to develop a new way of life animated by a Christian spirit.

The solution to this search for a new lifestyle was the establishment of a community of faith and goods at Sannerz in 1920. Under the charismatic guidance of Dr. Arnold, the Sannerz community sought to actualize the radical Christianity set forth in the Sermon on the Mount, to constitute simultaneously a social movement and a church. The community modeled itself on the early Christian church and, in addition, engaged in farming, the publication of religious writings, and crafts. During these years their doors were always open to the streams of people uprooted by the war, and for a while they served as a home for war orphans. As in the primitive Christian church community, the life at Sannerz was characterized by simplicity, poverty, a sharing of all goods, and an open door to the world's needy.

There was a great deal of discussion during these years, as there is in the United States today, of the possibility of infusing the established churches with ideas of social reform. However, Eberhard and his wife were firm in their conviction of the need to develop a revolutionary approach to the problems of the church and of social justice, for they felt that the established churches had compromised themselves unalterably in joining forces with wealth and the state.

The Society of Brothers, or the Bruderhof, traces its spiritual origins to the communal life of the early Christians in the first-century church and most particularly to the

Anabaptists of the sixteenth century with their pacifism, their concept of community, and their occupations as farmers and artisans.[7] When Sannerz proved too small to house the growing community, the brotherhood moved to a larger home at Rhon, and it was at Rhon that the Arnolds became familiar with the writings of the Anabaptists. When they discovered the Hutterite brothers and learned that Hutterite communities were still in existence in the United States, they felt a great desire to join forces with them. Eberhard Arnold journeyed to the United States in 1930 in order to elicit the financial support of the Hutterites and explore the possibility of establishing the Bruderhof in America. Although they were sorely disappointed at the amount of economic aid offered, they became united with the Hutterites, and Dr. Arnold was ordained as a Hutterite minister at the Stand-off community in Alberta.[8]

This was a very important crossroads for the fledgling community, for it guaranteed its longevity. Henceforth it was a member of a 400-year-old movement and as such could incorporate a set of tested procedures which would give a firmer foundation to community life than the guidance of a charismatic, but mortal, leader. The natural leadership of Eberhard Arnold was reinforced by establishing the Hutterite office of the servant of the Word, or elder, at the apex of a spiritual hierarchy. Furthermore, a set of graduated sanctions ranging from mild admonishment to exclusion would guarantee the unity of the community rather than the arbitration of a single man. Ultimately the Bruderhof was quite selective in borrowing from the Hutterites. It eventually rejected the rigidity of social customs such as the antiquated garb, the total isolation of Hutterite colonies, and the denial of modernization. Although the Bruderhof left the Hutterite church in the fifties over a combination of differences relating to biblical interpretations, economic decisions, and community politics, the Society of Brothers continues to maintain close relations with the Hutterite community at Forest River, North Dakota.

Because the Bruderhof at Rhon experienced great difficulties as a pacifist Christian community under the National Socialist regime, the brothers founded the Almsbruderhof in Liechtenstein. It managed to send its children there to avoid their education in a Nazi state. In 1937, two years after the death of Dr. Arnold, the National Socialist government dissolved the community and forced its members to leave the country. Along with the members of the Almsbruderhof, the fleeing members founded the Cotswold community in Wiltshire, England. However, on account of the war the English government objected to the presence of the Bruderhof with its predominantly German population, and once again the community decided to emigrate rather than disband. Canada turned them down, but Paraguay welcomed immigrants, so the community undertook an arduous wartime journey and in 1940 established the Primavera community in Paraguay.

The period of 1940 to 1950 was a time of isolation for the Bruderhof. However, this was not wholly unfortunate, for it welded a strong community out of an international membership. While in Paraguay, the brothers built three hofs, or colonies, Isla Margarita, Loma Jhoby, and Ibate. The environment was not propitious for missionary activity, although the Bruderhof did build and operate a hospital for the Paraguayans. Thus, it was spared the task of assimilating a new membership and could focus its energies on unifying its diverse membership and gaining strength from its growing population of youth.

As the war drew to a close, the brothers longed to break their isolation and engage in missionary activity. By the late forties some new members had trickled down from North America, and the Bruderhof had sent missions to speak in the United States. That country was experiencing a ripple of interest in community in the early fifties, and Bruderhof missionary speakers were very much in demand at church groups and college campuses.

In 1953 six members of the Bruderhof traveled to the

United States to speak, and to feel out the possibilities of financial aid and the purchase of land for a North American hof. The following year they were able to procure a large estate in Rifton, New York, site of the Woodcrest community. Five members of the Kingwood community and half of the Macedonia community, intentional communities which flowered in the fifties, joined the Bruderhof, bringing with them a new cultural outlook and a thriving toy manufacturing business, Community Playthings. From this point until 1958, the Bruderhof experienced a dramatic growth, peaking in 1956.

After a period of isolation the community revived its early character of an evangelical social movement with a heterogeneous membership. Former anarchists, communists, Quakers, and socialists flocked to join the Bruderhof. The Woodcrest community was the scene of work camps and conferences for thousands of guests, some of whom stayed on as members.[9] Like all intentional communities, the Bruderhof has experienced the problem of balancing the divergent aims of evangelism and expansion on the one hand and an orientation towards the inner life of the community on the other hand. It is the rare community which can combine these goals. Many suffer from pendular changes with a consequent strain among the members as they align themselves behind either goal. The Bruderhof was not exempt. In the peak of expansion the North American Bruderhof believed it could influence the entire intentional community movement, convert radical American youth, and still maintain good relations with the more progressive elements of the Hutterites. Meanwhile in Paraguay the Primavera community was distraught and confused over what they perceived as worldly accommodation on the part of the North American hofs. In their hunger for new members, the latter had welcomed hundreds of newcomers and even altered the requirements for membership by relaxing the necessity for a uniform confession of faith based on the Apostles' Creed.

Eventually the assimilation of a heterogeneous membership

posed severe problems for the Bruderhof, and between 1959 and 1962 the movement was rocked by a great crisis which affected the essential nature of the community, its structure, leadership, and membership. The issues were fundamental ones and included a choice between a return to the legalism and rigidity of Hutterite customs as against spontaneity, democratic versus authoritarian decision making, and a power struggle among the top leadership of the various communities.[10] The result was the closing down of the Primavera community and a significant reduction in membership in the Bruderhof as a whole.

The early sixties can be characterized as a period of reaction in response to the progressive innovation of the past decade, a time of withdrawal after social euphoria. As in all sectarian communities, but especially in the United States setting, boundary maintenance is an urgent matter. It represents a dike against a prosperous, sophisticated, and enticing culture.

Before the great crisis the Bruderhof considered itself an intentional community among intentional communities and maintained close ties with nonreligious seekers of community such as the kibbutzim. However, in 1959 it relinquished its membership in the Federation of Intentional Communities. At this time it regards itself as a church which is an intentional community and maintains relations only with religious communities.[11] The only period in which the community could sustain the dual character of church and social movement was during the lifetime of its founder Eberhard Arnold.

The basic goal of the Bruderhof is that of its Anabaptist forebears: to bear witness to the Kingdom of God by living the life prescribed by the Sermon on the Mount. The values embraced by the community include the unity which is symbolized by the Last Supper, love (agape, not eros), peace in the biblical sense, and purity.[12] The pattern of life in community is arranged to realize these values.

For the Bruderhof breaking down the barriers between men is the primary manifestation of a life of bearing witness.[13] It means sharing all possessions, for private property establishes walls between men. It also means the loss of self and its rebirth in community as in the kingdom of God.

Within the Bruderhof all material goods are shared according to need in the manner of the early Christians. When a member takes baptismal vows, he signs away all he owns forever and henceforth is dependent upon the community for all his needs. All goods are bought communally, from cars to shampoo, so that no member requires money. Meals are taken in common except for breakfast and certain suppers. Food supplies for family meals are distributed to families on a weekly basis, and linen and clothing are also purchased in bulk. The sewing room makes and repairs clothing as well. Needs and supplies are coordinated by the housemother, who distributes books, toilet articles, and various supplies on the basis of necessity lists drawn up by each member.

The Bruderhof is self-sufficient economically, and all three hofs are supported by the income from the toy manufacturing business, Community Playthings. Work as service is an essential part of community life and is shared by all as a practical expression of brotherly love.[14] All work is held in equal respect, whether it is performing the simple tasks of a shop worker or making decisions in the superstructure of community. Economic efficiency is not a virtue in the brotherhood, for work is assigned according to the spiritual and emotional needs of the individual and members are not accepted on the basis of their capabilities or productivity. Most important, the Bruderhof does not extend any sort of incentive for good work, for it would conflict with the goal of unity and hinder the dependence of the individual on the group.

In addition to Community Playthings, the Plough Publishing Company produces books of a religious nature. Aside from toy manufacturing and publishing, there are ten work departments at each hof. Six of these are exclusively for women: housemother room, kitchen, laundry, sewing room, cleaning crew, and baby house. The office, the school, and the archives employ both men and women. The housemothers supervise the women's work and the general welfare of the community as a household. One housemother distributes work, and another counsels women with their personal problems.

Life in the Bruderhof is not an alternative to family life as it is in some of the newly formed contemporary Christian communities. On the contrary, the Bruderhof does everything to strengthen the family. Each family has private living quarters, and there are special times set aside during the daily routine so that families can be together. Moreover, because community is total and includes work, play, education, and worship, Bruderhof families have more opportunities for spending time together than families in the outside world whose members work and learn often at great distances from home. Married parents are the dominant social class in the Bruderhof, and most families have several children, for a large family is considered wholesome.[15]

The rearing of children, however, is not the exclusive concern of the parents but belongs to the whole community. Children spend the day in either the baby house, the kindergarten, or the primary school. They are generally in the care of the young, unmarried women, for work is a time for unmarried women to express their love for children and for the married women to be away from the children. The children in community have a happy, although sheltered, life. From the early years their play and their learning are integrated into the community life. A child spends a good portion of his day throughout his youth with his cohort group, the group of children born within the same year.

Up to the eighth grade education is in community, but then the young people are sent to the public high school. This daily foray into the world outside will help them prepare for the decision between life in community and life outside. The brotherhood does not want any spiritual birthright. They must go through the same novitiate and take the same baptismal vows as members coming from the outside. The brotherhood does not wany any spiritual deadwood and takes only those members of a generation who feel called to a life in community, generally 75 per cent of the cohort group.[16] This policy constitutes a major difference with communities such as the Hutterites and the kibbutzim. In these cases, the most complete socialization process has been unable to prevent either a spiritual regression after the founding generation or, as in the case of the Hutterites, a lapse into an ethnic religion.

Bruderhof youth must have taken their membership vows to the community before they may marry. Because of the intimacy of a life in community, no dating or courtship is allowed. A boy communicates his interest to a servant of the Word, who in turn speaks to a housemother. It is the latter who will speak to the girl about the offer of marriage rather than the prospective groom. Bruderhof marriages are indissoluble because they are subordinated to the spiritual unity of the church community. This is made clear in the marriage vows, which stress the dependency of the marriage relationship upon the brotherhood of the collectivity.[17]

Though the Bruderhof still has some of its original members and is beginning to raise the fourth generation of sabra, the majority of members are converts who have joined in the past ten years.[18] Membership is open to anyone who asks, and thus the brothers come from a variety of religious backgrounds: Catholic, Jewish, Protestant, and Hutterite. The diversity of backgrounds and an open membership have prevented the regression of the Bruderhof into a culture religion like the Amish or the Hutterites.

The population of 750 is divided among three hofs: Woodcrest in Rifton, New York, Oak Lake in Pennsylvania, and Evergreen in Connecticut. A fourth community is under construction. Members identify with the Bruderhof as a whole, rather than with the particular hof. There are complete sharing and frequent exchanges of visits between the hofs.

Although the Anabaptist branch of Christianity abhors hierarchy and the professionalization of any religious function, the Bruderhof, like the Hutterites, has a system of social control as comprehensive as a totalitarian society, and an authoritarian system of governance. Agreement on the goals of the community, a unity which is the chief reward for the renunciation of self, and an extremely thorough socialization process provide the legitimacy for an oligarchic leadership. Since the goal of witness is manifested in the most humble routines of daily life, all life is sacred, and spiritual leadership is all-encompassing.

The Bruderhof hierarchy is an adaptation of the Hutterite system of leadership and is shaped like a pyramid. The gradations of the hierarchy are distinguished by the degree of access to information and the scope of decision making.[19] The elder is at the apex of the hierarchy and is also known as the *Vorsteher,* or chief servant. The elder is David Arnold, son of the founder, and he functions as spiritual leader of all three hofs. Each hof has one or two servants of the Word. They must have three qualifications: the gift of spiritual discernment, a strong personality, and sensitivity to sources of interpersonal problems. Servants function as spiritual leaders, administrators, and communications centers.[20] Since there are no legitimate channels of communication by-passing the servants and since no interest groups are allowed, the servants are privy to all information about personnel. However, although there are no reserved spaces of individual privacy and although social control is as pervasive as in a totalitarian system, it is wielded for spiritual ends which are freely accepted by the membership.

Communication flows up the hierarchy, but its downward flow depends upon the discretion of the servant. For instance, a brother in trouble may seek help from a witness brother. Unless the matter is quite trivial, the latter is obliged to inform the servant. However, the servant may or may not speak to the brotherhood as a whole, to a few members, or he may keep the information to himself.

Below the servants are the stewards, who act as financial advisers to the servants, and from three to seven witness brothers, or servants.[21] Witness brothers act as the servant's liaison to the work departments. Together, these three top grades of the hierarchy serve as executive committee for the hof.

There are also three grades of ordinary brotherhood members and three grades of nonbrotherhood members. The middle level of the hierarchy includes married brotherhood members, single decision-making brotherhood members, and nondecision-making members. The lower portion of the community structure is composed of novices, older teenagers, long-term guests, children, and excluded members.

Choosing a servant and witness brothers is the task of the upper hierarchy and requires complete unanimity.[22] Although the servants have indefinite tenure, there is considerable turnover because of the extraordinary demands and pressures of such a position. A servant can be removed from office by the hierarchy who selected him, and more rarely by the brothers. However, it is infinitely more complicated to depose than to select a servant or witness brother.

Although there are many circumstantial issues which require decision making, there have been three fundamental issues, matters of major importance which have affected the basic nature of the community. The fact that they cross-cut rather than reinforce each other has mitigated the severity of their impact on unity. The first of these issues refers to the choice between a spiritual-emotional approach or a legal-rational approach to building community.[23] As in the matter of outreach or pietistic withdrawal, orientations are never final. For instance, the early years of the Bruderhof at Sannerz stressed the spiritual-emotional approach, and the incorporation into the Hutterite church in 1930 signaled a change to a legal-rational orientation. The second major issue revolves around the choice between a democratic or oligarchic organization for the community, and the third hinges on whether to focus on the inner life of community or on social outreach.[24] These conflicts have been reflected in the power struggles and the crises which have punctuated the history of the community. However, the impact of crisis is mitigated by a context of peaceful change. The majority of changes in custom occur through the technique of controlled acculturation, a slow and constant evolution of customs which allows the simultaneous impressions of progress and continuity, suggesting an organic growth of policy.[25] Although no interest groups or factions are allowed in community, the method of acculturation keeps the hope of eventual change alive for proponents of all outlooks.

The Society of Brothers has also borrowed from the Hutterite's a system of social control or sanctions designed to handle deviance from communal norms. It is common to many religious communities that deviance is concerned more with attitudes than with behavior and that sanction is regarded as service rather than punishment. The attitude favored in the Bruderhof is that of complete identification with the community as opposed to the self, the spouse, or one's children. Joy, the eagerness to participate in community activities, openness to admonishment, and a childlike spirit are model attributes as against aloofness or a desire for solitude.[26] The socialization process inculcates reverence for the collective self as good, the individual self as worthless, and makes openness about one's inner self a virtue. The aim of social control is more to anticipate potential deviance than to sanction it. The orders, or sanctions, adopted from the Hutterites range from mild admonishment or criticism to various degrees of exclusion from community prayer meetings or brotherhood meetings, to the more drastic resort of exclusion.[27] The causes for this last resort have generally been recalcitrant pride, power, or sex. These sanctions are exceedingly effective since the joy of participating in community and the experience of unity as the Kingdom of God on earth are the primary reward of living in community.

The chief criticisms which have been leveled at religious communities of this type refer to escapism, and the loss of individual identity, a primary value in Western culture. The brothers would answer the first charge by pointing to the great struggle and sacrifice of life in community.[28] For

them building community is making history, not escaping it
or bending to the events in history. This is corroborated by
apostates who point out that after having experienced a life
in common, life outside seems pale and joyless.[29] Many
casual observers of community express concern at the possibility of losing individual identity within the collective. In a
very real sense, living in community requires that one renounce
worldly identity. This involves renouncing professional
ambition or placing it on a lower level of priority than serving
Christ. However, in losing this self, the communitarian finds
a much larger self or becomes a more perfect reflection of
Christ, so that most members appear as more substantial
persons than are common in the larger society. They seem
more loving, generous, and open than most people. Community
is an organic body and as such is greater than its parts. The
fact of participating in community as the Kingdom of God on
earth is the reward for the renunciation which group living
entails. Certainly, life in community demands that each
member be concerned with the problems and needs of all
other members as if they were his own and requires that
burdens will be shared by all according to their abilities.

The issue of freedom is also one which must be addressed.
The liberal definition of freedom as the possibility of making
a selection among alternative courses of action, leaders, and
policy processes does not exist in the Society of Brothers.
Rather, freedom is defined by the community in the conservative tradition, as a liberation from one's baser self to
a higher self capable of participating in an organic union of
selves. In religious terms, the community requires a liberation
from one's ego to a clearer reflection of Christ. It is a matter
of choosing between incompatible values: between the deep
satisfaction of sharing all one's life activities with the same
group of people, and the freedom to choose among alternatives including membership in a variety of specialized
groups. The total commitment of the self and a state of
moral dependence on the collectivity are not compatible
with the freewheeling individualism fostered by Western society.

Koinonia Partners

The concept of a Christian lifestyle based upon the Sermon on the Mount has inspired a variety of experiments in community. The tension between church and world can be construed in differing lights, and the institutional containers for peace, love, and sharing are manifold.

Koinonia Partners in Americus, Georgia, is heir to the Anabaptist, or Free Church, tradition with its elements of prophecy, congregational decision making, reliance on the Scriptures, and commitment to a life in common patterned on the early church. Ostensibly, its goals are similar to those of the Bruderhof. However, social regeneration is at the very heart of Koinonia's existence: for Koinonia, community is a means and not the *sine qua non* of a radical Christian lifestyle. The true significance of the Koinonia community lies in its unique blend of pietism, with its concern for perfection or authentic existence, and the social gospel focusing on a world to be saved. The late Clarence Jordan, founder and guiding light of Koinonia, was a man ahead of his time in his perception of the church as both a prophetic and a healing community and in establishing a firm link between personal salvation and social reform. As a prophetic community, Koinonia must address itself to the problems both of the world and of the community of believers. This involves two distinct levels of knowledge; prophecy and perception, an awareness of redemptive history and of current social problems. Thus, Koinonia functions as a community of study, with each member bearing equal responsibility for spiritual perception and knowledge of the facts. In exploring modes of social change, Koinonia is attracted by the examples of Gandhi, Martin Luther King, and the Berrigans.

Clarence Jordan believed that Christians should be distinct in the social order, and his interpretation of the Christian witness was quite specific. Koinonians were to practice the brotherhood of all men, the sharing of goods, and conscientious objection in a society characterized by racism, competition, and militarism.[30] The Bruderhof defines the Christian witness as the loss of self and its rebirth in a community sharply demarcated from an evil world; Koinonia defines its loyalty to Christ and acquires its identity through an intense involvement with a dynamic world. Koinonia's concern with poverty and racism reflects the crisis nature of these problems. The nature of its commitment, one of reconciliation, is such that its efforts will always parallel the needs of the social order. Thus, Koinonia is not only distinctive for racial tolerance and sharing of resources, but also for its efforts to achieve peace in a time of war, and as a model of human fellowship in a fragmented, technological society. For Koinonia, the battle is not a political one but revolves around the spirit that informs contemporary institutions. Clarence Jordan believed that patterns of mutual obligation were moral issues which should be confronted within the church as a fellowship of believers. This linkage between personal redemption and the problem of justice bears a very important message to contemporary man.

The Koinonia Farm community was founded in 1942 as a practical realization of Jordan's ministry. He defined that ministry as one of reconciliation; of God and man, rich and poor, black and white, urgent needs in the deep South of the early forties.[31] He had all the attributes so necessary for community building. In addition to his personal charisma, his competence as a New Testament scholar and as a Baptist minister, he was a graduate of the Georgia State College of Agriculture.[32] He enrolled in agricultural college rather than in law school as his parents had hoped, because of his deep commitment to social justice. He intended to alleviate the twin evils of racism and poverty by equipping himself for partnership with the victims of sharecropping. The rare combination of perception, practicality, and drive which was to guide Koinonia until Jordan's death in 1969 were already apparent in the young student.

During his student years Clarence Jordan dreamed of realizing his Christian commitment through a fellowship of believers who dedicated themselves entirely to sharing and community service.[33] While completing his doctorate in theology, he took steps to establish a fellowship like that of the early Christians who shared their lives and resources and distributed them to the needy. This fellowship was described as a *koinonia* in Acts. The Koinonia established in 1942 on a Georgia farm was to serve as a resource for the rural poor, an island of peace and racial harmony in a sea of inequality and racial division.

Clarence, his wife, and the members of the young community exhibited not only the courage to defy prevailing social practice by their partnership with the poor and black, but persistence as well. The story of the farm community's years of harassment by the Ku Klux Klan, of the economic boycott by the surrounding community, and the charges of subversion by the government have been recounted elsewhere. Suffice it to say that the public hostility which spelled an untimely end for many community experiments in the past failed to affect the Jordans' commitment to a reconciliation of men within contemporary society.

By the early fifties Koinonia had attracted a number of young radical Christians, and the membership was plunged into experimentation with community two decades before the community movement flowered in the United States. The families at Koinonia pooled all their resources and shared all facilities. New members either had to dispose of their possessions and cash before they arrived or turn over their resources to the community. From then on the community was accountable for their basic needs. Decision making was the responsibility of the entire group, and many hours were spent talking over issues of faith and economics. Various forms of worship were explored as well as Koinonia's relationship as church to the local Baptist church. However, that problem was solved when the Baptist church severed its relations with members of Koinonia because of their views on race.[34]

Koinonians regard their community as a family, not as a

structure. In contrast to the Hutterites and the Society of Brothers, they do not consider community as the only right way to live. Therefore, when the troubles of the fifties assailed Koinonia, when the barn burnings and the endless harassments by the local population steadily depleted the membership, the Jordans refused to move. The living church as a model of reconciliation in a divided society was more important to the Jordans than the preservation of community. Therefore, the Jordans watched the membership melt away, and remained where the need for brotherhood was so great.

In 1967 the community was at an all-time low. With only two families remaining, the Jordans were ready to sell the farm. However, a fortuitous encounter with Millard Fuller, a former businessman in search of a new life, spelled a new start for Koinonia.

In 1968 a meeting was held at the farm with some close friends: a founder of the Reba Place Fellowship, Bob Swann from the Committee for Non-Violent Action, Ted Braun of the United Church Board for World Ministers, and a dozen more men with experience in social action and the ministry.[35] The result was a plan for a new vision of Koinonia, reestablished as Koinonia Partners, Inc. The concept of partnership embraces a variety of practical undertakings from farming to sewing, in which people of different backgrounds can work together. It is Koinonia's solution to the problem of mutual obligation in a highly competitive and individualistic society.

Koinonia Partners functions as a nonprofit organization with a board of directors to implement its objectives. It has developed three programs to express its new mission of reconciliation: communication, instruction, and the Fund for Humanity.

The communications ministry is carried out by three members of the community who spread the radical ideas of the Gospel to the far corners of the United States. They seek speaking engagements at universities, regional conferences, and individual congregations. The backgrounds of the communicants differ widely. Ted Swisher is a recent graduate of

Princeton University. Ladon Sheats is a former top executive with IBM, and Millard Fuller, a founder of Koinonia Partners, was a lawyer and businessman who made a million dollars before changing his commitments. This tall, lean man steams from conference to conference with high-powered but well-regulated energy, a modern Simon Peter who has rechanneled his managerial skill.

In addition to the communications ministry, there are three full-time "neighbors" to the local community. Throughout the week they circulate through the town of Americus and its surroundings, seeking out people who need help of any kind. It may take the form of repairing a leaky roof, helping a youngster with his homework, or driving someone to the doctor.

One of the most imaginative community undertakings is the Fund for Humanity, which serves as a channel for the redistribution of land and capital between rich and poor. In the words of Clarence Jordan, "What the poor need is not charity but capital."[36] The fund purchases land and redistributes it according to need rather than ability to pay. It holds land in trust for families to farm and thus serves as a means to reassert that land is God's gift to all men and should be used justly. The intention is also to allow participants in partnership farming and industries to plow back money into the fund, so that, in sharing, a poor man can become a man with a mission.

Money for the fund comes from gifts, noninterest-bearing loans, and voluntarily shared profits from the partnership industries and farming. The fund does not seek government support or foundation grants since the goal is to create a spirit of partnership and sharing among individuals.[37]

The fund provides capital for the farming industry partnerships and the housing program. Each farming partnership consists of up to four partners. Land is used free of charge, and partners pool their labor and machinery. The partnerships serve as a means of involving community members with nonmembers. For instance, the peanut crop is farmed by Ed

Young, a young member, and Bo Johnson, a resident of the village adjacent to the farm. They borrowed money from the fund in order to start their crop and will return that amount plus any profits beyond their needs for livelihood.

Among the most urgent needs of the Americus area are adequate housing and steady work that pays a living wage, the chief goal of the partnership industries. Clarence Jordan's sojourn as a minister in an urban ghetto had convinced him that the best way to cure urban ills was to provide a way to prevent the rural exodus which swelled the ghettos in the first place. A pecan shelling plant and a candy and fruitcake mail order business employ around 40 people. A sewing operation which produces ladies' knit pants employs between 15 and 20 people. Bill Londeree, a former manager for Arrow Shirts, is running the industry cooperatively with its employees.

Nestled in the quiet of a pine grove adjacent to the farm is an entire village constructed by Koinonia's housing program for local people suffering desperate need. The village consists of 26 homes laid out on ample homesites. Each house has three bedrooms, a bath, kitchen, and living room. In most cases, they replace jerry-built shacks with roofs like sieves and no running water or sanitation facilities. For those locked in poverty they represent hope and dignity, a springboard to a new life. The terms for purchase are a 20-year, no-interest mortgage. Without the heavy burden of conventional financing, monthly payments average from $25. to $32. The Fund for Humanity assumes the onus of interest. The village includes a playground and a child development center with a capacity for 20 children; an anonymous gift has enabled Koinonia to plan an expanded center with a capacity for 60 children. Currently the children of the community and of Koinonia village attend. An expanded program will be particularly welcome in a state which provides no public kindergarten. The future center, which is being designed by the University of North Carolina School of Architecture, will be a multipurpose structure housing the adult education programs as well. Debbie Boggs, a recent Syracuse University graduate in special education, is managing the child care program.

A second village is currently under construction. It was designed by Don Mosely, a Koinonian who has served in the Peace Corps. It will have a series of two-story homes with the second floor projecting slightly over the first. Each house will have one-half acre or more of land so that the occupants may keep animals or raise a garden. The new village has a number of unusual features which will enhance the quality of daily life. The houses are oriented towards park strips rather than roads, so that the village children will be able to enter the play area without crossing a street and can be watched by their parents from the front porches. An old gravel quarry nearby will be turned into a roadside park.

Today the community of Koinonia includes 28 adults and 24 children. There are seventy permanent residents in all, including the volunteers. The maximum size is set at approximately 120 members. Beyond this point, the membership would rather create a second Koinonia than sacrifice the quality of life in a small community.

Membership is open to anyone willing to accept the demands of commitment to a Christian lifestyle. This entails a very modest standard of living, a difficult step for many people. Most members have joined because they were attracted by the incorporation of Christian values in practical life. In the words of one member, "The church only talks about loving your neighbors, giving up your possessions and loving your enemies . . . this group of people is trying to live that way." Although they are welcomed, there are very few black members at Koinonia. The community's low standard of living is a partial reason for this low representation. Since most black persons in the area have spent their lives in dire poverty, they are hardly in a position to reject material values.

The age span of the membership, from 18 to 80, and the great diversity of backgrounds lend a richness to community life. Although families predominate, there are several houses for singles on the farm. These singles tend to be the white middle class, college-educated youth who form the core of communitarians across the country. The difference lies in their commitment. Most of these youths have already spent a few years at Koinonia, and their permanent commitment is clear. The religious background of the older members ranges through Amish, Catholic, Protestant, and Hutterite. The range of socio-economic backgrounds is as broad and includes former executives, engineers, an anthropologist, a lawyer, and a farmer. Of the original members, Florence Jordan and the Wittcampers remain.

The community's children attend the local schools. Although establishing a school in community was an issue in the fifties, the membership decided against dissipating their energies or hindering their goal of reconciliation. Thus, the Jordans' son was the first white child to graduate from the local black high school.

Each year a large corps of volunteer workers streams into the community, spending a few months to a few years working on the farm or the housing program. As conscientious objectors, Mennonites may perform their years of alternate service at Koinonia. Volunteers are incorporated into community life by sharing housekeeping with the single members and by the Wednesday night sharing meetings with the membership.

The style of life at Koinonia is modest. In contrast to some of the newly formed youth communities which seek a stark living standard, Koinonia does not consume an inordinate amount of energy in self-denial. The simplicity of daily life is balanced by the immeasurable richness which results from fellowship and the sharing of purpose.

Equality rather than uniformity is emphasized in living standards. Each family has its own particular needs and receives according to its requirements. No one has a washing machine or dishwasher, and cars and bicycles are used in common. However, the community engages in much less extensive pooling of resources than the Bruderhof. Married members possess modest homes quite similar to those in Koinonia village, and the single members share houses.

The emphasis at Koinonia is more on sharing through work in community than on sharing of resources. All members participate in community work, even mothers with young children. Members work in either the day care center, the adult education program, or one of the partnership industries or farms. Women rotate the chores of preparing the common midday meal, holding sewing or adult education classes, or working in the office. Although several people hold managerial positions relating to the farm, the housing program, or a partnership industry, no one receives a salary. Each family receives a weekly allowance according to its need, and no community member receives enough to have a taxable income. Each house of singles receives a weekly food allowance plus seven dollars per person per month. The differential between productivity and allowances is plowed back into the Fund for Humanity. Thus, Koinonia expresses brotherhood by sharing not only within community, but also with the surrounding community by providing jobs, housing, and services.

It is the case in all the religious communities discussed in this chapter that the founding of community and the cement for the unity of the early years has been the task of charismatic leadership and diversity of talent. The founders of the Bruderhof, the Reba Place Fellowship, and Koinonia had, in addition to religious training and personal magnetism, a diversity of practical talents so necessary to keep community functioning on a day-to-day basis. The second generation of communitarians is apt to rely upon either the adoption of a firm set of procedures or collective leadership for decision making.

The establishment of Koinonia Partners created a board of directors which does not reside in the community but which appoints a Koinonian as coordinator for decisions relating to the farm. In addition, there is a division of responsibility within Koinonia according to talent and inclination. This is possible because of the small size of the community and the wealth of talent it contains. The membership meets every week to make decisions, and these meetings are generally characterized by a vigorous exchange of ideas, although consensus is the norm for adopting policy.

The most pressing current issue in the community is one which must be faced by all religious communities at some time, the choice between the economics of faith and the economics of realism. Koinonia enjoys a tax-exempt status. However, it is deliberating whether to pay its current arrears on the phone tax bill, which it views as a source of funds for the Vietnam War. The amount of arrears is such that the issue comes close to a choice of either continuing or closing down the farm's operations. The nature and style of antiwar activities conducted by the community are also moot. Other issues hinge upon economic options such as the opening of a bakery. There is some discussion regarding idealism and lifestyles. Some of the older members of the community believe that a comfortable style of living, plain but adequate is necessary for dignity, while the younger members stand on a matter of principle in favor of a very bare living standard. The selection of any course of action, however, is always a matter of prolonged study, discussion, and then decision in a thoroughly democratic fashion. Direct democracy is possible because of the small size of the community and the basic agreement on goals.

Members who differ on the nature of commitment have left Koinonia for a community life more commensurate with their aims. For instance, some families have left Koinonia to exchange a community life with minimum structure and a focus on social outreach for the unity, peace, and cloistered atmosphere of the Bruderhof.[38] At Koinonia the individual is not subjected to a group conscience, mutual admonishment, or the effacement of individual desire on behalf of unity as in the Bruderhof. Although members are encouraged to speak frankly at meetings and although everyone must share responsibility for knowledge and prophecy, they are not responsible for one another in daily affairs. The concept of a theological family is construed much more loosely at Koinonia than in the Bruderhof. Rather than the total social control of the latter, Koinonia affords large areas of privacy for families and individuals. However, among the singles in community there are various attempts to develop the intimacy of family.

Koinonia maintains close relations with the Bruderhof, the Hutterites at Forest River, the Reba Place Fellowship, and the new Christian communities which are being formed. These communities help each other to weather financial, economic, and social crises, and exchange memberships when there are shortages of personnel. In keeping with Koinonia's openness and its involvement with social and political issues, it has close contact with Quaker antiwar groups, the Catholic left, and the intentional community movement as a whole, including such widely different communities as Twin Oaks. In addition, there is a great deal of visiting among communities. Younger members of Koinonia may spend a month or two at Forest River or at Woodcrest.

Koinonia's relations with the surrounding community of Americus have slowly improved if the absence of physical violence can be thus construed. Nobody shoots at the community any more, but there is still a very grudging acceptance. Recently a member sought a job at a county school and was turned down on the grounds of her member-ship in Koinonia. The community is filing suit on her behalf. The civil rights movement and integration in the deep South have not affected the separation between the races. Members of the surrounding white community rarely communicate with members of Koinonia, for anyone associating with either a black person or a Koinonian will be socially excluded from the white community. There are two worlds in the deep South, and Koinonia aims to shake the complacency and injustice of the white culture. It scores small successes along the way, such as the cosponsorship of an integrated little league team. Koinonians are willing to spend a lifetime in the pursuit of such achievements.

Koinonia stands as a unique model of reconciliation in a deeply fragmented society, but it is a model which cannot be widely adopted because of the nature of the commitment it requires. However, the message of renewal it projects can have only a salutary influence on American culture, for it aims at a change of spirit and not at members to swell the ranks of groups seeking power. Its ministers are fishermen for a Christ-centered concept of mutual obligation and not for a particular subculture.

There are important differences between Koinonia and other community groups. Many of the new communities seek renewal through communal living and alternative economic systems. They hope to wring spirit out of a new way of life rather than the reverse. Moreover, Koinonians focus upon widening their reach to extend partnership to all men, whereas groups like Twin Oaks tend to cherish their distinguishing characteristics in Sorelian fashion.

The pitfalls to which Koinonia is prey attend many communities of a radical Christian nature today. They include the question of the confluence of a radical Christianity and radical politics, an issue which has not yet confronted Koinonia, but which is a reality for the Catholic left in South America, for instance. There some members of the church have concluded that it is impossible to realize God's will in a deeply corrupt society and therefore have committed themselves to extensive social change entailing an alliance with Marxists.

The Reba Place Fellowship

The Reba Place Fellowship is the oldest urban intentional community in the United States. It was established in 1957 by a group of Goshen College graduates and Professor John Miller, an Old Testament scholar who had studied the idea of community for years. Mennonite church historians at

Goshen had rediscovered the Anabaptist movement in the early fifties. It was on the basis of this exciting scholarship that the idea arose of developing a church based upon a life in community. Accordingly, John Miller began to gather around him a small group dedicated to a complete sharing of goods. As a consequence of his unorthodox economic plans, he was asked to leave the college, a request that was not without irony. Ten years later, when Reba Place was well established, Professor Miller was invited to teach at Goshen once again.

From an original membership of nine families and a dozen single members, the Reba Place Fellowship now includes forty adults and thirty children. It is a radical Christian church based upon the Anabaptist tradition and considers itself an alternative to the broader society. Like Koinonia Partners, the Society of Brothers, and other communities within the Anabaptist movement, Reba Place practices the lifestyle suggested by the Sermon on the Mount: commitment to Christ, sharing of resources, and mutual responsibility of the members.

As an Anabaptist church, Reba Place rejects infant baptism in favor of the committed, intentional discipleship of Christ in which each member bears responsibility for prophecy and witness and in which the group of assembled believers acts as receptacle for the Holy Spirit. Membership in the community is attained by the expression of a commitment in the form of baptism. Although the procedure of baptism may vary, the essential questions posed to the prospective member during the baptism refer to the person's intention to do God's will in all areas of his life, a recognition of Jesus Christ as the source of God's will, and a covenantal relation with the body of Christ, or church, as the fellowship of believers. This means that each member will be open to his sisters and brothers in Christ and will both give and receive admonishment.

Full membership is preceded by a period served as intentional neighbor. A family or person considering membership will rent an apartment in the immediate vicinity of the fellowship and spend a certain period of time participating in community meetings and worship. The length of time spent in this fashion depends upon the particular needs of the prospective member. Sometimes a person may spend two years as an intentional neighbor and then decide against membership. Or perhaps an intentional neighbor will spend only a few months in this status before he comes to a full decision regarding his commitment.

Because life in community is not institutionalized, members are continually confronted with the nature of their own commitment. One member relinquished her membership for a year and a half although her husband remained a member, because she perceived her participation as motivated by duty rather than intent. Eventually she rejoined with a clearer sense of her own commitment.

The establishment of community, especially an experimental community without a model to guide its formative years, requires a membership which combines the attributes of leadership and talent. Not only does Reba Place include many professionals in social service and teaching, it also has a high proportion of members with training in theology. Among the fellowship are former ministers of the Presbyterian church, the Church of the Brethren, and the Methodist church. Each had experienced disappointment and a sense of limitation within the institutionalized church. These members share a desire for innovation, relevance, and especially the realization of their commitment in everyday life.

Although there are some single adults at Reba Place, the fellowship is mainly composed of families and includes children of all ages, from infants to college youth. There is also a broad spectrum of ages among the adults. Recently the community has purchased a small farm where three of its families live and work. The rationale for this undertaking was to provide a more healthful and suitable location for the children and for community living. Interestingly enough, the group living on the farm is attracted by Skinnerian principles of behavior modification and has sought to incorporate these within the Christian framework.

The fellowship is located in the city of Evanston, Illinois, in the area bordering Reba Place. The building at Reba Place housed the entire membership during the early days, but now accommodates only the Sunday worship and Friday night suppers. A few single members live on the second and third floors of the original structure. Directly behind the Reba Place house is the day care center run by the fellowship. Each family has an apartment in the immediate vicinity, but the fellowship owns all the housing. Members live in close proximity so that they are able to share their daily lives with maximum ease. There are many occasions for community gatherings, but there is also considerable informal exchange outside of these gatherings as the members are committed to openness and mutual concern.

Because the membership is so large, it has been divided into three subgroups for the purposes of governance, both to insure intimacy and to facilitate decision making, which is achieved by consensus. Decisions are contingent upon unanimity.

Wednesday evenings are the chief decision-making meetings. Members assemble within the three subgroups, which are demarcated on the basis of proximity of housing. Between meetings one or two members of each subgroup meet together for the purposes of coordination. The membership as a whole meets once a month, or more often if necessary, in order to consider policy as a whole body.

The leadership for each subgroup amounts to no more than facilitation and opening and closing sessions. The requirement for the position of facilitator is a sensitivity to the feelings and needs of the membership rather than personal charisma. The basic philosophy of the community militates against the concentration of power in a single person. The priesthood of believers is construed as the variety of gifts at Reba Place. Each person is believed to be endowed by God with a particular gift of spiritual insight or a special capability. No

one gift is sufficient, for the church requires the contribution
of each believer in order to come into being. Thus, equality is
assured on the principle of "from each according to his
ability," and talents based upon a forceful personality are
accorded no more weight than those based upon the ability
to listen quietly. In other words, a total and sincere humility
is demanded of all members so that a biblical scholar may learn
from the member who has barely completed a high school
education.

In practice, certain members may hesitate to offer their
thoughts or opinions in front of a person whom they consider
as more competent than themselves. This has been a problem
for some of the women in the community, although the fact
that they recognize it as such constitutes a step towards its
solution.

One of the dangers of consensus in a religious community
is that it can lapse into conformity. Where the unity of the
group is aimed for and where its achievement is perceived as
a sign of the Holy Spirit, an individual may hesitate to put
forth an opinion. The individual who expresses himself may
bear the responsibility of disrupting unity. The result may be
the holding back of individual concerns until they reach crisis
proportions and are expressed in the decision to leave. On the
occasion of such a decision, previously silent members will
admit that they had similar needs. An example of this is the
decision of a couple to leave on the basis of their feeling that
spirit was insufficient in the community. When they admitted
this, other members came forth with the same reflection.
This same couple is planning to join the Bright community in
Ontario, which is currently experiencing a spiritual renewal.
There are no hard feelings when members leave. On the
contrary, contact remains close, and former members frequently return for extended visits. This is not the case in the Bruderhof, where departure is often accompanied by bitterness.
As a church community, matters of faith and policy inter-
twine, and the system of governance reflects this unity of
concerns. Thus, the Wednesday night discussions focus on

issues relating to all aspects of community life. Since the community is not institutionalized, changes in worship and daily life are open-ended, and any of the practices described is subject to change according to the sense of the membership. For instance, there are differences over the changing nature of the membership. However, since membership depends upon a commitment to Christ, it is more a question of reassuring the older members that standards are being maintained. The form of baptism is also a topic of discussion, for there are no hard and fast rules. The tension between individuality and conformity is also moot. This is a difficult problem in a community where the individual ego is considered detrimental to unity but which nevertheless places a high premium on individual gifts. Finally, members have varying attitudes towards the political order. Most members vote, but differ on the amount of interest displayed in politics and social change.

The community is continually in search of more relevant modes for expressing its commitments. Therefore, discussion is far-reaching, with the reservation that there is no long-range planning or policy making. The community's faith requires that the church live in the present with no thought for the future.

The Sunday night meetings include the intentional neighbors as well as the full members. These are meetings of the entire fellowship, and they focus upon personal matters and worship.

Friday night is the weekly fellowship meal. This is an occasion for the entire membership to dine together. Prior to the meal there is a period of sharing during which guests are introduced and the spiritual or personal experiences of the members during the previous week are related.

Friday night is also coffee house night. One of the couples of the community opened up the basement of a fellowship home as a coffee house. Here students of nearby Northwestern University or any interested person can come to talk with members about matters of concern to them, social or personal issues.

Each Saturday the male communitarians provide their service for community maintenance jobs on a rotating basis. Although this is an excellent way of managing personnel resources, the primary purpose is a format for community members to meet and work together.

Sometimes there are worship services on Saturday nights, depending upon whether most of the membership is present in community at that time.

The Sunday worship service has been developed in reaction to what the members perceive as rigidities in the institutional church with its emphasis on forms. Therefore, it is experimental and aims at expressiveness. Usually the service opens with songs which have been composed by the membership. These are accompanied by a guitar and tambourines. A short excerpt from the Bible is then read by one of the community members, and this is followed by a period of sharing similar to the Friday night sharing. This enables members to contribute their unique gifts or insights to the community. Then there is a short play enacted by members on a rotating basis and depicting an episode from the Bible. This portion of the service is intended for the children and is followed by a question period for them. Since the children do not receive any formal religious instruction, this is an occasion for them to have a formal exposure to the community's faith.

Children are not considered community members. When they reach adulthood, they must produce the same expressions of commitment as members coming from the outside. There is no parental pressure on the children to remain in community, a reflection of the concept of the discipleship of Christ and also a reaction on the part of many to their previous religious backgrounds.

Reba Place is unique among religious communities because its male members and some women members have outside jobs. Only one member works in community full time. This is Virgil Voth, spiritual leader and coordinator of community affairs. Perhaps because of the unusual demands of community life, many members have a combination of capabilities. There is a professor of sociology who is also trained for the ministry. Many members work in the field of mental health or as social workers. At one time eight members of the fellowship were working at the Chicago state mental hospital. In some cases, this capability was acquired in order to serve the needs of the emotionally disturbed who sought membership in the community. Other jobs held by the membership include teaching remedial reading, library work, and computer programming. Most members feel that contact with the outside world is a positive benefit and prevents the community from becoming ingrown. However, some members crave the closer fellowship that working in community brings.

The salaries of the various members range from six thousand to eighteen thousand dollars a year. These are placed in a common treasury, and the membership draws out allowances on the basis of need. Homes and cars are held in common. The members live modestly, but their living arrangements are secondary to their purposes in community.

A major issue being debated by the community is the possibility of purchasing two vacant storefronts in the neighborhood. These would become a community workshop where members could work alongside the mentally disturbed and the handicapped in a sheltered environment. The idea was developed by a member who is a psychiatric social worker and who regards his job as a means of keeping in touch with society's needs.

Although Reba Place has generally more of a pietist flavor than Koinonia, which is fully dedicated to social problems, it serves as a healing as well as a prophetic community. Its doors are open to those in serious need, and at one time the community served as a halfway house for a mental institution. However, that experiment terminated with the suicide of one of these patients. Reba Place now includes a number of members with various emotional problems who have been referred to the fellowship by churches of all denominations. This entails a heavy personal and spiritual commitment on the part of the members who enjoy mental stability. It is also a very moving witness to the covenantal relationship of all members, for they participate in community on the basis of genuine equality.

The membership of a troubled family has inspired a very interesting experiment in the extended family. A couple with three children of their own have enlarged their family to include a mother and her six children who have had a history of misfortunes. The combined family now includes two mothers, one father, and nine children. The household functions smoothly on the basis of rotation of chores and the full participation of the children. The father of this enormous family, Julius Belser, is a psychiatric social worker and therefore well equipped for the demands of an extended family. However, his motivation for this undertaking is to be a witness to his faith.

Reba Place community fulfills an urgent need of modern society: an environment in which the troubled can experience love and dignity. Not only are many such people institutionalized for a lack of an alternative environment which is sufficiently sheltered, but their spiritual needs are totally ignored.

Reba Place looks forward to the creation of many Christian communities. As an expression of the desire for an alternative society witnessing the Kingdom of God. Reba Place administers the Shalom Fund dedicated to helping the establishment of new communities. Recently it donated $5,000 to a Memphis group for the purchase of a house. That small community was founded in 1971 by a former drug addict who experienced a sudden and dramatic conversion to Christ and found his calling in establishing a Christian community in the South. Members of this small group visit Reba Place for joint Bible study just as members of the latter will travel to other communities for interchange and suggestions.

The fellowship is sending a member to live at the Church of the Redeemer in Texas, whose congregation of several hundred is living communally. Reba Place feels that it has much to learn from the innovation and viability of the Texas experiment.

There are very close ties between Reba Place and Koinonia Partners. One of Reba Place's founding families, the Zooks, moved to Koinonia when the partnership was established. There are also frequent exchanges of visits with the Hutterites at Forest River, the Bright community in Ontario, and the Society of Brothers. In the fall of 1971 Reba Place hosted a conference of Christian communities which included one of the new communities of the Jesus movement. The latter are traveling among the more established communities to learn the ins and outs of economic viability.

Interchange is beneficial to all Christian communities, as their attributes are often complementary. There are many differences between Reba Place and Koinonia Partners, ranging from setting, membership, and governance, to interpretation of witness. Reba Place is located in an urban environment and depends upon the outside jobs of its members for economic support. On the other hand, Koinonia is dedicated to the solution of rural problems in the deep South and embraces an economic system based upon cooperative farming and light industry. The membership at Reba Place includes very few of the new communitarian youth one finds at Koinonia, but more persons with a Mennonite background. Reba Place has more of a pietist orientation than Koinonia and emphasizes its nature as a close family with the practice of admonishment. In contrast, Koinonia achieves its identity through its distinctive social practice and its outreach. In its concern with the crises of contemporary America, it also functions as a community of study.

The Brotherhood of the Spirit

The Brotherhood of the Spirit is an expression of the hunger for mysticism experienced by many contemporary American youth, an exotic solution to the search for purpose and community. According to one of the members, "Humanity as a

whole has lost sight of the knowing that gives life reason."
The life of this community revolves around fellowship and
a communion of a purely mystical nature.

The primary reality at this Massachusetts community is
that of "inward seeing," to use the words of a medieval
mystic. The contemporary world stops at the gates of the
Warwick residence of the community where psychedelic signs
warn the visitor to leave drugs, alcohol, and tobacco behind.
Within the Warwick community there are no television sets
and very few tokens of a technological society. The buildings
and even the furniture have been designed and built by the
members as if to symbolize the fact that the Brotherhood of
the Spirit represents a new beginning and a new life for each
person.

The four-story structure at Warwick houses 132 people.
It contains an enormous inner room surrounded by a balcony,
which functions as a rain room for the community's children
and as a theater for the adults. Across a broad field is a
building for cooking, eating, and meetings; it also has two
floors of bedrooms. A studio building directly behind is
reserved for meetings. There are other residences for the
remaining 170 members. Northfield house is designed for
women who have recently given birth, pregnant women,
toddlers, and small children, and Gill house accommodates
members of the community's rock band, *Spirit in the Flesh*.
The residences at Northfield, Turners Falls, and Warwick are
considered schools by the community, for members are housed
according to spiritual progression. "The first school is Warwick
House where we learn that perfect thought exists. Northfield
is the house where we learn to recognize a perfect thought.
At Turners Falls we learn to manifest the thought all the
time."[39]

The Brotherhood of the Spirit was founded by Michael
Metelica in 1967 and now includes 300 members. Michael
Metelica is in his early twenties and seems no different from
his fellow communitarians. He grew up on a farm near the
Vermont border, not far from the community, and led a

fairly uneventful life typical of small New England towns. However, he claims that feelings of transcendence and cosmic visions in his preschool years were intimations of his future role as a spiritual leader. At the age of 16 he left high school and hitchhiked to San Francisco to join the Hell's Angels. He soon became disappointed with his life among that group and returned to his parents' home in Leyden, Massachusetts, after a year. There he constructed a treehouse where he lived a solitary life of meditation, absorbed in trying to recapture his childhood visions. During this period he met Elwood Babbit, a local medium, who convinced him of his mission to establish a new religious movement. Michael and his treehouse became a magnet for local youngsters, and a year after his return from California, Michael and his followers constituted a group of twenty-one. By the spring of 1970 the group had swelled to 70 members, all of whom were crowded into a single residence at Heath, Massachusetts. Several months later the Brotherhood of the Spirit started the construction of their Warwick residence and purchased a large house in Northfield, Massachusetts. Since that time the community has boasted a history of spiraling successes, a growing membership, and increasing assets. Aside from the four homes and 75 acres of farmland, the community has recently purchased an entire block of buildings in the town of Turners Falls. These include a movie theater, bowling alley, and four storefronts, all destined for various community enterprises.

Although new members continue to swell the ranks of the brotherhood, the turnover in membership is very low and many of the original members remain. The age span of the membership extends from a dozen infants to an elderly man and includes a large group of teenagers. No one is turned away provided he accepts the conditions of entering the community and is willing to relinquish his resources to the group. Prospective members are tested in the daily group meetings at Warwick. After two months of provisional status, the community votes on whether to admit the person to full membership. Michael Metelica has the option to overrule any decision or even to shorten the period of provisional membership in certain cases.

At the Brotherhood of the Spirit, there are few of the college-educated, middle class youth which constitute the chief membership of so many new intentional communities. The community includes a person with a Ph. D. and two with masters' degrees, but a number of the members have barely completed high school, and many have dropped out of college during their first year. The community attracts young people who have troubled lives and for whom no sufficiently sheltered noninstitutional place exists in society. It has welcomed juvenile delinquents and people with mild psychological problems.

The brotherhood is noted for its appeal to youth with drug problems and responds to the needs of these youngsters by giving them a sense of their own importance and of broader purpose as embodied in the community. It also serves as a haven for pregnant teenagers, or for mature women who did not make all the difficult hurdles which mean acceptance in society, such as a high school education or a stable marriage.

Anne, an attractive woman of thirty, has been at the brotherhood with her toddler daughter Tao for a year and intends to stay there permanently. Tao is residing at Northfield with the other toddlers while Anne lives at the Warwick residence. Sharing the responsibility of child rearing is welcome to a person who is separated from her husband and emotionally troubled. Anne with her problems, her failures, and her terrible need for love and acceptance is a typical member of the Brotherhood of the Spirit. In a totally unplanned manner the community serves as a haven for the world's rejects, constituting a small society which has few behavioral norms.

Some members have been drawn to the community by strange visions. One young member dreamed that he saw "Brotherhood of the Spirit" etched in cathode-ray tubes on a computer. The following week, when a salesman called to offer him a second-hand computer, he perceived this as an affirmation of his vision and departed for Warwick.

The standard of living at the brotherhood is rather spare but adequate. The community supports its large membership in a variety of ways. The rock band directed by Michael Meṭelica, *Spirit in the Flesh*, supplies a portion of the community's income. In addition, fifty or more members bring in cash through such outside jobs as plumbing, electrical work, construction, teaching, and nursing. John Pollard, the brotherhood's business manager, has a master's degree in business and makes all the financial decisions for the community, from the purchase of equipment to the spending money for each member. He is assisted by Alan Harris, who is in charge of purchasing food and supplies for each house. A 43-year-old mother of four, a former systems analyst, takes care of the accounting for the community. Since all members are required to turn over all their property on joining the community, the brotherhood is responsible for all the needs of each member.

The community operates a variety of small businesses near its four locations. These include a pool hall, the Rebirth Dance Studio in Brattleboro, Vermont, an antique jewelry store in Amherst, the Rough Edge Leather Crafts, Lumière Photo Studio, Krishna Electric, Cold Zap Refrigeration, a bakery, and an ice cream shop.

Some of the members grow vegetables for the community. They also cooperate with local farmers by exchanging their services, such as bagging or grading, in return for fertilizer and supplies. Over the years these members have become successful farmers. At the 1972 Franklin County Fair, the community won 14 prizes in the vegetable display in addition to prizes in art, baking, and flower arrangement.

Despite the considerable array of economic pursuits, the community has no system for allocating responsibility among the membership. Each member who is able must work, but may choose any occupation. In the economic sphere the brotherhood practices a true anarchism by relying upon the interest and responsibility of each member to accomplish community tasks. Generally, members are loath to discuss such matters as subsistence and governance because they regard the communion of their membership as the primary reality of their life.

The visitor to the Brotherhood of the Spirit is immediately struck by the atmosphere of cheerfulness and warmth. Members hug each other with brotherly gusto and by their emphasis on affect appear to be reacting to an unfriendly world. However, this harmony and apparent mystical union of each and all is difficult to maintain. The primary reality of the brotherhood is the breaking down of boundaries between people established by roles, formality, rules of interaction, and status. The brotherhood uses the resultant intimacy as a source of social vitalization for the community. It is achieved through the group meetings, which are designed to dissipate customary reserve. Meetings are scheduled daily, before breakfast and after dinner, or at any time a member so desires. Although community business is discussed at these meetings, they are primarily devoted to easing tensions among the membership and insuring that the community functions smoothly.

At least once a day the group gathers in order to achieve a feeling of spiritual communion. At first the participants sit quietly in a circle. During this period of quiet the individual prepares himself for communication by emptying himself of thought. Then certain individuals will feel moved to carry on a quiet exchange, or an individual with a personal or spiritual problem will feel comfortable enough to bring it up for discussion. There is no formal adjournment of such meetings. There is a core of persons concentrating, and participators on the margins of the group flow in and out of the room. Afterwards the energy and satisfaction released from such a session flow through the most routine chores of daily life.

The harnessing of energy in such a manner is possible because members of the Brotherhood of the Spirit agree on the values and beliefs of the community and because each member participates fully, maintaining the intensity of the communion.

It is also possible because all members join in giving a positive interpretation to the experience. During these meetings members often speak of being on the brink of a certain experience or of feeling fear. The mutual trust of the members and the agreement on the goals of the group is a way of overcoming the fear of a communion which is essentially unfamiliar. The resultant unity and euphoria are the recompense for relinquishing the protection of formal roles and modes of behavior. The wholehearted participation of all members in these sessions results from the fact that the community demands unity of belief and values regarding interpersonal relations. People are judged on the basis of their attitudes rather than by their behavior. A hostile, querulous, or aggressive person is highly visible in the community and usually turns out to be a temporary visitor.

In its search for communion the Brotherhood of the Spirit has assimilated important techniques from the drug culture and the Quaker religion without institutionalizing them.

The joy of unity is difficult to sustain for long periods of time and is vulnerable to periodic depressions in which the accumulated tensions of intimacy are reflected in disunity and disarray. Gripe sessions are scheduled on the basis of the need to release these tensions. During these sessions a member may be told that he exudes hostility and there will be an angry exchange. However, the member initiating the exchange directs his comments in a totally controlled way. These dialogues function as catharsis and are intended as service.

Although the brotherhood professes a strict equality among members, seniority operates as an important factor in conferring status within the community. A core group of original members, including Michael's wife Jeanne, has no official power but wields considerable influence. Michael Metelica is not only the spiritual leader of the Brotherhood of the Spirit (he has proclaimed himself founder of the New Church of Christ of the New Age); he appears to enjoy unlimited power and to act as court of appeals for even the smallest issues. The community can be fairly characterized as a dictatorship with legitimacy residing in Michael Metelica's alleged spiritual powers.

Although the community stresses the importance of appropriate attitudes among the members, there are few actual restrictions on behavior. Members must relinquish their property on joining the community and may not indulge in alcohol, tobacco, or drugs. Nor is any sexual promiscuity tolerated. Members who wish to cohabit or to have children must marry. There have been several marriages among members which have been performed in local churches.

The children in community enjoy great freedom. In 1971 the school-age children voted to terminate the free school run by the community and to attend the local public schools instead. The smaller children are free to select certain adults to care for them while their parents work or when a parent wishes to be relieved of responsibility for a period of time. Preschoolers may attend a community nursery staffed by their mothers on a rotating basis.

The membership of the Brotherhood of the Spirit is large enough to wield considerable influence in local politics. In Warwick the brotherhood constitutes a near majority of town population and could either influence the town govern- ment or swamp the school system. However, the com- munity regards contemporary society on all levels, local or national, as thoroughly corrupt and as a field for missionary activity rather than for political participation. Much as the sectarian communities, the brotherhood distinguishes itself from what it considers an immoral society.

The Brotherhood of the Spirit devotes a great deal of its energies to outreach. A portion of the large membership is constantly on the move, bearing the message of peace and brotherhood. Their main outreach is through the rock band and the songs composed by Michael Metelica. Some typical titles are "The Meek Shall Inherit the Earth" and "The Blind Leading the Blind." The band makes recordings for Metro- media and travels from one end of the country to the other gathering up young and old converts or leaving the message of fellowship for those it does not convert. The brotherhood welcomes the attention of the media and has been on television several times. It also publishes a magazine devoted to the exposition of its beliefs.

The brotherhood directs its missionary activities to a variety of groups. Members have entertained the Hell's Angels in New York and have spent the entire day riding the crowded New York subways introducing people to each other. They have even passed out leaflets at a Catholic college in Worcester. Recently they have set up a coffee house and poolroom in the town of Greenfield, Massachusetts, so that they can reach an older population. They are inspired by intense fervor and untiring optimism, convinced that heaven on earth will be achieved in their generation and that their message will be received by the entire world, not just the United States.

The substance of the belief spread by the Brotherhood of the Spirit includes reincarnation, the Aquarian Gospel, and the Seven Immutable Laws of the Universe. The origin of these laws is very simply attributed to "conditions observed by the membership in life situations." Briefly, these laws include *order* within the universe, and a *balance* between the mind as positive and the brain as negative, for the brain has the possibility of destroying spirit. *Harmony* is the third law, and the fourth law refers to *growth* from the carnal to the celestial, which is directed by the free will. The fifth law, a *perception of God,* tells the faithful "to look ahead into that which is unseen and believe in the reality of the unseen which does operate but which does not control the free will of an individual spirit." *Spiritual love* and *compassion,* the sixth and seventh universal laws, bring man into an understanding of and harmony with the universe.[40] The purpose of these laws is to achieve unity among all men.

The Aquarian Gospel, written by Levi H. Dowling, is the source of the metaphysics animating the seven laws. According to this philosophy, all primary substance of spirit is pervasive and constitutes "universal mind." When the mind of man is in accord with the universal mind, man enters into a conscious recognition of the Akashic impressions.[41] According to the Aquarian Gospel, man is both a thought of God and a seed who holds within himself the attributes of God. Though he has to suffer trials on earth, ultimately man will be saved. His flesh and even his soul will fall away as so many dried petals, and man will unfold in the Holy Breath.

The path to universal mind is a spiral one, for man achieves perfection through repeated reincarnation. Members of the brotherhood speak easily of their thirty former lives which form the substance of their memories and which are perceived as attempts to reach balance of spirit. Michael Metelica is convinced that he was formerly both Peter the Apostle and Robert E. Lee. He also believes that there is a visible aura around each person's head which changes to reflect one's spiritual progress. Apparently, only he can interpret the changes in color and intensity of these auras.

The beliefs of this community are deeply anti-intellectual. Its members view the source of all evil, whose supreme manifestation is the separation of men, as the intellect, the brain. They consider Western rationality as the source of the world's troubles and would alleviate these through mystical experiences.

Although the beliefs expressed by the Brotherhood of the Spirit are somewhat bizarre, the community provides an interesting model for changes in interpersonal relations, as well as acting as a haven for the troubled.

As a model for change in interpersonal relations, the brotherhood demonstrates the retrieval of affect in a controlled manner. It has explored new ways of bridging hiatus between institutionalized or game behavior and spontaneity, without the use of drugs or alcohol.

Communities such as the Brotherhood of the Spirit provide repose and relief from the bewildering complexities of modern society. As retreats for the restoration of the self, they replace families, for most members come from families unable to perform this function for their members. Depending upon one's outlook, one can either refer to the

Brotherhood of the Spirit as a place where anyone who wishes may work for self-renewal and fellowship or as a haven for society's failures. The brotherhood attracts many people who would otherwise fill the dreary institutions society has built to hide its weaker members, and gives them both a feeling of their own worth and a sense of participating in a highly successful and dynamic venture.

THREE

ANARCHISM, DECENTRALISM, AND THE NEW RURAL COMMUNITIES

Anarchism

There is no coherent set of ideas one can refer to as communitarian thought. The ideologies and premises underlying the various contemporary communities are as diverse as the experiments themselves. They range from new visions of Anabaptism, through the social thought of B. F. Skinner, the Aquarian Gospel, the revival of anarcho-syndicalism preached by the new collectives, to the anarchism which inspires many rural communities.

For many people the term "anarchist" evokes the specter of bombings, terrorist practices, and revolutionary ideology. However, this is a misconception, for anarchism does not oppose order or society. Rather, it opposes external authority, power, and coercion in favor of voluntary cooperation and self-imposed restraints. Anarchists attribute chaos and disorder to the state and trace all moral and social evils to the existence of government. Anarchism is essentially a philosophy of society, a society without government in which the regulation of public affairs and the adjustment of diverse interests occur by free and spontaneous agreements concluded between individuals and among territorial and professional groups. Its proponents believe that justice and freedom will prevail only when the state is eliminated in favor of the voluntary association of groups for production, consumption, and the satisfaction of the various needs of civilized men.

Anarchist thought embraces a variety of doctrines, practices, and attributes towards social change. However, the unifying spirit or theme in anarchism is that of rebellion against the established order. This rebellion may take the form of change through peaceful means, as in the creation of communities actualizing alternative values. On the other hand, it may espouse a form of symbolic violence, as in syndicalism, or it may constitute a purely philosophical opposition to a particular status quo. The starting point of an anarchist position is generally the evaluation of contemporary society with respect to the fulfillment of human potential, freedom, and justice. Thus, it is a movement which acquires its identity through its attitude towards contemporary events and the ideas prevalent on the left in the spectrum of political thought.

While anarchism shares with socialism its concern for egalitarianism and labor, Marxism and anarchism animate rival strains in left-wing thought. Classical Marxism embraces anarchism as a political philosophy yet contradicts it by its socialist ideology. For Marx the goal of history and the highest form of society is a stateless form. However, the road from the "realm of necessity" to the "realm of freedom" is the dictatorship of the proletariat. The anarchists, however, do not believe that the construction of a new state is necessary in order to abolish the old one or that a workers' revolutionary state is a necessary step in transition to a stateless society. On the contrary, the temporary state may prove as repressive as the system it has replaced.

Nor do anarchists look more kindly on the moderate socialists who would achieve reform by evolutionary means and through governmental institutions. They believe that freedom must be achieved integrally, and their rebellious spirit brooks no compromise. Piecemeal reform is a sham for anarchists, who see each evil in society as fulfilling a function essential to the political system as a whole. For instance, they would consider that prison reform fails to touch the reason prisons exist at all, which they perceive as the unequal distribution of property. Besides, they would claim that even a democratic socialist government hinders justice and genuine community, for any system of external authority, even if controlled by the people, is inherently corrupt. Irrespective of its constitution, the state is by definition alien from the society it governs and has a life and needs of its own. By sustaining the military and, in some cases, private property, the government prevents people from cooperating. It keeps its citizens so spiritually impoverished that they cannot fulfill their social propensities as human beings.

Anarchists in industrial society perceive repression not only in the government and its military establishment, but also in the multinational corporations and the bureaucracies which create foreign and domestic policy for an unwilling society. For contemporary anarchists, the public schools and the mass media have replaced religion as the chief falsifiers of truth. Above all, they oppose the inertia of rigid institutions. their imperviousness to the needs and desires of ordinary men.

Since a systematic program or even guidelines require some sort of executive authority, anarchists suggest no program. Since social progress is incompatible with authority, the new order will be ushered in by each and every one making it and living it. "Go ahead and live" is the advice of Mildred Loomis, a founder and guiding spirit of the Heathcote community. The anarchist vision is one of self-regulation and cooperation. It takes flesh when each person grasps his destiny and attains self-sufficiency through his own efforts and a purely voluntary and spontaneous cooperation with others. Sectarian communities share with anarchist thinkers their passion for egalitarianism, a belief in decision making by consensus, and the desire for a loose federation of communities as the new order. However, they part company over the questions of freedom and self-regulation. For the sectarian communities freedom implies liberty of conscience, but tempered by obedience to the state in secular matters. In addition, sectarians regard freedom as the liberation of the higher man from his worldly self of ambition and pride. On the other hand, anarchist philosophers such as Peter Kropotkin consider sociability rather than the Hobbesian axioms as the law of nature. For Kropotkin unbridled individualism is not natural but a peculiarly modern growth fostered by the state. In its quest for complete power, the state destroys all institutions in which either self-reliance or mutual cooperation is practiced.

If the new rural intentional communities seem like new wine in old bottles, it is partially because anarchism evokes certain aspects of conservatism. Both schools of thought agree that the individual and society will flourish in direct proportion to the curtailment of government activity.

Decentralism and the Social Thought of Ralph Borsodi

At a recent conference sponsored by the Heathcote School of Living, a crowd of 400 packed the recreation hall of a world fellowship camp to overflowing. People stood four rows deep at the entrance and others lined the aisles in order to hear a lengthy speech delivered by an elderly scholar and economist, Ralph Borsodi. The subject of the two-hour address was decentralized industry and decentralized agriculture, alternative means of livelihood which would insure both liberty and security to those who practiced them. This model for a new life appeals to the feeling of powerlessness experienced by many young people today, particularly those who turn to community.

Decentralism and homesteading represent one of the older branches of the community movement and are the product of the depression years, the ideas of Ralph Borsodi, Henry George, and Lewis Mumford's critique of the city. Homesteading was the refuge of the radicals of the thirties, such as

Helen and Scott Nearing. One might question associating this phenomenon with contemporary communitarianism and apolitical youth, who are chiefly concerned with the transformation of the family, of sex roles, and of lifestyles. But these two movements converge in their anarchist philosophies and in their radical rejection of contemporary society. They are separated in time by the postwar generation which labored to achieve the American dream of the fifties: the home, the car, and the economic independence prized as the opportunity of a free society. The youth of today, on the other hand, have tasted the affluence of the postindustrial society and found it wanting. They oppose it for what they have condemned as its spiritual vacuousness and for its threat to the environment, rather than for political reasons. Although the foundations of their disaffection differ, there has been a considerable amount of influence and cooperation between the two generations of communitarians. The Heathcote School of Living, run by a disciple and contemporary of Ralph Borsodi, Mildred Loomis, has helped countless young adults learn the fundamentals of homesteading and has spawned a variety of intentional communities throughout the United States, including the May Valley Cooperative in Renton, Washington, Sky View Acres in Pomona, New York, and Nethers in Virginia.

Dr. Ralph Borsodi was a consulting economist for the Du Pont Corporation and R. H. Macy & Co. in the early thirties, when he was invited to assist Dayton, Ohio, cope with the depression along the lines suggested by his program for homesteading in his book *This Ugly Civilization*. His answer to the social agencies serving the thousands of unemployed was to help families by getting them on the land in model communities. There they could produce their own food, clothing, and shelter. As a result of the Dayton experiment, which foundered over a combination of problems, not the least of which was bureaucratic delays in funding, Borsodi concluded that education in self-reliance would have to be an integral part of community building. For this purpose he founded the School of Living in Suffern, New

York, in 1936, as well as homesteads which have served as models for communities all over the United States. Since then he has devoted himself entirely to a critique of industrialized society and the dissemination of decentralist ideas. During the twenties and thirties Borsodi's ideas received little attention. Today his program has struck a responsive chord among the many youth who are critical of urban society and anxious for a better life. Decentralism differs from anarchism only in the emphasis it places on the abolition of government. Decentralists are content to reduce government to a bare minimum of activity, whereas anarchists look forward to the complete elimination of the state. Decentralists agree with anarchists that both religion and government erect barriers to the good life. They believe that the former evades life's great problems, and burdens the search for morality with dogmatism; governments are an excuse for the exercise of power, keeping their citizens in a state of dependence and actually hindering the development of the arts, education, and any institutions in which man can cooperate for their real needs.

However, as with Marxism, the main thrust of Borsodi's social critique is aimed at the debasement of work. His visions evoke the utopian strains of Marx: "Labor must be self-justifying, the means to life and the end of life. . . . When it is only a means to life, it becomes a curse."[1] However, his explanation for the blight and social misery attending industrialization is not the class domination of the means of production, but the centralization of those means. Borsodi does not reject technology or the achievements of modern science. Properly managed, decentralized, and geared to a homestead economy, they can be life-enhancing. Unlike Marx, however, he advises the workers to leave the city and return to the land. But he also urges them to bring along labor-saving machinery.

Borsodi was one of the earliest critics of the consumer society in his insistence that true happiness comes from producing not as much as possible, but as little as possible.

He criticized the capitalist system for regarding production as an end in itself rather than as a means to a fulfilling life.[2] Under the capitalist system, he claimed, men are forced to consume an endless array of useless and prematurely obsolete goods, despoiling natural resources in the process. Mass production, the most characteristic feature of capitalism, destroys culture by imposing uniformity of tastes and depersonalizing labor. In exchange for robbing men of fulfilling labor, the system provides an empty leisure and a spiraling consumption.

In 1932 Borsodi advocated an industrial counterrevolution. All mass-produced goods which could be turned out on a homestead, such as clothing and processed food, should no longer be purchased. Forty years later communities of youth and middle-aged persons are producing their own food and necessities. They are disengaging themselves from the economy by refusing careers in favor of subsistence farming and crafts, eschewing therefore the most characteristic products of American technology, from cars to education.

For Marx freedom means collective control of the means of production by the workers. Borsodi believes that men will be liberated when the family, not the working class, retrieves its destiny from the jaws of a capitalist, consumption-oriented economy by assuming responsibility for its livelihood, its education, and its culture. "Move on a homestead," he advocates. "Develop a garden and an orchard . . . acquire livestock and the machinery necessary to produce the basic necessities of life."[3] Homesteading is less time-consuming than any other occupation. With the time thus saved, one can work at crafts or in a profession and earn just enough to purchase items which cannot be produced on the farm. This is the foundation of the good life: escape from the urban turmoil to the peace of the country and a self-sufficient life on the land. During the depression, when many people suffered penury, the Borsodi family enjoyed a comfortable life on their homestead. Moreover, the latter with its extended family or network of families is also a refuge for its ill, elderly, and unemployed members.

The homestead advocated by Borsodi need not be limited to the extended family, but can be established by any group of individuals. However, he stipulates that the membership must be large enough to insure a rotation of work, and also continuity while members are absent for travel or study. It must also be small enough to allow administration by common consent. Work on a homestead eliminates excessive specialization and the dichotomies of physical and mental labor, work and play. Borsodi attests that such a life is enjoyed every day and every moment.[4]

Today there are hundreds of farming communes and communities throughout the east and on the west coast of the United States: Packers' Corners in Vermont, Montague community in Massachusetts, the Weavers in Maine, the Oxford community in New York—the list is endless. They represent a version of Borsodi's reaction to the fragmentation and artificiality of life in a highly industrialized society. However, they are also the products of this society, because it has provided mass education at the university level and hence a generation well versed in social critique. In addition to the expansion of higher education, the wealth of American industrial society has prolonged the period of youth as the time available for experimentation in lifestyles.

The new rural communities hold many of the same values as the homesteading movement which flowered in the thirties: they favor natural childbirth and breast feeding; a life close to nature; self-sufficiency in the necessities of life, thus avoiding waste and overconsumption; health and nutrition through organic gardening; a simple and tranquil lifestyle; and fulfilling interpersonal relations.

The Green Revolution

While Ralph Borsodi was engaged in building homesteading communities for the unemployed in Dayton, Ohio, he met a young teacher who was searching for ways of coping with the causes of the depression. Borsodi convinced her that a decentralized society of rural communities was the answer, and after a year at his School of Living Mildred Loomis became a devoted advocate of his ideas. Today she refers to herself as "a dropout of the thirties." For the past forty years she has paralleled Borsodi's efforts by sponsoring conferences on community building and seminars on homesteading, publishing, speaking, and serving as a personal example of the "green revolution."

The "green revolution" means a lifestyle without coffee, potato chips, soft drinks, most meats, alcohol, and tobacco. It means a sober diet of raw and cooked vegetables grown in an organic way and guaranteeing a vigorous and healthful existence. Its proponents believe that good health and clean living are akin to morality and the good life. The homesteader grows his own food and is practically self-sufficient in pro-curing his subsistence. This occupation is both healthful and pleasurable, carried on in the open air amidst the peace and beauty of the country. It is intended to stand as an example of order and serenity compared to the frenzy of modern life in urban centers. Self-reliance is the motto for all facets of life under the Green Revolution. It aims to prove that one can eschew the marketplace entirely and even the government itself, an outlook which is basically anarchist. The homesteader educates his children under the free school system, and the only concession he makes to the state is in paying taxes for the land. However, even this act is contrary to the fundamental beliefs of these revolutionists, for they subscribe wholeheartedly to Henry George's views on the land. The decentralist position can best be summarized in a quotation from Mildred Loomis's *Go Ahead and Live.* [5]

The Green Revolution moves opposite to the Red Revolution, not bloody and violent, but quietly via persuasion and education. Not through government and the state, but through personal and family action. Not through control of some people by other people, but free of external controls. Wherever individuals, agencies and institutions in Russia or elsewhere distort and dominate the purpose and activities of other individuals, there the Red Revolution is active. Wherever individuals decide and implement their own purposes, they are part of the Green Revolution.

When Dr. Borsodi withdrew from the School of Living in order to devote himself to compiling his ideas in a major work, he suggested that Mildred and John Loomis take over the school. From 1945 to 1965 this community of sixteen families with a school as its center was located at Lane's End, Ohio. There the school taught health and nutrition, organic gardening, and skills related to homesteading. In the words of Ralph Borsodi, "The goal of education will be how to live, not how to succeed or make money; the content will be real problems of living, not academic subjects; the method will be families building and living together around a school."[6] Since 1943 the community has published a monthly newspaper, *Green Revolution,* which promotes the concepts of intentional community, organic gardening, the trusteeship of land, and decentralism.

In 1965 the School of Living was transferred to Freeland, Maryland, and is currently known as Heathcote Center. Although retired as director of the School of Living, Mildred Loomis is still active in organizing conferences, speaking, and writing. Age has not eroded her rebellious temperament, and she continues to advocate, with undiminished fervor, a life outside the "system."

Heathcote Center

Heathcote is located on 37 acres of meadows and woods in Baltimore County, Maryland. True to decentralist principles, the community holds the land in common and provides most of its own food. None of the members earns enough money to pay income taxes, and the community is practically self-sufficient.

Heathcote is managed by a board of trustees who are not all residents of the community. The president of Heathcote,

Tim Ryan, lives on his seven-acre homestead in Chapel Hill, North Carolina, which he also uses as a small school of living and from which he heads a movement to buy and secure land for holding in trust. The chairman of the board, Don Newey, is director of *DEVCOR,* a consumer-producer cooperative for farm products. Another board member, Erick Hansch, is on the staff of the International Independence Institute in Ashby, Massachusetts. The remaining members reside at Heathcote. Funds for the school are partially supplied by the proceeds from Tim Ryan's landscaping business.

The administration of daily life at Heathcote is accomplished by its 15 or so residents according to anarchist principles. There are no leaders, no procedures for making decisions, and no plans for a division of labor. Members build their own dwellings and are usually involved in their own projects for the community. Everyone "does his own thing" occupationally, and people accept responsibilities for the newspaper, the garden, building projects, and housekeeping "spontaneously." Meetings of the membership are held frequently, generally once a week for business and once a week for personal relations. When decisions are called for, they are reached by consensus.

There is no agreement on goals among the residents of Heathcote. Some of them incline strongly towards School of Living principles, while others agree only on the adoption of communal living as an alternative to the "system" and the nuclear family. Because of the variety of motives which bring people to the community and the considerable turnover in residents, Heathcote functions as a haven as well as a school of living. Once refreshed and with a new awareness of their goals, Heathcoters move on, either to form communities of their own or to seek a community in which they can settle. Most leave with a knowledge of the fundamentals of gardening and related skills.

The motives which bring people to Heathcote are the varying themes of a generation of youth alienated from their society's goals and institutions. Some see Heathcote as an opportunity to regain a sense of personal worth through such achievements as growing one's own food and learning how to be as self-reliant as possible. Unhappiness with an employment situation or emotional isolation brings others. Some are college dropouts, and many flee the noise, dirt, and crime of the city. "The world appears too hostile, too diseased, too dissociated in the city. . . . Its economic rat race, its machines which have taken over, its drug addicts . . . have put too many of us over the edge."[7] Most of these people seek to reestablish connections between man and nature, work and well-being, which the complexities of modern society have obscured for them.

The population of Heathcote is highly transient. Aside from Mildred Loomis, who no longer resides permanently at Heathcote, the oldest resident has lived there for five years. Ten have stayed on for two years, and the others average a stay of from a few weeks to a few months. Permanent residents are those who have remained at Heathcote for more than a few months. Some of them refer to the turnover with a certain optimism and claim that a permanent state of flux functions as a guarantee against constraint. For these people, community means the environment in which self-regulation can flourish.

The different generations at Heathcote agree on the value of education modeled on Summerhill, natural childbirth, and breast feeding, as well as the virtues of organic gardening. However, the youthful generation of Heathcoters shares the views of its more radical contemporaries on the nuclear family.

A former editor of *Green Revolution* told an inquiring couple that more than 75 per cent of the married couples entering community will either separate or alter their monogamous status.[8] Couples in community experience tensions between the desire for prolonged intimacy with one person and an intense relationship with the community as a whole. Because it focuses on interpersonal relations, Heathcote provides the security and companionship which these youth perceive as the value of the family.

But there seems to be a deep hiatus between the School of Living principles, developed by the board of trustees, and the majority of residents at Heathcote who regard the community as an experiment in group living. The School of Living exists to promote its views of the good life and to help others achieve it: nonexploitive economics, including the trusteeship of land, health, security, nonviolence and independence. On the other hand, the communards at Heathcote concentrate on health through nutrition, meditation, and interpersonal relations. They share no commitment to the community as a source of purpose or responsibility. At Heathcote the central issues of community, mutual obligation, and the relation of the individual to the collectivity, is skirted. It is the individual who decides in his own manner when and how to participate in community and what shall be the nature of his relations with the totality. Given these characteristics, one can describe the residents of Heathcote more accurately as a communal (free as opposed to blood-related) family rather than as a community

Communities and Families

Given the lack of emphasis on generally accepted and hence authoritative purpose and mutual obligation or responsibility, the term "commune" or "communal family" seems a more appropriate description of groups such as Heathcote.* As a family, Heathcote provides its members with emotional security. Unlike a member of a biological family, the member is free to express himself regarding roles and style.

Community, however, is concerned with many crucial aspects of man's life: family, livelihood, education, and perhaps, though not necessarily, religion. These are integrated in a socialization process in which the institutions

---

* See page 3.

of the community are consistent with its purposes and principles. It was the discontinuity between purpose and procedure in American life which inspired community building in the fifties. The Federation of Intentional Communities (FIC) summarized its perception of the hiatus in this manner: "The common order and practice prevail, while the teaching and preaching within that order forever broaden the gap between experience and life."[9]

The Federation of Intentional Communities, which flowered in the fifties, stressed democratic methods and encouraged theorizing and dialogue on the principles as well as the practices of community. But the rural community movement today, unless inspired by ideology or behaviorism, avoids conceptualizing and prefers to focus on practical details.

A loose definition of intentional community was adopted by the FIC in 1953. It sets as criteria for community a minimum size of three families or five adults, an organization sufficient to assure a recognizable social entity, and shared land or housing, or sufficient geographic proximity of members to insure continuous fellowship. Among the basic concepts of community articulated by the FIC are: sharing in a whole way of life; the importance of the spirit animating community; and the necessity of active participation in community for the maturity of the person and of the social order.[10] At that time intentional community was conceived as the seed of a new social order inspired by the principles of mutual concern, pooling of resources, democratic and nonviolent methods, and a concern for balance between the worth of the person and the social whole.

Although the FIC dissolved in the late fifties, partially because of an abrupt break with the group by the Society of Brothers, its member communities are still flourishing today: Celo, May Valley Cooperative, the Reba Place Fellowship, Koinonia Partners, Gould Farm, and Tanguey Homesteads. The Vale in Yellow Springs, once a model of intentional community, has dwindled to a very few families. However, the resource center associated with it, Community

Service, Incorporated, continues to keep the flame of intentional community alive by the prodigious efforts of its director Griscom Morgan.

The intentional community movement in America has been characterized by alternating periods of proliferation and decline. The flurry of community building in the post-World War II period was inspired by a rebellion against what communitarians perceived as the uncharitableness and impersonality of modern life, much as today's community movement. However, this protest against the social order and urban life was not influenced by such a broad spectrum of political and religious thought as is today's communitarian movement. The latter has been inspired by such diverse currents as Eastern mysticism and popularized versions of Maoism. While contemporary communitarians share with their forebears the inclination to experiment in new modes of life and while their revolt against the broader society is inspired by similar motives, profound differences separate them. Today's rural communitarians have skirted the basic issues of community tackled by the FIC. The communitarians who flock to conferences on intentional community and who listen to Dr. Borsodi with such rapt attention have not confronted the problems of authority and of procedures for adjusting their interests and handling conflicts. While they yearn for humaneness, this yearning is diffuse. They seem to lack a clear perception of the philosophy and practice of humanism when compared to such groups as Gould Farm or Koinonia Partners.

Contemporary Rural Communities

In the late sixties hundreds of farm communities and communes were formed in the eastern United States as well as on the west coast. They proliferate in New Hampshire, Maine, Vermont, Massachusetts, and Virginia. The back-to-the-land people are as invisible to the broader society as the rural poor. However, the majority of the 400 people attending a regional homesteading conference in New Hampshire in the spring of 1973 were representing community farms. They were a bare suggestion of a large movement. In addition, the age span of the movement has broadened in the past few years. From being a phenomenon of young adults in their early and mid-twenties, homesteaders now include groups in their thirties and forties with children of primary school age, and a sprinkling of former professionals in engineering, systems analysis, and teaching. The Alpha community even includes three members in their early fifties.

Although the age span of rural communitarians is broadening, their socio-economic origins remain those of white middle class, college-educated Americans. There are no black or ethnic Americans represented in this movement. While the latter constitute a majority in the large urban centers, their recent migration from a grueling life in rural areas does not make them ready candidates for rural communities. They are hardly free to reject an abundance and participation which they have never tasted.

A variety of motives has inspired the return to the land and community living. These include the revolutionary aims of the rural collectives, dissatisfaction with urban life and traditional work roles, and the pursuit of a decentralized economy. While the politically inspired groups constitute a highly distinct strand of communitarians, most rural groups share the desire to establish a new economic system based upon equality, cooperation, and ecological balance.

Many of the rural communitarians who are in their mid-twenties and over are former political activists who have exchanged their political goals for the more personal aim of a new lifestyle. Weary radicals whose years of pickets, vigils, and peace walks have borne them little fruit flock to rural communities. Serious schisms among the radical leaders of the sixties have left the movement rudderless. Also, the shift in emphasis from politics to culture is partially inspired by gaps in national leadership on such issues as poverty and race. For communitarians, no populist seems to have emerged to continue the leadership of Robert Kennedy, and there is no churchman of national stature who has continued Martin Luther King's efforts at reconciliation and social progress. Therefore, they have postponed politics while they strive to change the value structure which informs contemporary society. Most rural communitarians believe that a thorough transformation of attitudes must precede the shaping of a new reality.

All rural communities are attempting to establish an alternative economic system based upon the communal ownership of property, the trusteeship of land, and the distribution of food and other products through marketing cooperatives. It is in the development of marketing cooperatives and similar activities that the apolitical rural communities and the radical political groups known as collectives converge.[11] The former have established cooperatives in order to effect a culture change in which competition and personal success will be eliminated as values. The latter regard cooperatives as a means of reaching untapped population sectors and "raising their political consciousness." Because most rural communities are focused upon their own small society at the expense of the larger political system, they are quasi-anarchist. They have turned their back on a government dedicated to purposes they do not share and have effected a psychological retreat into the backwoods of contemporary society. The rural collectives, however, are political in inspiration, although they appear to share the same dreams of social justice which had animated rural communitarians before their retreat from society.

The development of a decentralist economy is not the only goal of the new rural communities. Some of their members have turned to farming as an escape from the urban environment with all its complexities and frustrations. They see in farming a simple life in which satisfaction is derived from one's immediate surroundings and one's work. Acquiring self-sufficiency is highly appealing to a generation which feels excluded from the formulation of foreign and domestic social policy. Rural communitarians perceive their nation's destiny as impervious to their influence. As a result, they seek outlets for their creativity and their thirst for participation in creating a lifestyle which has all the excitement of pioneering days.

Farming requires a broad spectrum of skills, which contrasts with the specialization of functions and competences imposed by a technological society. The new farmers echo Marx's dream of an end to the alienation of man produced by the division of labor which fragments his life. For Marx the springs of revolution lie in man as frustrated producer, unable to express his creative potential in material life. He believed that every social division of labor infringes on freedom, for it enforces occupational specialization as a way of life. To be free, man needs a total life experience: the possibility of creative self-expression in many fields of activity. Physical work has acquired a new mystique among contemporary young adults. In addition to the romantic appeal of the primitive, they have been influenced by Marcuse, who insists that capitalism has eliminated the physical and sensual aspects of work in order to isolate man from nature and render him more amenable to political control.[12]

Life in a small rural community is intended to provide a model of sound ecology. Communitarians maintain a very low consumption of energy, appliances, and cars, compared to the broader society. This is their answer to pollution and dwindling resources, and they hope that other groups will follow their example.

If the new communities farm organically, it is also because they are interested in the end product, pure food, as well as in ecology. Communitarians immerse themselves in canning, storing, and preserving with a gusto which may seem strange to their parents who consider such tasks drudgery. The suspicion of these young adults towards processed food is highly reminiscent of that of the European homemaker confronted with a strange array of "packaged products" in a supermarket as opposed to the fresh produce of the farm market. In fact, the lifestyle of these farm communities has a certain flavor of the turn of the century in western Europe. Although the inspiration may be intellectual or political, the prudence and thrift which filtered into European middle class society from its assimilated peasant social climbers is readily apparent in these communities.

Despite their flavor of conservatism, farm communities are also the scene of the contemporary sexual revolution, as both sexes are attempting to broaden and redefine their roles. It is not uncommon to find a man in charge of the community's toddlers while the women are manning the tractors in the fields. It is a widespread practice in these communities to categorize chores not along sexual lines but according to time required and other characteristics, rotating all chores equally among the members. In some communities a strict equality between the sexes is the norm. In others it is still an ideal to be strived for.

Child rearing is generally regarded as the responsibility of the entire community, although some communities lean toward a greater role for the parents. Aside from the liberation of women, the rationale for communal child rearing is that the child so raised will profit from the interest and models of several adults rather than being limited to one or two parents. Community children seem to thrive on the freedom of a life in the country, and appear generally cheerful and self-reliant. The school-age children of the Brotherhood of the Spirit decided against a free school in community in favor of the local public school. The Saddle-Ridge Farm children have also opted for public schools. It would not make sense for the parents to have engaged in a total effort to reshape their lives only to impose a solution on the children. The Skinnerian communities alone are dogmatic about child rearing.

Rural communities avoid the pleasures of modern entertainment. The most successful and long-lived shun drugs, alcohol, and many of the minor pleasures American society has come to take for granted. Even Twin Oaks, a community based upon the social theories of B. F. Skinner, is adamant against the use of drugs, and curiously enough television, for it is considered the purveyor of the false values of consumerism and violence. Square dancing, music, volleyball, and similar homespun activities fill the leisure time in community. The adventure of building a life on the land with a new group of people seems to have eliminated the need for large doses of passive entertainment such as television.

The New Collectives

While the communitarian movement as a whole represents dissent from the social order and can be characterized as apolitical, the new collectives[*] represent the crystallization of the New Left of the sixties into novel forms of political dissent. Frustrated with the tactics of protest, this group has seized upon the development of community as a new strategy for revolution. These proponents of community define the term in anarcho-syndicalist manner, as the common consciousness of oppression. By espousing community they are combining revolutionary politics and revolutionary culture, for they claim that building a collective is "living the revolution." In other words, the community serves as both a model of the postrevolutionary society and a base of operations against the broader society.

Nestled in the Vermont countryside is a federation of collectives known as Free Vermont. At its center are radical collectives which regroup veterans of the Weathermen, the SDS, and various antiwar organizations. The federation developed intercollective cooperative services such as a book and seed exchange, a medical traveling group, an organic restaurant, a cooperative garage, and even a "free farm" on land demanded of and donated by a small Vermont college. So concerned were some of these groups with their Sorelian purity that they even established a children's collective in

---

* Collectives are defined as a group organized around a work project, political goals, or both. See note 11.

order to educate them within the "emergent" culture. An intercollective newsletter appears with great irregularity and contains practical information on farming and essays with a revolutionary bent. Its precursor, *Free Vermont,* was mainly devoted to promoting a radical political view. Member "tribes," as they referred to themselves, convened periodically, but this practice was short-lived. Before the dissolution of the "inter-tribal organization," these groups regarded themselves as a potential red base in case their political movement would ever develop into a territorial campaign.

Member collectives proved as ephemeral as the broader organization. An example is the Red Clover collective, which had a brief and checkered existence. It was founded by a group of radical filmmakers and former political organizers, and was intended to function more as an organizational base than as a community farm. A constant change of goals, the vagueness of its plans, as well as its unease in the countryside, contributed to its demise. The dispersed membership eventually found new homes in other groups. Ironically, throughout its existence Red Clover was subsidized by the heir to a food marketing corporation.

The philosophical underpinnings of the collectives within Free Vermont derive from the visions of anarcho-syndicalism manifested by the Weathermen in the sixties and the utopian ideas expressed in the "triple revolution."[13] From the SDS these groups have retained the focus on participatory democracy and on culture as the substance of revolutionary politics. They regard themselves as the womb of a new culture in the state of gestation.

Collectives share with the community movement the desire to create alternative economic institutions based upon cooperation and equality and a concern for ecology and organic farming. However, the fundamental reason for life within the collective is to free members for activity on behalf of social change. This consideration also explains their dogmatic insistence on communal child rearing and on the "smash monogamy" campaign. While they regard the nuclear family as the most characteristic institution of the old order and are willing to indulge in considerable experimentation to modify it, they are primarily interested in channeling the affect and resources dedicated to that institution. Living in collectives frees people to devote a considerable amount of time and energy to political work. This technique is similar to the monopoly of affect engaged in by various types of authoritarian systems in order to fasten the state's grip on the citizen. Such calculated monopoly of affect serves the dual purpose of channeling each person's energy for particular ends and preventing the development of opposition within the group.

A typical collective in the Vermont area has been in existence for six years. It includes a dozen or so adults ranging from teenage to middle or late thirties, and eight or more children. Toddlers and infants sleep in their own quarters and the children are raised in community or in a separate children's collective. Certain members maintain outside jobs, in a local restaurant, for instance. Relations with the neighbors are excellent and carefully cultivated. Their interests may converge to the point where the collective will vote with local conservatives in order to oppose a rise in school taxes. The conservatives may be interested in arresting social change while the syndicalists wish to hasten the demise of the old order.

Collectives are more prevalent in urban areas, for there they have a broader field for outreach. A typical example of the cross-fertilization of community and collective is a collective located in an eastern urban center. It maintains a farm in the country, growing organic food and selling it at advantageous prices to black communities and blue collar neighborhoods as a means of politicizing them. One of the key members is also involved in community action in the inner city. He is a former professional and a long-standing member of SDS, in which he served as a consultant on community organization. In his current capacity he organizes local groups for elections and helps establish new communes. His particular collective serves as a resource in organizing skills for intentional communities and as such is in constant touch with the community movement all over the United States. The long-term political goal of such groups is to develop the political consciousness of the new communes and communities in order to use them for promoting social change.

Radical collectives consider themselves the base for the creation of a new society, instruments to attain political influence among certain population groups, and means of sinking roots in a locality. They allow their members to pool economic assets, free their political energies by the sharing of chores, and serve as resource for a variety of organizing activities. They represent a distinct strand on the fringes of the community movement, although their members are in contact with intentional communities throughout the country. However, they are remnants of the New Left politics which developed in the sixties, rather than a branch of the intentional community phenomenon as such, although they may be frequently identified with the latter by unwitting observers.

Springtree Community

The Springtree community is located on 100 acres of rolling pasture and woods outside of Scottsville, Virginia. A great gnarled tree with a spring issuing from its roots has given the community its name. The members of Springtree met at the Twin Oaks annual conference on intentional community in the summer of 1971. Shortly after, they purchased their farmland, which is only 25 miles away from the Twin Oaks community. The 200 people attending the Twin Oaks conference were either communitarians or persons in search of either a community or a compatible group to establish a community. Although the workshops on various practical aspects of community such as the construction of housing, were interesting and informative, the chief aim of the conference was to recruit new members and to promote intentional community. Indeed, most of the communities represented at the conference acquired new members and several new communities were founded, among them Springtree.

Springtree differs from the many farming communes and communities dotting the Virginia-Pennsylvania-Maryland area chiefly in age and outlook of its membership. Presently the community includes 12 adults ranging from the twenties to mid-thirties, and 8 children. Eventually Springtree hopes to include 14 families and broaden its age representation on both ends of the age spectrum. Several of the adults are professionals, some in the academic fields, and some younger adults are completing their university education by commuting from the farm. In fact, the membership continued its regular jobs, often commuting long distances, during the winter of constructing housing and farm. Perhaps because of their age, their job experience, and their motives for establishing community, they have evidenced a greater degree of commitment to community building than most groups.

Springtree is composed mainly of couples, some with children, some without, and a few singles. It is a small community rather than a communal family. The adults have thoroughly familiarized themselves with child rearing practices in the kibbutzim and with Skinner's theories. Most of them have embarked on community chiefly to enrich the lives of their children by providing them with close contacts with other adults and children.

At Springtree the parents bear the primary responsibility for the children, rather than the community, and the members expect that throughout infancy parents and siblings will be the dominant but not exclusive influence. The community expected to have the children up to five share their parents' living quarters rather than placing them in separate housing as in the kibbutz or as projected for Twin Oaks. However, once installed at Springtree, the children from the ages of 3 to 9 preferred to room together, and their parents yielded. The community takes great pains to distinguish its flexibility from the dogmatism of child rearing expressed at

Twin Oaks. Unlike the kibbutzim or the Skinnerians, Spring-tree is careful to set a balance between community and self. The members do not regard child rearing as a perpetuation of community or as the actualization of social thought. Rather, they believe that community should provide a broad range of alternatives for self-development. One of the goals which binds the community is the common commitment to "permissive child-rearing," and a free school for its children.[14]

Springtree is currently holding a summer school for its older children as an experiment. Some of the novel methods pursued include having one lesson a day, i.e., mathematics on Monday, biology on Tuesday, geography on Wednesday, in an hour set aside for this purpose each morning. This plan will depend on the interest of the child. The community feels that it is more important for younger children to run and play than to study, and to learn through doing by actively participating in the life of the community. Children are encouraged to express their tastes and interests, and their parents take great interest in them. The younger children delight in exploring the woods and streams and bringing back turtles, leaves, and rocks for further investigation. Some of the older children have expressed a desire to learn to cook and therefore are scheduled in the kitchen duties one at a time. In the words of a member, "The children are one of the greatest joys of life at Springtree."[15]

The desire for such an environment has attracted new members. The most recent additions to the community have joined because of the responsible attitude of the community, its focus on children, and its flexibility. The community boasts no ideology or recipe for society, and its members assert that "we do not want to trade in our precious egos for the dubious benefits of a collective identity."[16] Members come from similar socio-economic backgrounds and share the same level of education. They have similar tastes and values, such as the wish to farm in an ecologically sound manner, to consume only natural foods, and to develop their own lifestyle.

The whole tenor of Springtree is one of moderation. Issues are handled on their own merits rather than on the basis of doctrine and are discussed on a regular basis each Sunday afternoon. The planning on the farm is done with care and on a long-term basis. The community does not expect to transform the social order within a decade.

The members of this new community have managed to erect communal housing, dig a well and septic field during a single winter, in addition to pursuing their professions and preparing a garden. One building houses the adult members and 3 babies and includes all facilities. The building was designed by an architect and is a long rectangular structure topped by a sleeping loft projecting over the first floor in a dramatic line.

The focus of the life in common at Springtree is the garden. The members have planted an early and late vegetable garden and an orchard. They plan to produce most of their own food with some surplus for cash income. However, their main efforts will be concentrated on producing wine grapes. They have purchased some French hybrid vines in the hope of generating a large cash income within a decade. The newsletters of this community are replete with all the details of the preparation of orchard and garden, the mulching and setting of asparagus, and the various combinations of fertilizers employed.

Most communities have overcome their inexperience in farming with the aid of interested neighbors. Springtree is no exception. Neighboring farmers have loaned their labor and equipment to the community and have offered their advice on a variety of practical problems ranging from thistle eradication to raising goats.

The members of Springtree will pursue their various professions in the Scottsville area in addition to their work on the farm. Although residents of Twin Oaks rotate low-skill jobs on the outside in order to generate the necessary cash income, they do so with extreme reluctance and with the hope of becoming self-sufficient as rapidly as possible.

Springtree does not share this desire to live entirely within the confines of its own community. However, its closest relations are with other intentional communities, and it exchanges frequent visits, skills, and advice with neighboring Twin Oaks. Eventually these two communities hope to engage in barter. Both participate in a round-robin newsletter which circulates among twelve farm communities scattered about Virginia and Maryland.

Full Circle Farm

If the story of Springtree exudes success and well-being, an account of Full Circle Farm is less bright. But each in its own way is characteristic of the intentional communities being formed in rural America. Full Circle Farm was established by five families, including 8 children, in 1970. Most of the couples had been married at least 10 years, and most of the members were professionals in either the academic field or the computer industry. None of them had ever farmed or worked an orchard, and not all the members were acquainted before the land was purchased.

The founding members pooled their resources to raise the down payment for a 110-acre tract priced at $550 an acre, a considerable financial commitment. At the outset there was a division between those members who wished to launch large-scale organic farming and those who preferred subsistence farming. The former prevailed, and the farm purchased expensive equipment on time. Full Circle was soon in debt because of its heavy commitments and financial mismanagement. The community had overextended itself. At one point its members were engaged in pruning in the orchard, raising a garden, tending children including two new babies, constructing housing, and maintaining outside jobs. There seemed to be little time for personal relations.

The ideals which inspired the establishment of Full Circle were to live a healthy life close to nature, to grow organic food, to reevaluate male-female roles, and to provide the children with the freedom and independence of a life in the country. Private property was to be eliminated in favor of pooled resources. A labor credit system was developed for household chores and child care in order to free the women.

As in the Springtree community, the couple at Full Circle Farm has retained its identity and each family has separate quarters, a trailer or a two-room apartment in the farmhouse. The main meal at noon is an occasion for the community to gather. In addition, weekly meetings are devoted to community affairs.

Recently the community experienced a period of crisis over financial affairs and some members quit, leaving behind sizable debts for the rest of the members to bear. It just so happened that those who left were the ones favoring the large-scale operation which had proved so burdensome. This particular issue was settled by departure. However, the group still suffers from a gap between the ideal of life in common and the propensity of some of its members to do their own thing economically, such as purchasing with community funds 4000 bushels of apples for a resale which failed to materialize. Some of the members have retained private funds which have enabled them to engage in such personal ventures as purchasing bees to pollinate the trees. Economically Full Circle is at odds over the ownership of the property and the status of private incomes.[17] The prime need seems to be for both the predisposition and the procedures to develop common goals.

Like many other rural communities, Full Circle seems to lack the capacity to compromise a variety of interests. This is the true test of community. Most fledgling groups solve the problem of diversity by the departure of dissenting members. The rationale is that intentional communities should be quite homogeneous and that the opportunity is always available either to find a congenial group or to establish a group oneself. This means that the cardinal problems of man in community—freedom, justice, mutual obligation, interest, and authority—are simply evaded.

Sunrise Hill: The Rise and Fall of Utopia

Because of the contemporary bias against theory and any conceptualization of community, the annals of contemporary community include only diaries and practical accounts of handling interpersonal conflicts, preparing a garden and erecting either buildings or a power supply. As a result, the movement has generated very little material on the visions of its founders. An exception to this is the chronicle of the Sunrise Hill community by one of its founders and members. His honest attempt to analyze the failure of the venture yields considerable insight into the problems and prospects of the community movement as a whole. Although it is an account of an unfulfilled dream, one must not condemn the vision of community or confuse that vision with the frailties of an enthusiasm untempered by method.

The members of Sunrise Hill met at a conference on intentional community jointly sponsored by the Heathcote School of Living and the New York Federation of Anarchists, held at Heathcote in 1966. Participants espoused such divergent goals as New Leftism, a life close to nature, mysticism, nudism, and psychotherapy.[18] However, this diversity did not preclude the development of close comradeship and empathy. In fact, 20 of the participants decided to anchor these feelings into a permanent community as an embodiment of the "new order." This intention became an immediate possibility when one person offered to donate his 40-acre homestead near Conway, Massachusetts, for the use of such a community. The property included buildings and gardens, and even boasted goats and chickens. At a series of meetings of the prospective communards, plans were aired for the establishment of a home industry, the construction of private shelters, and a school for the community's children which would be eventually open to paying outsiders.

Attempts were also made to develop goals for the projected community beyond the generally shared longing for a new order, a utopia of perfect freedom. That broad umbrella concealed disparate and vague visions on the potentials of intentional community as an alternative to mass society. There were as many interpretations of utopia as participants and as many suggestions for realizing millennium. However, since no decision-making procedure was established, a consideration of goals promised no immediate resolution, and debate on that issue was shelved. If deliberation would not clarify goals, perhaps they would emerge in the process of community building. This expectation was founded on the general feeling of optimism and fellowship which pervaded the preparatory meetings. After all, there was no problem which such an assemblage of sympathetic persons could not solve.

Thus, the goals of the community were not clearly articulated. Its establishment was indeed an act of faith, as claimed by one of its founders. The members hoped that love and mutual regard would serve as cement in the absence of purpose. The lifestyles and values of the founders, insofar as they exhibited certain common features, provide some insight into the unstated aims of Sunrise Hill. Much as some young adults turn to marriage as a solution to either personal or family problems, the new community was founded by rebels against the institutions and values of contemporary society, its competitiveness and impersonality. Many of the members had a history of occupational mobility in their vain attempts to find a social niche compatible with their values. Some of the married couples joined the community as a means of solving their problems in a new and congenial setting. All agreed, however, on community as a haven from the evil and violence of the outside world and as the seed of a new and more humane order.

The Sunrise Hill community was established as a trust with all members as beneficiaries and with three trustees administering community property and legally responsible for community activities. Land and buildings were communally owned, and all vehicles, tools, and equipment were used in common. Only personal items were retained as private property. However, individual assets such as cash reserves were not mandatorily pooled, but were left to the discretion of the owner. This led to inconsistency of practice, with some donating and some retaining private funds. The result was tension and ultimately conflict. Most communities today require a total relinquishment of resources, either before joining or on a phased plan, as proof of commitment, and thus have avoided thorny disagreements.

The cash income of the community was derived from the outside jobs of its members in construction, carpentry, waitressing, clean-up contracting, and other jobs. Most of this income was pooled, and members could withdraw money for necessities from the common treasury. On the inspiration of Heinlein's *Stranger in a Strange Land,* a petty cash box was kept by the main door where members could help themselves and record the amount and use on a sheet posted nearby. Most of the time the cash level hardly warranted such a practice. However, the low standard of living and meager cash flow was compensated by the adventure of building a new life. During its first few months the community functioned without a budget. Money was simply spent as needed and consequently the community incurred debts. Eventually, however, an accounting system was developed, as well as rudimentary financial planning. Economic viability remained secondary to the desire for a nonexploitive livelihood and the replacement of competition and private property with co-operation and sharing. Moreover, life in community permitted its members to dispense with the demands of specialization. In a single day communitarians performed a wide range of tasks from carpentry to gardening. In the absence of hierarchy and professionalization, the integrated personality would flourish.

The community moved to its quarters in the middle of summer, a time of euphoria and the enjoyment of the out-of-doors. Plans for sorely needed additional housing were temporarily shelved as the new communards lounged about a refreshing pond. In the warmth of summer the community practiced nudity as a "symbolic act of communion."[19]

Sunrise Hill developed a liberalized sexual code and found that in general the relaxation of sexual taboos reduced the desire for promiscuity rather than the reverse. The permanent partnerships of married couples were considered compatible with "inter-group love," and some members considered that this permitted married couples to reduce their social, emotional, and sexual demands on each other.[20] The sense of intimacy and warmth experienced in community was regarded both as cement and as a steppingstone to the kinship of all men. However, the adults at Sunrise Hill were in their late twenties and thirties. They had been the youth of the fifties, and the relaxation of sexual restrictions was less easy to achieve than among the emancipated youth of the current decade. As a result, the new freedom created frictions and ultimately resulted in the departure of a member.

As the flush of newness and warmth wore off, differences of views on religion, sexual relations, and ideology became apparent and generated conflict. Unscheduled group medita- tion was attempted as a means of alleviating interpersonal tensions. However, such practices could scarcely cope with conflicts of interest. Given the small size and intimacy of the group, serious personal conflicts among members exposed the fragility of community foundations and threatened its very existence. Since no means were devised to handle fundamental disagreements, the departure of the disgruntled proved the solution of the last resort. The first conflict was handled in this manner and thus set a deadly precedent for the evasion of responsibility. Dis- agreement focused upon child rearing, although communal child care was one of the primary goals of Sunrise Hill. The community's children lived together and members rotated in their care, although each child normally spent a considerable amount of time with his parents. The "nest program," or group care, was short-lived and foundered over divergence of views on child rearing.[21]

Sunrise Hill was an anarchist community. Its members had rejected politics but had developed no means of regulating their life in common: no procedures for compromising various interests or handling personal conflicts. Sunrise Hill was to be a haven of freedom, defined in practice as a refusal of all structure or any limitations on personal behavior. Members felt that work should not be scheduled or delegated but "spontaneously accomplished." The result was a lack of coordination, indecisiveness, and ultimately stalemate. Work was performed as a last resort, frequently out of anger as when one member spent hours washing dishes just in order to clear counter space for preparing a meal.

Nor was there any procedure for deciding policy. Decisions were made only under the pressure of urgency, and majority voting was rejected as a tyranny practiced in outside society. Sunrise Hill discovered to its dismay that when decisions are relegated to "spontaneous solution," personal friction results. Moreover, in anarchist communities there is a certain reluctance on the part of members to assume leadership roles. Meetings of the entire membership proliferated in order to discuss the myriad problems of utopia, and the lack of results created a sense of frustration at the time thus spent. All too late Sunrise Hill discovered that responsibility, authority, and initiative are necessary for the proper functioning of society . . . even a small society.

When the first autumn cold visited Sunrise Hill, the membership had dwindled to 12: three couples, two singles, and four children. By January the entire community had dispersed and the venture in Utopia had reached an untimely end. The chronicler of Sunrise Hill ruefully concluded that its members had more negative than positive ideas in common: that they had built community on visions of what the community should not be.[22] There was no clearly articulated purpose which could be authoritative, and the warmth of fellowship provided no substitute for the ultimate cement of value contained either in religious ideals or in political culture. Even if man rejects history and politics as a source of life in common, he must ultimately reinvent them.

As in many newly formed communities, the temper of compromise and the commitment to community which can contain a diversity of interests was sorely lacking at Sunrise Hill. Perhaps this is too much to expect of rebels opposing what they perceive as an overspecialized, standardized, and regimented social system. Having rejected society as a whole, the Sunrise Hill people sought to reconstruct it in toto, with no method and at once. Tackling extensive social change simultaneously rather than piecemeal and gradually is characteristic of many rural communities of the sixties. Thirsting for challenge, communitarians seek to build their own housing with primitive tools and to effect far-reaching changes in family and sexual relations with a group of previously unacquainted members. This means revising institutions, roles, and patterns of behavior: competitiveness to co-operation, jealousy to sharing, all in the context of meager financial resources. It is the sheer enormity of the task which sinks many a community.

However, failures due to lack of method or foresight should not invalidate the concept of community, nor obscure the periods of genuine satisfaction experienced by its members. The very fact that the dispersed members of Sunrise Hill have renewed their search for community, armed with the benefit of hard-earned wisdom, corroborates the intrinsic worth of their experience.

Communitarians of the seventies, such as those at Spring-tree, have access to the accumulated experience of the past few years, distilled from the mimeographed newsheets circulating within the movement and the increasingly frequent conferences featuring workshops on the more basic aspects of viability. However, there remains a deep reluctance to discuss or conceptualize the politics and processes of community within the movement. Communitarians approach their task pervaded by anti-intellectualism and often rely exclusively on the techniques of the encounter movement, on the substitution of psychology for politics, to cement their life in common. The search for community today constitutes a reach towards utopia, but utopians are by definition rebels against the social system as a whole.

The Revitalization of Rural America
Through New Communities

Most rural communities are convinced of their usefulness to the broader society in serving as a model for social change and in disseminating their views through their conferences and newsletters. However, one branch of the intentional community movement has actually developed a full-scale program directed to the specific problem of rural poverty throughout the world. In structure and aims this group represents a rather distinct variation of the community movement. However, it operates from the center of the movement and shares the basic premises of decentralism.

The organization which has launched this project, the International Independence Institute (III), was conceived in conjunction with Dr. Ralph Borsodi's International Foundation for Independence, a program dedicated to financing rural credit programs and community land trusts. The III is located in Ashby, Massachusetts, and directed by Bob Swann with a small staff of economists and social workers. It operates as a nonprofit educational corporation dedicated to the revitalization of economic and community life in the United States and in the technologically underdeveloped, primarily rural areas of the world. The philosophy of the III focuses upon the trusteeship of land and on a dramatic new concept of aid to the rural poor all over the world. The III provides a combination of agricultural credit on easy terms, education, and training to small farmers or farmers' organizations, rather than gifts of capital or goods. Underlying this new approach is the desire to foster economic growth at the grass roots level without disrupting social structures, urbanizing the rural poor, or commercializing the land. At the heart of the program is the linkage of land tenure, community organization, and ecological planning. This approach recognizes the similarity of problems attending both foreign aid and aid to the domestic poor, and responds to the new concern of unevenly modernized nations for regional development.

In addition to establishing pilot projects in community and extending foreign aid, the III functions as a research and publications center on economic and social development at the grass roots level. Among its publications are *A Guide to Setting up Land Trusts,* based partly on the model and experience of the Jewish National Fund in purchasing and leasing land to avoid speculation. It has also published a pamphlet "Rural New Towns for America." It is currently engaged in research projects relating to community-based credit and banking, and a community-based welfare/workfare system designed to remove the stigma of welfare and create new capital resources.

The foreign aid extended by the III helps support the program of the Farm Center International in Michoacan, Mexico. The Center provides low-cost credit to small farmers for the cooperative purchase of fertilizer, seeds, chicken, and pigs. The 100 per cent repayment of the small loans has sustained the confidence of the III. [23] It plans to support this program's expansion into other countries in Central America. The success of the program is proof to its sponsors that the rural poor in the world can become self-sufficient without the disruption occasioned by an urbanized modernization on the Western model.

This approach is of potential relevance to all those nations which have acquired independence in the past decade and a half. Typically, these countries suffer from a dual economy reflecting the former colonial administration and the untouched indigenous way of life. Foreign aid, which is mainly directed to the former sector and which has helped build a modern infrastructure, has broadened the gap between the rural and the modernized economy. An increasingly severe unemployment is one of the worst by-products of the policy of industrializing from the top downward by borrowing sophisticated Western techniques. Moreover, because of restrictive quotas imposed by industrialized nations, industrial production in newly independent and developing countries is limited to internal markets. However, the agricultural sector of these economies does not generate the income either for purchasing power or for the growth of small-scale processing and distribution services which could strengthen the economy. On the other hand, the modernized portion of these economies is characteristically burdened with overvalued exchange rates and the servicing of loans. The alleviation of hunger and unemployment in the countries could be met by fostering from below the growth of a bridge economy between the modern and traditional sectors, by helping enrich and diversify production. This has been the approach of the III. The organization is interested in fostering economic and social growth at the grass roots level and with the full participation of the local population, rather than from the top down by national policy makers.

This outlook has taken concrete form in the New Communities, Inc., a rural new town in southwest Georgia. It was conceived as a solution to rural poverty and as a means of preventing the migration of the rural poor into crisis-ridden urban centers. The goals of rural new towns as developed by the III include:[24]

To create an economically viable alternative to urbanization for landless tenant farmers, sharecroppers, farm laborers, and poor homesteaders.

To devise new methods whereby small farmers with limited resources may share in the benefits of modern farm technology and industrialization.

To make improved social welfare services available to rural families on an equitable basis.

To decrease rural poverty and economic dependence.

To encourage decentralization and community self-government which will permit the expression of life styles which are independent of those imposed from without or above.

To reduce individual economic insecurity by eliminating land speculation, absentee land ownership, and systems of tenancy whereby the user of the land is victimized, and by devising an alternative system of beneficial land trust ownership.

New Communities began with the leadership of Slater King and Charles Herrod, both of whom were active in the civil rights movement in Georgia. Sponsored by the III and the National Sharecroppers Fund, these men and a party of black leaders from the South traveled to Israel to study Israeli solutions to rural problems. They returned convinced of the relevance of those solutions to the American South. As a result of this experience, New Communities was incorporated in 1968 as a nonprofit Georgia corporation. Its board of directors includes representatives of the III, the Federation of Southern Cooperatives, the Southern Christian Leadership Conference, the Southern Rural Project, and a number of residents of New Communities.

In line with the philosophy of the III, the prospective residents played a major role in planning the community. The initial planning was funded by a grant from the Office of Economic Opportunity (OEO). With the help of loans and financial guarantees by national church groups and charitable organizations, the community acquired 5735 acres of land. Since then it has produced watermelon, squash, okra, peanuts, and soybeans, and the first 100 housing units have been erected. New rural towns are not conceived as self-contained units. New Communities hopes to provide additional employment for residents and nonresidents alike by attracting industries, commercial enterprises, and services.

The land acquired by the community is held in trust, but town residents have full and exclusive usership rights, subject only to a small user fee. These rights may be inherited, but not sold, leased, or purchased. Trusteeship is intended to eliminate land speculation and to guarantee land against repossession in times of hardship. The town raises the necessary development capital from government and private sources to modernize the agricultural production and to create a market-oriented infrastructure.

It is too early to judge the economic or political viability of New Communities. However, this approach to social change through the creation of institutions allowing social and economic self-sufficiency within the broader society is an imaginative one. It proves that local action need not be parochial and that community ventures can cope with economic and social inequities and the need for ecologically sound management of national resources.

A Community of Communities

Intentional communities in the United States have always considered their ultimate goal as a federation of communities stretching from one end of the country to the other. In keeping with decentralism, initiative and influence would be centered in local groups, with the parent organization serving mainly as a communications hub and resource center. The FIC served in this capacity, as did its more specialized branch the Homer L. Morris Fund, and Community Service, Incorporated, of Yellow Springs, Ohio.

For the past twenty years the Homer L. Morris Fund annual meetings have gathered together representatives of various intentional communities in order to share their experiences and report on their respective statuses. The purpose of the fund is to provide short-term loans at reasonable interest rates to tide communities over emergencies and to help finance undertakings that could not obtain backing from orthodox banks or loan institutions. The fund has helped 12 communities weather financial crises of various kinds. The most dramatic emergency occurred in the fifties at Koinonia. The fund helped tide that community through the dark years of bombings, burnings, and economic boycott.

In order to obtain a loan from the fund, a community must include at least three families and members must share a significant degree of their life. A ceiling of $3,000 is set on each loan, and a reasonable assurance of eventual repayment is required.

Community Service of Yellow Springs, Ohio, was associated with the development of FIC and has served as a resource center for intentional communities for the past 30 years. It conducts research and publishes material in such areas as the effects of urban living on social, mental, and physical health, comparisons of small community schools with "mass schools," the economics of small community, and the place of intentional community in pioneering social development. These studies tend to corroborate the outlook of Community Service that mass society has appeared historically as a symptom of social decay and that stable, small communities are the basis of a healthy social order. In addition to a substantial literature on intentional communities (guides to education and economics), the service circulates a quarterly periodical on small community. It also fosters pilot community projects in India, Appalachia, and Ohio, and has initiated programs to help American Indians retain their social and cultural heritage. Each August it sponsors a conference on community which is also hosted by the Vale community. The latter is the home of Griscom Morgan, who runs Community Service almost singlehandedly.

The Morgans are famous in the annals of community. Arthur Morgan is known chiefly as former president of Antioch College and as the man who transformed the moribund town of Yellow Springs into a thriving community. An eminent scholar and also an engineer, he continues to publish on matters of public interest despite his advanced age. His daughter-in-law Elizabeth Morgan founded and directed the Arthur Morgan School of the Celo community in North Carolina. For Griscom Morgan small community is a matter of faith. Throughout the long years of its ebb in popularity, he continued to practice, promote, and research intentional community with no other return than the satisfaction gained in the pursuit of humane values.

The Heathcote School of Living sponsors annual conferences

which include workshops on decentralized economics and homesteading skills. In addition to providing an opportunity for communities to share their experiences, these conferences have an activist mission. They serve to inspire and organize efforts to enlarge the intentional community movement. People from all over the country attend these gatherings, and they have proved so popular that a series of regional conferences has been launched to accommodate the large numbers of interested people.

A newcomer to the scheduled gathering of communities is the annual conference on community sponsored by the Twin Oaks community in Louisa, Virginia. These conferences serve to spread the message of intentional community as the wave of the future, and quite a number of communities trace their origin to these gatherings.

Visits among community members and a plethora of mimeographed newsletters keep the movement abreast of events between conferences. The spontaneous, ad hoc method of community interlink is characteristic of the intentional community movement of the seventies.

The New Communities and the Nation

Community farming constitutes a viable alternative lifestyle for young adults and thus helps foster a pluralism which is the lifeblood of a healthy society. However, unless there is communication among diverse groups and between small communities and the broader society, there is a possibility that the political system will become fragmented rather than plural and that stalemate will replace compromise. True community among men is comprised of unity in diversity, not just of individuals but of men in groups and of mutual obligation among groups. Thus, the true test of community lies in the extent and nature of its communication with other groups and its relevance to the broader society, for communities are no less subject to egoism than individuals and, in addition, are frequently tainted with dogmatism. Admittedly, the new communitarians are chiefly of white middle class origin with only a small representation of poor. The materialism which they reject may appear as the good life to disadvantaged Americans.

Although all rural communities insist that they are trailblazers in solving the problems of world poverty, communities vary greatly in the interest and resources they actually devote to the major problems of contemporary society. New Communities, established by the International Institute for Independence, serves the nation's rural poor and its minorities who have suffered from poverty and unemployment in a degree far out of proportion to their numbers. Community Service sponsors pilot projects in community in depressed areas and Indian-managed improvement programs.

On the other hand, the new homesteading communities are dedicated to cultivating their own Voltairean gardens while the socially deprived must await their millenary achievements. For all their stress on sharing as opposed to competition, the new mutuality is practiced within a constricted universe, and rural communities constitute a new corporatism of complacency and self-righteousness. They are more than faintly reminiscent of a suburbia which has become thoroughly sanitized against the pain and misery of urban life. "We have our own problems," they reply when questioned on their views on such matters. They seem unconcerned and uninformed regarding the needs and problems of the poor, black, or Chicano American and would rather discuss mulching or the construction of a new building.

While the communards have rendered a great service to American society by their perceptiveness in defining some major social problems, they have not followed through. It is ironic that in seeking to cope with a diminished spirit in the nation, they have indulged in considerable spiritual shrinkage themselves. Their search for purpose has been cast in a pioneering venture which excludes the real on behalf of the pseudovictims of the social order. Their absorption with baking whole wheat bread and clearing fields, "discovering" nature, display an inability to cope with the problems of our era and an ingenuity for escapism. Must Rome burn while communards seek vitality through organic foods and the warmth of fulfilling personal relations?

Homesteading is an alternative for the healthy, self-reliant, and adventurous. It is not everyone's dish, especially not those who fill the category of "weak" members of society: the elderly, disabled, and homeless. Having denounced competition in a ritual fashion, rural communitarians are apt to ignore its victims in society. However, while a carefully cultivated blindness can indeed render the poor invisible, it can also exacerbate their problems. The refusal to cast one's lot politically is equivalent to a political decision, for it accords undue weight to the wishes of the politically active without influencing them. Beating a psychological retreat from the political system because of its immorality is tantamount to leaving the problem of government to those who would exacerbate the very policies which communitarians oppose. What makes this abdication of responsibility all the more serious is that the young adults in community have enjoyed the benefits of an education which has prepared them for the responsibilities of participation and for the role of "attentive public." The refusal to participate in the political system disrupts the balance of political forces and deprives society of the capabilities and resources of a generation.

Political apathy is a feeble guarantee of self-sufficiency. In their carefully constructed self-quarantine from the political system and their inner focus, communities are prey to groups wishing to swell the ranks of extremist political subcultures. In order for any society to flourish, large or small, it requires a purpose above and beyond taking care of its own existence in the most humane manner. Men need broad goals to lend meaning to their life in common. If they fail to articulate purpose in order to manage power, they will become instruments of those who equate order with force at either extreme of the political spectrum.

FOUR

A   MODERN   UTOPIA

> They constantly try to escape
> From the darkness outside and within
> By dreaming of systems so perfect that
>   no one will need to be good
> But the man that is will shadow
> The man that pretends to be.

> *T.S. Eliot, choruses from "The Rock"*

The Social Thought of B.F. Skinner

Because of the fragmentation of life in modern society and the sheer complexity of problems besetting the political system, many Americans today find solace in the total solutions of utopian thought. It is no accident that a man such as B. F. Skinner will be widely read and his ideas hotly debated, for his social thought attempts to reduce the magnitude of crises facing American society to seemingly manageable proportions. He offers not only an insight into human nature through his theories of human behavior, but also a program for improving the human condition which assures man the primary position at the helm. "Man as we know him, for better or for worse, is what man has made of man,"[1] he claims. Man can design a new culture which will be peaceful and productive, and will insure the harmony of the whole with its parts. Laws from the science of human behavior will be the instruments of a culture in which people will be controlled by the consequences of their behavior.

Because Skinner is deeply involved in the search for a scientific method of studying human behavior and because he wishes to see this methodology attain the status of physics in the hierarchy of sciences, he has dismissed what he calls "traditional" approaches to the study of man. Political philosophy, history, theology, jurisprudence, and philosophy are all non-scientific and as far as Skinner is concerned of little help in either elucidating human nature or improving the human condition. As an environmentalist and an activist, he is impatient with disciplines which allow men to gain a critical distance from the issues which absorb policy makers. He insists that it is simply not possible to transcend contemporary society in search of the critical perspectives of time and space, for man is culturally determined and the self is but "a repertoire of behavior appropriate to a given set of contingencies."[2]

Although Skinner's social thought is inspired by a scientific study of human behavior, it follows the tradition of nineteenth-century utopian thought represented by Saint-Simon and Robert Owen. For Owen, as for his contemporary counterpart, man is a tabula rasa, and therefore the opportunities for improving the human condition by controlling the environment are virtually limitless. The science of psychology notwithstanding, Robert Owen and B. F. Skinner emerge as social reformers with striking similarities. Both men are inspired by a fervor for social perfection born of a desire to carry the techniques of industrialization to completion in society. They chafe at inefficiency as much as at the crime, poverty, and conflict endemic in their societies, and concur in absorbing the problems of politics into the design of a new social order. A scientifically designed community would need no government, for mutual obligation would be achieved by virtue of the transformation men would experience when society underwent reform.

Owen and Skinner define the concept of individual responsibility as the chief source of social evil. Skinner refers to the concept of "the autonomous man" as a fiction of philosophy and religion. Autonomous man is merely that portion of human behavior which has yet to be subsumed under the laws of psychology.[3] Man is neither good nor evil, and the thrust of social reform should be to produce not good men but better environments. "Under a perfect system, no one needs goodness."[4] In a similar fashion Owen attacks religion as the source of social ills, for it promotes the notion that each individual man forms his own character and is therefore responsible for his actions and feeling.[5]

The will of man has no power whatever over his opinions. He must and ever did, and ever will, believe what has been or may be impressed on his mind by his predecessors and the circumstances which surround him.

The improvement of society therefore must involve the entire social system: its institutions for production, socialization, and education.[6]

In those characters which now exhibit crime, the fault is obviously not in the individual, but the defect proceeds from the system in which the individual has been trained. Withdraw those circumstances which tend to create crime in the human character, and crime will not be created. Replace them with such as are calculated to form habits of order, regularity, temperance, industry, and these qualities will be formed.

Owen founded several utopian communities in England and America which were aimed at providing the perfect environment for integrating individual happiness with the good of society. At New Harmony, for instance, economic practices fostered cooperation rather than competition, and education elicited attitudes of mutual regard. Although Owen's many utopian experiments failed and are remembered chiefly for their failure, they were also a fertile source of ideas for broad social reform. The doctrine of universal, elementary, and free education originated in Owen's New Harmony. The first nursery schools in the country were established there, and the first women's literary club was founded by a prominent member, Frances Wright. From New Harmony she first proclaimed her stand of equal political rights for all regardless of sex or color, and through her the community became one of the earliest centers of the abolitionist movement.

As Owen does, Skinner shifts the focus of responsibility for social evil away from the individual to the institutions and practices of the culture. He is a thoroughgoing determinist in his claim that "whatever we do and hence, however we perceive it, the fact remains that it is the environment which acts upon the perceiving person, not the perceiving person who

acts upon the environment."[7]   Hence, he concludes that man
is not a moral animal in the sense of possessing a special trait,
although he may build a kind of social environment which induces him to behave in certain ways.

Skinner's instruments of perfection are based upon his explanation of human behavior. As our knowledge of the laws
which govern it increases, the inner man—i.e., those unexplain-
ed areas of human behavior currently referred to as the will—
must yield to these laws until the inner man disappears altogether. Ethics, philosophy, such "obsolete traditional ideas,"
are all based upon a dualism of inner and outer man which
Skinner believes is without foundation. For him there is no
inner psyche or autonomous decision-making mind, and hence
there are no inner virtues or moral men. Once men abandon
these notions of free will and dignity, they can apply operant
conditioning to structure a social environment that will work.
The measure of a culture is that "it works" in the sense of
eliciting the support of its members.

According to Skinner, behavior is shaped and maintained
by its consequences. Most human behavior operates on the
environment, and the responses it produces are labeled operants. Operant behavior operates on the environment to produce consequences. The specific consequences of operant
behavior may replace the explanatory functions now assigned
to purposes, intentions, and states of mind. An operant response affects the environment in such a way as to generate stim-
uli which feed back to the organism. If the rate of response
increases as a result of the feedback, the latter is called reinforcing. Positive reinforcers are judged more effective behavior modifiers than negative reinforcement (punishment
for doing something other than what is desired). In other
words, behavior in support of a culture can be elicited in a
more efficient manner by a system of rewards, or positive
reinforcers, than by punishment.[8]

This theory was developed by Skinner through the use of
pigeons in the controlled environment of a laboratory. However, he defends his inference to complex systems from simple systems and the use of organisms below the human level

for research pertaining to humans. His defense is the argument that in all sciences advances take place from the simple to the complex and that since animal behavior is simpler than that of humans, its study enables one to get at the basic processes more easily.

Skinner takes great pains to argue the irrelevance of the Western tradition of Greek and Judeo-Christian political thought. He characterizes it as obsessed with eliminating control and therefore as a miscalculation, for all human behavior is in truth controlled. He insists that the great issue for man is not to eliminate control, for that is not possible, but to make it visible. According to this interpretation, the liberal tradition in political philosophy aims to eliminate control but in so doing only renders control invisible and the controlled blissfully unaware of their servitude.

By characterizing the whole of Western political philosophy in a narrow way as the attempt by the "literature of freedom"[9] to eliminate intentional control, Skinner equates a tradition which has shaped our political systems for four thousand years to the narrowest of anarchist outlooks. In fact, the questions posed by the earliest political thinkers referred precisely to who will control, how, and for which ends. Both anarchism and laissez-faire liberalism represent strands and episodes in a rich and varied history of political philosophy.

Having reduced the tradition of Western political thought to the "literature of freedom" aimed at eliminating intentional control, Skinner also reduces the concept of government to "the power to punish."[10] Like Owen, Skinner wars against punishment because of its objectionable by-products and because of its inefficiency. He defines punishment as either the withdrawal of a positive reinforcement or the presentation of a negative one. Punishment may suppress undesirable responses, but does not subtract them as positive reinforcers do. In other words, one may divert but not wholly eliminate undesirable behavior by punishing it. Further, punishment has such unfortunate by-products as severe anxiety. The most effective technique of control is to condition objectionable behavior by means of positive reinforcement. Like Plato's philosopher king, who fashioned a constitution for the perfect society, Skinner will engineer the perfect culture through the operant conditioning of its citizens.

Plato explained the superior capabilities of the philosopher king through myth and an elitist apology. As a scientist, Skinner can scarcely resort to such justification for the designer of social reform. In fact, he reduces the role of designer on the grounds of his environmentalism and his deep distrust of the individual. The individual may indeed control himself, and the evolution of culture may be accelerated through a knowledge of the laws of operant conditioning. However, the self-control exerted by the individual, such as his abstention from harmful but delicious food, is but an instance of the arrangement of stimulus conditions that facilitate behavior. Man controls himself and others by working with the variables of which behavior is a function. However, ultimately control emanates not from the controlling individuals but from the variables in the environment and the history of controlling persons. In other words, the activity of man controlling is merely a reflection of past conditioning. In such an explanation of the design of reform, purpose is not a quality of behavior, but a way of referring to the variables which control behavior. The individual does not direct his behavior towards the future. He only emits responses which in the past have been reinforced under similar circumstances. Skinner believes that the concepts of reinforcement, operant behavior, and conditioning of operants will eventually explain all human behavior and that they are the ultimate tools with which to construct the perfect society.

In discussing government and the "literature of freedom," Skinner has established the terms of his polemic by assigning very narrow definitions to politics and philosophy. By loading the dialogue, so to speak, he wins. Just as Thrasymachus in Plato's *Republic* was brought to confess his erroneous path to success, Skinner's countless opponents subsumed under the umbrella of the "literature of freedom" must succumb to the verdict of obsolescence from a science which will soon reach the advanced state of physics.

However, the problem of value remains, and a philosopher king about to give birth to an advanced culture must grapple with the unscientific questions of goals and purpose. Failing this, he will be classified with the social Darwinists. Nevertheless, Skinner believes that he has exploded a myth by classifying value and purpose as prescientific views of human nature. Values, he claims, are actually man's feelings about events, and these feelings are facts. Good can only mean good facts, positive reinforcers, or "what group members find reinforcing as the result of their genetic endowment and the nature of the social contingencies to which they have been exposed."[11] Things are good because of the contingencies of survival under which the species evolved, and all value judgments refer to the reinforcing effects of actions. This means that ethical judgment refers to the customary practices of a group. The source of value, therefore, lies in the cultural environment, the contingencies consequent on human behavior. This is true for all areas of human behavior, even religion, for Skinner claims that a person does not support religion out of conviction but because of the contingencies arranged by the religious agency. Since there is no independent source of norm resulting from philosophy or theology, survival is the only value by which a culture may be judged. This position eliminates vast areas of policy from government: the matters of adjusting ends and purposes, and dealing with conflicts of interest. The substance of decision has narrowed to a studied selection of the most efficient means to a given end. For instance, in a "scientific" society one would no longer question the aim of a foreign policy, but rather concentrate on creating those conditions which would elicit supportive behavior. Success is its own value, and hence the problems which man must grapple with in managing his life are greatly reduced. If behavior in all areas of life can be regulated by scheduled reinforcement, man will be absolved from asking questions about the goals of his existence and taking responsibility for the answers. He will, indeed, be beyond freedom and dignity.

Some of the features of a good culture are elucidated by Skinner in his *Beyond Freedom and Dignity.* A successful culture maintains civil order and defends itself against attack, arranges economic contingencies to maintain enterprising and productive labor, and induces its members to maintain a safe, healthful environment and a population density appropriate to its resources and its space.[12] As an afterthought, he admits that it will also need the support of its members and thus must provide for the pursuit and achievement of happiness. The key to survival, however, is the propensity constantly to review and experiment with current practices.

Skinner's characterization of a good culture is broad enough to include most existing cultures. Nor does the question of support for a system or the happiness of its members provide a yardstick for distinguishing among systems. The Soviet Union has arranged social contingencies so that support of the system is a sine qua non of participation and has transformed happiness into an ideological matter. Skinner corroborates this practice in his claim that "if Mao has succeeded in making signs of progress toward a greater China positively reinforcing, then it is possible that the Chinese feel freer and happier than most young Americans."[13]

The survival of a culture can indeed be guaranteed in many ways. One need not take the Chinese example. There is always the advice of Machiavelli or Aristotle's essay on how to preserve tyranny and avoid the disaffection of the governed. Skinner would explain obedience to a political system merely by an analysis of the "relevant behavioral repertoires."[14] Since he has expelled value from a study of man in society, obedience cannot be justified in ethical terms, and authority will be supplanted by operant conditioning.

Skinner's search for utopia reflects the widespread desire of contemporary youth to substitute psychology for politics in building a life in common. Much as the latter shun the procedures and purposes expressed in political culture in favor of encounter techniques, Skinner's utopia will be achieved by behavior modification. "We have the physical, biological and behavioral technologies needed to save ourselves. . . . The problem is how to get people to use them."[15] The most important task of the utopian designer is to insure that the survival of the community is important to its members.

Skinner approaches the task of utopia as he does the problem of studying human behavior: he extrapolates from a simple to a complex system. "The simplification in utopian writing is nothing more than the simplification characteristic of science."[16] The practice of utopia is worthwhile for men, he believes, because it emphasizes experimentation. Even if it is not possible to design a successful culture as a whole at this time, it is possible to design better practices in a piecemeal fashion. Because of their small size, isolation, and internal coherence, utopian communities are useful laboratories for experimenting in the practices of education and socialization. Changes and experimentation are well-nigh impossible in a broader society with its "specialized reinforcers" (police, priests, teachers) and "codified contingencies" (laws).[17] A utopian community, however, can factor out all these complexities.

Walden Two

Because Skinner regards his discipline as a tool with which to shape as well as to understand human behavior, it is not surprising that he has focused his ideas on the search for the perfect society. A utopian community is an ideal vehicle of reform for thinkers who reject both power and compromise as a means to human purpose. Although Skinner insists that his Walden Two is distinct from previous utopian communities because it is "scientific," one need not take this claim at its face value. Saint-Simon and Owen also labeled their utopias scientific, and Skinner can be included in the utopian tradition which flowered in such nineteenth-century figures as Fourier and Etienne Cabet.

The key figure in *Walden Two*, the founder of the perfect community, is Frazier, a scientist and mouthpiece for Skinner's views. Two professors, Castle and Burris, tour the community and reflect the approval and disapproval of outer society in their remarks. Frazier treats them to lengthy explanations and occasional corrections as he shepherds them about. As a philosophy professor, Castle plays the role of devil's advocate in his support of personal freedom and democracy. His personality is carefully sketched to embody all of Skinner's contempt for that discipline. Burris, however, is enlightened. He is highly sympathetic to the experiment and ultimately leaves his job to join Walden Two.

The focus of *Walden Two* is similar to that of previous Utopias: the integration of social and individual well-being and the management of labor and leisure to enhance both the individual and society. However, the emphasis is clearly on the social order, for the fundamental task of Walden is "to find the best behavior for the individual so far as the group is concerned and to induce him to behave in that way."[18] Robert Owen founded New Harmony for similar reasons, "to give a new existence to man by surrounding him with superior circumstances only."[19] He believed he had the "science of society" in his grasp which would help him to remodel all social institutions from marriage to education and to create happy and intelligent human beings. His rationale for New Harmony was an environmentalist one.[20]

Each individual comes into certain existing circumstances which act upon his organism, especially during early life. Each individual may be trained to either beneficial or bad habits. . . . Feelings and convictions are formed for the individual by the impression of circumstances.

Skinner develops an identical explanation for Walden Two.[21]

The behavior of the individual has always been shaped by society, whether on the basis of theology or ideology. The individual is helpless to resist, for it commences when he is a vulnerable infant. Why not shape behavior according to the results of experimental study?

What kind of person will emerge from Walden's "superior circumstances"? Skinner's new men and women display a combination of traits not frequently encountered in the outer world. Because Walden has substituted administration for politics and because Skinner abhors power, the people at Walden display no bent for becoming leaders or exercising control over their fellow communitarians. Utopia is a world without heroes, for the individual finds ample fulfillment as an agent of the community and therefore seeks no personal aggrandizement. However, this does not mean that Waldenians are conformists or automats, for self-expression is encouraged in styles of dress and in leisure pursuits. Barbara, a young observer, notices that the women at Walden look as if they come from foreign countries. Burris finds himself suddenly surrounded by a crowd of people and is moved to exclaim:[22]

They were delightful people. Their conversation had a measure and cadence more often found in well-wrought fiction than in fact. They were pleasant and well-mannered, yet perfectly candid; they were lively, but not effusive.

The reader is suddenly reminded of an upper class turn-of-the-century salon, vibrant with wit and ready intelligence, but sheltered from the boisterous lower class. However, the citizens of Walden are modern. They display a lively experimental attitude towards their habits and customs and are constantly alert to the possibilities of improving their domestic technology. For instance, the visitors admire the staggered schedules for dining, and the trays contrived to transport tea without spillage. The citizens of Walden live in communal housing, and children live separately from their parents. Cooperative living is highly economical and frees members of the community for the leisure which is central to the quality of life at Walden.

The community replaces the family not only as an economic unit but also as a social and psychological entity. Just as in the kibbutzim, Waldenians believe that abiding personal affection is much more than a romantic rationalization of a crude economic unit and that group care of children is better than parental care.

Skinner believes that most people are ready for marriage and procreation at an early age. This maturity is translated into a sex problem in outer society, but at Walden the community encourages and supports marriage and childbearing at the age of sixteen. Most young women are then finished with childbearing in their early twenties and can devote their adult lives to interesting professions. Walden practices a complete equality among the sexes so that a young woman can look forward to a full and early participation in community life.

Because husband and wife are spared monetary worries, and because they come from the same culture and have had the same sort of education, marriages are quite successful at Walden Two. Socialization in community is designed to make persons happy and easygoing. However, before embarking on marriage a prospective couple visits the manager for marriages, who compares their interests, school records, and health. If there is any serious discrepancy, the applicants are advised to choose other partners. Persons are able to accept such decisions with equanimity because there is plenty of opportunity for other liaisons at Walden and because they have been trained not to develop unreasonable, stubborn attachments to others. Marriages are secure from the temptations of communal living at Walden because friendship between the sexes is encouraged. Therefore, men and women need not become lovers when they only want to be friends. If trouble does occur, the taboo against gossip protects the wronged mate. Besides, the destructive impact of such occurrences on the persons involved is much less than in outer society. Jealousy and wounded pride are emotions which have been conditioned out of the residents of Walden Two.

The children at Walden do not live with their parents. "Home is no place to raise children," Frazier exclaims.[23] The control of behavior is an intricate science which requires years of training and which is simply not available to the average mother. Therefore, the delicate process of child rearing is left to the experts, both male and female. Even though parents may work in the nursery for a few hours, personal dependency is avoided. "Love and affection are psychological and cultural, and therefore blood relationships can be happily forgotten."[24] Every adult at Walden regards every child as his own, and every child thinks of every adult as his parent. Thus, the childless do not suffer for their lack, and children are not left to rely on those who happened to bear them.

All infants are cared for in the lower nursery. There they are placed in temperature controlled plastic cubicles so that they may avoid the frustration of clothes and linen. "When a

baby graduates from our Lower Nursery, it knows nothing of
frustration, anxiety or fear. . . It never cries except when sick,
which is very seldom, and it has a lively interest in everything."[25]
The upper nursery houses children from one to three years
and is arranged both to provide space for play and learning
and to shelter the child from the frustrations which create
negative emotions such as anxiety or fear. Robert Owen also
advocated an "infant school" where the child would be raised
in an atmosphere of mutual regard, safe from the careless handling and temper of his parents. Skinner and Owen believe that
life in the outer world deluges the infant with frustrations before he is able to handle them. At Walden obstacles are introduced carefully and gradually so that the child develops a
strong tolerance for the frustrations he will encounter in his
life. Thus, the aim of early education in community is to
build tolerance for annoying experiences by designing a series
of adversities concomitant with the child's capacity for self-
control. A hungry child will learn to wait before touching a
steaming bowl of soup, and a toddler may defer licking a lolli-
pop.

All ethical training is completed by the age of six. By that
time control over the physical and social environment can be
relaxed, and the child left to control himself. There is no
punishment at Walden. In the outer world punishment selects
the strong and produces many pathological personalities in
the process. In utopia adversity is geared to build strength in
all the members of a community.

As the child grows up, he moves from one age group to another without the abrupt changes and problems experienced
by children in the broader society. The Walden system is arranged so that the child emulates other children slightly older
than himself. Thus, much of his early education can be accomplished without adult interference. Between the ages of three
and thirteen, the child gradually assumes responsibility for
his room, clothes, and dining arrangements. Education at
Walden is informal by most standards in practice today. The
child learns at his own pace, and the community as a whole
with its fields, workshops, and laboratories is his school.

Rather than being isolated from the life of the community and placed in a formal institution, the child integrates work and learning at an early age and is gradually brought into a full participation in community life. There are no serious gaps between facets of life at Walden, no practices or institutions which are dysfunctional.

Work is part of the good life at Walden Two. A communal existence with its shared facilities avoids the duplication of effort and hence the necessity for long working hours. Most Waldenians work only four hours a day and in that short period are as productive as a man working eight hours in outer society. This is so because people work better during the first four hours of the day and because they are more highly motivated when working for themselves than for a "profit-making" employer.[26] In contrast to modern society, which eliminates "weak" members from the labor force, Walden provides appropriate employment for all its citizens, including the elderly, women, and children. There are no occupationally disabled and no leisure classes at Walden.

Although the people at Walden live well, their personal wealth is small and the community has a low consumption of goods. Communal living allows its members to share appliances such as cars, and the community is self-sufficient in food and many other necessities. Far from being alienating, labor in community is life-enhancing, and the relationship between one's work and community well-being is clear. Thus, Walden has eliminated the expensive pastimes developed in modern society to dull the pressures and frustrations of life. There are no bars or taverns at Walden Two.

Money is not needed in Walden because the community provides food, clothing, education, medical services, and entertainment for the individual. Labor credits replace cash as the medium of exchange. In return for goods and services, members contribute twelve hundred labor credits a year, or four credits for each of three hundred work days. Jobs are evaluated in terms of the willingness of members to undertake them. In the long run, when all values have been adjusted, all kinds of work are supposed to be equally desirable, or the whole system will be reassessed. The goal of the economic system is to break even and yield a comfortable and satisfying life for all members rather than to make a profit. In addition, Waldenians enjoy the opportunity of pursuing a variety of occupations and thus avoid the boredom of work experienced by so many in the broader society.

Because the energy and intellect of the individual are not spent in long working hours and worry over subsistence, he enjoys a rich and satisfying leisure in Walden Two. The citizens of utopia revel in a leisure "for art, science, play, the exercise of skills, the satisfaction of curiosities, the conquest of nature and the conquest of man."[27] Walden is a bustle of theater groups, string quartets, and art exhibits. Given the leisure, the opportunity, and the appreciation of others, Frazier explains, any person can develop artistic capabilities. The unique balance of work and leisure in utopia eliminates the necessity for postponing enjoyment.

In the nineteenth century Count Henri de Saint-Simon believed that his design of utopia spelled the twilight of power. Once man has erected the New Order based on a knowledge of the science of society, politics, that despicable art, will give way to administration. In a similar manner Skinner also dismisses politics as the path to the good life. Given the techniques provided by the science of human behavior, man has the means to create the good life for everyone. "Keep out of politics and away from government. . . . It is not the place for men of good will or vision."[28]

Just as in Saint-Simon's New Order, government in Walden Two is a technocracy devoted to high administration. A board of six planners is responsible for policy making and for supervising the administrative agencies under the managers. Since there is no separation of powers in Walden, the planners also perform certain judicial functions. Planners are chosen by the board itself from names supplied by the managers and usually include three women. They receive six hundred labor credits a year for their services which leaves them short two credits a day, one of which must be earned in physical labor. Like

Plato's ruling class, they receive no rewards of wealth or distinction for their services, only the satisfaction of exerting themselves for the good of the community. In the absence of popular control, the limited opportunity for personal gain is supposed to curb any expansionist tendencies on the part of the planners. Skinner echoes Plato and Saint-Simon in his desire to render responsibility totally pure by separating it from the instruments and the will to power. Like Saint-Simon's scientists and industrialists, the planners are experts, and it is their expertise which qualifies them for governance.

The daily affairs of Walden Two are the province of the managers, specialists in charge of the divisions and services such as food, health, play, dentistry, dairy, industries, the nursery, and the school. Because they are specialists like the planners, they are not chosen by the citizenry. They are selected by the planners on the basis of ability and concern for the welfare of the community and have achieved their position via intermediate posts which provide the necessary apprenticeship.

Scientists form another administrative category. They conduct experiments in plant and animal breeding, the control of infant behavior, and educational processes, engaging in pure science only in their spare time.

None of these three categories enjoys any special privileges or titles which set it apart from the general body of workers and which form the basis of class distinctions in other societies. As in the kibbutz, experts must also perform physical labor and menial tasks as a health measure and to keep them attuned to the needs of the ordinary person.

Walden Two functions for the benefit of all as opposed to a competitive society in which Skinner sees one man's gain as another man's loss. He believes that personal ambition and the urge to power are not inherent in man, but the results of faulty environmental design. Social contingencies are arranged in Walden so that no person will seek his own ends at the expense of the community. The possibility of tyranny will be socialized out of the Waldenians. Individuality has lost its glamour along with its dangers, in community. This fact, plus the absence of rewards for the exercise of responsibility, will provide a check on both planners and managers. In addition, competence will provide its own restraint. Just as Plato insisted in his *Republic*, a truly competent man, whether he is a doctor or a ruler, is by definition concerned with the well-being of his subjects, and therein lies his ultimate check.

Plato, Saint-Simon, and Skinner share a contempt for democracy and its foundation on the wisdom of the average man. The average person may know what he wants, but he does not know how to achieve it or even how to assess the competence of experts. Government, Frazier points out, is a highly specialized task for experts, and most people are just as happy to be governed in this fashion.[29]

In Walden Two, no one worries about the government except the few to whom that worry has been assigned. To suggest that everyone should take an interest would seem as fantastic as to suggest that everyone should become familiar with our diesel engines. Even the constitutional rights of the members are seldom thought about, I'm sure. The only thing that matters is one's day to day happiness and a secure future.

Frazier takes issue with two features of democracy: its emphasis on majority rule through elections and its trust in the inherent goodness and wisdom of the common man. In relying on rational man, democracy fails to account for the fact that man is determined by the state and not the reverse. Frazier emits an anguished sigh on behalf of the suffering minority in democratic states. Elections do not really ascertain the will of the people. "The chance that one man's vote will decide the issue in a national election is less than the chance that he will be killed on the way to the polls."[30] There are no elections at Walden, for the people are not qualified to choose or even evaluate the experts who govern. They can only tell the experts how they like their life. This information is communicated by studies and through carefully established channels for individual protest to the planners and managers. In turn, the managers will automatically heed the grievances of the people, as an engineer will lend his immediate attention to a defective engine. Besides, as Frazier points out wearily in response to

Castle's insistence on the benefits of democracy, the people of Walden live under conditions striven for but never attained under democracy. All citizens share equally in the community wealth, and there are no barriers impeding the mobility of the talented.

In *Walden Two* Skinner takes issue not only with democracy but with all forms of government. First of all, government relies on force to achieve its ends, and therefore it cannot provide good environments for men. Second, since men in power can never admit that they are wrong, they cannot maintain an experimental approach. However, experimentation is the only source of improvement, and therefore, Skinner concludes that politics can never establish the good life. The liberal reformers who seek power are at bottom only concerned with imposing their views on others.[31]

Why don't they build a world to their liking without trying to seize power? Any group of men of good will can work out a satisfactory life within the existing political structures of half a dozen modern governments.

Since Frazier has only contempt for history, he is unaware of the harrassment endured by experimental communities in the past and takes for granted an environment which tolerates his own. One wonders whether Frazier would allow a group experiment opposed to the basic social order if the entire country were ruled by Fraziers.

There also remains the problem of providing for the national defense and conducting international relations. Frazier deftly parries the criticism of his lack of concern with the outer world by claiming that Walden "is but a grand experiment in the structure of a peaceful world."[32] Like Owen, Skinner believes that once all men can witness the improvements wrought in community, they will at once adopt this example. Apparently, at this level behavior need not be cultivated. Faith and rationality will fill in.

The good life will be ushered in not by politics but by the constant experimentation of experts in designing temperaments and personalities which will sustain a peaceful, creative social life.[33]

The control of temperament? Give me the specifications and I'll give you the man. What do you say to the control of motivation, building the interest which will make men most productive and most successful? Does that seem to you fantastic? Yet, some of the techniques are available and more can be worked out experimentally. Think of the possibilities! A society in which there is no failure, no boredom, no duplication of effort.

Skinner has a rather frightening ailment for a scientist. He thinks he is God, and Frazier admits to Burris that he feels his position to be similar to God's. It is somewhat better, though, because he is not disappointed by his children as God is with His.

One is left with a feeling of deep unease after visiting Walden Two through Frazier. He assures us that politics has been left behind because it is useless and that values have been eliminated in favor of a scientifically planned society. Yet life is highly politicized at Walden, and choices are constantly being made, which means that values are still operative. The charming people at Walden Two are balanced and cultivated. Conceivably, they could have had other characteristics. However, even when men are agreed on their goals in society, the allocation of resources must be decided; who gets what . . . when . . . and how . . .

One has the feeling that Skinner understands neither the limitations of science, the nature of value judgments, nor the political implications of having scientists apply their discoveries to the solution of human problems. Although Skinner insists that he has exorcised power from Walden Two, the act of making a decision for society is a form of power. And not only is power involved in such an event, but value as well. The ethics which Skinner rejects may involve a different level of reality from experimental science, but its focus on the articulation of goals for human society is as important for man as the development of hypothesis in a controlled laboratory environment. In eliminating this area of thought, Skinner treats the larger questions of man's existence as derived from practical issues and elevates social norms into ethical standards. The choice exercised in decision is not merely the technical matter of weighing evidence and following the path indicated by evidence. Choice involves values, and even science as a human endeavor is not divorced from human purpose.

Skinner's combination of behaviorism and activism is highly reminiscent of Marx's skillful bridging of historical determinism and revolutionism. Neither man derived his activist goals from the social sciences, and for both the leap from determinism to social transformation is provided by a dramatic act of will and hope. Since the future society will not evolve inexorably from present circumstances, history requires a midwife.

But if science does not contain the answers to the values men pursue in society, then the scientist is not necessarily qualified for leadership. And since it is ultimately the individual who experiences culture and society, it is his desires, tastes, and feelings which are important. If one is concerned with the person, and such a concern is as axiomatic as the concern with culture, a form of government which allows the influence of individuals is preferable to a government of experts. Under a democratic system a citizen obeys laws because they are established in accordance with procedures which he supports and because their substance is in accord with his own moral values. It is in this sense, the congruence of values between governed and governing, that the survival of a system depends on the support of its members. More important, the adjustment of values will be mediated by and not for the individual.

Like Plato, Skinner assumes that an identity of interests between the individual and the collectivity can be engineered without the mediation of the individual   by myth in the case of the *Republic* and by behavior modification in *Walden Two*. Both men are reacting to the divided and tumultuous societies in which they live, and conclude that disagreement or divergence of interests is so harmful to society that it should be eliminated. In trying to exorcise conflict by operant conditioning, Skinner falls into the tradition of utopian thinkers who seek to redesign men and society to produce a condition of peace and harmony.

One factor which accounts for Skinner's wide popularity is that he crystallizes in his writings many of the values and prejudices espoused by contemporary youth. When *Walden Two* first appeared in the late forties, it was greeted with derision. Today a portion of the younger generation has welcomed it to the extent of emulating features of Walden, not because they find it novel but because it contains values which they have articulated themselves.

Communitarian youth who admire Skinner are deeply attracted by his search for a better life in *Walden Two*. Like Frazier, they are concerned with equality between the sexes and the benefits of child care in a communal setting. They believe that the human condition can be improved by transforming the institutions in which men work, learn, and socialize new generations.

These youth are conducting the search for a better life in a manner reminiscent of *Walden Two*. They display a deep-seated bias against politics, which stems from their notion that government is equivalent to coercive power and that power is evil. They would rather approach their life in common as a problem to be solved by administration. A logical result of this outlook is a strong bias against pluralism, for the latter requires carefully worked out procedures in order to survive. Rather than cope with the diversity of interests and philosophies animating men today, sections of communitarian youth would retreat into a corporatist society where each community erects its psychological barriers against the outside. Given the homogeneity of outlooks and ends within the small community, all that is needed to maintain cohesion are the popularized techniques of psychology: "group rap" and encounter.

Skinner has dispensed with history because he believes that an objective history is not possible, that history can teach us nothing about human nature, and that therefore we can make no real use of it as a guide. For the activist the pursuit of non-instrumental knowledge is a waste of time. The bias of youth against history, however, is born of a sense of despair at the course of foreign policy and at their inability to influence it. Closely related to their rejection of history is the tendency of many young adults to avoid discussions of political philosophy, with its questions of freedom and responsibility, in favor of sociology and psychology, on the grounds that abstraction is of no use to man. It is as though they desperately seek to reaffirm their influence if only by the curious act of limiting their universe of discourse in time and space. They have willed the world away like the young Quaker who set himself on fire in front of the White House.

The abstention from political philosophy is no guarantee against the dogmatism which Skinner and his followers wish to avoid. A good Waldenian cannot question the validity of operant conditioning, just as a good communist cannot discuss his trinity of historical materialism, democratic centralism, and the dictatorship of the proletariat. These axioms are enforced in Soviet society not only by persuasion but also by making them existentially functional, just as Skinner's axioms of operant conditioning are functional to his utopia. Closing the universe of discourse in the search for truth has as its sequel the closed society.

Twin Oaks

ORIGINS

Reflecting on the social accomplishments of a new revolution, Lenin once remarked that theory is gray, but the tree of life is green. The intentional community of Twin Oaks represents the practice of Skinner's behavioral revolution as well as part of the alternative culture of new communities. Skinner's ideas inspired the founding of this community, and his social thought forms the core of belief animating its institutions. Members have corresponded with him, advertise and sell his *Walden Two*, and await his eventual visit with eager anticipation.

However, Twin Oaks is not a fictional embodiment of social thought. It is a pioneering venture in intentional community, and its heterogeneous membership displays a more relaxed attitude towards utopia than the fictitious Waldenians who lecture all visitors. The annals of this community are flavored with accounts of the kinks in "perfection," a new building flooded, the fiasco of a veal enterprise, and the precipitous fall of a member from a treehouse. And if Waldenians repair to their rooms before dinner in order to dress, the members of Twin Oaks may be dashing for a quick refreshing huddle in the steam dome. The moderate and cultivated person who lived a life of calm competence in Walden Two has been replaced by Tom Sawyer, and that gracious Miss Meyerson is driving a tractor.

Ever since *Walden Two* appeared, small groups of people have come together in order to plan a similar utopia: graduate students like Frazier and psychologists heady with the new possibilities for a peaceful society. Twin Oaks community was founded by the efforts of two such groups: Walden Pool of Atlanta, Georgia, and Walden House of Washington, D.C. *Walden Pool* was a newspaper organized to elicit interest in an eventual Walden Two and to find the people, land, and money to start such a community. Walden House was an urban commune aimed at founding a community on the model of Walden Two. The economies of group living enabled its members to start an investment fund for the eventual purchase of a farm. It also served as a recruiting center as well as a home for Walden Two enthusiasts.

Two other groups were simultaneously working towards a new society. Living Research was founded to educate and prepare prospective members for community life. Another group met with Skinner in the fall of 1965, and together they compiled a list of all the people who had written to him about *Walden Two*, almost two hundred. It was this group which organized a national convention in 1966 at the Walden-Woods Conference Center in Michigan. The eighty-three persons attending reviewed *Walden Two* and the concepts of behavioral engineering, and conducted workshops on all phases of community. The interminable lectures and the proliferation of working committees were reminiscent of an academic gathering, but the results were hardly proportionate to the hours of discourse. However, the high point of the conference was a tape-recorded message from Skinner congratulating the

participants on the timely quest for community. The United
States is the strongest power in the world, he explained, yet it
continues to propagate international violence, perpetuating
"aversive control" instead of exploring other alternatives.[34]
The message suggested that the science of behavior could be
applied to the most urgent problems of the times and that the
design of culture on the model of *Walden Two* was a commen-
dable approach. Although the conference generated considerable fervor for utopia, it ended without achieving agreement on
either the goals of a community or the methods of achieving
a new society.

A follow-up conference in Racine, Wisconsin, comprised
chiefly of behavioral scientists and professional people, proved
equally inconclusive. As a result, fifteen people from Walden
House and Walden Pool convened in January 1967 to discuss
the possibility of actually establishing a small community. They
agreed that it should be modeled on Walden Two and constitute a small society rewarding neither selfishness nor wealth
and insuring complete equality. They believed that the time
for community was ripe, for they were convinced that the economic and social fabric of society was deteriorating and that
the government had neither the intention nor the ability to
carry out reform. Their dream became an immediate possibility
when a friend offered a loan to purchase land in the farm belt
around Washington, D.C. The terms were generous, and the
community would enjoy a three-year period of grace before
repayment.

The prospective utopians selected a 123-acre farm near
Louisa, Virginia, which included two creeks, a woods, pastures,
and tillable land. The majestic oaks dominating the farm inspired the name of Twin Oaks. In recruiting prospective members the founders wisely advertised for persons interested in
the pioneer aspects of community life and warned against ex-
pectations of a Walden Two with all the amenities of Skinner's
fictional society.

In June of 1967 a blue-green and white bus crammed with
furniture, appliances, a printing press, a skunk cage with a
skunk, and even a beehive bore the new utopians to their land.

Because the farmhouse temporarily lacked power, the first night in heaven was spent under the apple trees.

The early years at Twin Oaks were devoted to learning how to distinguish weeds from vegetables, building a workshop to house a new hammock industry, initiating a labor credit system and a superstructure of planners and managers. There was even time for rearing four-year-old Elliot with positive reinforcement.

A NEW SOCIETY

Along with the buildings, the orchard, and the new crops, Twin Oaks has constructed an entirely new society in miniature. The members of Twin Oaks regard their community as the first step towards a new order, the first of a series of communities which will form a new society from the bottom up. Each visitor to this small universe is handed an attractive prospectus which explains the community as "an attempt to create a culture which produces happy and useful people, a people who cooperate with one another for the general good and who deal with problems in a peaceful and rational way." All the evils of a corrupt and immoral society have been banished at Twin Oaks, for it brooks no institutions which embody egoism, exploitation, or aggression. Twin Oakers claim with pride that competition and "sexism" have been exorcised and replaced with an equality more complete than one could ever dream of in the outer world.

Like Skinner's Walden Two, Twin Oaks is embarked on the design not merely of an ideal community but of a new culture for all mankind. It is through the techniques of behavior modification that the goals and organization of work, the institutions of family and governance, and new norms of interpersonal relations will permanently insure that now elusive state of happiness. However, members of Twin Oaks experience both the pride and burden of their model, Walden Two. Issues of the community newsletter, *Leaves,* bristle with debates on points of resemblance and difference. To the outside observer it appears that the broad goals and techniques of Walden Two

animate Twin Oaks while the actual substance of the good
life is strikingly different. Indeed, the membership is steeped
in the theory of behaviorism. Conversations are laced with references to "circumstances in the past environment," "positive
reinforcers," and the "extinction of negative behavior." But
Twin Oaks is adamant on its uniqueness. It regards itself as
Skinnerian, but as an original interpretation.

It is mainly in the tone and elements of daily life that Twin
Oaks differs from its prototype. The good life is fellowship,
the adventure of pioneering a new movement, and the more
immediate pleasures of sex and a relaxed pace of life in the
country. Slowing down the tempo and pressure of life in a
modern society and enlivening it with play constitute a new
road to well-being for communitarians. In themselves these
values may not seem original or even revolutionary, but in
the context of an urbanized society in which the metropoli-
tan frontier is the focal point of development and individual
opportunity, such a lifestyle appears singular.

While the tone of life in Walden Two is calm and studied,
an air of burlesque pervades Twin Oaks and masks the seriousness of community building. Evenings the members gather to
chuckle over the amplified crunch of corn shucking from the
community's radio station or to witness the presentation of
a six-act play entitled *Adventures in Sanitation*. The hilarity
and high spirits which characterize daily life at Twin Oaks are
notably absent in Walden Two with its busy crews of scientists
and technicians.

Twin Oak's unique relationship to Walden Two is apparent
in attitudes towards marriage. In Walden Two couples married
at an early age in order to cope with the problem of adolescent
sexual frustration. Thereafter the community arranged "contingencies" to support the couple as a source of abiding affection. At Twin Oaks monogamy is not highly regarded, for
it is considered in conflict with the community's stand against
personal possessiveness and its emphasis on sexual freedom.
There have been nine married couples in community at one
time or another, and currently there are three. However, only
one of these shares a room or spends much time together, and

they do not consider their relationship exclusive. Three of the nine couples who have been members of Twin Oaks have eventually separated, but Twin Oakers do not consider the community responsible for the break-ups. They trace the source of trouble to the partners themselves and to their own concept of marriage as a confining and outmoded institution. Twin Oakers assert that by providing fellowship as well as economic support community living has eliminated the need for marriage.

Ideology aside, there are informal pairings in the community. Pairing is fairly fluid and most communitarians would claim that jealousy or possessiveness are not major problems, although they have caused the departure of some members. Generally, instances of tension arise as a result of changing or multiple relationships. In such cases, the community tries to provide various techniques for easing pride. One of these is scheduling relationships and another is for the members of a triangular relationship to spend time together as a trio. However, the greatest hedge against jealousy, according to Twin Oaks, is strong community disapproval of such feelings. Apparently no one receives sympathy or support for pangs of jealousy. Besides this negative restraint, the fact that lack of possessiveness constitutes a moral standard in community helps members to curb their possessive impulses. In a more practical vein, the constant stream of visitors helps to ease the resentment of some of the unpaired communitarians who do not appear to enjoy that state.

Sex is regarded as an important part of the good life at Twin Oaks, and the community has taken a firm stand in favor of sexual freedom. There are no regulations or taboos such as one finds at the Brotherhood of the Spirit, for instance, and there have been a variety of unconventional arrangements which have functioned harmoniously. The only community norm regarding sexual practices stipulates that pressure or seduction is contemptible and that the desire for sex must be mutual.

As in Walden Two, a purely platonic relationship between the sexes is common and highly valued at Twin Oaks. The rich interpersonal life is one of the primary attractions of life in community, and many people have joined Twin Oaks in search of friendships as well as out of conviction.

The family as a center of affection, economic security, and the socialization of children has been replaced by the community. The relationship between an older member and her adult daughter is evidence of the new pattern. The daughter lives at Twin Oaks most of the time. However, most people are not aware that they are mother and daughter. Like Walden Two, Twin Oaks intends to eliminate any sense of identity between children and their natural parents as it commences the socialization of a new generation.

The elimination of sexism in daily life is part of the sexual revolution being waged at Twin Oaks. As soon as the members began the business of a life in common, women turned towards chores outside of their socially ascribed roles, in construction or animal husbandry, for instance. The men followed suit by learning sewing and housekeeping. A few years ago a young member broke new ground in Virginia by becoming the first female student in a cattlemen's school. Recently a young member commented on the presentation of *The Women's Film* at the community and somewhat gloatingly mused on the irrelevance of the message. "Women are not exploited at Twin Oaks, but even if we were a little bored by the film, perhaps we needed to be reminded what it's like for our sisters in American society."[35] Members have sought to eliminate desirability to the opposite sex as a measure of worth or status, and women are encouraged to ignore standards of beauty. They claim that because these standards are ignored in community, "We know that we are all beautiful."[36] According to these members, the rivalry between women has been replaced by the "joys of sisterhood." As in the nineteenth-century Oneida Community, the practical, boyish attire of the women (pantaloons and cropped hair in the latter case) has not impeded an active sex life among members.

In addition to new concepts of sex roles and the family, equality is one of the primary values which the community wishes to realize in the new order. Twin Oaks is no haven for the personally ambitious or for those who wish to act as leaders.

The community has sought to provide a set of conditions which will allow each person to flower, and no member is singled out or receives any distinction because of his occupation, individual achievements, or personality. The labor credit system prevents the development of sexual or occupational hierarchies, for everyone must earn the same amount of credits, and labor credits are distributed according to a scale established by personal preference. A reader of the community newsletter who inquired about profiles of the membership was delivered this reply: even if Dr. Skinner were a member, he would be referred to merely as fred, and then his managership and perhaps his hobbies or interests would be included in his profile but certainly not his accomplishments. Members experience no desire for individual distinction. No titles are used, neither "mother" nor "doctor," last names rarely, and first names, which keep changing, are not capitalized. Community members sign correspondence with their first names followed by "for the community." Another example of this phenomenon is the case of a young artist at Twin Oaks who does not sign the handsome sketches which adorn the various buildings. The grounds for this omission are not the desire for self-obliteration, but a sincere intent not to use talent for personal enhancement. There is no danger of a tyranny ushered in by personal charisma at Twin Oaks.

The community is not merely interested in establishing selected values but is deliberately approaching the broader task of redesigning the entire cultural environment with its resultant "behavioral alternatives." The organization of work is central to the establishment of a utopian environment. At Twin Oaks work is intended to provide choice, responsibility, cooperation, personal growth, and most of all, happiness. Much like Karl Marx, the behaviorists at Twin Oaks regard specialization as the prime cause of servitude and alienation experienced by modern man. And as in the Marxian heaven, the acquisition of responsibility and multiple skills constitutes the road to self-perfection.

Therefore, communitarians actively promote the universalization of skills, and the Twin Oaks behavior code includes the obligation of skilled persons to communicate their competence to those interested.[37] Both instructor and apprentice earn labor credits for their efforts. The attendant behavioral alternatives are as important as the competences. For instance, an experienced worker will refrain from snatching a power saw from a novice. The result expected from this self-control will be mutual regard rather than mutual irritation, and a tension-free learning experience for the beginner. "Well made" is not a value in community. A member who happens to be earning his labor credits at the electric sander may have only a sketch of the finished product by which to gauge his results, and these will not be evaluated by the community. As long as a hammock or any article functions, it is deemed sufficient by the community and no pride in craft is aimed at.

Apprenticeship helps eliminate any work-preference advantages that a specialist might have, and the member with a long career behind him will not necessarily be given any special consideration over one who has not completed high school when both select the same occupation. Whether a member wishes to concentrate on carpentry or auto mechanics, he acquires this skill on the grounds of interest rather than aptitude. Most important, of course, is the view that acquiring a variety of competences and concomitant "behavioral alternatives" is a major source of well-being.

The behavior code regarding the communication of skills is also motivated by some very practical concerns. Twin Oakers have learned from the experiences of their formative years that specialization does not necessarily further the survival of the group. The person who specializes in farming, for instance, may fall ill or demand extra privileges. Worst of all, he may eventually leave the community and thus create a serious gap in available skills. During the first years of the group's existence, its survival was frequently jeopardized by the departure of highly skilled members.

A careful balance of work and leisure is the aim of utopia, although many utopian communities of the past never survived long enough to realize it. At Twin Oaks the work week is thirty-five hours, and this includes housekeeping chores. The shorter working day, the rotation of housekeeping activities, and the fact that work is performed on the premises mean that communitarians enjoy more leisure than most people in the broader society. In addition, work hours are staggered throughout the day so that no one works for several hours in a row. On a typical day a member rises at 8 or 8:30 A.M., breakfasts, and will weave hammocks from 9 to 11 A.M. Then he may take a short swim in the river which cuts through Twin Oaks's land, and rest until lunch. In the afternoon he will spend a few hours helping to construct a new building or working in the orchard, and still enjoy leisure hours in the later afternoon. Perhaps he will be on clean-up after dinner. The revising of work schedules and labor credit systems is a major preoccupation at Twin Oaks, and it is animated by the personal preferences of each member. As in Walden Two, productivity is enhanced because each member works at an occupation which he has selected and because fatigue is eliminated by shortening and staggering work periods.

In Walden Two, happy communitarians devoted leisure hours to chamber music, the theater, and other arts. The members of Twin Oaks also provide their own entertainment, but prefer the washtub bass, fiddle, and recorder to the violin. The raucous sounds of "Mrs. Pringle's Pig Favorite Bluegrass Band" or a hastily mustered a cappella fill their evenings. Twin Oakers also enjoy folk dancing and impromptu plays. For the daytime there is a swiming hole by the South Ana River with hammocks nearby and a steam dome. A creaky rowboat is also available for those who like to fish. In keeping with Twin Oaks's bent for equality sports are played in a noncompetitive fashion with no winners and no losers.

Twin Oaks has a constitution which embodies the entire set of purposes realized in community, much as the Bill of Rights of the United States Constitution. However, they are not conceived of as negative restraints on authority in the manner of classic basic rights, but rather as economic and social rights which depend upon the activity of an agency. These rights include: communal child care, or "the right to a neurosis-free childhood"; behavioral engineering, or "the right to be taught the elemental techniques of self-control": the right to a labor credit system, or "equal opportunity to choose one's own work and have a share of leisure time"; and the Aristotelian privilege of being "governed sensibly by people of ability and good will," or the right to a planner-manager system of government.[38]

As a result of these purposes, there is little differentiation in the social structure of Twin Oaks. There is no distinction based on age, occupation, or education. Planners and managers are the only separate categories. However, there are so many divisions that almost everyone either is or has been a manager. Besides, a planner or manager receives no special reward or distinction for filling his post. He must earn the same number of labor credits as any other member. Since labor credits are the only remuneration a member receives and since all members must earn an equal amount, they cannot become a source of status.

In contrast to many other utopian communities, Twin Oaks has not turned its back on modernization. Technology is favored in this community because it frees the individual for the good life, and Twin Oaks boasts modern kitchen appliances which lighten the burden of feeding fifty people each day. However, the community insists that technology must be inserted within their society without transforming it and must be strictly limited so as to avoid the pollution and consumerism it considers endemic in contemporary society.

Just as at Walden Two, experimentation in all phases of life is highly valued at Twin Oaks, and the members are continually revising their methods of calculating labor credits and schedules in order to make labor more enjoyable. A variety of methods to develop a happy and cohesive membership has been employed, such as mutual criticism, but no procedure for achieving unity or even for governance is allowed to acquire the status of hallowed tradition.

The community provides for change on the fundamental level as well as in the informal processes governing daily life. Twin Oaks wishes to absorb as many members as feasible in order to spur the community movement. However, it prefers to split into daughter communities rather than expand indefinitely. In spurning size, the community is turning its back on mass society just as it does in avoiding specialization. As in Walden Two, fission is the answer to success. In 1972 the community established Merion, a new branch, and it looks forward to many more.

MEMBERSHIP

The increasing number of members and the diminishing rate of turnover are indications of a successful community, and Twin Oaks is proud of its statistics in these matters. During the first few years of its existence, the membership turnover was 70 per cent, and the average stay was only three months.[39] Some causes of turnover included the desire for a higher standard of living, which prompted one member to form a new community, the reluctance to defer children, and a clash over ideals such as equality versus professionalism. Generally, the declining rate of departures seems to have coincided with the improvement in such amenities as food and housing. However, community hopping can also be regarded as a by-product of the great mobility of an experiment-prone, American population. Historians of migration patterns in the early American colonies have also discovered considerable colony hopping!

Twin Oaks has opened its doors to itinerant youngsters in search of adventure and freedom from parental control. However, in order to avoid problems with the law and with parents, the community requires a letter of permission from one parent before admitting a minor. But the community by no means disparages the young. On the contrary, as in *Walden Two*, thirteen is regarded as the official coming-of-age in Twin Oaks rather than the legal eighteen or twenty-one. From that point on a teenager will be regarded as an adult and will participate fully in community. Far from excluding them as members, Twin Oaks considers them useful members if only because they will have been partially socialized in community and will have assimilated its values to a greater extent than members who joined when adults. One of the current planners is nineteen, and one of the "old-timers" joined at the age of sixteen.

From an initial membership of eight, the community has expanded to fifty, exclusive of the ten or so visitors who arrive each week. There is a long waiting list of prospective members because the community cannot possibly accommodate everyone who wishes to join. A core group of founders exists within the membership but exerts no special influence.

However, the issue of membership is fundamental to intentional community and has occasioned both arguments and experiments at Twin Oaks. Membership is generally open to all who seek it, with certain reservations. Personality types such as the aggressive person who is eager to exercise his leadership ability are generally avoided. During the period of provisional membership, anyone who is highly critical of the group, who consistently fails to do his full share of work, or who asks for special privileges before finally joining is likely to be excluded. On a more fundamental level, Twin Oaks is not interested in members who will not support the goals of the group or who would dilute its identity as a Skinnerian community. Whether they regard themselves as such or not, they are a political society and therefore must strive for some consensus on values and methods.

The period of provisional membership is set at six months. During this time a new member enjoys full membership status, except that he may retain his financial assets and he may not vote on those rare occasions when a vote is called for. Also, he may be asked to leave if the full members do not approve of him, whereas a full member may be expelled only for specific reasons set out in the bylaws. When the six months have expired, the new member signs a contract with the community. It includes financial arrangements and a clause to the effect that anything produced by members or in their possession is considered community property, whether the interest on a savings account or a work of art. Incoming members may either donate their money outright or lend it without interest, but there is a three year cut-off on withheld assets. During this period departing members may recover the principal of savings or bonds if it is still available, while leaving the interest to the community. The contract also includes an acceptance of the community's bylaws and behavior code and guarantees the member an equal share of any benefits the community may provide. A member may keep private property, defined as those articles kept in a member's room. Bicycles or cars become community property even in the provisional period in order to avoid envy and dissension.

Throughout the first three years of its existence, Twin Oaks has included members with children at various times. A former member even gave birth in community, but mother and child eventually departed. Each time new members with children arrived, problems developed over the issue of parental versus communal authority and the diversion of scarce labor resources to child care. Even the most convinced communitarians found it impossible to relinquish their entire parental responsibility to the group. Their periodic interference frustrated those members earning labor credits with child care, not to speak of the arguments which burdened planners' meetings. One parent refused to allow a teenage member of the community to take her baby on car trips during her child care period. Also, it seemed as if the members with children joined at a time when the community had a great deal of work to spread among a relatively small membership. There were the hammock orders to fill, the houses to construct, and the planting in addition to the task of building a communal life. To the busy members, diverting scarce labor to sixteen or more hours of child care each day seemed a luxury that a fledgling community could ill afford.

Beyond the questions of resources and conflicts of interest lies the more important issue of socialization. Twin Oaks regards itself as the harbinger of a new order and as such is dedicated to creating the culture for an entire generation. It is the desire to socialize a generation according to Skinnerian principles which led the community to exclude children until it was able to produce its own. In 1970 the members decided to postpone a new generation for a period of three years.

Maya, the first community baby, was born in March 1973, and a sibling is expected a few months hence. The overjoyed communitarians have constructed a Skinnerian air crib, and a children's building is nearing completion. The building is under construction in the wooded area a few minutes away from the main complex of houses. Several buildings will eventually enclose a courtyard and a safe play area for toddlers. The current design accounts for ten children between infancy and five years. This number includes the children which the community will accept from the outside as well. When they reach the age of five, the children will move into a second building which will include a large indoor active play area, rooms for quiet play and sleeping, a kitchen, laundry, and an area for the adults who sleep in at night.

Maya is truly a communal child and is being socialized to consider all fifty adults as his parents. Since all community adults are parents, they are all engaged in child study meetings to bone up on positive reinforcement and the extinction of negative behavior. However, a core of around fifteen members cares for the baby. They are called metas after the metapalet (child attendants) of the kibbutz, and they are also intended to eliminate what the community regards as the "sexism of motherhood."

On a typical day Maya enjoys the loving care of six metas. The first meta arrives before the baby awakes, at 7 A.M. He takes care of the morning feeding and change of clothes. There is also time for cuddling and play before the arrival of meta number two. Each attendant takes a four-hour shift. However, the person on night shift is nursing Maya and therefore shares her room with the nursery.

Despite the months of study and preparation, the community greeted the small newcomer with all the nervousness of new parents. However, the communitarians look forward with anticipation to a generation which has the traits of cooperativeness, honesty, and generosity.

The membership of Twin Oaks is drawn from the white middle class and has an age spectrum ranging from seventeen years to the mid-forties. Educational backgrounds include several high school diplomas or the equivalent and several masters' degrees. There is a sprinkling of former professionals among the members, including a former engineer and systems analyst, a speech therapist, an artist, and several teachers. However, this particular group has not set the tone of life, and the only evidence of its professional history is the impressive library which lines the upper and lower halls of Llano, one of the residences. These people are now immersed in farming, cattle raising, and auto mechanics, and the observer is hard pressed to recognize them as former professionals. Equality is not just a pious phrase at Twin Oaks.

What motives inspire people to pull up stakes and join a Skinnerian community? Surely they were not all thirsting for a heaven called Walden Two. Nor is the community a panacea for the anguish of the children of affluence. ronnie, a former ranch hand and police officer, read about Twin Oaks in the *Modern Utopian* and was attracted by behaviorism and a planned society.[40] A friend of ronnie's was excited by his glowing reports and came for a visit. She stayed because she decided that the Twin Oaks approach to reform is more effective than her former efforts in radical politics. Quite a few members have arrived at the community on the heels of a deep disaffection with radical politics. If there is no room for young reformers in the political system and if anti-system activities are both dangerous and ineffectual, why not start building a new order immediately? One member served in the Air Force and worked as a TV commercial writer before starting a Walden Two in Colorado. When that failed, he joined Twin Oaks. Anthropology and psychology students have descended on Twin Oaks for research projects and remained because they were impressed with the quality of life and the philosophy of the community. The oldest member of the community, kat, was a member of Walden House and a founder of Twin Oaks. She is a dedicated communitarian and proponent of Skinner's social thought. As a convinced Skinnerian she takes great pains to deemphasize her considerable competence and experience in community. However, while espousing a bias against leadership, kat has worked tirelessly to keep the community functioning and has provided the drive which serves as fuel for so many new communities.

The fact that she is both more articulate and more know-ledgeable than most about community gives the impression that she has considerable influence. However, this is not cor-roborated by the facts of daily life. She was recently turned down as a planner by two-thirds of the membership in order to avoid the accretion of undue influence by a single member.

Most members of Twin Oaks are there because they favor communal property, cooperative economics, behavioral engine-ering, liberal sex norms, and a life which is both peaceful and dedicated to social improvement. Like utopians through the ages, they are imbued with missionary fervor and look for-ward to a time when society as a whole will enter heaven.

THE NEW PERSON

The road to heaven on earth is paved with operant con-ditioning and self-management. Twin Oakers insist that their way produces good human beings; cooperative, loving, and peaceful. Selfishness and competition have become "extinct" because the community no longer reinforces these attitudes, and because the only avenue to personal gain is through im-proving conditions for the community as a whole. Take the problem of sloppiness. Rule 9 of the behavior code stipulates that members should clean up after themselves. When sloppi-ness became rife in year four of utopia, a program to reinforce neat behavior was introduced. Each participant in the program purchased M&M chocolate candy with his meager weekly al-lowance. Anyone could secure an extra M&M by noticing a violation of rule 9 or by remembering to pick up after them-selves. The whole community attacked the litter and sprawl as members earned the M&Ms for not throwing cigarette butts on the lawn, remembering to scrape their plates after dinner and removing coats from the backs of chairs. Within a short period of time, a modicum of neatness was restored without any "aversive control."

Psychology classes and community behavior modification programs are supplemented by self-management. The happy person, Skinner affirms, has learned to control his social behavior, moods, and emotions. The practice of keeping self-management notebooks constituted another episode in the production of "good human beings." Dr. Matt Israel, director of the Behavior Research Institute, a corporation devoted to the development of behavior technology, paid a visit to Twin Oaks in 1970. Dr. Israel is a close friend of Skinner and is working towards the establishment of a Walden Two in the Rhode Island or Boston area. The high point of his visit was the display of his detailed self-management notebook which contained a daily account of his complete behavior as well as an indication of progress according to a four-step system for changing behavior.[41] The latter involves pinpointing undesirable behavior, recording its rate, and changing it by administering either a self-reward or a self-penalty. Matt Israel fined himself for a particular misbehavior and found it most fitting to contribute his penalty money to Twin Oaks. It was characteristic of Twin Oaks to emulate the practice of personal notebooks in a perfunctory and temporary manner.

While most members are not inclined to keep graphs in order to plot their behavior, they are nonetheless involved in other forms of behavior modification. One member has been trying to overcome feelings of inadequacy. But she is accomplishing this by learning new skills rather than by observing her behavior. New-found capabilities in carpentry and animal husbandry have inspired her own approval as well as that of the group. Another member is trying to eliminate jealousy by noticing instances of tense facial muscles and increased sweating that indicate jealous feelings.[42] Keeping track of these experiences has made her increasingly aware of their occurrence. She now reports a marked decrease in their intensity and frequency. Community support and approval as well as the vision of one's own progress act as reinforcers in changes of behavior.

Personal friction is bound to arise among the members of a community even if it is dedicated to developing self-control. Because Twin Oaks is as all-encompassing as a religious community, smooth interpersonal relations are fundamental to its functioning. Therefore, the community relies as much on parapsychological techniques as on governance for achieving unity.

In the past Twin Oaks has resorted to a variety of methods to handle the problem of friction. In the first year of community, a "generalized bastard" received complaints from members and attempted to solve them. Then a mutual criticism program based on the method developed by J.H. Noyes of the Oneida Community was instituted in 1969. Each week a different member volunteered to be the subject of criticism. That member sat quietly as each person related what he liked or disliked about him. However, strict ground rules protected the subject. Criticism was to be expressed courteously and in a helpful manner, and the subject could halt criticism at any time if it became unbearable. No member could volunteer any name but his own for criticism, and no visitors were allowed except at the express invitation of the subject.

When mutual criticism proved no longer useful, the community modified it into a "feedback" system. At a feedback meeting all participants were potential subjects, from two to five people might be the focus of attention. However, they were not required to listen in silence. They might respond, complain, or object as they were moved. Eventually, feedback also was relegated to history. In line with its focus on experimentation, the community believes in using a variety of techniques to cope with problems of daily life.

Since the winter of 1972 a professional couple, both encounter group leaders, have visited the community at irregular intervals to help resolve interpersonal tension or to facilitate feedback meetings. Occasionally the membership journeys to the couple's Maryland home for combination seminar-encounter sessions. Groups of members have used their newly acquired facilitation skills on a weekly basis in community.

Sometimes psychological techniques have actually replaced politics at times of crisis. For instance, in the spring of 1973 the newly created Juniper branch of Twin Oaks was in the throes of an identity crisis. Discontent and disunity were traced to serious disagreement on goals. In order to cope with the disarray, Juniper scheduled a "personal goals workshop."

The Maryland couple conducted the workshop, which emphasized positive goal setting: defining lifetime goals, five-year
goals, and immediate goals for each member and for the community.[43] The technique also provided a method for working
out conflicts between possible actions at any choice point by
ascertaining how the probable results of each choice fit into a
set of goals. After three days of highly structured sessions, Juniper produced three lists of goals. Since each list was a long one,
goals were selected on the basis of group approval. Long-range
goals included the community as a "loving and caring family,"
and as part of the larger community movement.[44] Five-year
goals were as various as purchasing more land, launching ecological experiments, and redefining Juniper.[45] Lowering the
labor credit quota and the number of visitors were prominent
on the immediate list.

At Twin Oaks interpersonal conflicts reverberate at the community level because Twin Oaks is a Hobbesian society. It lacks
social groups which can articulate and aggregate interests and,
most of all, which can mediate between the individual and the
totality. Both entities are rendered more vulnerable by the absence of middle level groups.

ECONOMICS

Just as in the Bruderhof where the ideals of the community
take precedence over economic viability, economic growth in
itself is not valued at Twin Oaks. The community looks forward
to the day when it will attain complete self-sufficiency so that
members need not take outside jobs to bring in the necessary
cash income. However, even when this is achieved, the standard
of living will remain peripheral to the focus of life in community. The values of equality and cooperation dominate Twin
Oaks's economic system, and the satisfaction of the members
in their occupation takes precedence over efficiency. For instance, some occupations at Twin Oaks, such as construction
or printing, require skilled persons to fill them. However, these
jobs are open to any member who wishes to learn them. The

apprenticeship rule of the behavior code is implemented by granting labor credits to both teachers and students of a skill. Labor will certainly be wasted if a member spends long hours learning printing and then decides he does not really wish to sign up for it. However, the community feels that the loss of efficiency is more than compensated by the realization of equality and the possibility of selecting a satisfying job.

Twin Oaks currently supports itself through a combination of agriculture, light industry, and outside work. Agriculture provides the community with its milk, meat, vegetables, and fruit. The community also sells organically grown vegetables and wild greens to health food stores and restaurants in the Washington, D.C. area.

The diversity of industrial and agricultural activities is intended to protect the community against financial collapse and to provide a wide choice of occupations for its members. In 1971 the sale of hammocks manufactured at Twin Oaks yielded a quarter of its yearly income.[46] Outside work is still the largest source of income, providing a third of it. The rest is supplied by the smaller industries and services. The manufacture of hammocks is a low-skill light industry which does not require expensive plant to produce. The first hammocks were woven on the porch of the original farmhouse as soon as the members were installed. Other occupations include job printing; contract typing; writing, printing, and selling material about community; copper enameling and pottery; working for neighboring farmers in the haying season; and lecturing to college classes and other groups about community. Skills can be easily acquired in all these undertakings, so the community is not only able to realize its aims of equality but also to protect itself against a flux in membership.

There is a budget manager at Twin Oaks and a central treasury under the control of the planners. They hold monthly budget meetings which are open to the members and allocate budgets to the various managers. All funds are handled by the treasurer, who signs checks and keeps a petty cash box and a number of charge accounts in town. Members have no need of cash since the community provides all necessities from aspirin to the fee for the cattlemen's school currently attended by the cattle manager. In addition, each member receives seventy-five cents a week as a personal allowance to splurge on cokes or a movie in town.

Twin Oaks earns just enough to cover its expenses, and within limits it can gear its consumption to income. Generally, it spends between three and six thousand dollars a month on such items as farm and equipment maintenance, utilities and transportation, and raw materials for the manufacture of hammocks. Emergency funds can be derived from the sale of the cattle, the community's building fund, or a loan from the Homer Morris Fund. However, the community is keenly aware of its vulnerability to crises in health, finances, and the tolerance of the surrounding community.

Labor credits rather than cash serve as the medium of exchange in community. The labor credit system was adopted from *Walden Two* and is designed to give as much free choice of work as possible to every member and to adjust the amount of labor contributed to the desirability or undesirability of a job. Each member is required to earn the same number of labor credits per week. The hours vary with the work load and may range from twenty-five hours a week up to fifty-five if there is a large order for hammocks or if frost threatens a crop. There has been considerable experimentation to adjust the values of variety, specialization, and quality of work within the labor credit system. During the first few years of Twin Oaks's existence, variety was considered more important than either specialization or quality of work. Each member signed up for a day's work, and labor credits were adjusted on the basis of competition. The more people signed for a job, the lower the labor credits designated for that occupation. In 1970 the system was changed to emphasize quality over variety.[47] Now members sign up for a full week of gardening, dishes, or fence mending, and labor credits are granted on the basis of individual rather than group preference. Each member receives a list of all job categories and is asked to number them from one to forty in order of preference. On the basis of this information, the labor credit manager draws up individualized schedules and establishes different credits per hour for each preference. Work hours are staggered in each day so that no member works for several hours in a row. The pace of life is a leisurely one, yet tasks are accomplished. This is especially evident to members who leave the community for outside jobs. They often experience great difficulty in adjusting to the pace and the pressures of the outside world.

Each member must take turns at outside work. For a new member this may involve an eight week period, twice a year as the system of rotation is based upon the length of time spent as a community member. Even though a variety of jobs are taken, some much more pleasant than others, outside work credits remain the same for all workers in the interest of equality. Members may work for longer outside shifts if they wish as did one member who kept his teaching job for a year. However, this was a single exception. The fact of the matter is that Twin Oakers have a profound dislike for outside work. It means either two months or 12 hours a day away from the community. The commuter worker gets up at around 5:30 A.M., grabs a sack lunch and climbs aboard the red Ford van for the long ride to Richmond. Many members who commute daily in this fashion have settled for unpleasant, unskilled jobs such as outdoor painting. This fact added to the differences in pace between the community and the outside world have motivated some members to leave the community. However, Twin Oaks believes that any exceptions to this policy or exempting a member from outside work would result in division and injustice in the community. Therefore, it would rather lose some members over this issue than make distinctions which would conflict with its goals.

Some members with special skills prefer to move to another city in order to find a job that is commensurate with their aptitudes and which pays more than an unskilled, local job. This is not an easy choice to make, for members are deeply attached to the community and its style of life. In addition to the pain of a temporary absence, reentry also has its little miseries of adjustment. A returning worker often finds that considerable changes have taken place during his absence and that he feels like a visitor instead of a member. However, the joy and relief uniformly expressed by returning workers is striking evidence of the loyalty and support of Twin Oakers for their community. New members who take their first outside shift during the provisional membership period will be assigned their first managership upon return. For these members return means the beginning of deep involvement in community work and policy.

GOVERNANCE

It is no exaggeration to claim that Twin Oakers support their community because they are committed to its values and its methods rather than because it promotes their particular interests. The acceptance of the political values incorporated in Skinner's social thought is not a *sine qua non* of membership. However, only those persons who support his outlook are likely to feel comfortable at Twin Oaks, for its system of governance is adopted from *Walden Two*.

With some slight variations, the institutions of planners and managers at Twin Oaks are modeled on those of Walden Two. More important, the theoretical bases for an oligarchical system of government, the blend of elitism and contempt for democratic principles, are derived from Skinner's alter ego, Frazier. In the conciliation of purpose between the individual and the collectivity, it is the latter which prevails at Twin Oaks. The goals and identity of the community must be protected from the pressures of its members, rather than the reverse.

The constitution of Twin Oaks states that each member of the community has the right to be governed by people of merit and good sense: planners and managers. These are the decision-making institutions of the community. The three planners formulate policy on fundamental issues, act in a judicial capacity, and handle matters relating to the special needs of the members. They serve for eighteen months on a staggered basis, and replacements are coopted by the incumbents rather than elected. However, a two-thirds majority overrule is possible and in fact occurred when the board coopted kat as a member. The rejection of the oldest and most experienced member of the community as planner is evidence that there are some limitations on "merit" at Twin Oaks.

The planners appoint managers for all areas of community life that require supervision: health, kitchen, garden, cattle, library, budget, to name only a few. There are over thirty managerial positions, and most members hold more than one. Their terms are indefinite and depend upon interest and ability. For instance, the cattle manager, marnie, is highly skilled in this area, and her wish to remain manager is unopposed. However, recently a manager of the orchard was removed by the planners for incompetence. Vying for positions is unknown at Twin Oaks. Since there are more areas of responsibility than members, the latter can assume as much responsibility as they can handle. On the other hand, members who do not like responsibility are free to remain out of managerial positions if they choose. As in *Walden Two,* no recognition, prestige, or privilege is extended to those who have special abilities or positions. Nor do the planners and managers receive extra labor credits for their work. Their chief reward is the satisfaction of participating in the community and furthering its welfare.

As in an Aristotelian community, the population may voice its opinion on issues, but it is merit and quality which ultimately make the decisions. There is no voting at Twin Oaks, except on occasional emergencies. The membership makes its will known by polls, in group criticism sessions, and by speaking up at open planners' meetings. Generally, issues are publicized a few days before such a meeting so that all members will have a chance to reflect on an issue before attending the meeting. During a general meeting planners take note of all the opinions and at the close of discussion summarize each position so that the group knows it has been heard and understood. The planners meet alone to decide an issue. Final decisions are posted, along with clarifying statements. A petition of two-thirds of the membership may overrule a decision by the planners. This channel of appeal is a highly important revision of the *Walden Two* system, which provides for only individual expressions of opposition, thus eliminating any possibility of reversing decisions.

What guarantees are provided for the minority in a system designed to eliminate the "tyranny of the majority"? The minority has a personal rather than a procedural guarantee at Twin Oaks, the attention granted its views by the planners. However, the community does not take the harmony of the membership lightly. In the spring of 1971 it contracted a T-group firm from Washington, D.C., to study the decision-making process at Twin Oaks and to suggest a program for rationalizing it.[48] The result was a highly systematized and effective set of procedures to clarify information, test consensus, and achieve compromise. Ultimately, the community relies on the small size of the group with its face-to-face daily contact and its interest in the satisfaction of the members to provide some sort of assurance that the minority will not be totally ignored.

A behavioral code has been borrowed from *Walden Two* and is intended to protect the community against internal friction and external pressure. Twin Oaks claims that it is designed to be easily enforceable and considers it an example of the community's flexibility. (See Twin Oaks Behavior Code on page 187

The only enforced activity in community is work, and the only prohibitions are drugs and television. Drugs are banned from the community in order to protect it from local harassment, and television is barred in order to protect Twin Oaks from what it perceives as the violence, consumerism, and sexism of the outside world. Expulsion is the ultimate sanction for noncompliance with these regulations. However, before resorting to such a drastic measure, the community uses various programs of positive reinforcement to correct deviant behavior.

Although Twin Oakers agree on the goals of culture design through behavioral engineering, communal property, and the labor credit system, there are some fundamental issues which divide the community. Skinner notwithstanding, even a utopian community cannot dispense with politics. The major question assailing the community is the expansion of the group versus the quality of life, with the attendant issues of member-

ship and the allocation of resources. The expansionists stress
the missionary role of the community and would like to see the
community lifestyle available to as many people as possible.
In practical terms, this might mean building another dormitory
rather than expanding the living room, increasing the number
of visitors at the expense of the group's privacy, or establishing
a biannual conference on communities rather than devoting
labor credits to building private rooms. Generally, the line between the stake a member has in a growing successful community
and his personal benefit is difficult to establish, and discussions
of this nature are apt to arouse intense emotions. In the last resort, the planners decide, but their stand depends on the tolerance of the members and the issue is a recurring one.

Some typical matters considered by the planners are the
issues of whether people who leave the community and then
decide to return should make up the labor they missed while
gone, whether a leave of absence may be granted a member, or
whether the appointment of planners and managers should take
place in an open or closed planners' meeting. The community
has experimented with both solutions to the latter question.
The pragmatic, experimental attitude towards procedure and
the bent for compromise displayed at Twin Oaks softens the
oligarchic features of its institutions to a certain extent.

There is no serious dissension at Twin Oaks. Religion and
ethics have been supplanted by the principles of behavioral
engineering, which everyone accepts, and the membership is
satisfied with the institutions of governance. Moreover, the
universalization of skills and the achievement of equality have
eliminated a host of related issues. Generally, the substance of
policy refers to the allocation of scarce resources, and facilities,
within the community. Given the limited funds and labor hours,
how much of each should be allocated to the hammock industry or the strawberry patch? Some other moot issues regard
the allocation of scarce private rooms, the use of a community
vehicle for personal errands, and the use of pesticides on the
strawberries. . .

Although Twin Oaks confronts a different type of issue from
those usually debated in outer society, the pattern of commun-

ity policy is all-inclusive. Twin Oaks makes decisions affecting the entire life of its membership: their leisure, health, education, travel, and procreation. Whether the member who suffers from a cold may have orange juice or not will be decided by the health manager. Whether a female member may bear children is a community decision, as is any project for special training or education. As in the Bruderhof, where the smallest matters of daily life are considered issues of faith, the Twin Oaker lives in a system where government and society coincide and where society must reflect ideology. The individual is free to do what society permits.

Twin Oaks shares a basic premise with democratic centralism: while individual opinions are important to the group, since the latter depends upon the support of its members, individual responsibility is not. The community's support for an oligarchic system of government is based upon a set of assumptions regarding the governing process, the capabilities of individuals, and the nature of representation. Like Frazier, the community rejects the premises of democratic theory: that the individual is a rational being, that the individual should mediate the congruence of his own and the social well-being, and that politics and ethics are closely connected. A founding member of Twin Oaks refers to decision making as a highly specialized job which requires intelligence, dedication to the interests of the group, and sensitivity to the needs of its members.[49] These qualities are found only in a very few people. Moreover, decision making by large groups is impractical, she contends, since no large group is sufficiently informed on a wide variety of subjects.[50] Expertise, not common sense, is the only justification for the exercise of responsibility, and the ability to govern referred to in the Twin Oaks constitution includes both specialized knowledge and dedication to the goals of the group.

Twin Oaks has no more confidence than Skinner in the ability of the average person to make an intelligent choice. It assumes that most people will place their own interest above that of the community, and that those genuinely concerned with the long-term interests of the community will always be in the minority and hence will always be overruled in a majoritarian system .[51] The common man, backbone of democratic systems, is held in very low esteem by the community. Typically, he is perceived as weighing issues according to superficial criteria, such as whether he likes the person who raised the issue or not, and as only marginally interested in government, preferring his private concerns. If he is as selfish and limited as depicted, then truly he is incapable of either managing public affairs or selecting his representatives.[52] Twin Oakers claim that election is no way to select the representative of the people and that the representation under a democratic system is a sham. They consider that the behavior of voters is always irrational, that most people select their representatives on the basis of intuitive feelings rather than sound judgment. Among the common men it is essentially personality, and not convictions or character, which earns votes.

At Twin Oaks representation means acting on behalf of the long-range goals of the community and manifesting the strength to resist popular pressure against those goals.[53] Twin Oaks exhibits a distaste for majority rule similar to Plato's scorn for the mob. However, Twin Oaks's view of democracy is based upon a misunderstanding of that system of government, especially its guarantees of minority rights through the courts, its decision-making procedures, and frequent elections.

It is not without a certain irony that a community so passionately devoted to the pursuit of equality is grounded in elitist views of human nature. Like the good philosopher king who knows what is best for his subjects, the community rules for the good of its members. Secure in this benevolence, the individual is free to pursue his own interests . . . within the limits of his capabilities.

THE TREE OF LIFE

The visitor to Twin Oaks must turn his watch forward one hour, for the community is on Daylight Saving Time while the surrounding area is on Standard Time. Until the establishment of a community of communities, Twin Oaks will remain a cultural colony as described by one of its members. Whereas Walden Two participated in local politics, using its large block of votes to get the "best man through," Twin Oaks remains aloof from politics, for it is profoundly hostile to the broader society. But community's relations with local people, especially with neighboring farmers, are excellent, and it is generally accepted in the town of Louisa, for it brings business to the local merchants. However, Twin Oaks is keenly aware that its very survival depends upon the nature of its relations with the local community and therefore has devoted considerable energy to developing good relations with the sheriff and the health department. A concern for survival in a southern location is one reason why there are no black members at Twin Oaks.

The bulk of the community's contact beyond its premises is with other intentional communities, at conferences or at informal gatherings. The members of Heathcote spent Thanksgiving at Twin Oaks, and the two groups exhange members for brief periods of time. The Springtree community is a short drive from Louisa, and as one of the most successful intentional communities, Twin Oaks perceives intimations of the new order in the burgeoning community movement.

How does Twin Oaks consider its less structured counterparts in the so-called hippy communes or the radical movement constituted by fragments of the New Left? Twin Oaks has been invaded by streams of visitors from the very beginning of its existence, and these have included members of both groups. While long-haired itinerants from the hippy communes are tolerated by Twin Oaks, the community takes issue with their aversion for both organization and work. And while Twin Oaks may agree with the radical movement's assessment of contemporary society, they part company over tactics and goals. Twin Oaks is staunchly opposed to the use of violence and very much concerned with the safety of its experiment. Hence, it does not wish to associate with a movement which either frightens the establishment or incurs "repressive" measures.

Twin Oaks is constantly grumbling about the visitor problem. However, the community has it well in tow, for no one can descend on the premises without prior written request,

and overnight guest facilities are limited. The community conducts tours of the property for a fee on weekends in order to
cope with the curious tourist. However, visitors are both an
important source of potential members and an equally important link with the outside world. Despite its disdain for contemporary society, Twin Oaks has acquired from it a keen sense of
public relations. It welcomes "friendly" coverage from the
media as a means of spreading the message of intentional community, and its own publications promote community and
convey the success of Twin Oaks.

As it enters its sixth year of existence, Twin Oaks exudes a
feeling of success and well-being. The membership is growing
at an increasing rate and the turnover has stabilized. The standard of living has improved from the spartan first years, and
many members boast private rooms. Instead of the usual diet
of brown rice and beans which fill the tables of new communities, Twin Oaks enjoys an abundant and varied fare. A cardinal
feature of the new life in utopia is the careful balance of work
and leisure, the easy pace of life for accomplishing a variety of
tasks. No one at Twin Oaks suffers from the pressure, boredom,
and fatigue of life in modern society, and Twin Oakers appear
uniformly cheerful and content.

The most important indication of success at Twin Oaks, and
the image Twin Oaks strives to convey, is one of growth and
steady progress. Each issue of *Leaves* reports another improvement: a new crop planted, a root cellar completed, another
new building, and plans for expansion. Currently (summer of
1973) a new building is almost completed. It includes a spacious office, a hammock shop twice the size of the present accommodation, and a large upper story of private rooms. Following the practice of naming each building after a community, the latest construction is referred to as Ta Chai, a well-
known Chinese commune. While Ta Chai is nearing completion, the community is absorbed in constructing a children's
building and plans for an enlarged kitchen and dining facility.

Because Twin Oaks is building a new order and not merely
a new community, it would rather help establish new communities than expand indefinitely on the premises. In 1972 it pur-

chased an eighty-seven-acre tract of land with a farmhouse not far from Twin Oaks. With this purchase it launched Acorn Project, the first instance of fission. Eight members of Twin Oaks have moved to the new property along with three new members to form a separate branch of a greater organization called Merion.[54] It has a common economy with Twin Oaks (Juniper branch), but a separate budget for domestic consumption. Although each branch will follow the principles of *Walden Two* for labor, governance, and child rearing, it is expected that decentralism will inspire experiments on a domestic level. Perhaps certain branches will emphasize small size or a vegetarian diet, or even practice mysticism. The community talks of creating a new branch each year, allowing a constant incorporation of new members and benefiting from the experience and direction of Twin Oaks.

B. F. Skinner was scheduled to visit Twin Oaks in October 1971, but an overburdened agenda forced him to cancel at the last minute. If he ever does visit Twin Oaks, he will have the strange experience of returning to past dreams revised. As in Walden Two, there is a music room where the community assembles nightly to hear Twin Oaks's news from its own broadcasting station in the Oneida building, but the evening fare will be hard rock, not chamber music. Meals are taken on a staggered schedule, and the kitchen in Llano boasts a steam table to keep meals hot for long periods. However, Twin Oakers dine casually out of doors, accompanied by dozens of hungry pets, rather than in well-appointed dining rooms. Nor do the members dress for dinner or for pleasure as in *Walden Two*. The "community clothes" in Harmony's loft provides jeans. underwear, and sweatshirts in all sizes and states of repair. Skinner would be pleased with the extensive library lining the corridors in Oneida with its sections on psychology, physics, Russian, and French, but he might balk at the thin carpet of bugs if he settled down in Oneida's living room for an evening of reading.

The greatest difference between Walden Two and Twin Oaks is one of spirit. Frazier has not appeared at Twin Oaks, and if he did, he would find no cooperation in executing his plans for society. He might even be disgusted with the banter, the steam dome, and the cheerful disarray. The members of Twin Oakes consider the structure of their life in common with a certain degree of utilitarianism, and this has watered the Skinnerian dogma somewhat. Besides, there are no social scientists in the community. At Twin Oaks the tree of life is green.

The Smaller Tree

Because the search for utopia has become a way of life for so many young adults in the seventies, it is no longer surprising to hear of a group of young people or professionals spurning the wealth and status sought by their parents in favor of the rewards of reconstructing society. There is a Walden Three community today, and a host of them are in the planning stage. Matt Israel, director of the Behavior Research Institute, has developed a proposal for a Skinnerian community in the Boston area. The Behavior Research Institute operates the Center for Behavior Development, a residential treatment center for autistic, retarded, or emotionally disturbed young adults, and this will serve as the economic base for the new community. The aim of Dr. Israel's project is to develop an experimental community which is both therapeutic and relevant to the good life for normal adults. However, the very nature of this project and its intellectual definition of the good life limits its appeal to professionals in the field of medicine or psychology.

The Walden Three community includes nine members and is located in the heart of downtown Providence, Rhode Island, rather than in the spacious rural setting depicted in *Walden Two*. Although it was established in 1970, its founding members had dreamed of such a miniature society ever since they first read *Walden Two* in high school. The core group of founders met while attending Ohio State University and were inspired to establish the community by their study of utopia for a sociology class. The group was joined by a young woman who has spent two years living in a kibbutz. All the members are relatively young; the age span ranges from nineteen years to twenty-five. At one point the community almost recruited a fifteen-year-old and a middle-aged farmer. However, legal problems prevented it from assuming the responsibility for a minor, and the farmer's wife was notably unenthusiastic at the prospect of a life in community.

Walden Three has close ties with the Twin Oaks community, and the members frequently exchange visits. Both groups are convinced Skinnerians and boast a similar system of governance and a long-range behavior modification program. It is mainly in tone and emphasis that differences are apparent, and this can be partly traced to the membership. For instance, the communitarians at Walden Three place greater stress on the social thought of B.F. Skinner and take great care in patterning their life in common on the Skinnerian model. However, this reliance on shared ideals does not extend to the smaller details of daily life. Walden Three does not set its clock either behind or ahead of standard time, nor is it concerned with establishing community clothes or with spending much energy on this type of project. On the other hand, Twin Oakers take great pains to distinguish themselves as unique variants of Skinnerian thought. Also, they set great store on the smaller aspects of community life. In part, this can be traced to the greater heterogeneity of the Twin Oaks membership with regard to age and socioeconomic background. Given this diversity, agreement on ideology is harder to muster, and the sense of commonality that community clothes provides, for instance, helps form the cement for Twin Oaks.

Like Twin Oaks, Walden Three intends to defer children until the community has acquired a certain degree of economic viability. At that time child rearing will be a communal venture and will follow the pattern established by Skinner in *Walden Two*. However, most members are highly critical of the nuclear family and would have established communal child rearing even without the benefit of Skinnerian thought.

The procedure for accepting new members is highly informal compared to that of Twin Oaks. Prospective members spend from one to three weeks living with the community. They are then requested to leave for a period of time while the community forms a decision. No contracts or formal agreements are signed when a new member is accepted. Whether it is a rationalization of their current status or a matter of conviction, Waldenians insist that they do not regard size as an indication of success. Rather than growth, this group emphasizes the harmony and compatibility of its members.

Daily life in Walden Three reflects the preferences and attributes of the membership. Waldenians are a sober group. They spend their leisure time reading, sewing, baking, and sifting through their voluminous correspondence on the community rather than indulging in the noisy games which fill the free hours at Twin Oaks. Privacy is an essential part of the good life in the Rhode Island community. In contrast to many of the newer communities, Twin Oaks included, Walden Three feels that a daily period of solitude is necessary for everyone's well-being.

That the founders were inspired by Plato's *Republic* is evident in their stress on the necessity for the perfect correspondence of the individual and society as the anchor of the good life. The members of Walden Three are expected to participate in community not only by contributing to its economic viability, but also by developing their own behavior and working actively towards the harmony of the group. They frown on encounter groups and the methods employed by Twin Oaks to promote membership cohesion. Rather than what they describe as short-lived and tyrannical methods, Waldenians stress long-term behavior modification programs in general and self-management in particular. Members spend a period of time each day recording and assessing their behavior. They even carry strings of colored beads as reminders of habits and practices to stress or eliminate.

Waldenians practice the planner-manager system of *Walden Two* not only for its intrinsic merits, but also because they consider structure as essential to longevity and success. The planners at Walden Three appoint managers on the basis of their skills and special experience. However, each member holds two managerships, given the small size of the community As in Twin Oaks, the labor system is in effect, and tasks are allocated on the basis of personal choice without distinction of sex.

It is mainly in Walden Three's relationship with the broader society and in its attempts to secure its livelihood that it differs from Twin Oaks. Walden Three holds all property in common from small appliances to a large library of utopian literature. As in Twin Oaks, private property is categorized as the personal effects stored in each member's room, and within the limits of its income the community provides for all the needs of its membership from medical care to clothing. However, while Walden Three is absorbed in establishing an alternative social system, it wishes to participate fully in the broader economic system. Waldenians have launched a successful printing business, catering to newspapers, magazines, and universities and are apt to scoff at the craft activity favored by Twin Oaks. The bulk of their income comes from the printing business so that only three of the members need to hold outside jobs.

In the first year of community, most of the members worked at outside jobs of a low-skill nature, such as a nurse's aid or a packer in a local jewelry factory. At that time income yielded a rather spartan living standard, but the group managed to found a handsome publication, the *Communitarian.* As in many contemporary communities, the challenge of creating a new society offset the low standard of living.

Three years later, in the spring of 1973, Waldenians were able to purchase a twelve-bedroom house with the proceeds of their business. This move will allow the group to expand its membership without violating its concern for the privacy of each person.

The members of Walden Three look forward to the day when they will be able to purchase a farm and found a new town as part of a new and decentralized technological system. They are devotees of Murray Bookchin, anarchist thinker, who advocates scaling economic activities to communal settings where feasible. The family of David, a founding member, operates a small iron foundry, and he plans to apply his experience with this business in a new setting. Research and industry will play an important role in Walden's new town as will the related values of efficiency, rationality, and constant experimentation towards the good life. From Skinner Waldenians have borrowed the view that a properly managed technology can liberate man from burdensome occupations and provide the foundation for a high quality of life.

Both the Skinnerian communities have a rather ambivalent relationship to the broader society. In a sense, Twin Oaks and Walden Three are mirror opposites. Despite its search for utopia. Walden Three has no desire to sever its ties with the outside world. Its members read the newspapers, vote, and enjoy watching television. They are realistic about their economic dependence on society and consider the relationship to be of mutual benefit. Twin Oaks slams the community door with great fanfare, turning its clocks ahead, and barring radio and television. However, it depends upon visitors to accomplish a fair amount of labor and upon outside jobs to remain economically viable. Even more perplexing to the outside observer is the desire of that community to advertise its success in the very mass media it scorns.

The members of Walden Three are united by their struggle for viability and their dreams of a new society. Like Twin Oaks, they take great pains to distinguish themselves from radicals and from what they perceive as faddist communities, particularly those inspired by mysticism. Religion, they claim, is an escape mechanism for persons unwilling to reform their behavior and for groups wishing to avoid coping with social problems. Heaven's place is on this very earth . . . in a Skinnerian community.

TWIN OAKS BEHAVIOR CODE

1. We will not use titles of any kind among us.
2. All members are required to explain their work to any other member who desires to learn it.
3. We will not discuss the personal affairs of other members nor speak negatively of other members when they are not present.
4. We will not publicly grumble or gripe about things we think wrong within the community.

5.   Members who may have unconventional or unorthodox views on politics, religion, or national policies are requested to stay clear of such topics when talking to non-members.

6.   Seniority is never discussed among us.

7.   We will try to exercise both consideration and tolerance of each others' individual habits.

8.   We will not boast of individual accomplishments.

9.   We will clean up after ourselves after any private or individual project; we will not keep articles longer than we need them but will return them to their proper places, so that they can be enjoyed by other members.

10.   Individual rooms are inviolate. No member will enter another's room without the other member's permission.

FIVE

CONCLUSION

The intentional community movement today is in the midst of an extraordinary expansion. New communities are being formed in both urban and rural areas of the United States, and the age span of the membership is lengthening to include the middle-aged and the elderly. They are all animated by a profound disaffection from the social order. However, the grounds for their dissent from the status quo are highly diverse, ranging from anarchism and Anabaptism to behaviorism.

Whether Christian or decentralist, the new intentional communities embody dreams of perfection and a bent for experimentation. As experimental communities, they constitute laboratories for social change: sheltered, isolated environments in which new social institutions and new behavioral norms can be developed. As utopian communities, they seek to mold social reality to the norms of social doctrine, whether Skinnerian or anarchist. Self-sufficient miniature societies such as Twin Oaks or Walden Three constitute a search for perfection which is based upon the expansion of knowledge in psychology. They intend to root out all social evil and to establish an order in which men will be governed by the consequences of their behavior. The rural communities which dot the eastern seaboard and the west coast seek a new economic balance and a return to the principles of the polis. On the other hand, Free Church communities embrace a radical Christianity based upon convenantal fellowship, sharing, and mutual responsibility.

Despite their diversity, all intentional communities cherish their small scale and their vision of a social order composed of a loose federation and grounded in a new humanism.

A New Subculture

Through its increasing number of publications, conferences, and meetings, the various strands of the community movement are converging to form a national cultural phenomenon which goes far beyond the fleeting instance of a rebellious youth culture. This has occurred spontaneously and without the development of either a bureaucracy or systematized media.

In the decade of the seventies, the community movement largely represents an anarchist crack in the cake of American political culture. It is a subculture in the sense that it includes a full range of institutions and services as alternatives to the broader society: economic, educational, medical, legal, and communication. Just as the communist subculture in eastern Europe protects its members from the taint of bourgeois val - ues by providing them with "pure" communist art, cinema, and services from cooperative housing to clothing sales, the community movement envelops its members with a total if diffuse social system. Because anarchism is the political philosophy espoused by the gathering of communities, the communitarian subculture has no alternative political institutions other than those of its more radical fringes in the collectives. Therefore, it proposes no alternative programs or decision- making institutions. While it holds goals and institutions which differ from those espoused by the political system, it hopes to promote these through peaceful means, via example and persuasion.

Communitarianism qualifies as a subculture both because of its all-inclusive scope and because of its extent, for it is a movement which can claim hundreds of thousands of adher-

ents throughout the United States. Another salient feature of
the community movement is the curious resemblance of its
rank and file to the ideologies of leftist movements in other
modern political systems. Like socialism in western Europe,
the community movement appeals specifically to the more ed-
ucated and definitely to the middle class.

Just as the ideological subcultures, such as socialism and communism provide, the community movement embraces certain
fundamental premises as the axioms framing the evolution of
discourse and practice. Behaviorally oriented communities,
collectives, and anarchist communities categorically reject government as a source of social or economic reform. The behaviorists eschew politics in favor of functional administration and
operant conditioning. The anarchists look toward a spontaneous social management of contemporary crisis, and the collectives aim at a total transformation of the system through violence and guerrilla tactics.

A second premise in the communitarian spectrum of assumptions concerns the equality of all men. This value is expressed
in a variety of matrices: in the relations between the sexes, in
the desire to avoid specialization of skills in economic life, and
in the universalization of roles. Purely practical considerations
buttress this value. A community which is not overly dependent upon either the leadership or skills of certain members
will be able to survive a turnover in membership. Conversely,
the person should be able to achieve a sufficient degree of
emotional autonomy to remain unaffected by changes in personal relations within a community. Rather than stressing the
uniqueness of each individual, the movement (religious groups
excluded) stresses the similarity of persons. The resident of
Twin Oaks, for example, believes that behavior defines the
person and that behavioral engineering can produce a certain
type of individual. Proper socialization can render the individual open to a whole spectrum of satisfactory personal relations and liberate him from "stubborn attachments."

A third axiom of the new community movement is the value
of a life in harmony with nature.[1]

Harmony, cooperation and interdependence are the values the communitarian movement is struggling to restore in a society whose political and economic system exploits and violates man and nature.

Gaining subsistence from the land without the use of chemical fertilizers or pesticides has become an important ingredient of the good life which communitarians advocate. They believe that small-scale organic farming and the trusteeship of land will eliminate the exploitive, dominating relationship of man to nature. The land need not be the sole source of subsistence, but most communities strive to maintain palpable links to a rural setting. The Reba Place Fellowship maintains a farm and enjoys an urban-rural link.

The new communities (religious groups excepted) practice a new morality which promotes freedom and spontaneity in sexual relations. The latter is a part of the transformation of the institution of marriage, the rejection of permanent partnerships and the nuclear family. The economic and socializing functions of the family are assumed by the community, and the individual will receive the affection, support, and sex he requires from the group. These new practices and behavior patterns have attracted single adults of all ages and circumstances to the community movement.

Although many communitarians have not read Marcuse's *One Dimensional Man,* most of them have pinpointed consumption and the differentials in living standards as the barrier to community and the source of widespread malaise in contemporary society. Advertising and obsolescence are barred from the gates of intentional communities. There are few television sets to be found in the new communities and no luxuries. It is not possible for a community member to distinguish himself from the group by means of access to material goods and services, for all communitarians live modestly. They depict themselves as liberated from the compulsion to buy products they do not need and hence as free to focus on the search for the good life.

Leisure is as important as fulfilling and useful labor in the community movement. Although a new economic system

based on cooperation, equal distribution, decentralized production, and marketing is part of the good life for the new
communitarians, leisure is of equal importance in the design
of such a life. Communitarians carefully calculate the hours
set aside for pure enjoyment, for fishing, square dancing, or
music, and will not allow the desire for increased productivity
to encroach upon them. Twin Oaks recently lowered the number of weekly working hours in order to allow more free time
for the members.

Despite its burgeoning population, the new community
movement has developed no alternative political institutions
or programs for achieving or wielding power. It has opted for
an existence in the interstices of political society.

The Measure of Community

There are a variety of ways in which intentional communities may be assessed, and communitarians themselves have
subjected their experiments to critical review. If the chronicler
of Sunrise Hill concluded that agreement on goals is essential
for the survival of a community, a member of the Washington
Free Community arrived at the opposite conclusion. Rick
Margolis, spokesman for that community, claims that it is more
important for the core group of a community to be committed
to each other than to an idea.[2]

This is one of the most destructive aspects of utopian or visionary thinking, for the relationships of the people to each other is filtered and mediated through the mental structure of what they should be doing.

Rick Margolis discovered that dogmatism is harmful to mutuality. However, like many rural communitarians, he also confused the concept of the family, a personal commitment, with
the political or social commitment of community.

The assessments of these two communitarians refer to the
longevity and viability of communities. Survivability may be
included in the spectrum of measuring rods of evaluating communities if it is considered along with other criteria. Viability

is a function of the goals and structure of a community and to a lesser, though not unimportant, extent to the tolerance of the broader society. Within a true community, membership is valued as an end, not just as a means to an end, and the authority of its ruling group is legitimate because it is based upon shared views of purpose. A group with less dedication to common purpose than Koinonia would not have survived the hostility of Americus.

Frequently the combination of hostility from the surrounding society and the demands of a pioneering venture suffices to bring an experimental community to an untimely end. External hostility caused the nineteenth-century Kaweah community to close down, and the Morningstar Ranch in California disbanded in 1971 because of pressure from the local health department. External hostility has caused the Hutterites to engage in endless migrations from Europe to Canada to North Dakota and back to Canada again. In itself, external pressure may not impair a community experiment. However, when local authorities and even the media criticize or misrepresent a new community, they intensify the difficulties of developing new institutions and behavior patterns.

Although most intentional communities aspire to a diversified and self-sufficient economy, they are generally too small to transcend the laws of the broader economic system. Economic failures are not uncommon among intentional communities. Even if Sunrise Hill had managed to contain the severe strains among its membership, it would have foundered over economics, for it failed to produce enough to keep pace with even a meager consumption. A lack of funds may constitute a serious threat to a fledgling project like New Communities, of Georgia. On the other hand, religious communities must be on constant guard against the dangers of economic success. The Bruderhof found it necessary to curtail its operations in Community Playthings in order to maintain the priority of its faith.

Those communities which are committed to a set of religious ideals have survived longer than any other type. The Hutterites have maintained their life in community for almost five hundred years. Their younger relatives in the Society of Brothers are entering their fourth generation and are in the midst of constructing a fourth community in the United States. However, both these groups have persisted not only by their faith, but also by their authoritarian structure and a rigid regulation of daily life. There is a danger that the combination of authoritarianism and strict isolation from the broader society may cause a community to slip into cultural primitivism.

At the opposite end of the spectrum, inadequate structure and the lack of goals has frequently spelled the death of anarchist communities. An overriding issue for every society, intentional communities included, is that of the relationship among men in their efforts towards common goals. The anarchist communities claim that men will come together fortuitously once the restraints of procedure and organization are removed, and that in an anarchist community individuals will automatically work for the good of the whole. This untempered optimism is reminiscent of the early liberal philosophers such as John Locke, who believed that discrete individuals, those happy atoms endowed with reason and imbued with middle class values, would be guided by an invisible hand toward the well-being of the entire community. Having observed that the institutions and procedures which were devised to protect the rights of the individual against the weight of society have ceased to serve the citizen and have become preempted by certain powerful interest groups, anarchists would eliminate procedure altogether. However, the demise of Sunrise Hill demonstrates that in addition to spontaneity one of the chief characteristics of anarchist communities is their short life. Anarchist communities which survive their spontaneity are prey to a variety of subcultures in search of new members to augment their power. And communities which refuse to come to terms with their political relationship to the broader society may find themselves in unanticipated conditions of subservience.

The Skinnerian Twin Oaks is one of the oldest and most successful of the new intentional communities. The members attribute this longevity to the structure of their life in common and to their firm views on the good life. They point with considerable pride to an increasingly stable membership, the birth of communal offspring, and expanding property. Within Skinnerian communities the quest for social integration is based upon a combination of oligarchical rule and the coincidence of political and social spheres. At Twin Oaks the decision-making power of the community extends to the most minute details of daily life, from the consumption of orange juice to the allocation of private rooms. In each case, the balance between individual and group is mediated by the community rather than by the person.

One of the measures of community is the ability to accommodate and adjust a plurality of interests. Neither the behaviorally oriented communities nor the homesteading communities appear able to contain diverse interests. Although the grounds for such monolithisms are not ideological, both types of community practice a narrow corporatism. They would rather resort to the departure of some of their membership than allow for the expression of diverse interests.

Between the extremes of authoritarian governance and anarchism, Koinonia Partners and the Reba Place Fellowship practice direct democracy and are able to include divergent interests within the framework of their goals. Both communities have managed to execute important changes in their structure in response to their Anabaptist commitment and their perception of needs within the broader society. This flexibility has enabled the communities to survive periods of great change and crisis without serious splits among the membership. Because they combine a willingness to experiment with their focus on a Christian lifestyle, they have not been prey to the schisms and bitterness experienced by communities such as the Society of Brothers or the Hutterites. In fact, the Reba Place Fellowship and Koinonia Partners exhibit the bent for experimentation and flexibility so ardently sought by Skinnerian groups. However, this trait is a result of the value placed on the person as expressed in the philosophy of these communities and of the practice of direct democracy. When experimentation is imposed from the top down according to the superior insights of a particular social doctrine, rigidity will ensue rather than flexibility.

The true test of a community lies in the nature of its communication with other groups and its relevance to the broader society. One of the greatest pitfalls of intentional communities is that of isolation; those which survive for more than a few generations may become fossilized. Communities which have links to the broader society, either by constantly incorporating new recruits, like the Society of Brothers, or by serving society, have demonstrated the greatest vigor. The Skinnerian communities and anarchist groups have defined their small societies in a Sorelian fashion. They strive to maintain an absolute distinction between themselves and the surrounding society. However, because the Skinnerians wish to form the nucleus of a subculture, they maintain links with the outer world in order to proselytize. Anarchists seek no influence within the broader society, either to gain converts or to promote their own interests. They are content to remain in the interstices of the social system, in the shadow of its tolerance and prey to radical groups in search of untapped sources of power.

Communities vary greatly in the interest and resources they devote to the problems of contemporary society. Koinonia Partners is devoted to the mitigation of racial and economic inequities in the Deep South, while its urban counterpart, the Reba Place Fellowship, has focused on the spiritual needs of urban society's distressed person. New Communities, established by the International Institute for Independence, is aimed at stemming the flow of rural emigration by making land and economic opportunities available to the rural poor. In Ohio, Community Service, managed by Griscom Morgan, is sponsoring Indian-managed improvement programs and community action programs for southeast Appalachia.

At the opposite extreme are the homesteading communities and the Skinnerian communities which are devoted to cultivating their own back yards. Their enclavism is more than reminiscent of certain suburban communities which appear uninterested in the needs of the broader society.

The Uses of Community

The search for community is an expression of man's hope that he can live with his fellows in brotherhood and that he can construct an order that will foster a sense of mutuality. The success of this attempt ultimately depends upon the nature of the dialogue between intentional community and society.

Although the relations between intentional communities and the broader society vary widely, even those communities which exist in self-imposed isolation are of value to the political system because they serve as barometers of social crisis and laboratories for experiments in social change. Although the formation of intentional communities constitutes an act of rebellion against society, it is a peaceful and viable form of dissent in a political system whose tolerance of dissent is subject to fluctuation and in which radical dissidence has been revealed as dangerous and futile.

Communitarians render a great service to contemporary society by raising the question of the goals of life and by their experiments in organizing economic and social institutions to insure human growth and well-being. Like John Stuart Mill, they aim to dispel "the deep slumber of decided opinion," for "to discover to the world something which deeply concerns it and of which it was previously ignorant: to prove to it that it had been mistaken on some vital point of temporal or spiritual interest is as important a service as a human being can render to his fellow creatures."[3]

In their search for a new mutuality and a new balance of work and play, intentional communities broaden the choice of values and institutions for society as a whole. And in reacting to social ills and attempting to meet them head-on, no matter how fumbling the attempts, intentional communities inspire reforms. Visions of perfection are fertile ground for the diffusion of new practices in the broader society, whether the infant schools established in the nineteenth-century New Harmony or the alternative custodial care adopted at the Brotherhood of the Spirit. A major eastern city and its surrounding towns has initiated pilot programs of foster families for adolescents in distress and for alcoholics. The new child-adult relations forged in community will ultimately inspire viable solutions to the overburdened and isolated nuclear family and to the troubled people without families.

The broadening of sex roles in community will help enlarge the choice of careers and lifestyles available to adults and benefit the contemporary search of both sexes for new identities. Some communities include men who assume roles traditionally ascribed to women, such as child care. On the other hand, women in community have a greater opportunity to explore their abilities and interests than in the broader society, where cultural values and the practices of certain occupations restrict them. However, this does not entail a rigid recasting of roles, for all communities maintain a division of labor and there will always be men who prefer their more traditional roles and women who prefer housekeeping to construction. In community, however, it is the individual who makes the choice and who bears the consequences of his decision, for there is no one to blame for the nonfulfillment of cherished goals when the opportunities are available. The absence of cultural values to guide men and women in shaping their lives means both a boost to individualism with its increased burden of responsibility and a decrease in the casualties society has sustained in relegating nonconforming persons to its margins. There is no easy solution to the equality and the identity of the sexes. However, the small community is an eminently appropriate setting for exploring alternatives and devising new ones. The tension and self-doubt which attend all individuals engaged in social innovation is assuaged by the support of the community.

Communitarians are moved by the same concern for freedom and well-being as John Stuart Mill, who advocated a society which tolerates a variety of lifestyles.[4]

There is always need of persons not only to discover new truths, and point out when what were once truths are truths no longer, but also to commence new practices and set the example of more enlightened conduct and better taste and sense in human life.

NOTES

Chapter One

1. J. F. Harrison, *Quest for the New Moral World: Robert Owen and the Owenites in Britain and America* (New York: Charles Scribner and Sons, 1969), p. 89.
2. Ibid., p. 218.

Chapter Two

1. *Wellesley Townsman,* May 13, 1972.
2. Franklin H. Littel, *The Origins of Sectarian Protestantism* (New York: The Macmillan Co., 1968), pp. 46-47.
3. James Leo Garrett Jr., *The Concept of the Believers' Church* (Scottdale, Pa.: Herald Press, 1969), pp. 15-34.
4. Littel, op. cit., pp. 101-108.
5. Ibid., pp. 111-137.
6. Ibid., p. 97.
7. Emmy Arnold, *Torches Together* (Rifton, N.Y.: Plough Publishing House, 1971), p. 115.
8. Ibid., pp. 141-153.
9. Benjamin Zablocki, *The Joyful Community* (Baltimore, Md.: Penguin Books, 1971), pp. 93-98.
10. Ibid., p. 98-110.
11. Ibid., p. 110.

12. Ibid., pp. 169-172.
13. Ibid.
14. Ibid., pp. 130-138.
15. Ibid., pp. 116-122.
16. Ibid.
17. Ibid.
18. Ibid., p. 239.
19. Ibid., pp. 201-211.
20. Ibid.
21. Ibid.
22. Ibid., pp. 201-211.
23. Ibid., p. 217.
24. Ibid.
25. Ibid., p. 216.
26. Ibid., p. 277.
27. Ibid., p. 223.
28. Eberhard Arnold, *Why We Live in Community* (Farmington, Pa.: Plough Press, 1967).
29. Zablocki, op. cit., pp. 158-164.
30. Dallas Lee, *The Cotton Patch Evidence* (New York: Harper & Row, Publishers, 1970), pp. 26-34.
31. Ibid.
32. Ibid.
33. Ibid.
34. Ibid., pp. 67-85.
35. Ibid., p. 206.
36. Ibid., p. 208.
37. Ibid., pp. 208-217.
38. Ibid., p. 99.
39. *Free Spirit Press,* vol. 1, no. 2, pp. 26, 27.
40. Ibid., pp. 28, 29.
41. Ibid.

Chapter Three

1. Ralph Borsodi, *This Ugly Civilization* (New York: Harper & Brothers, 1933), p. 432.
2. Ibid., p. 18.
3. Ibid., p. 297.
4. Ibid., p. 337.
5. Mildred J. Loomis, *Go Ahead and Live* (New York: Philosophical Library, 1965), p. viii.

6. Mildred J. Loomis, "From a Drop-Out of the 30s to Today's Young," *Central Issues* (May-June 1971) vol. 55, no. 4, p. 5.
7. *Green Revolution,* vol. 9, no. 12 (December 1971), p. 5.
8. Ibid., p. 4.
9. "The Intentional Communities," 1959 Yearbook of the Fellowship of Intentional Communities, p. 8.
10. Ibid., pp. 2, 3.
11. Collectives are defined as groups organized around work projects, or political goals, or both. *Vocations for Social Change* (September 1971).
12. Herbert Marcuse, *One Dimensional Man* (Boston, Mass.: Beacon Press, 1964).
13. "The Triple Revolution," in *The New Left*, edited by Priscilla Long, Porter Sargent, Publisher, Boston, Mass., 1970.
14. *Springtree Newsletter* (April 1972), year 1, no. 3, p. 3.
15. Ibid.
16. Ibid.
17. *Communitas,* no. 1 (July 1972), p. 15.
18. Gordon Yaswen, "Sunrise Hill Community: Post Mortem" (unpublished paper), p. 15.
19. Ibid., p. 7.
20. Ibid., p. 12.
21. Ibid., p. 14.
22. Ibid., p. 29.
23. International Independence Institute Newsletter (October 1971), p. 3.
24. Shimon Gottschalk and Robert Swann, "Planning a Rural New Town in Southwest Georgia," *Arete* (Fall 1970), vol. 1, no. 2, pp. 4, 5.

Chapter Four

1. B. F. Skinner, *Beyond Freedom and Dignity* (New York: Alfred A. Knopf, 1971), p. 206.
2. Ibid., p. 199.
3. Ibid., pp. 202-206.
4. Ibid., p. 67.
5. Robert Owen, *A New View of Society* (Glencoe, Ill.: Free Press, n.d.), p. 107.
6. Ibid., p. 59.
7. Skinner, op. cit., p. 188.

8. Ibid., pp. 84-96.
9. Ibid., pp. 31-37.
10. Ibid., p. 98.
11. Ibid., p. 104.
12. Ibid., p. 152.
13. *New York Times,* August 11, 1972.
14. Skinner, op. cit., p. 199.
15. Ibid., p. 158.
16. Ibid., p. 154.
17. Ibid., p. 155.
18. B. F. Skinner, *Walden Two* (New York: The Macmillan Co., 1970), p. 105.
19. Owen, op. cit., p. 27.
20. Ibid.
21. Skinner, *Walden Two,* p. 105.
22. Ibid., p. 28.
23. Ibid., p. 142.
24. Ibid., p. 143.
25. Ibid., p. 98.
26. Ibid., p. 60.
27. Ibid., p. 88.
28. Ibid., p. 194.
29. Ibid., p. 70.
30. Ibid., p. 265.
31. Ibid., p. 195.
32. Ibid., p. 236.
33. Ibid., p. 292.
34. "Experimenting with *Walden Two,*" Twin Oaks Community, Louisa, Va. (from *Walden Pool,* June 1966).
35. *Leaves* of Twin Oaks (February 1972), p. 10.
36. Ibid., (April 1972), p. 7.
37. See Appendix.
38. "Twin Oaks," a descriptive brochure of the Twin Oaks Community, Louisa, Va.
39. *Leaves* (June 1972), p. 2.
40. Ibid., (April 1972), p. 5.
41. "Experimenting with *Walden Two*" (January 1970), pp. 5, 6.
42. *Leaves* (June-July 1973), p. 11.
43. Ibid., p. 5, 6.
44. Ibid.
45. Ibid.
46. Ibid., (June 1972), p. 10.
47. "Experimenting with *Walden Two*" (October 1970), p. 3.

48. T-groups are training groups in human relations skills. The idea was developed by an M. I. T. psychologist, Kurt Lewin, in 1947.
49. "Experimenting with *Walden Two*" (January 1970), pp. 7-9.
50. Ibid.
51. Ibid.
52. Ibid.
53. Ibid.
54. *Leaves* (June 1972), p. 1.

Conclusion

1. *The Center Magazine* (July-August 1971) vol. 55, no. 4, p. 71.
2. Rick Margolies, "On Community Building," in *The New Left,* edited by Priscilla Long, Porter Sargent Publisher, Boston, Mass. 1970, p. 372.
3. John Stuart Mill, *On Liberty* (New York: Henry Regnery Co., n.d.), p. 34.
4. Ibid., p. 80.
5. Ibid., p. 80

INDEX

Almsbruderhof, 46
Anabaptism, 31–32, 40–43
Anabaptist communities, 9–10
Anarchism, 87–90
Anarchist communities, 13, 16,
    195
    structure of, 33–34
Aquarian Gospel, 84–85
Aristotle, 23
Arnold, David, 52
Arnold, Eberhard, 44, 45

Behaviorist communities, 30–31
    structure of, 34–35
Borsodi, Ralph, 7, 90–94, 96
Braun, Ted, 59
Brotherhood of Spirit, 19, 40,
    76–86
Bruderhof *see* Society of Brothers

Children of God, 38, 39
Chief servant *see* Vorsteher
Church communities, 9–10
Church of the Brethren, 43
Collectives, 106–109
Communal family, 99

Commune, 99
Communitarianism, 190–193
Communitarians, 19
Community, 99–100
    measure of, 193–197
    uses of, 198–199
Community Playthings, 16, 47
Community Service, Incorporated,
    100–101, 126, 128, 197

Decentralism, 90–94
Dowling, Levi H., 84

Farm Center International, 122
Federation of Intentional Communi-
    ties, 48, 100–101
FIC *see* Federation of Intentional
    Communities
Free Church, 40–43
Free Church communities, 10–11,
    13, 15
    radical Christianity and, 32–33
Free Vermont, 106–107
Full Circle Farm, 34, 113–115
Fuller, Millard, 59, 60
Fundamentalist communities, 38–39

Fund for Humanity, 60, 61

Gaskin, Steven, 40
Go Ahead and Live (Loomis),
   95–96
Green revolution, 94–96
Green Revolution, 96

Hansch, Erick, 97
Harris, Alan, 80
Heathcote Center, 34, 96–99
Heathcote School of Living, 91,
   96, 126–27
Herrod, Charles, 124
Homesteading, 90–92, 129
Hutterites, 43, 45, 194

Infant schools, 26
International Foundation for
   Independence, 121
Israel, Matt, 168, 183

Jesus Movement, 39
Jesus People, Incorporated, 39
Jordan, Clarence, 41, 56, 57,
   60–61

King, Slater, 124
Koinonia Partners, 10–11, 16,
   56–57, 196, 197
   Anabaptism and, 32–33
Kropotkin, Peter, 28–29, 90

Labor credit system, 172–73
Living Research, 152
Llano community, 20, 27
Loomis, Mildred, 7, 89, 91, 95
Lost Tribes of Communism, 27
Love Inn *see* Jesus People,
   Incorporated

Margolis, Rick, 193
Marx, Karl, 104
Mennonites, 43

Merian, 182
Metelica, Michael, 40, 77–79,
   82–83, 85
Mill, John Stuart, 199
Miller, John, 67, 68
Morgan, Arthur, 126
Morgan, Elizabeth, 126
Morgan, Griscom, 101, 126
Morris Fund, Homer L., 125–126

Nethers, 19
New Communities, 123–125, 128,
   197
Newey, Don, 97
New Harmony, 19, 25, 132
New Testament Missionary
   Fellowship, 38
Northfield house, 77

Operant behavior, 133
Owen, Robert, 19, 26, 27, 131–132,
   139, 142

Pentecostal Spirit movement, 38
Plato, 22–23, 146
Plough Publishing Company, 49
Polis, 22–24
Pollard, John, 80
Primavera community, 47

Quakers, 43

Radical Christianity, 31–32
Reba Place Fellowship, 9, 11, 16,
   33, 67–76, 196, 197
Red Clover collective, 107
Religious communities, 16
Republic (Plato), 22–23
Rural communitarians, 28–29
Rural communities, 13–14, 15,
   16–17, 101–106
Ryan, Tim, 97

Saint-Simon, Henri de, 144

Sannerz community, 44
School of Living *see* Heathcote
  School of Living
Sectarian communities, 30
Self-knowledge, 25–26
Shalom Fund, 75
Sheats, Ladon, 60
Skinner, B.F., 26, 34, 182
  social thought of, 130–138
Society of Brothers, 9, 10, 11, 12,
  13, 16, 30, 44–55, 195
  Anabaptism and, 32
Spirit in the Flesh, 80
Springtree community, 16–17,
  19, 34, 109–113
Summertown, 19, 40
Sunrise Hill, 27, 34, 115–121,
  194
Swann, Bob, 59, 121
Swisher, Ted, 59–60
Swiss Brethren, 43

Turners Falls, 77

Twin Oaks community, 15, 19,
  34, 35, 105–106, 195–196
  adolescents in, 9
  behavior code, 187–88
  children in, 9
  economics of, 170–74
  governance of, 174–79
  labor credit system, 172–73
  membership of, 162–67
  origin of, 151–54
  person developed in, 167–70
  as a society, 154–62

Vale, 100–101
Vorsteher, 52
Voth, Virgil, 73

Walden House, 152, 153
Walden Pool, 152, 153
Walden Three, 22, 24, 183–87
Walden Two (Skinner), 138–51
Walden-Wood Conference Center,
  152–53
Warwick house, 77
Wideman, Jacob, 43
Woman suffrage, 25
Woodcrest community, 47
Wright, Frances, 20, 132

ADDICTION

ALSO BY G. H. EPHRON

Amnesia

ADDICTION

G. H. Ephron

St. Martin's Minotaur
New York

www.minotaurbooks.com

Library of Congress Cataloging-in-Publication Data

Ephron, G. H.
    Addiction / G. H. Ephron.—1st ed.
        p.   cm.
    ISBN 0-312-26677-4
    1. Forensic psychiatrists—Fiction.   2. Mothers and daughters—Fiction.
3. Teenage girls—Fiction.   I. Title.

PS3555.P49 A65   2001
813'.6—dc21

                                                            2001034895

First Edition: September 2001

10 9 8 7 6 5 4 3 2 1

M

To Molly, Naomi, Jerry, and Sue

Acknowledgments

Special thanks to our spouses, Susan and Jerry, for their love, support, and for the time and space that writing takes. Thanks to our agent, Louise Quayle, for her encouragement and insightful suggestions, and to our editor, Kelley Ragland, with whom we are so fortunate to get to work.

We are grateful to writing pals Connie Biewald, Donna Tramantozzi, Nancy Tancredi, Lynne Viti, Pat Rathbone, and Maggie Bucholt, and to Hallie's daughter Molly Touger, for reading the manuscript in progress and offering their honest critiques. Thanks to Lorraine Bodger for her help in shaping the characters and the plot, and to Carolyn Heller for a deft hand with the final polish. Thanks to Sumi Verma, Lissa Weinstein, and Carolyn Ferrucci for their supportiveness, and to Bruce Cohen for helping us shed one pseudonym. And thanks to Buzz Scherr for helping us get the legal details right.

ADDICTION

1

MATTHEW FARRELL stumped onto the stage of the Medical School amphitheater, folded his six-foot-plus frame, and sat on the chair opposite me. He clutched a near-empty Evian bottle in both hands. His Save the Whales sweatshirt gaped around his thin neck as he glanced quickly at the screen behind us on the raised stage. The electric blue of the slide background reflected off his face, turning the pimples on his forehead purple. He didn't seem to read the canary-yellow words. *Asperger's Syndrome.*

He stared down at the bottle, squeezing it and releasing it in a slow, steady rhythm. He avoided eye contact with me or the second-year students who filled the hall, all squeaky clean in their shirts and ties, sweaters and ponytails.

"Dr. Zak," my colleague, Dr. Kwan Liu, stage-whispered to me from the side of the stage, pointing to his Rolex. I checked my Timex. We'd finished with the lecture portion of our presentation, and it was time to get on with the clinical interview. We had only about fifteen minutes before our audience would summarily abandon us to their various obligations.

I cleared my throat and waited for the whispering in the hall to subside. I introduced Matthew to the audience and thanked him for agreeing to come and help our medical students better understand Asperger's syndrome. The plastic bottle went *pok* as he released it. "I'd like to ask you a few questions," I said.

I could feel the audience of second-year medical students strain forward into the silence.

"You like to ask questions," Matthew said, staring at the bottle. The words were delivered in an automaton voice, each syllable taking up as much space as the next.

There was uneasy laughter in the hall. "Yes, I guess I do like to ask questions. I thought I'd ask you if you are having any problems."

"That's what you thought," he said, and waited patiently, presumably for me to tell him more about my thought processes.

"Are you having any problems in school?" This time, I'd phrased the question so it was harder to misinterpret.

"Yes, I'm having problems." I could understand how teachers who encountered Matthew Farrell found themselves barking "Look at me when I talk to you!"

"What kind of problems are you having?"

"Kind of problems . . . hard problems."

"Do you have trouble with your schoolwork?"

"I do okay," Matthew said, still addressing the water bottle.

"Do you like hanging out with other students?"

He shrugged. "They laugh, and I don't know why. Maybe they are laughing at me." Matthew concentrated on the bottle as if it were a crystal ball. I waited. Finally he added, "Makes me do things I should not do."

Things-he-should-not-do included throwing a chair through the window of his high school English class. That's why he was spending a few weeks with us in the Neuropsychiatric Unit at the Pearce Psychiatric Institute, getting evaluated and having his medication adjusted. It was fortunate for the students attending the lecture—a live patient makes a much stronger impression than just a psychiatrist and a psychologist lecturing at you.

"Matthew, I'm going to show you some pictures." I clicked the remote control and a photograph of a smiling man was projected onto the screen behind us. "Please, look at his face and tell me what this man is feeling."

Matthew stared at the screen, tilted his head to one side, and stared some more.

"How does this man feel?" I repeated.

"His glasses are crooked," Matthew said at last.

The second photograph was of another man, his face twisted with rage. "And how does this man feel?"

"He needs a shave," Matthew offered.

And so it went, through a half-dozen pictures. No matter what the facial expression — from surprise to sadness to disgust — Matthew commented on some physical detail.

"Matthew, now I want you to repeat this: People who live in glass houses shouldn't throw stones."

There was a pause. Matthew repeated the phrase.

"Good. Now tell me, what does that mean?"

"What that means . . . Throw a stone and you'll break the glass house."

"Anything else?"

"People will get angry at you. Say you should not do that."

After some more questions, I thanked Matthew and the aide escorted him from the lecture hall. We still had a few minutes before the hour was up.

I called on a young Asian woman with a close-cropped cap of glossy black hair, her hand raised tentatively. "His speech sounds almost like deaf speech. Is he deaf?"

It was a good question. "The simple answer is no," I responded. "But he takes what he hears literally. He's deaf to nuance, to inflection, to the emotional content of speech. And forget about humor, sarcasm, even anger — goes right by him. And in a sense, he *is* deaf to emotion. As you saw from his responses to the photographs, he can't interpret emotions in the faces of others. He can't express emotions either. The monotone voice, the flat demeanor — they don't give us a clue about his inner state."

A young man who could have doubled for Tom Cruise asked,

"He seems withdrawn, depressed. Would you treat him for depression?"

"You're raising a very important point. It might appear that Matthew has an emotional disorder. But Matthew's problem isn't primarily psychiatric. It's likely caused by a brain dysfunction involving the right hemisphere. In his case, it's developmental, though you can get similar symptoms in stroke patients."

I glanced at Kwan. He picked up without missing a beat, "If we only pay attention to the psychiatric presentation, we might prescribe Prozac or another SSRI." When it worked, Kwan and I were like a team of relay runners, passing the baton back and forth, our narrative flowing like a single stream of consciousness. "But in this case, an antidepressant is contraindicated. It could end up making him more distant from his own emotional states, feeling more out of control, possibly suicidal."

"What's the prognosis?" The question was called out from the back corner, an area usually occupied by faculty who drop in when one of our weekly lectures piques their interest. "Are there treatments, drugs? How do they do out in the real world?"

Surprise turned to pleasure as I recognized the voice, saw the face. It was Channing Temple. She still wore her straight blond hair pulled back from her face. She'd never been exactly pretty, but she had the kind of looks that made an impression, made you listen when she spoke. We'd been friends for years. Back in college, I'd been in love with her.

She delivered her question standing up, canted forward with a finger raised. It was a stance she'd used to good effect when I'd first laid eyes on her. She was twenty years old, grilling the university provost about institutional investments in tobacco stocks. Today, her tone had none of the in-your-face brashness that irritated the provost to the point where he found himself, much to the students' delight, red-faced and screaming back at her.

There was a hesitancy to her voice that made me pause before answering, take a few extra seconds to edit the usual blunt way I allow myself to talk to doctors about mental illness. Asperger's syndrome is a difficult diagnosis, and I wondered if her question was personal.

Before I could phrase a response, Kwan answered. He always likes to get in the first word—and the last. "There is no cure, per se." The unvarnished words made me cringe. "There are medications to help control the anger that arises out of their frustration with the world." At least that sounded a bit more encouraging.

I added, "In terms of treatment, we might try cognitive behavioral therapy to help the individual use his intellect to adapt. We can work with them, teach them to notice what they *don't* notice— facial expression, for example—and get them to take a step back and ask questions whenever they're perplexed. The good news is, there's potential for living a satisfying life."

Channing mouthed, "Thanks, Peter," and sat.

I nodded back. I tried to remember the last time Channing and I had gotten together socially. It might have been a catered dinner at her and Drew's Back Bay town house—could that be right, two years ago? It might even have been the last party I went to before my wife, Kate, was killed.

Since Kate's death, I'd avoided parties—and old friends, too, for that matter. I was working long hours, keeping busy, and generally keeping to myself. I'd seen Channing from a distance, run into her at meetings. She'd left a message on my voice mail some weeks earlier, but it had been business—she'd called to recommend a resident for a rotation on my unit. Fortunately or not, the Pearce Psychiatric Institute is so big that it's easy to avoid anyone you don't work with directly.

If I'd been my own therapist, I'd have explained that grief has to be felt in order to be worked through. You can dull the ache for only so long with busyness. Remove the anesthetic, and the pain returns double. But I was lousy at taking my own advice.

Kwan thanked the students for coming and reminded them of the agenda for next week's lecture. Channing stood at her seat. She waved at me, pointed out to the lobby, and held up one finger. Even from a distance, her face seemed strained with anxiety. I nodded and smiled back.

• • •

I waded into the lobby and poured myself a cup of coffee from a large metal urn. Kwan was already there, helping himself to a cookie. He glanced up at me and tsk-tsked. "How many cups is that for you today?"

I took a sip and grimaced. The coffee tasted boiled. "One too many."

Channing emerged into the lobby. When she saw me, her expression morphed from pleasure to hesitancy. *No, I wanted to whisper, it's not your fault that we've become strangers.*

She came over. We did a little awkward dance where she went left and I went right, and we ended up air-kissing nose to nose instead of cheek to cheek. She laughed. "Peter, it's so good to see you." She put her arms around me and hugged hard. She still smelled of citrus. "We've missed you."

I held up an empty coffee cup.

"No thanks. They never have any tea at these things," she said, "and when they do, the water's usually tepid."

"Ah, another tea aficionado," Kwan said. "So few of these Philistines understand."

I knew it was killing him to know what kind of relationship I had with Channing Temple. Friends, just friends, I would have told him. But he'd have guessed we were once much more.

"Hi there, Kwan," Channing said. "Long time no see." They executed a flawless, cheek-brushing-without-colliding air kiss. She let her hand linger on his arm. "Mmm, nice fabric. Nice suit. Armani?"

"No, but close. Some of us try," he said, eyeing the Harris tweed jacket I'd bought in England a decade ago.

"At least mine still fits."

Kwan sniffed. "Oh, so now I know why you never wear a hat—can't find one big enough to cover that swelled head of yours."

Before I could come up with a snappy retort, he tugged at his vest, gathered his dignity, and turned to talk to a group of medical students.

"What brings you to a lecture about Asperger's syndrome?" I asked Channing.

"Actually, you were on my mind," Channing said. Her hair was wound around and anchored to the back of her head with ivory chopsticks. It was a severe look that emphasized her strong chin and prominent cheekbones. There were lines now, etched around her eyes and along the upper edge of her thin lips. "The other day, Drew brought me a beautiful spray of orchids, and I was putting them in a vase, the one that Olivia made with Kate." She put her hand on my arm. "You know how terrible we feel about what happened."

I nodded and blinked. Sympathy still threw me. I hate being out of control.

"That vase, it's really quite lovely," Channing went on.

"Kate thought Olivia had talent," I told her. I remembered the night of Channing's party, Kate had offered to teach potting to her quiet, gawky preteen daughter, who seemed to evaporate into the corners of the home. Kate had enjoyed the "lesson," and she'd been looking forward to another one.

"Then it seems like the very next day," Channing went on, "I see your name on a bulletin board in the cafeteria announcing this lecture. Asperger's syndrome. I've been seeing articles about it in the popular press."

"It's actually an old syndrome with a new diagnosis—wasn't in DSM-III," I said.

"Something like dyslexia for interpersonal nuance," Channing said.

"Exactly."

Channing lowered her voice and took a step closer. "Peter, I had an *aha* in there, listening to you." For a plain, severe-looking woman, she could become quite beautiful when she turned on, lit from within. "Know how you can be an expert in something, but when it's someone you love, someone in your own family, you turn stone-blind? Well, as you were talking, I realized—that's Olivia. She's been seeing a therapist, tried antidepressants."

I led Channing over to the window, away from the crowd. "Are you concerned about anything in particular?" I asked, the clinician kicking in.

"It's everything in particular. You wouldn't recognize her. You could say that she's using her appearance to make a statement. And her behavior—she's turned moody and dark. She comes home, goes upstairs. Wham, shuts herself into her room. Spends hours alone."

At sixteen, how I'd longed to have a room to close myself in and the world out. But in a one-bedroom apartment—my brother and I slept in the bedroom; my parents slept on a foldout sofa in the living room—there's only so long you can lock yourself in the bathroom before someone threatens to kill you.

"I know what you're thinking," Channing said. "What do I expect from a seventeen-year old? You don't have to tell me this is normal. And God knows, it would probably help if I'd experienced good mothering when I was her age."

I remembered. Channing's mother had killed herself when Channing was still in grammar school. Shot herself in the head. But there was no bitterness or self-pity in Channing's voice. It was just a fact, something she'd learned to live with. Once we'd stayed up most of the night, looking through Channing's family photo albums and comparing childhoods. I'd been struck by the change she'd undergone, before and after her mother's suicide. As an eight-year-old, she'd flirted with the camera, sturdy and buoyant, her blond hair short and soft around chubby cheeks and mischievous eyes. A year later, she looked away, morose and brooding. Her hair had grown long, stringy bangs creating a veil over her eyes.

"But Livvy's turning more and more inward," Channing went

on. "Blows hot and cold like that." Channing snapped her fingers. "She says nothing she does is good enough for me—but the truth is, she's the one who's so ashamed of her own work that sometimes she refuses to even try. When she has to do something that seems hard, she has an anxiety attack.

"When she's in her room, she's on her computer. Hard to believe she's my daughter." Channing gave a wry laugh. "It's all I can do to answer my e-mail. What do they do in chat rooms, anyway?"

"You probably don't want to know," I said.

"Probably not. What I do know is that she's in another world, all the time, one I don't understand at all"—her voice broke—"one I can't reach into."

I squeezed her arm. "She has friends?" I asked.

"I really don't know," Channing said wearily. "She doesn't bring kids home. But she goes out. I think she's got computer friends. If you can call that friendship. Who knows who they are. I worry. She's so young and inexperienced."

Channing was the one person who'd always had everything under control. Figures—it would take a teenage daughter to throw her off-center.

"Peter, I'll bet if you spent even fifteen minutes with her, you'd be able to give us a better sense of what's going on."

I knew what was coming. I should have stopped her right there, invoked the unwritten rule: Thou shalt not treat friends or their relatives. That's if she'd been a casual friend or a colleague. But Channing was much more than that.

"Please. See her informally," she begged.

I knew what Kate would say: "If you can't help your friends, then what's the point of the fancy degree?" And I remembered a picture in our photo album of Kate playing with six-year-old Olivia at a picnic in the Berkshires, one of the few times we'd seen Olivia when she was very young. The two of them sat beside a puddle, making mud pies. A pair of kindred spirits. On the ride home, Kate had talked about the daughter we'd have one day, and how she hoped our little girl would be as open to life's possibilities as Olivia.

Kate and I never did have that little girl—or little boy, for that matter. There was always a reason why *now* wasn't the right time.

"You say she's seeing a therapist?" I asked.

"Daphne."

"Daphne?" I was surprised, yet not surprised. Daphne Smythe-Gooding was Channing's longtime mentor.

"I know, I know. But she analyzed me more than fifteen years ago, and she'd never spent much time with Olivia. Besides, she's a brilliant clinician. . . ." Channing's voice trailed off.

"But?"

"Let's just say the chemistry doesn't seem to be working. Lately, seems like I have to drag Livvy, kicking and screaming, to her sessions with Daphne," Channing said, avoiding my eyes. "Besides, Daphne's a psychiatrist, like me. We come at this from a different angle than you would as a psychologist. Maybe ours is the wrong angle, in this case. If you spent even five minutes with her, I think you'd see things both of us miss." She looked at me, her eyes pleading. "Nothing formal. Just a casual meeting, and then you tell me I'm being an overanxious parent."

I chuckled lightly, but I knew better. Whatever it was that Channing was sensing in Olivia, it was probably real. Perhaps not Asperger's syndrome, but something with a name, and hopefully a treatment.

"I'd be happy to see her. Informally," I said.

"How about this weekend?" Channing rushed on, as if she was afraid I'd change my mind if I thought about it for ten seconds more. "Saturday night. It's my birthday, and we're having some people over to celebrate. Olivia will be there."

"A party? Doesn't seem like the ideal place to talk to her," I said. The last party I'd been to at their house was a suit-and-tie affair, the kind a teenager would rather clean her room than attend.

"I want you to get a fresh impression. If she knows you're evaluating her, she'll clam up. Say you'll come."

Saturday I had plans for a quiet dinner with Annie Squires. Annie was a private investigator. For years I'd worked with her and attorney Chip Ferguson evaluating defendants, until I helped them defend Ralston Bridges, a sociopathic killer who violently objected to my diagnosis. Turned out, no one ever called him crazy and got away with it. After a jury pronounced him not guilty, he took his revenge by stalking and killing my wife.

After that, I retired from forensic work. Permanently, I thought. But then I let Chip and Annie talk me into defending a man accused of murder. The prosecution's entire case rested on the memory of his ex-wife, who'd survived a gunshot wound to the head. In the end, I wasn't sorry I'd taken the case. It helped me put a few of my own demons to rest.

"Are you free?" Channing asked.

She glanced at my left hand. I fingered my wedding ring. "Actually, I have a date," I said.

"You're seeing someone?"

The question gave me pause. I wasn't ready to think of myself as *seeing* anyone. Over the last six months, Annie and I had had a couple of dates and a bunch of near dates. A few times, she'd had to cancel because of her work. I'd had to cancel because of my work.

Our last date had been by accident—we'd run into each other at Wordsworth's in Harvard Square and gone out for drinks, which turned into dinner, which might have turned into something more except Annie had plans to see her sister that night. Since then, Annie's time had been occupied working and moving her office and Chip's to a renovated building near the Cambridge Courthouse. They were going into private practice.

I'd been busy. She'd been busy. I knew if I didn't get off the dime, she'd soon be getting busy with somebody else. But I wasn't sure I was ready yet for a serious relationship.

"That's wonderful! Bring your friend," Channing said.

Visions faded of juicy grilled steaks and that bottle of Turley zin I'd been saving. Not to mention the rest of a long, empty evening waiting to be filled.

"Please, come," Channing said.

"Sure, can do," I said finally. At least I'd still be seeing Annie.

Relief flooded Channing's face. She took a business card from her jacket pocket, wrote quickly on the back, and handed it to me. "Here's where we are." I recognized that precise, backward-slanted handwriting, more printing than script. "It's right near our old house. Saturday night. Seven o'clock."

I walked Channing out. We plowed through the clouds of smoke that hung under the Corinthian columns at the front of the building. Nurses and doctors who knew better were huddled there, getting their nicotine fix. We crossed the pristine grass quadrangle, flanked by five, perfectly proportioned Greek Revival buildings, holding their own in the shadow of towering modern medical buildings that crowded in from behind.

As we headed down the path toward the parking lot, Channing had her head down. She was holding her coat together under her chin, her shoulders hunched against the cold. March in New England can be so discouraging. More cold nasty weather when we're all good and sick of it.

Channing gave a furtive look behind her before she spoke again. "You saw the note in *JAMA*?"

"What note?" There was a pile of unread journals on my desk, including the last four issues of the *Journal of the American Medical Association.*

"I'm amazed no one's shown it to you. A team from Hopkins dismissed my research as"—with two fingers, she drew quotation marks in the air—"'too flawed to be meaningful.'"

In polite scholarly circles, the phrase was the ultimate insult. Her detractors—and there were many, since Channing minced few words when it came to exposing the questionable practices of others—were probably rubbing their hands together with glee.

A pair of doctors passed us going in the opposite direction. One of them nodded and then resumed his conversation with his colleague. "They're all talking about it," Channing said, lowering her voice. "They're treating me like a car wreck they don't want to get involved in. It makes me so goddamn mad. And it's complete bullshit. When I got a call from the team that reviewed my research, they told me their results appeared to be confirming mine. A month later, it's like 'Never mind, her research is corrupt.' I want to know what happened to change their minds."

I smiled. Here was the old Channing, the maverick who followed her own compass — which probably explained why she'd run the Drug and Alcohol Rehabilitation Unit for years but had never officially been named director.

"What's the study about?" I asked.

"I was reporting the preliminary results of a pilot project — about twenty subjects. A treatment for addiction. We got patients fresh out of detox programs — they take care of the easy part, the physical addiction. Then we focus on the psychological craving." Channing's voice was animated and enthusiastic. "Keep them for two weeks. Treat them with a compound called Kutril."

"What is it?"

"You're going to laugh. It's actually a highly concentrated extract of kudzu, combined with Trilafon."

"Kudzu? Isn't that the vine that's devouring the state of Florida?" I envisioned a viscous green potion.

"That's it. Actually it's the root that's medicinal. The Chinese used it at least as far back as the first century A.D. to inhibit the desire for alcohol."

"You're serious, aren't you?"

"Completely. There had been trials with rats that showed promise. Imagine if it works for humans? Kudzu isn't even a prescription drug! And Trilafon has been on the market for nearly thirty years. It's cheap. We've got a company in New Jersey making up batches of the compound in pill form."

Trilafon was one of the first antipsychotics developed. It tranquilized without sedating. "What about side effects?" I asked. I recalled that was one of the reasons doctors had stopped prescribing it.

"From long-term use, yes. This treatment is short and intensive — patients take a dose every four hours the first day. Every eight hours for a week. Twice a day for a week. Then we discharge them with a dose a day for two weeks. Then nothing. Kills the craving right from the beginning, and it doesn't seem to return, even after the treatment is discontinued."

"What's the success rate?"

"We just finished analyzing the results of the full-blown study. It confirms the findings of our pilot. Eighty percent after six months. Sixty-five percent after twelve months."

I whistled. That was impressive.

"The only serious adverse events we had were two patients who had seizures, which were then well controlled with Neurontin."

"Can it be administered outpatient?"

"Perhaps. Eventually." Channing glowed with satisfaction. "Sounds like a magic bullet, doesn't it? Talk to the drug companies, you'd think it was a subversive plot to put them out of business. Acu-Med went ballistic when they heard. And oh, big surprise, one of the guys who submitted that note to *JAMA* used to work for them." She gave a disgusted sniff. "Wouldn't surprise me if he's still on retainer."

"They're probably trying to develop a prescription drug to do exactly the same thing."

Channing's eyebrows rose in surprise. "Peter, you're starting to think like me. Actually, they are. Liam Jensen is running the clinical trials." Jensen was a doctor who worked with Channing in the Drug and Alcohol Rehabilitation Unit. Channing slowed down until a middle-aged couple walked past. "I've got most of my final report drafted. The final stats are being reviewed now."

"Sounds like you think they're out to get you."

"You think I'm being paranoid?"

"It's not paranoia when you're surrounded by assassins," I said. "After all, you're the one who's still fighting greed, injustice, and the American way. I think you've got it written into your job description."

Channing didn't smile. "How much longer, I wonder? You've heard the other allegations against me?"

"I haven't." I tried to keep my head out of the noxious cloud of gossip that floats around the Pearce.

"You're probably the only one, then. They're questioning my clinical judgment."

Clinical judgment — a euphemism vague enough to cover just about anything. That and *not a team player* were the terms used to brand those who didn't go along or get along.

"They're saying that I behaved inappropriately. Got too close. Violated the boundaries."

I paused, midstep. "You?"

Channing laughed. "Oh, come on, Peter. I'm not that much of a prig." She gave me a sideways glance. "Well, maybe I am." She took my arm and pulled me forward. "Anyway, some people find it credible. The worst part is that these allegations are being made in a way that I can't confront them. Character assassination by innuendo."

We stopped near the edge of the parking lot, at the foot of an enormous concrete lion. The creature had his mouth open, his mane curling about his head as he hugged a shield emblazoned with the word *Veritas*. Channing glanced up at the beast and shivered.

"Truth," she said, spitting out the word. "I know that's what this place is supposed to stand for. But sometimes I wonder if we're embracing it or devouring it whole."

• • •

By the time I got back to the lobby outside the lecture hall, someone had disconnected the coffeepot and carried it off. I scooped up the last cookie crumbs and ate them.

"I didn't realize you and Channing Temple were such good friends," Kwan said, coming up behind me. He was munching on what must have been the last Lorna Doone on the tray.

"Actually, we met ages ago. Back when we were both undergrads."

"I wonder if she'll weather the storm," Kwan said.

"The article in *JAMA*?"

"That, and they're saying she . . ."

I held up my hands. "Don't. I know as much as I want to know."

Kwan put his hands over his eyes, then over his ears, then over his mouth.

"Right," I said. "Besides, it's all bullshit. And she's an old friend."

"Ah," Kwan said, as if that explained something. "She's married, isn't she? Is he one of *the* Temples?"

"Huh?"

"Boston Brahmins. Old money."

"Sounds right."

I knew Drew Temple didn't have your typical day job. When people asked him what he did, he'd mumble something about managing property and financial assets. I'd always found him pleasant but distant. Part of it was the age difference—people sometimes assumed he was Channing's father, especially early in their marriage. And part of it was just who he was.

"Back Bay, I'll bet," Kwan said.

I fished Channing's card from my pocket. Kwan pounced on it. He whistled. "Marlborough Street. Nice neighborhood. Saturday night?"

"She's having a dinner party."

His eyes drifted over to my Harris tweed jacket. He eyed my fish tie as if it were an actual dead fish. "You're not going to wear that, are you?"

I flicked away an errant cookie crumb. "Not swank enough?"

"Not Marlborough Street enough. This calls for a good suit. And, Peter, I know for a fact that you don't own one. In fact, I think you don't even know what one *is*." He checked his watch. "Let's see. Tuesday. If we get over there this evening, you'll have it in time."

"There where? In time for what?"

"In time to save you from yourself. And permanent disrepute."

I could have said no. I tell myself I don't care about appearances. And most of the time, I don't. But at just that moment, as I was pushing him away, my hand touched the sleeve of his jacket. The fabric was soft, fine, nothing short of amazing. On top of that, I happened to look up and see the two of us reflected in the enormous gilt-framed mirror that hung on the wall opposite. That suit made Kwan—a fairly short person who avoids exercise the way some people eschew dirty socks—look tall and broad-shouldered. My trusty Harris tweed made me—a tall person with decent shoulders who feels rotten if I go more than a couple of days without rowing or running—look rumpled and squat.

If he'd waited a day, I probably would have backed out. But later that afternoon, before I'd had a chance to act on second thoughts, I found myself being helped out of Kwan's Lexus by the valet parking attendant at Neiman's.

Just as at Filene's Basement, there's a long escalator ride down into the men's department. But the similarity ends there. No beehive of activity to descend into. No one trying to push past us on the escalator. Instead, there was orderly calm, subdued chamber music, and the air was subtly infused with musk.

"Ah, Dr. Liu! A pleasure to see you again," said an impeccably dressed fellow who materialized the moment we reached the floor. His face had a mannequin look about it, perfectly arranged, wrinkle-free, the eyebrows just a touch darker than you'd expect them to be. "What can we do for you today?" The royal We.

"Actually, nothing for me. I've brought in my colleague, Dr. Zak, for his first real suit." The salesman tilted his head a micron and appraised me. The smile stiffened, and he stroked his chin. I wondered if his skin felt laminated.

"Certainly," he said, and pulled something from his pocket and squeezed it twice to make a loud but somehow unobtrusive clicking sound.

I started to head for the exit—I didn't need this. But Kwan blocked my way. A smaller, younger man appeared. He quickly measured me and wrote a bunch of numbers on a little pad.

"Color?" the salesman asked, now addressing the question to Kwan.

"We're starting a wardrobe. I'd say a basic gray, chalk stripe."

The salesman glided off and reappeared with two suits. He held one up. "Here we have a Brioni. Classic but contemporary." The suit was three-button, dark gray with a muted stripe. "They weave their own fabrics in Milan. Hand-tailored, of course."

I felt the fabric. The words *subtle yet lush*, right out of a clothier's ad, sprang to mind. There was a handwritten tag just visible from the sleeve. "Five thousand dollars?" I croaked. My first car had cost less.

Poker-faced, the salesman put the suit aside and held up the other one. "And here we have a Canali. Understated elegance. Fine detailing, of course. More, uh, affordable." The final word came out raspy, as if saying it hurt.

"How much more affordable?" I asked.

"Just try on the damn suit, Peter," Kwan growled. "It's not going to kill you."

"I wonder if I might suggest," the salesman offered as he carried the suit toward the dressing room, "a shirt and tie to try with it?"

When I came out, Kwan did a double take. "Peter? That you in there?"

I stood in front of the mirror, and a stranger gazed back. Could have been the medical director of the hospital. Or James Bond. Depending on my frame of mind.

I took it all—the suit, the shirt, the tie. I held my nose and handed over my credit card.

"Great purchase," the salesman oozed. "You'll wear that suit for five years."

He made it sound like an eternity.

THERE WAS a storm the night of Channing's party. When I got to my car, the windshield had become a glaze of ice. My fingers turned numb as I hacked away at it with a dull plastic scraper when what I needed was a blowtorch.

I had plenty of time to speculate about what I'd find when I met Olivia. From ebullient toddler, to mousy preteen, to what? I hoped a normal youngster, rebelling in the time-honored way in which adolescents differentiate themselves from their parents. I longed to be able to reassure Channing: This too shall pass.

By the time I had cleared the car windows, I was late. I was supposed to pick up Annie on a street corner near the Cambridge Courthouse—she'd worked all afternoon, setting up her new office. I hoped Annie wasn't freezing to death. I drove as fast as I dared, taking yellow lights as invitations to speed.

Annie looked like a dandelion puff, her curly, reddish hair back-lit by the streetlight, her face clouded with dragon's breath. Instead of her usual jeans and leather jacket, she had on a full-length coat that looked like one of those sleeping bags that are supposed to keep you warm, camping out overnight on Mount Washington. She slid into the car, leaned over, and gave me a light kiss on the cheek. Her lips were icy.

"To Marlborough Street, Jeeves," she said, shivering. "And can you crank up the heat in this old car of yours?"

I'd almost finished restoring the 1967 BMW. I was taking my time, hammering out the rear quarter panel—I'd done it once already, but a run-in with a red Firebird in a parking garage had left it in need of further straightening. After that, there wouldn't be much left to do. I'd miss working on the car at quiet, ungodly hours, long before any sane person willingly contemplates crawling out of bed.

"I do love that leather smell," Annie added, inhaling. "Mmm. So comforting."

I inhaled too. But it was Annie's scent, watermelon and rose water, that I was enjoying.

I caught Annie eyeing me. "I was glad to hear from you," she said.

"It's been—" I paused, trying to remember how long it had been.

"Six weeks," Annie said.

"No."

Annie laughed. "No one can accuse you of rushing into anything. Though I have to say, I was disappointed at the change of plans."

I reached over and put my hand over hers. An electrical charge zapped up my arm. "A quiet dinner for two would have been nice," I said.

"Next time," Annie replied, and put her hand on my knee and squeezed.

It was with considerable effort that I continued toward Back Bay—down Memorial Drive, across the Harvard Bridge—instead of making a U-turn and heading back to my place.

This stretch of Mass. Ave. was undistinguished—a row of run-down restaurants, convenience stores, and bars. As soon as we turned onto Marlborough Street, the landscape changed. Trees reached up from either side of the street, not quite forming an arching trellis overhead. Electrified gas lamps cast a soft light on tidy rows of town houses, the cornices lined up in soothing, nineteenth-century uniformity.

The parking was residents-only, but even a resident would have had a hard time finding a parking spot that night. We ended up at a meter on Clarendon and walked back.

We stood on the sidewalk and gazed up at the house. Annie exhaled. "Wow."

"Wow," I echoed. "They used to live a few blocks away. But that house was about half the size of this one."

The formidable, gray granite town house had a double staircase going up to an arched doorway with windows on either side. A crystal chandelier sparkled through one of the windows.

Annie scrunched up her shoulders and pulled the collar of her coat around her neck. "This place is going to make my teeth itch."

I smiled and wondered what Channing would make of Annie. The two couldn't have been more different, and neither one was much like Kate. On the surface at least. Physician, private investigator, artist. Still, each one was about as independent and self-sufficient as a person can get.

We mounted the steps. The brass fittings—banister, wall-mounted mailbox, and door knocker—looked as if they'd just been polished. I rang the bell. The front door was drawn open by a young man in a tuxedo who looked as if his teeth itched, too. Probably a student working for the caterer.

Overflowing floral arrangements were grace notes in the generously proportioned, high-ceilinged entrance hall. There were French doors on either side; one led to a parlor, the other to a book-lined study. The entryway continued past a curved staircase to the back of the house.

It sounded as if about two dozen guests were there already. I recognized some colleagues from the hospital. The ones I didn't recognize were probably Drew's friends—stockbrokers and real estate developers, most likely.

I glanced up the stairs to the second-floor landing. No Olivia.

Annie shed her coat like a gray cocoon. She wore a short, sleeveless dress. The black velvet hugged her like a second skin. I tried not to stare. She looked spectacular. I was doing what women say they hate, staring at her legs, the swell of her hips, her breasts, giving her the once over from the bottom up. When I got up to her face, I realized she hadn't noticed. Or if she had, she didn't mind. She was looking at me, open-mouthed, as if I'd just swallowed a goldfish.

She touched the lapel of my new suit and whistled. "You clean up good."

I laughed out loud. "Speak for yourself!"

"Peter, I'm so glad you could make it," Channing said as she flowed into the room, holding a half-filled champagne flute. Her face was flushed, and she tripped over the hem of her voluminous maroon skirt and then quickly recovered her footing. Some champagne splashed onto the Persian carpet.

This time I executed the Kiss without bumping noses. I handed her a bottle of 1986 Calon-Segur, velvety red, just ready to drink. "For a special occasion," I said. "Channing, this is . . ."

Annie smiled sweetly, "Annie Squires — criminal investigations, missing persons" — she raised an eyebrow at me — "lost loves."

Channing laughed. "How appropriate," she said, and extended a long, elegant hand. Annie gave her a solid handshake back. "I'd definitely like to hear more." She leaned in toward me and lowered her voice, "Peter, you must promise to rescue me if I disgrace myself. I got beeped last night, and I barely slept a wink. I feel like roadkill, and this" — she held the champagne glass at arm's length — "is going straight to my head."

"Peter!" Gray-haired and distinguished in a red plaid dinner jacket and black bow tie, Channing's husband, Drew Temple, came toward us, two glasses of champagne in hand. With his six-foot-plus frame, he had to stoop coming through the doorway. "Delighted you could make it." When he smiled, the lines in his face deepened.

We took the champagne, and I introduced Annie.

Annie shivered. "You still cold?" I asked, and put my arm around her. Then I felt the draft, too.

We turned. The front door had been pushed open. Channing went over to the young woman who'd stepped into the hallway.

"Chan . . ." the woman stopped herself. "Dr. Temple," she said, and extended a stiff arm. The bracelets on her thin wrist jingled.

Channing took her hand and squeezed it. "Jess, I'm so glad you could make it. Let me take your coat."

The woman slipped off her wool coat. Beneath, she wore a short black sleeveless dress, like Annie's. I looked around. Most of the women at the party were wearing practically the same outfit. With her long neck, narrow waist, aristocratic nose, and the way she held her head slightly tilted, the young woman reminded me of a blond Audrey Hepburn. The same innocence mixed with sophistication. Definitely not Audrey Hepburn was the battered backpack she set on the floor, and the small tattoo, maybe a butterfly, that adorned her ankle.

"You look very pretty tonight," Channing told her. Then, she put her arm around the young woman and presented her to me. "This is Jess Dyer," she said, emphasizing the name as if it was one I should know. But it didn't ring a bell.

"Pleased to meet you," I said, shaking her hand. She had long fingers, like the slender toes of a wading bird. I introduced her to Annie.

"Dr. Dyer. The resident I told you about," Channing reminded me.

"Oh, right! You'll be starting your Neuropsych rotation next week," I said remembering the message Channing had left me a few weeks ago. "We're looking forward to having you." We were always understaffed. A good resident was an extra doctor on the unit, one with a not-yet-jaded perspective.

"Believe me, I'm looking forward to it as well," Jess said.

"She's unusually talented," Channing said. Jess blushed. "That's why I recommended she work with you. She's interested in testing."

That was unusual — psychiatrists are generally content to leave testing to psychologists.

At the top of the stairs, a gangly, dark-haired girl peered down. She vanished before I could get a good look. Even from a brief glimpse, I realized I never would have recognized her as Channing's daughter.

"I'll be there, bright and early Monday morning," Jess said. Then she excused herself to find the powder room.

Channing watched her leave. "Smart, very empathic. She's been through a rather difficult year. Just needs a bit of centering. Ballast. The kind of mentoring I got from Daphne when I was doing my own residency."

How much centering, I wondered? I hoped this young woman wouldn't turn out to be an extra patient.

"Is Daphne here?" I asked.

A peel of laughter rippled from the adjoining room, followed by, "Oh, sod off, Liam. You can't be serious."

Channing raised a finger. "That's her, in the flesh."

We peered into the neighboring room. There was Dr. Daphne Smythe-Gooding, her straight, shoulder-length white hair gleaming against shoulders-to-floor dark silk. "She's looking well," I said.

"She certainly seems to have come out of mourning."

Daphne's husband had died the previous summer. Robert Smythe-Gooding had been only sixty years old. He and Daphne were icons of solidity at the Pearce. Robert, the brilliant researcher; Daphne, the scholarly clinician. When I first arrived at the Pearce, he was chief of psychiatry. Everyone assumed he'd be in line to become director of the hospital. Then, there had been some kind of reshuffling that had the whiff of scandal about it, and he was shunted aside to a new position, director of clinical trials.

I'd seen it happen many times since. Hearsay about drugs disappearing under a particular unit director's watch. A doctor rumored to be sleeping with his patients. Gossip about an administrator's mishandling of funds. Who knew if the stories were true? The dirty little secret at the Pearce was that though senior staff rarely got fired, they got "promoted" into meaningless jobs, assigned "special projects." The rumor mill managed attrition by grinding away at reputations. Eventually, the person disappeared from the org chart, leaving barely a ripple.

That wasn't what had happened to Robert. At first the new position had no real duties. Single-handedly, he'd written grant proposals and spearheaded research projects. He recruited doctors to work with him, courted the National Institute of Mental Health, the pharmaceutical companies, and the foundations. When the money started to roll in, it became apparent that research was going to be key to the institute's survival.

Robert had been director of clinical trials right up until his death. Cancer, metastasized to the brain. Daphne was at his side constantly in his final months, until they'd both disappeared from view. A few weeks later, I saw the obituary. I was glad for him. Cancer like that usually means a lingering death.

"Didn't I hear that Daphne's been named director of clinical trials?" I asked.

"Yes. Of course, she's been doing the job for a while anyway. Robert was trying to carry on for as long as possible with the same old routines, but he was failing. Refused help from anyone but her. Cantankerous old son of a bitch." Channing smiled at the memory. "Still, I never expected her to defect to the dark side."

It was typical Channing. She had no trouble seeing the issues her patients faced in every shade of the color palette. Medical ethics were another story. She saw a monochromatic battlefield, inhabited by armies of black hats and white hats.

There was another peel of laughter. "I almost don't recognize her these days," Channing said.

Daphne seemed smaller than I remembered her, somewhat tentative in the way she stood, with her head tilted to one side. She was holding a wine glass in one hand, but her other hand seemed to float away from her side, as if she were groping for something that wasn't there. Perhaps without her husband beside her, she felt off balance. That wasn't so unusual. Six months after Kate's death, I'd only just begun to come to terms with the loss—two years later, I still had trouble defining myself as "alone." When my dad died, I remembered, my mother took more than a year to bounce back. Dad had been the one who had organized their social life, initiated friendships. No one was more surprised than Mom when she turned out to be a natural schmoozer.

A waiter slid by with a tray of hors d'oeuvres. Daphne helped herself to what looked like a stuffed mushroom. She didn't eat it. She just held it. It anchored that free, fluttering hand in place.

"She's gaining back some of the weight she lost, too," Channing went on. "For a while there, we were afraid she was going to disappear entirely. You should go say hello. She's always been a big fan of yours."

"Me? She barely knows who I am," I said.

"Peter, I can assure you, she knows all about you."

I felt my face get a degree warmer. Daphne had analyzed Channing during her residency. If Channing had discussed her former lovers, which surely she had, then Daphne knew more about me than anyone had a right to know. I caught Annie watching me speculatively.

Liam Jensen, a senior psychiatrist who worked on the Drug and Alcohol Rehabilitation Unit with Channing, was expounding to Daphne and to a small group of listeners; ". . . a new treatment for alcohol and drug dependence." Jensen was hinged over at the hip, his upper body dipping, his waxy nose pressing the point home. "Today we can detox patients with Librium, but the rate of recidivism is discouraging. DX-200 actually diminishes the psychological dependence."

As we approached, Daphne ate the stuffed mushroom she'd been holding, then reached out her hand to Channing and pulled her close. She gave her a wry smile and rolled her eyes in Jensen's direction. "Of course, Channing is working on a different treatment for the same thing," Daphne said.

"Kudzu vine," Jensen said, pursing his lips with distaste.

"Witch doctor's brew," Channing said, a mischievous gleam in her eyes. "We'll see which one proves more effective. At least we know which one is more expensive." Channing seemed to savor their rivalry. Jensen did not look amused—but then, he was a dyspeptic kind of guy.

A man asked, "And the potential market?"

Daphne broke in. "Dr. Jensen has his priorities. Wouldn't be wasting your time on anything insipid, would you, Liam?" Under her breath, she added an aside to us, "Besides, he owns the bloody patent." Now she sounded like the old Daphne, self-assured, razor sharp.

Jensen gave a thin smile. "Conservatively speaking"—he paused—"hundreds of millions of dollars, in this country alone."

The last words came during a little gap in the party noise, and an assortment of heads lifted and angled in Jensen's direction, harvesting his words.

Across the room, Drew Temple was talking to a woman maybe in her early thirties. Between the form-fitting, pale-blue suit, the suntanned skin, and the dark hair that hung like a long, straight curtain, she didn't look like a hospital type. She reached up and smoothed the collar of Drew's dinner jacket. He glanced about and caught me watching. He took a wooden step back and gave a self-conscious cough.

Just then, Channing announced that it was time for dinner and led the way into the dining room. The fellow who'd taken our coats was removing one of the place settings and rearranging the chairs to camouflage the hole where it seemed Olivia wouldn't be sitting. I found myself seated between Daphne and Channing.

Annie ended up across the table, next to Liam Jensen. Jess Dyer sat on Jensen's other side. He put his arm around the back of Jess's chair, and they spoke quietly for a few moments. Then he picked up his empty wineglass and she picked up hers. They touched the glasses together in a silent, symbolic toast.

I quickly got into a back-and-forth with Daphne and Channing about how come smart liberal women in politics don't get any respect, while smart conservative women do, with forays into abortion rights and gun control. No one commented on Olivia's absence.

Channing talked about a white-water–rafting trip she was planning for the spring. "Aren't you terrified?" Daphne asked her.

"Completely. That's what makes it exciting."

I had forgotten that aspect of Channing—the side that courted her fears. An edge that years of wearing a suit and carrying a briefcase hadn't worn down. She'd once shown me the gun her mother used to kill herself. She kept it cleaned and oiled. Learned to shoot like an expert. She used to say anything you could master loses its menace.

Channing pushed away from the table and picked up her cup. She gave a bright smile to the other guests who'd followed her lead and were standing as well. "Shall we take our coffee into the parlor?" she suggested.

As we passed the foot of the stairs on our way to the living room, I said, "Olivia must still be up in her room. Shall I go up?"

Channing sighed. "It sure doesn't look as if she's going to come down."

"Which door?" I asked.

"Top of the stairs, first door on the left. Make up some excuse."

AT THE top of the stairs I ran into Jess, emerging from a doorway across the hall from Olivia's. She seemed startled to see me, her eyes large and bright. "Just using the ladies," she said, as she zipped up her backpack.

Of course, that was the perfect excuse for bumbling into Olivia's room.

Olivia's bedroom door was ajar. I stood in the hall, listening to the tapping of her keyboard. I nudged the door open an inch more. She was sitting at a desk facing me, staring intently at a computer screen. Olivia looked nothing like the lively six-year-old or the mousy preadolescent I remembered. A long neck and bony elbows stuck out of her loose black T-shirt. But the hair was what you noticed—black spikes with poster-paint red streaks running through them.

She took off her round, wire-rimmed glasses, picked up a bottle of eyedrops from alongside her keyboard, tipped her head back, and squeezed some drops into each eye. She had a leather lace tied around her wrist and silver rings on all her fingers, including the thumb.

She set the bottle down and blinked back the drops. Then she righted herself, put her glasses back on, and began to type. She stopped abruptly, her eyes flickering from her keyboard to the screen. Then another burst of typing. She took a blister pack of pills from her pocket, squeezed one out, and knocked it back without water.

I rapped on the door. She gave a startled jerk, and her face twisted in anger. She quickly dropped the pills into her desk drawer and said, her voice shrill, "Jesus Christ, can't you leave me . . ." When she saw it was me, she turned wary, the tendons in her neck stretched taut, her face hard and still—like an animal, suddenly aware it's being stalked.

"Bathroom?" I asked.

Her face went blank. "The can's at the end of the hall," she said in an expressionless voice. I saw immediately why she reminded her mother of Matthew Farrell—the flat demeanor punctuated by explosions of rage.

"I'm Peter Zak. Do you remember me?" I asked. Olivia gave me a blank look. "I met you when you were a little girl. And then a while back, you came over to my house and my wife helped you make a ceramic pot. That was almost three years ago." She narrowed her eyes to a squint. "You've grown up since then."

Her expression turned sour. I could hear the unsaid "Duh."

I glanced around the room, trying to find a toehold. A poster caught my eye.

"You a Nirvana fan?" I asked.

"Kurt Cobain," she said. *Now go away*, her body added as she turned back to her computer.

Cobain, a sensitive, obsessively driven young man who had stuck a shotgun in his mouth and pulled the trigger, was not a great role model.

"Mind if I have a look?" I asked.

She shrugged. I entered the room. The cloying, minty odor of patchouli took me back to my undergraduate days when we used herbs and incense to mask the smell of pot. Only slivers of wall were visible between the posters of rock groups and newspaper photos of Eric Harris and Dylan Klebold—alienated kids who'd worn black trench coats to define themselves, and then made names for themselves by shooting down their high school classmates. I lifted the picture of Eric Harris. It was tacked over a magazine photo of a blond model in a pink, Cinderella prom dress.

There were also pieces of lined paper, tacked in random spots on the wall. I looked more closely at one. It was a list, written in purple ballpoint pen in careful childlike handwriting. It was dated about two months earlier. There were twenty-five numbered items. The first one was "Brush teeth," then "Appointment with Dr. D." I scanned down. "Buy a birthday present for Mom," "Math home-work," "Term paper," "Make bed." Another list was pinned up nearby, likewise a hodgepodge. Clearly, here was Olivia trying to get organized, struggling to build a structure around her life. But anyone would have been overwhelmed by so much detail. Where to begin?

On the adjacent wall, there was a little gallery of photographs printed from a computer. I recognized one. A woman in black with a mournful face and long flowing hair stood intertwined with the sinuous trunk and limbs of a tree.

"This is beautiful," I said. "Annie Brigman's work is quite ex-traordinary."

"You know Annie Brigman?" Olivia asked, her voice betraying a hint of interest. She fingered the stack of silver rings on her thumb, took the top one off, slid it back on.

"I wish I knew her better. I had a chance to buy one of her photographs a few years ago, but I blew it."

"For reals?" She stood and drifted over beside me. "Her photo-graphs are so, like, totally emotional." Olivia looked as if she needed a good night's sleep. Despite the shot of Visine, her eyes were still bloodshot, and her hand shook as she raised it to the image. The bones stood out like carbuncles at the base of her painfully thin wrist. I wondered what pills she was taking. "It's like, if she photographed you, it would be so scary because you'd get a picture of your insides."

"That's a very perceptive observation," I said.

She glanced at me and quickly looked away, the door slamming shut again. I wondered, was there a prom princess or a female Kip Kinkle hunkered down behind Olivia's in-your-face outsides?

Then I noticed a computer printout under an empty water glass on the table beside her bed. The splashy title: Snuff It. It was the subtitle that caught my attention: Suicide Methods. That and the yellow highlighting.

Olivia stood with her head tipped against the wall, gazing at the Annie Brigman photograph, her finger tracing the undulating lines that merged nature and woman into a single form. Despite the blunt, chopped-off black hair, Olivia's resemblance to her mother was striking—the strong profile, the intense eyes. When she stopped slouching and carried herself tall, the resemblance would be even stronger. I wanted to ask, did she feel depressed? Angry? Did she ever think about killing herself. But this wasn't the right time.

. . .

I left Olivia in her room and went to find the bathroom, which was, as promised, at the end of the hall. My chat with Olivia had left me shaken. The fact that she was intrigued by social outcasts and deviant teenagers didn't, by itself, concern me. At her age, trying on different personas is healthy. But the combination of that with annotated literature on the how-to's of suicide set red lights flashing.

I returned to the top of the stairs and looked down. Drew was at the front door, saying good-bye to guests. The door on the opposite side of the landing from Olivia's was ajar. I heard, "A resignation. That's what I want. Enough of this dangerous incompetence." It was Channing. Her voice was low and intense, the wine's softness gone.

I couldn't make out what she said next, but the response was loud and clear. A man's voice, the words clipped and carefully enunciated. "It's not something we want to air in public. It could damage the hospital. And at such a critical time."

I took a step closer to the door. I knew I was eavesdropping, but I couldn't help myself. "Critical to you," Channing said.

"And to the hospital—"

"And to the drug companies. Don't forget the drug companies. The ones that pay those nice, fat consulting fees. Oh, no, it wouldn't look good at all."

"Right. You're too high and mighty—and rich—to take their consulting fees," he shot back. "But you know as well as I do, the Pearce would have long ago been turned into a housing development if it weren't for their money."

The house had turned dead quiet. Olivia poked her head out of her room, her expression wary. Drew and Annie were at the base of the stairs; Jess and Daphne, now wearing their coats, stood near the front door. They were all looking up the stairs, straining to hear.

The man continued, "Don't threaten what you're not prepared to do."

"I'm prepared. Believe me, I'm prepared. A man is dead. And everyone thinks . . ."

"What difference does it make what everyone thinks?"

"It would make a difference to him. And it makes a difference to me."

"You're so sure of what's right and what's wrong."

"Why not? What have I got left to lose?" Channing said, her voice laced with disdain.

"You have no one to blame for that but yourself."

"You son of a bitch," Channing hissed.

There was a pause. Silence. I could barely hear the clatter of dishes from the kitchen. Then, the man's gasp of outrage. "What the hell do you think you're doing?" he bellowed.

That was enough for me. I entered the study to find Channing and Dr. Liam Jensen confronting each other. Jensen was clutching the stem of a brass floor lamp, his face filled with rage. The lamp was lifted six inches off the floor, and I had the distinct impression that he was a hair away from wielding it like a club. His normally waxy complexion had turned florid. Channing was holding an empty brandy snifter, and cognac dripped from Jensen's beaky nose. More was spattered across the lapel and one perfectly padded shoulder of his pale-gray suit jacket.

When he saw me in the doorway, Jensen set down the lamp and released his hold. He coughed, pulled a handkerchief from his pocket, and blotted his face, then his jacket.

I stood close to Channing. "You okay?" I asked.

"I'd like to kill the bastard," she said under her breath. Then she looked up and saw Drew peering in from the doorway. Annie, Jess, and Daphne crowded behind him. Channing backed up until she bumped into a wing chair and sank down into it. She put her head in her hands. "Oh, God, now I've gone and done it." I put my hand on her shoulder.

"Here, Liam, let me take your jacket," Drew said.

Jensen looked as if he didn't trust himself to say anything. He took off his jacket and handed it to Drew.

"Cold water," Channing said wearily. "Before the stain sets. You don't mind, do you, Peter?" She looked up at me. "Take it to the bathroom at the end of the hall." Drew handed me the jacket. "Cold water should take care of it, but you have to treat it right away. If that doesn't work, take it down to Verna in the kitchen. She'll know what to do."

I left, holding the jacket. Cold water. I started toward the end-of-the-hall bathroom and stopped halfway there. I looked down at the jacket on my arm and recognized the silky brown Brioni label. I promptly turned around and trotted Jensen's jacket directly down to the kitchen and the ministrations of Verna.

• • •

As Annie and I walked back to the car, I felt a cold sweat on my forehead, the aftermath of the adrenaline rush kicked off by the altercation. It left me feeling uneasy, as if the entire evening had somehow ridden off the rails. *Dangerous incompetence. A man is dead.* Who were they talking about? And whose resignation did Channing want?

"Any idea what that was all about?" Annie asked.

"I haven't any idea," I said. I hoped Channing hadn't been added to one more enemies list.

We got back into the car. I started it and cranked the heater, though I knew it would be at least ten minutes before anything but cold air would be blowing on us. Annie yawned and hugged herself.

"Tired?" I asked.

"Not really. It's only eleven. Want to go somewhere for coffee?"

Her stockings hissed against each other as she crossed her legs. Her knee emerged from between the flaps of the coat. I didn't feel like coffee.

"Not especially," I said.

Annie tilted her head and smiled. "Mmm," she said, "neither do I, actually."

I was out of practice. With Kate it had been so uncomplicated, so natural, like a slide down the rapids and at the end coming up gasping for air. It had been a long time since I'd gotten from where I was to where I wanted to be. Even a few months ago, guilt and the feeling that I was being unfaithful looking at another woman would have made it impossible for me to feel what I was feeling now.

All I could manage was, "Hey, you," as I reached over and touched her face.

She turned her head and tasted my index finger. I closed my eyes. "Hey, yourself," Annie whispered.

I put my hand on her leg and caressed, the intense feeling in me wanting, needing, to get out. Annie took my hand and pushed it a few inches higher up her thigh. I wrapped my other hand behind her head. She smiled and closed her eyes, her lips parted, her mouth inviting. I meant to kiss her gently, but it came out hard and urgent. She pressed her body hard against mine. I pushed my hand further up her thighs, and her legs parted.

Annie heard the beeper go off before I did. "Must be yours," Annie said, gasping. "Mine's at home."

I didn't want to let go, to fish out my beeper. But I did. It's amazing how fast obligation can deflate desire.

I had to wipe the steam off my glasses before I could see the emergency code 900. "Great. Perfect timing." I groaned. "I go for a week without a beep and now, at this very moment, there's an emergency. I've got to go in."

I grabbed a rag from under the seat and swiped the moisture off the windshield. Annie arranged the flaps of her coat and shivered. "Next time, let's skip the party."

"We'll pick up where we left off, at my house, with dinner and a good bottle of wine."

"Um-hmm," Annie purred. "And no beepers."

"No beepers," I said, kissing her lightly on the mouth. "This is completely infuriating," I said, my face close to hers.

"My mother always said, all good things come to those who wait."

"Bullshit."

I dropped Annie at her apartment, taking time for one last kiss. Regretfully, I watched her scurry up her front steps and disappear inside.

• • •

The drive across Somerville was uneventful. I turned onto the landscaped grounds, past the gold embossed sign. PEARCE PSYCHIATRIC INSTITUTE EST. 1804. The serpentine access road was deserted, the few remaining elms like a ghostly honor guard.

I parked, opened the car door, and heaved myself out. The emptiness was palpable. Only a few other cars were in the lot, clustered under a flickering streetlight. I inhaled the metallic, bitter cold and turned my collar against the wind.

I hurried up the hill. The rolling lawns were threadbare with patches of ice waiting to melt. Austere Victorian buildings that housed the units were right at home in the bleakness, but more recent additions, redbrick-and-glass monstrosities, looked naked and uncomfortable without any foliage to soften their contours.

I hopped onto the back porch and let myself in. A blast of overheated air hit me in the face. Instantly, my glasses fogged. I wiped them as I strode down the hall, past the dining area where the patients ate, past the once-gracious living room with its grand piano and not-so-grand vinyl sofas and chairs. In the glare of fluorescent lighting, the pink walls were nearly the color of vomit.

A thin voice warbled from the reception area, "I left my hearrrrt . . ."

I could hear Nurse Gloria Alspag's coaxing counterpoint — "Mr. Fleegle, you can't stay out here without anything on" — which prepared me for the scene when I rounded the bend and got past the half-dozen patients who were watching the show.

Though I'm nominally in charge, Gloria is the backbone of the unit. She looked very tired, her shirttails hanging from her tan trousers, her short hair standing up as if she'd been running her fingers through it in frustration. She was waving a blanket like a bullfighter brandishing a cape, while skinny old Samuel Fleegle, stark naked, nimbly avoided it.

A night nurse herded two patients back to their room, while three more drifted out to take their places.

"Olé!" one of the watching patients cried. Others shouted encouragement.

". . . in San Francisco . . ." Mr. Fleegle held a mop handle and crooned into it. "Above the blue . . ." There were little bits of white hair on his chest, like wisps of cotton balls, stuck to it. He was concave in the front and behind, the muscles atrophied in his derriere and chest. His face was flushed as his voice gathered strength.

Gloria gave me an exasperated look. "Mr. Fleegle, you're waking everyone up," she said reasonably. "Please, sit down and be quiet."

Just then Mr. Fleegle saw me standing there in my good suit. He raised his hand and wagged an index finger. "Waiter," he said, his voice aloof and polite. "Could you get us two Manhattans?" He licked his lips. "With bourbon."

I approached him and put my arm around his frail shoulder. "Mr. Fleegle, I'm so sorry, but we can only serve you at the bar,"

I told him, stepping into his delusion, hoping that in doing so, I'd be able to lead him out of it. "Why don't you sit here?" I maneuvered him gently over to the geri-chair Gloria had been trying to get him into.

Mr. Fleegle willingly sat down and saluted me. He seemed unfazed as Gloria shoved the tray in place to keep him from getting up.

He finished the song, holding one last tremulous note. Then, there was blessed silence and a scattering of applause. He waited expectantly, tapping his fingers on the tray in time to invisible music.

Gloria wheeled him into the dining room, where we could at least close the door. "How long's he been like this?" I asked.

"A couple of hours. Ever since his brother came in this evening, he's been getting happier and happier. We found an empty pint of Four Roses in his room. I've tried everything." Gloria sank down into a chair and rested her head on the table. Mr. Fleegle had started the song over from the beginning.

It didn't seem as if Mr. Fleegle, after a lifetime as an alcoholic, should have had such an extreme reaction to a pint of booze. Still, metabolism changes as a person ages. Then I remembered. "Didn't Kwan put Mr. Fleegle on the Zerenidine trial?" I asked.

"Started him about a week ago."

"That's probably it. Seems as if the drug binds to the same receptor sites that metabolize alcohol. Makes the alcohol much more potent and, I'm afraid as we're about to see, for a much longer period of time. Good thing he's a happy drunk."

Gloria lifted her head off the table. "How much longer?"

I shrugged. "An hour. Maybe a few."

"A few?" Gloria said.

"I need to help get the rest of the patients back to bed. Besides, there's really nothing to do but wait it out. He should be fine by breakfast, though he'll have a helluva headache."

Mr. Fleegle's voice reached another quavering crescendo. Gloria moaned. "And so will I."

SUNDAY, I awoke around noon, alone in bed. It wasn't what I'd hoped for. As I lay there, Channing's argument with Liam Jensen came back to me. The anger, the threats. I ran their words through my head. Most of it didn't make much sense. Someone was dangerously incompetent. Someone was dead? The only clear part was that whatever it was, Jensen wanted to hush it up, and Channing didn't.

I was still lying there when the phone rang. It was Channing.

"So, what did you think?" she'd asked, her voice taut with anxiety.

"About Olivia or Liam Jensen?"

"Never mind Liam. That's under control."

"He didn't seem under control."

"He's wrong." There was a pause. "What about Olivia?"

I pushed the hair out of my eyes and swung my feet over the edge of the bed. "I saw Olivia for such a short period of time, it's hard to . . ."

"Peter, think who you're talking to. I know all the disclaimers."

"Sorry. Habit." My mouth tasted foul. I got up and headed for the bathroom. "Well," I started, "based on a minimal amount of data and a very cursory inspection, she seems like a normal, disaffected teenage girl. For the most part."

"And the rest?" Channing asked, picking up immediately on the hedge.

I squeezed a taste of toothpaste onto a finger and licked it off. "She seemed edgy, overly moody. Could just be that she's not getting enough sleep."

"That, too."

"I saw Olivia taking a pill. Is Daphne prescribing anything?"

"She had her on Prozac a while ago. But nothing now."

"Well, it would be a good thing to find out what Olivia's medicating herself with. It could be contributing to the moodiness," I said, leaning heavily against the bathroom door. "And she's attracted to the photographs of Annie Brigman."

"Who's that?"

"A photographer from early this century. Beautiful images of young women, yearning to merge with nature. There's a mysterious eroticism in them. That alone wouldn't concern me. But she also had some material about suicide."

"She knows her grandmother killed herself."

I went back and sat on the bed, resisting the impulse to lie down again. "Channing, she has this sheet about *how* to commit suicide, with sections highlighted."

"Oh," Channing said. It was like the sound of the air going out of a balloon. She knew as well as I did that for an adolescent, an obsession with suicide is a danger signal.

I said gently, "Some of the literature suggests that, for whatever reason, suicidal behavior runs in families."

"Don't you think I know that?"

"I could easily be wrong. I talked with her for less than ten minutes, and—"

She cut me off. "Will you do a more formal evaluation? Please."

"Wouldn't you rather take her to someone who isn't a friend? Someone who can be completely objective?"

"I need someone I trust."

"Why not Daphne?"

There was a pause. "I'm not asking you to be her therapist. I just want someone who can give me hard information. Besides, Daphne . . ." She broke off the thought. "I want another opinion. I can't send her to someone I don't know. I wouldn't trust them. You, I trust. Please, Peter," she went on, "do this for me. Take care of Olivia. Say you have some time to squeeze her in this week when she's on spring break."

I found myself thinking about what kinds of tests would help me understand Olivia. Those long, dysfunctional lists of to-do's on her wall suggested a processing problem. Cognitive tests would help me understand how she was making sense of the world. I tried not to think about the conflict I might have to face, dealing with Daphne, who, like most analysts, saw things in terms of drives and emotions. Especially if my take on Olivia didn't square with hers.

My datebook was on my dresser. I opened it. There was a time slot free late Monday morning. "How about you and Olivia meet me tomorrow in the cafeteria, around eleven? We can talk, then I'll take her for a few hours."

"Great. Thanks, Peter. I really appreciate this."

• • •

When I arrived at work Monday, I detoured to the closet behind the nurses' station and gouged the clot of mail out of my mailbox. Most of it was glossy advertising and pamphlets from the drug companies, plus an embossed invitation to an all-you-can-drink dinner at the Ritz—all I had to do was endure a thirty-minute "analysis" of current treatments for anxiety.

I turned the card over. No stamp, no address. Just a handwritten "Dr. Zak, hope to see you there." Had to have been hand delivered by one of the sales reps. It annoyed the hell out of me, the carte blanche access these guys had to the unit.

I threw it all away. I continued down the hall to our conference room. I barely registered my colleagues already assembled inside. All I saw were the holes that had been punched in the walls and the dangling wires left behind by a small army of workers who'd commandeered the room a few weeks ago and then vanished without a trace. I'd called maintenance four times. Each time, someone different had promised to send the workers back right away to finish the job. Well, right away had come and gone. Didn't they realize we had to work in this room?

"Peter, you're looking tense already," Gloria said, putting her hand on my arm and peering into my face. She looked relaxed and rested, despite having worked all Saturday night. Her khaki pants and white shirt were crisp, her short dark hair damp, the comb lines still showing.

I still hadn't recovered from Saturday's all-nighter. "You need a cup of coffee," Gloria observed. She already had her own oversize mug.

She was right. It felt like a tension wire was pulling my eyebrows together. I took off my glasses and massaged the bridge of my nose. I'd had a cup — or was it two? — a few hours earlier. Since then I'd gone for a run, showered, shaved, and sanded a couple of rust spots off my car.

I left my briefcase at the head of the table and made a quick trip to the coffeemaker. When I returned, Gloria, our social worker, and our music therapist were ready to get started. Our psychology fellow and a senior aide joined us. Kwan strolled in on a wave of aftershave. He was carrying a cup of tea and a glazed doughnut. He was impeccably turned out, as always, in a dark three-piece suit.

I sat down and pulled out the rounds book. Conversation quieted and then turned off. All eyes focused on the white board listing the eighteen beds on the unit.

Before we could get started, there was a tentative knock at the door, and Jess Dyer poked her head in. Catching my eye, she pinked up. When she saw everyone else, she blushed more.

"Dr. Dyer, please come in," I said, my voice formal. "We were just starting rounds."

She slipped into the room. Today, in her dark suit with her blond hair pinned up, briefcase in hand, she looked older and more substantial than she had at Channing's party. In fact, she looked like a psychiatrist.

"This is Dr. Jess Dyer, our new resident," I announced.

Kwan sprang up, pulled over a battered Windsor chair, and gave a courtly bow. It was the same respectful way he treated patients. Jess nodded thanks, took a seat, and hurriedly pulled out a pad of paper and a pen.

I turned my attention back to the white board. "Let's start with Mr. Fleegle. A seventy-five-year-old alcoholic." Jess was writing. "Mr. Fleegle had a reaction to a new antipsychotic drug Dr. Liu is conducting trials on, late Saturday night —"

"Sunday morning," Gloria corrected.

"Right. Very early Sunday morning. Seems like the Zerenidine interacted with some whiskey someone snuck in to him."

"He shouldn't have been drinking," Kwan groused as he slumped in his chair, chin sunk into his chest. He'd have to report the adverse event — that's what they call it when a drug being tested does something unexpected. This one could be a major setback for the Zerenidine trials, and Kwan would be the unfortunate messenger.

"How's Mr. Fleegle doing?" I asked. "Any more hallucinations?"

"No. He seems pretty normal," Gloria said. "Normal for Mr. Fleegle, at any rate."

"Poor Pharmacom," Kwan said. "They have such high hopes for Zerenidine."

"Poor Gloria!" I said. "She was in here for hours trying to calm him down." As for me, there were several things I'd rather have done than catch Mr. Fleegle's lounge act. "I thought the Zerenidine trial was almost finished."

"I need to enroll five more subjects in the next two weeks. So I'd appreciate any help any of you" — he nailed me with a hard look — "can give me." Two weeks wasn't much time.

"I can help," Jess offered. "I coordinated research for Dr. Temple while I was on the Drug and Alcohol Unit."

"Really?" Kwan seemed impressed. He dug around in his pocket and passed Jess his business card. "Let's talk later today, Dr.—" He hesitated.

"Dyer. D-Y-E-R," Jess said as Kwan wrote.

It was a small thing but definitely an indication of how preoccupied he was. A young, attractive resident shows up and Kwan hasn't got her name written at the top of his meeting notes. All he'd written on the blank sheet was the numeral 5 large and underlined.

"We had some more excitement on Sunday night," Gloria said. "Patients partying in the tunnels."

"Our patients?" Kwan asked.

"No. A bunch from the Drug and Alcohol Rehabilitation Unit. They broke into one of the decommissioned buildings. Must have felt pretty safe because they had a boom box, a couple of bottles of cranberry juice they'd helped themselves to, popcorn, marijuana, and some vodka."

I tried not to laugh, but I had a vision of Mr. Fleegle nursing a sea breeze, waving a cigar, and crooning "Melancholy Baby" to a group of rapt patients in hospital johnnies.

"Dr. Destler is not amused," Gloria said. "You've got a manifesto in your e-mail this morning."

That news made everyone quiet for a few moments. Arnold Destler was chief bean counter at the Pearce. He'd been bustling around for the last four years, "bringing the Pearce into the twenty-first century," as he put it. Not surprisingly, you mentioned his name and the reaction was never lukewarm. People saw him as either our savior or as the Angel of Death, who was turning the Pearce into an institution not worth saving.

Gloria took a dim view. Whenever Destler's name came up in private conversation, she'd start muttering. "The man's a psychopath. Someone ought to put him out of his misery." In morning meeting, though, she just sat there tight-lipped. She was convinced Destler had spies everywhere reporting back to him.

"Looks like we had a few discharges over the weekend," I said, noting the erasures on the white board.

"Four patients discharged, one admitted," Gloria said.

That gave us three empty beds—a welcome breather, as long as it didn't last. Though even a few days below capacity made me anxious. With our razor-thin financial margins, we were under constant pressure to maintain a census of at least 95 percent.

I glanced at the list on the board. "Lydia Small."

"Admitted Sunday," Gloria said.

"A new patient?" Kwan asked, his voices prickling with interest.

I reached behind me for the chart and scanned the admitting record. "Seventy-eight years old. Police picked her up chasing her sister down the street with a carving knife. No clothes on. They brought her to the ER, delirious. No history of violence. They had her in restraints but couldn't get her calmed down. They did a rapid neuroleptization."

"Must have knocked the hell out of her," Kwan said.

"A rapid what?" Jess asked.

"Neuroleptization," Kwan and I chorused.

Kwan went on, "Means they gave her a half milligram of Ativan and a half milligram of Haldol. Then after an hour, doubled it. After that, doubled it again. Standard operating procedure with a violent patient."

"Then they throw up their hands and ship her to us," I added.

"She's completely out of it this morning," Gloria said.

"No surprise there," I said. "Is her blood work back?"

"Not yet," Gloria answered.

Kwan sat at attention. "Sounds like a perfect candidate for the Zerenidine trial."

Now I was sure he was preoccupied. Leaping from symptom to treatment wasn't his style. He was the one who held off treating a patient who'd kidnapped and threatened to kill his mother-in-law. The guy kept insisting she was an alien. He held the police at bay for eight hours before they were able to capture him, book him, and deliver him to us. Knee-jerk response would have been to dose him with antipsychotics, but Kwan waited and evaluated. Turned out he was right to wait. The guy had been forgetting to take his thyroid medicine. Severe hypothyroidism made him delirious, not demented. We restarted his medication, and three weeks later, he was as normal as the rest of us.

I was relieved when he added, "Let's wait until her blood work comes back before we decide. She'll need to be off the benzos for at least twenty-four hours anyway." He turned to Jess. "Dr. Dyer, please call the lab as soon as we're done here and make sure they get her test results to us, ASAP." Jess took notes. "Then, if she's coherent, talk to her about the study and get her consent. In the meantime, find out who can give permission if she turns out not to be competent."

Next, we discussed Matthew Farrell. Kwan said, "We've just started him on Adderall." Jess looked up. "A-D-D-E-R-A-L-L. It's a fairly new psycho-stimulant. Supposed to be a more effective treatment for patients with Asperger's syndrome."

I added, "Helps with concentration, anger control."

Kwan doodled on his paper. "I wonder how he'd do on Zerenidine. . . ."

I snapped the file shut. "He's only eighteen years old! And he doesn't fit the profile."

Kwan raised one finger. "Bursts of anger." Two fingers. "Out of touch with reality."

"He's not out of touch with reality. You're the one who's—"

"Can we get on with rounds?" Gloria asked pointedly. "I thought we were supposed to be talking about patient care. You two are going at it like a pair of bull elephants."

That brought the meeting to a full stop. "O-kay," I said. "Point well taken."

We resumed and got through the remaining patients on the unit without further acrimony. But the tension was still there. I knew it would be, until Kwan's Zerenidine trial ended and he could stop sizing up each new patient as a potential research subject.

Research had become a fact of life at the institute. The money, the prestige that came from being in the forefront in the fight against mental illness—it was all intoxicating. Individual doctors profited. The institute profited. We used to worry about the danger of finding ourselves in bed with our patients. Now we had an entirely different bed partner to worry about—the drug companies.

IT WAS after eleven by the time I got to the cafeteria to meet Channing and Olivia. The place smelled like Fridays at P.S. 181—baked haddock and canned corn. I scanned the cavernous room. A squadron of Formica tables was arrayed on a field of putty-colored linoleum. I'd expected to see Channing sitting there tapping her fingers on the tabletop to get me to move along, move along. I'd expected to see Olivia looking self-conscious as only an adolescent girl can look when she has to be seen in public with her mother. But the place was deserted.

I went through the food line, bypassing a muffin that looked as if someone had sat on it. I got a cup of coffee and took it to a table near the entrance. I sat down to wait. The coffee tasted vile, but I drank it anyway.

I checked my watch. A quarter past. A little role reversal. I'd always been the late one—only one of our many incompatibilities that seemed, in retrospect, fairly trivial. For a woman with the soul of a rebel, Channing had very buttoned-down habits. Under the Indian-print bedspread in her incense-laden dorm room, the sheets had been tucked in with hospital corners, sharper than any drill sergeant's. Shoddy research methods? Not likely. But then, it was unthinkable to me that she'd be late.

Now it was twenty past. I used the house phone in the lobby and called her office. It went directly to the automatic answering system. I hung up and called her beeper instead. I punched in my office number.

I hung up and stared out the window. It would soon be lunchtime. People were starting to drift toward the cafeteria in ones and twos, small groups, But none of them was Channing. The Drug and Alcohol Rehabilitation Unit was just across the lawn. Channing's office was one of the windows under the ornately trimmed roof overhang, just beyond the topmost branches of a magnificent, two-hundred-year-old oak.

I checked my voice mail. There was a message. But not in response to my beep. Channing left it while I was in morning meeting. I kicked myself for not checking my messages. It just hadn't occurred to me. When it's important, I usually get beeped.

"Peter, I'm running a bit late. Why don't you come over and find us in my office, instead of in the caf. I might need your help to extricate myself."

I dumped out the remaining coffee and headed over to her office. The exterior of the building that was home to the Drug and Alcohol Rehabilitation Unit resembled the one that housed our unit. The interior was another story. The lobby's mahogany paneling glowed. The walls looked recently painted. An actual brass chandelier hung from the ceiling medallion, not the fluorescent boxes that hung from ours. No question about it, they were doing something right.

I pressed the elevator button and waited. No creaks and groans from ancient machinery heeding the call to action. I could barely hear anything. I waited. I pressed the button again. Then I punched it four times hard, as if that would make a difference. It was reassuring. With all the money they had for paint and chandeliers, the elevators still didn't work.

I followed the EXIT sign, entered a stairwell, and started up the three flights of stairs. There were banister railings on the outer wall. On the inside, where the staircase wound around an air shaft, there was a wall of elaborately turned, closely set wooden spindles that ran from the treads to the ceiling. The spindles formed a wall preventing suicidal patients from flinging themselves off the steps and down to the basement floor. The central air shafts in our unit stairways were protected, too, but by a wall of ugly, prisonlike gray metal bars.

I took the stairs two at a time, pushed open the fourth-floor door, and tried to orient myself. Up here there were fresh carpeting and brass wall sconces as well as overhead lighting. No wonder the elevator hadn't come. The door was propped open with a wastebasket. Someone downstairs was banging on the elevator doors. I removed the basket and watched the doors slide soundlessly shut.

I continued along the hall of medical offices. A sign about halfway down said CHANNING TEMPLE, M.D. All staff offices had double oak doors, separated by an air pocket for soundproofing. The outer door was open. I listened. No voices. Whatever Channing needed extricating from was either over or taking place very quietly.

I knocked on the inner door. There was no answer. "Channing?" I said hesitantly. I turned the knob and pushed the door open. "You in there?"

There was a shrill, metallic sound, like feedback from a sound system. I froze. A tinny voice whined, "Please hang up and try your call again. If you need assistance, call the operator. Please hang up now. This is a recording."

I exhaled. The phone was off the hook. I peered into the spacious office. Channing's desk was facing me in front of a pair of windows. The base of the phone was on the desk, alongside a laptop computer. I crossed the room and found the receiver, lying on the floor. I set it back into its base.

There was a sharp, metallic smell, almost like something was burning. But there wasn't even an ashtray on the desk. The laptop drive hummed.

The back of my neck prickled. I could hear rapid, shallow

breathing. I turned around slowly. Olivia was standing behind me, pressed against the opposite wall at the corner of the room. Between the black lipstick and the dark around her eyes, she looked like a scrawny wet raccoon in her skinny jeans and black T-shirt. She stared at me, her pupils dilated.

Beside her, partially obscured now by the open door, Channing was sitting in a leather and teak chair that faced the desk. Her eyes were closed, and her blond hair hung loose and soft against a red headrest. In her lap were the ivory chopsticks she had used to anchor her hair.

My stomach turned over. I knew she wasn't resting. And only the chair's headrest was red. The seat and back were a creamy butterscotch.

"Kate?" I choked as I heard my wife's name emerge from my throat. I was looking at Channing, but I was seeing Kate, lying in a pool of blood on the floor of her studio. I felt as if I were captured in the merciless flash of a strobe light, my face held in a grimace of disbelief. Not dead. Please, God, not again! Why was I always too late?

I watched my hand reach out to touch Channing's face, as if the fingers, the slivers of white at the end of the nails, belonged to someone else. Her cheek was cool, soft, the flesh yielding. I wanted to back out of the room, reset the clock to when I was in the cafeteria, and start over.

As I drew my hand away, Channing tipped to one side. Olivia screamed as blood, bone, and brains smeared across the back of the chair.

I wanted to lash out, to strike whoever was responsible for this, the way I'd beaten and nearly killed my wife's murderer. I looked from Olivia to Channing, then back to Olivia. There was no one to beat on.

That's when I realized Olivia had her fingers wrapped around the barrel of a small silver handgun.

"Mom, I didn't mean for this to happen," she whimpered. She

pressed herself against the wall and slid down to the floor, hugging her knees and rocking.

"Hullo?" It was a woman's voice from the hall. "Channing? Is everything all right?" A clipped British accent. It was Daphne. She started into the room and saw me. "Oh, that you, Peter? I thought I heard—" She froze when she saw Olivia. Then Channing.

"What's happened?" she demanded. She put a trembling hand to her throat and stood very still. She seemed to shrink and grow hunched over. "Channing!" The word came out like a strangled cry.

Olivia made mewling noises and tucked her head down.

"Were you..?" Daphne started to ask Olivia, then thought better of it. She turned to me. "Was Olivia here when this happened?"

It took a few seconds to find my voice. "I don't know," I said. "I just got here a minute ago myself."

"Oh, God."

"She and Channing were meeting me . . ."

"Meeting you?" she murmured. She steadied herself against the desk, drew herself up. "Have you rung up Security?"

"Not yet." I picked up the phone.

Daphne went over to Olivia. She crouched alongside her. "Livvy. Let me have the gun," she said firmly, placing a hand on Olivia's shoulder.

Olivia flinched. She tilted her head and looked at Daphne without expression.

"Please, Olivia," Daphne coaxed, holding out her hand. Olivia seemed to shrink from it.

I dialed. The phone rang once.

"Give me the gun," Daphne said, her voice steady.

Olivia looked at the gun, as if seeing it for the first time. Her fingers tightened around the barrel and the gun wavered.

The phone rang again.

With what seemed like extraordinary presence of mind, Daphne took off her sweater, wrapped it around her hand, and took hold of the butt of the gun. With her other hand, Daphne pried loose Olivia's fingers. When she had the gun, Daphne stood, stepped over, and set it on the floor beside Channing.

Security picked up after the fourth ring. "This is Dr. Zak," I said. My voice sounded calm. "I'm in 407, the Drug and Alcohol Unit. There's been"—Daphne coughed and looked at me expectantly—"there's been an accident. Dr. Temple is dead. Call the police"—I felt my voice breaking up—"and come right away."

I hung up before they could ask any questions. I closed my eyes but opened them immediately. The horror in the room was preferable to the memory of Kate that came roaring back to me, her throat slit, her life's blood spilled on the cold cement floor of her studio.

"They're on their way," I said.

I steadied the tremor in my shoulders. I tried to focus on the top of the desk—the phone, the computer, a neat pile of purple file folders, the gleaming metal letter opener, its handle engraved with an elegant Gothic C, a glass paperweight with a miniature bouquet of glass flowers entombed inside, an empty white porcelain mug with the blue-and-white Acu-Med logo.

A beep from the computer cut the silence. Olivia's head jerked up. I rotated the laptop around to face us. Fat black words scrolled across a brilliant red background. "Can't live with myself. I'm so sorry."

I touched the mouse. Instantly, the message disappeared, replaced by a sky-blue background, white clouds, and a white rectangle with the message *You have new mail.*

• • •

From the hall came the heavy sound of feet. A security guard arrived. The heavyset African American had a fist-size ring of keys jingling at his waist, his walkie-talkie squawking static. He scanned the room. When he saw Channing, he approached gingerly. Dealing with gunshot victims isn't exactly standard operating procedure for our security personnel. He touched her neck. Then he unhooked the walkie-talkie and spoke into it. I caught the words *ambulance* and *police.*

"Has anyone touched anything?" he asked.

"I used the phone," I said.

The guard glanced at Olivia, then raised his eyebrows to me in a question.

"Dr. Temple's daughter," I said.

"Poor kid," he replied. "She wasn't here when it—?"

"No, no," Daphne rushed in with the answer. "Thank heavens."

"I think we should step outside and wait," the security guard said.

Daphne crouched alongside Olivia and put her arm around her. Olivia pulled away. "Come on. Let's go outside and wait for the police," Daphne said.

Daphne talked to her quietly and stroked her head. Olivia was dry-eyed, in shock, her face pale. She stared at her mother's lifeless body, then at me. Daphne pulled her to her feet and guided her from the room. Olivia submitted, stiff-legged. I followed them into the hall.

A few minutes later, I heard sirens approaching. Soon after that, there were footsteps on the stairs. The security guard met the two uniformed police officers and my old friend Detective Sergeant Joseph MacRae as they emerged from the stairs. MacRae, whose compact, powerful frame would have made better sense in jeans and a sweatshirt, wore a brown suit that puddled a bit at the ankle. His red crewcut might actually have acquired a fleck or two of gray in it since our last encounter—one in which we'd developed a grudging respect for each other. Our head-butting in the Sylvia Jackson case had convinced him that the memories of a victim with traumatic brain injury may not be what they appear to be. And he'd convinced me that not every cop is as clueless as he seems. He was the kind of guy I'd much rather have with me than against me.

MacRae gave me a surprised look of recognition. Our eyes locked briefly, and he gave a quarter-inch nod before he charged the door. Daphne stood, blocking the way. She drew herself up, stiffened her face. "There's been a suicide," she said firmly, clipping her words. It was the old Dr. Smythe-Gooding, scourge of hospital residents and senior administrators. "Dr. Temple has shot herself. Please, before all hell breaks loose, promise me that you'll handle this case without unnecessary grandstanding to the press. Her family and the institute will appreciate your discretion."

She dropped MacRae in his tracks. He flashed his silver badge. "Detective Sergeant Joseph MacRae. Of course, we'll follow standard police procedures."

"Dis-cre-tion." Daphne enunciated each syllable. "Right?"

"Right," MacRae muttered, gritting his teeth.

Just then, there was a crash. Olivia was no longer with us in the corridor. MacRae pushed Daphne aside, and I followed him inside. The room had turned cool, and the acrid smell was gone. Through the broken window, blue lights from the police cruiser pulsed against the tree branches. Olivia was sitting on the floor, covered in blood. She breathed heavily; her face was flushed. She held a shard of glass and drew it along her inner arm, creating another long, bright red line.

"Olivia, no!" I cried out. I took hold of her wrist and held firm. She dropped the glass. It wasn't until Olivia screamed in pain that I realized how hard I was holding her, much harder than was necessary to keep her from hurting herself. I picked her up in my arms. She was trembling.

She stared at me, terror in her eyes. "We're going to get you somewhere safe," I told her. "No one's going to hurt you. Please, don't struggle. We need to stop the bleeding."

"Take her to Admissions, Peter," Daphne said. I started off. "I'll telephone and have someone meet you in the foyer downstairs," she called after me.

"Hold on . . ." MacRae bellowed.

I hurried to the elevator and stood there, listening to the sound of my own breath heaving, like the bass line to Olivia's shallow, rapid panting. MacRae caught up with us.

"This is Dr. Temple's daughter," I said before he could ask. Olivia had gone limp in my arms. "She was here when I got here. Dr. Temple was already dead." It was, strictly speaking, the truth.

"I'll need to talk to her," he said. "And I'll need to talk to you, too."

"It can't be right now," I told him. "You can see that for yourself." The elevator door opened. I stepped in and turned to face him. He had his mouth open and his arm half raised, but he let the doors slide shut.

A pair of burly mental-health workers were waiting for me in the lobby with a gurney. I set Olivia down, and they strapped her in place. As we went out onto the walk, a police officer emerged from the shrubbery carrying Channing's laptop computer. I realized then how the window in Channing's office had broken—Olivia had thrown the computer through it.

The police officer shouted. MacRae appeared at the open window. The officer held up the laptop. Now Olivia screamed and strained to sit up. She was staring, wild-eyed, at the police officer. One of the straps came loose. One of the men held her down, and the other one snapped the buckle and pulled the strap taut. She was no match for them.

Olivia kept screaming as we ran the quarter mile from the Drug and Alcohol Unit to Admitting. By the time we got up the ramp and inside, her voice was hoarse and her head was thrashing from side to side.

Nurse Dot O'Neill and the admitting doc were expecting us. Nurse O'Neill was a formidable figure of indeterminate middle age, monolithic and apparently without joints. She inspected the slashes on Olivia's arm and didn't seem impressed. She leaned over Olivia and held her by the shoulders. "Ms. Temple, you need to calm down and relax," she said, her voice low and soothing. "We're going to dress your wound and try to help you—"

Olivia spat at her.

Calmly, Nurse O'Neill wiped her face. She gave me an irritated look. The admitting doc nodded, and Nurse O'Neill went to the med room and came back with a hypodermic syringe. She pushed up Olivia's sleeve, steadied herself, and jabbed the needle in. Slowly, she depressed the plunger. Even before the syringe had been withdrawn, Olivia started to go limp. Within moments, her face went from screaming red to pink. She seemed to shrink as her body turned slack. Her eyelids fluttered, and her eyes lost their focus.

I called hospital personnel from the lobby and got Drew's phone number. I stood there, holding the phone to my ear, but I couldn't dial. The numbers I'd written on the pink message pad seemed to swim together. My knees buckled, as if someone had given them a chop from behind. I sat, my head buzzing. How could this be happening again? Another woman I cared for, killed violently.

I barely heard the dial tone disappear, then chimes and the voice, "Please hang up the phone and try your call again. . . ." I could see the door to Channing's office swing open. There, sitting erect in the butterscotch leather chair, my wife, Kate, was staring back at me, eyes wide open. Something about her look made me snap to.

Ralston Bridges had created a scene that pointed to me as my wife's murderer. Was that happening again? Had someone created a scene that was supposed to make it look . . . look like what? Like Channing had killed herself? Only Olivia walked in, just as I had? And like me, she was too late.

When I looked at the piece of paper again, Drew's phone number was in perfect focus. I punched in the numbers. His assistant answered. She put me on hold.

As I held the phone to my ear, I noticed the smell of coffee. I sniffed. It was my hand. I looked down. There was blood all over my shirt, on my trousers. My stomach turned over. But where had I picked up the coffee smell? I didn't remember spilling any on myself while I was waiting for Channing in the cafeteria. Had to have been from somewhere in Channing's office.

Drew's assistant came back on the line. "I'm sorry, he's off-site." She promised to page him and get him to return my call ASAP.

It was another thirty minutes before Drew called back. Apologizing, he said he had his beeper turned off. I told him what had happened. He didn't say anything. Just that he was on his way, and thanks for being there for Olivia.

I was waiting on the front steps when he pulled up in his silver Mercedes and parked in a tow zone. He looked tired, his dark suit rumpled, his ice-blue silk tie loose at the neck. His bloodshot eyes gleamed, slightly manic. That's what it was like, those first few hours. You sped along on some chemical the body produced to make you numb and functional, leaving you unprepared for the full body-slam of grief that would flatten you later. And then, even months later, a little detail, a smell even, could catapult you into despair.

"I'm so sorry," I said. I grasped his hand in mine and put my other hand on his shoulder. What else was there to say?

"Did she suffer?" he asked. He smelled unwashed, musky under a veneer of aftershave.

At least I could answer that with certainty. "No."

Drew pulled away. "Did she leave a note? Anything to explain . . ." He looked haggard, his jowls hanging loose from his jaw.

I told him about the message on her computer screen. "Can't live with myself? I'm so sorry?" He echoed the words in disbelief. "That's it?"

"I didn't see anything else."

"But that explains nothing." He blinked, held his hand over his mouth. "I can't believe . . ."

"Maybe she was under some additional stress?"

Drew looked at me, stone-faced. "She was angry, Peter. Not suicidal."

"Olivia was there," I told him. His face collapsed. "It's not clear when Olivia arrived or what she saw," I said gently.

He just stood there, staring up at the building, his arms dangling useless at his sides. "Olivia's in there?" he asked.

A cell phone rang. Then again. It wasn't until the third ring that Drew roused himself, pulled it out of his pocket, and answered it.

A look of annoyance crossed his face as he listened. He turned away from me and cupped his hand over his mouth.

"I can't talk now," he said, his voice impatient. A pause. "She's dead, all right?" He exhaled a sigh. "I don't know. I'll call you later." Then a softer, gentler "Promise."

He turned back. He seemed confused, as if he didn't know what the next thing should be. "Would you like to see Olivia?" I suggested.

He nodded, grateful. "Is she okay?" he asked.

I licked my lips. "No, she's not."

"She didn't try to—" Drew started.

"She's fine now. She threw a computer through a window and cut herself with broken glass. She's being evaluated."

Drew was already moving up the front steps. I followed him. In Admitting, Dot O'Neill presided from the nurses' station.

"I'm looking for my daughter," Drew said.

"This is Olivia Temple's father," I told her.

She indicated down the hall. "One-twelve."

Drew rushed ahead of me. He pushed open the door to the room and took a step inside before freezing. A nurse and two doctors already filled the small space. Olivia was on the bed. Her forearms were bandaged and her eyes were half closed. The nurse was taking blood while the younger of the two doctors was listening to her chest.

"She's been sedated," I told Drew.

"For God's sake," Drew sputtered, "she's just a kid."

"She tried to harm herself," the older doctor said as he wrote in her chart. He looked at Drew. "You're the young lady's father?"

Drew swallowed. "Yes."

"We have her stabilized. Rapid pulse rate, dilated pupils, high blood pressure, cold sweat." He tilted his head to one side and squinted at Drew. "Do you know if your daughter is taking any drugs or prescription medication? Diet pills?"

Drew looked dazed. "Nothing that I know of. Beyond the occasional No-Doz. You know kids."

The doctor sniffed, waited a beat before saying "Mr. Temple, we found about a half-dozen Ritalin tablets loose in her pocket."

"Ritalin?" Drew seemed genuinely astonished. "I thought that was for hyperactive kids."

"Drew, perhaps her psychiatrist was prescribing it?" I suggested.

"If she was, then I knew nothing about it. And I don't think my wife did either."

The doctor added, "She also had about a half-dozen physician's sample packs. Ritalin, Ativan, Prozac." He made some notes on his clipboard. "We haven't got her blood work back yet, but it looks like she should be admitted to the Drug and Alcohol Rehabilitation Unit."

I tried not to explode. I'd explained the circumstances when I'd checked her in. Couldn't they communicate one thing from the front desk to back here? I swallowed my irritation. "We can't do that," I said. "Her mother ran that unit. And her mother just died. Can you admit her to the Neuropsychiatric Unit?"

"Neuropsychiatric?" Drew asked.

"We were going to evaluate her anyway"—I paused—"to rule out Asperger's." I was improvising. She didn't need to be admitted to rule out Asperger's, but that was the kind of verbiage we needed. "Now, she's made a serious suicide attempt and needs to be in a safe place where she can get the help she needs. She should be admitted under the care of Dr. Kwan Liu."

"Suicidal depression. Rule out Asperger's." The doc wrote as he said the words. Then he shot me a questioning look. "I suppose. If that's what the family wants, given the circumstances."

Drew seemed at a loss for words. Finally, he said to me, "Whatever you think is best. . . ." His voice faded out. "Can I talk to her?"

"You can try," the doctor replied. "She's heavily sedated."

Drew pulled a chair up to the bed. He ran his hand gently across Olivia's face, sweeping back a few strands of hair stuck to her forehead. He leaned close and whispered, "Olivia? Can you hear me?"

There was no response.

He bowed his head. "Oh, Livvy. I'm so sorry all this is happening. I'm so—" His voice broke. He put his hands to his face and shuddered. "It's going to be okay, baby." He pulled a handkerchief from his pocket and blew his nose. "Everything is going to be okay," he said into the handkerchief.

I put my hand on his shoulder. "Do you need anything?" I asked him. "Want me to call anyone?"

He shook his head. I left him sitting there with her.

I WALKED back across the hospital grounds, unaware of anyone or anything except the anger and disbelief roiling inside of me. Why was this happening? I couldn't help wondering, if Channing hadn't shown up at our lecture at the Medical School last week, who would have found her?

When I got to my building, I took a look back across the rolling lawns to the Drug and Alcohol Rehabilitation Unit. The lights atop the emergency vehicles were flashing—police blue, ambulance red and white. I winced as two white-suited men emerged from the building, carrying what looked like a body bag. That's how they'd taken Kate out of our house. Ralston Bridges had gone out on a stretcher, and Kate in black plastic. I'd nearly killed him when I rushed upstairs belatedly to find her already gone, her throat slit. I struck him with an iron rod from Kate's work table. Then I kicked him, over and over. If it hadn't been for my mother, I'd have still been kicking him, long after he was dead.

I turned and pushed my way through the crowd of gawkers standing on the steps. "Do you know what happened?" a woman in a dark coat asked as I squeezed past.

I didn't trust myself to speak, so I just shook my head. They'd all find out, soon enough.

I went upstairs. I wanted to go into my office, close the door, and be alone. But Daphne was in the hall waiting for me, pacing up and down. She was ashen-faced, her eyes rimmed with red. "How's Livvy?" she asked.

I found my voice. "Stabilized. Drew is with her."

I opened my office door and followed her inside. Even though the room was overheated, Daphne shivered as she took a seat and pulled her sweater around her. "It's too awful," she said. "Too bloody awful."

She reached into her skirt pocket and came up with a package of cigarettes. "Do you mind?"

With a trembling hand, she edged a cigarette from the pack. I went around behind my desk to sit, ducking so I wouldn't hit my head on the sloping ceiling. I opened the little window an inch.

Daphne held the cigarette between her lips, took out a lighter and lit up. The tip of the cigarette quivered, then it glowed red as she inhaled. She held her breath and closed her eyes, then exhaled gently. It had the same effect as the shot had for Olivia. Instant calm.

"Olivia didn't do it," Daphne said.

"She was holding the gun," I said.

"Codswallop." The word exploded in a puff of smoke. "There's got to be another explanation." She took a long drag and coughed.

I pushed over an empty mug. "Such as?"

"It seems perfectly obvious. Channing killed herself. Olivia came in, found her. For some reason, she took the gun. We found her holding it by the barrel."

I wanted to scream at her, "Channing would never commit suicide." It wasn't possible. But shoddy research methods and improper behavior were equally impossible. Daphne's explanation did account for the scene I'd stumbled into. "You really think Channing committed suicide?" I asked, keeping my expression bland.

Daphne looked past me.

"Has she seemed distraught?" I asked.

"We talked yesterday." Daphne stared at the cigarette. "I was all wrapped up in my own problems. Nattering on about moving from my house into a flat, now that . . ." She waved the cigarette in the air, leaving behind a scribble of smoke in the air. "It's just the sort of thing Robert used to manage. . . ." She hardened her face, but a tear trickled down her cheek. "Of course, if Robert were still with us, I wouldn't be having to move." She stopped suddenly, as if embarrassed by the stridency in her own voice.

"I'm sorry," I said, feeling as if there should be something more I could say but not knowing what.

"When Robert died, I felt like I'd lost one of my arms," Daphne said. "Now I've lost the other." Smoke pooled at the ceiling. "I should have seen it coming. If only I'd been paying attention."

"Seen what coming?"

"You haven't spent much time with her lately, have you, Peter?" It wasn't an accusation. "Channing was very good at making the world think she'd got everything battened down. But underneath it all . . . she was in crisis. The pressure of her work. The hatchet job they did on her research in *JAMA* that was a profound shock to her. Olivia possibly headed for a psychological break. Drew . . ." Daphne left the name hanging. "She asked me to prescribe some Ativan to quiet her nerves."

It was typical Channing. She could easily have prescribed it for herself, but consulting another doc was more aboveboard. "Lots of people need help once in a while," I said.

"But for Channing? To ask for a sedative?"

I agreed. "She'd have to be pretty upset."

Daphne said, "She clearly was. And perhaps she was taking more than she should have."

We sometimes talk about Ativan as "dehydrated booze" because it affects the same areas of the brain as alcohol. It disinhibits. Throwing a glass of cognac at a colleague seemed very out of character. A sedative turning Channing Temple suicidal? A week earlier, I'd have dismissed the possibility outright. Now I wasn't so sure.

She was under tremendous pressure. Her daughter was troubled. Add to the mix the rumors of impropriety. I realized that the hesitancy I sensed in her when we met after the lecture probably had nothing to do with me and my loss.

"Channing." Daphne breathed the name. She loosened her hold on her sweater and leaned back. "She was remarkable, even as a resident. Bright. Insightful. Honest to a fault." Daphne laughed. "She'd smite me for saying those words. 'Can't be honest to a fault, Daphne. Contradiction in terms,' " Daphne said, her voice flattened out into an American accent. "She's always been an excellent psychiatrist, and I don't see why anyone would say otherwise. Her patients will be devastated. Particularly . . . oh, my." Daphne took a last puff, and then stubbed out the butt against the inside of the cup. "I wonder — "

"What?"

"Channing was working with a young woman. Suicidal. She came to me about it, afraid she was losing her perspective." Daphne focused on a spot somewhere in the air between us. "She felt a strong kinship with this woman. But it dredged up a lot of issues for her. Issues I thought we'd put to rest years ago."

This did make suicide seem a bit more plausible. "You're suggesting Channing was getting too close to this patient?" I asked.

Daphne's eyebrows raised. "Was I?"

"She discussed the case with you?"

Daphne picked at her sweater sleeve, pulling away brown pills. "Well, only in general terms." Maybe Daphne didn't want to add another boundary violation to the pile of true and untrue transgressions Channing could no longer defend herself against. "Peter, I've always had a supervisory relationship with Channing. She was scrupulously discreet, and I have no idea who the patient is. But I can't help wondering if she wasn't experiencing the effects of projective identification."

Projective identification. It was a concept I'd once dismissed as far-fetched — until it happened to me. I was working with a patient who was obsessive about germs. He wore rubber gloves all the time, couldn't stand to be touched. Every night, he boiled all the door-knobs in his apartment. I was seeing him twice a week when I found myself rubbing my own hands together, wiping them over and over against my trousers, unable to shake the feeling that they were dirty. I'm sure the stress I was under made me more suscep-tible—Kate had been dead only four months.

It's something therapists refer to as feeling "lost in familiar places," when you become enmeshed in your patient's feelings, even though you know they have nothing to do with you. If I'd been my own therapist, I could have explained it—something about his need to wash his hands connected to my feelings of guilt, which, like the blood on Kate's studio floor, I couldn't wash away. Sounds so logical, now that I can hold it out at a distance and examine it. At the time, there was nothing logical about it.

Channing was at about the age when her own mother commit-ted suicide, if I remembered correctly. If she was identifying with a suicidal patient, then perhaps stress, combined with the sedating effects of the drug, altered her judgment, reducing her resistance to suggestion even further. I wondered if the autopsy would find more than therapeutic levels of Ativan.

Everything pointed to suicide. I could chew on the possibility, appreciate all the contributing factors, but I couldn't make myself swallow.

"Let's say she was suicidal," I said. "Why pick that particular time to kill herself, when she knew Olivia was about to meet her at her office?"

"I can't explain it, I confess." Daphne rolled a bit of brown sweater fuzz between her thumb and forefinger.

I couldn't explain it either. I couldn't accept it. She'd never have left her daughter to find her, the way she'd found her mother.

"As much experience as I have with human behavior," Daphne said, "there are still moments like this when I find myself at a loss to explain."

We sat there in silence. I was missing a budget meeting that I'd spent an hour yesterday preparing for. Today that seemed unimportant. I turned on the desk lamp. The little pool of light only intensified the surrounding gloom.

"Has Olivia been admitted?" Daphne asked.

"To the Neuropsychiatric Unit."

"Neuropsychiatric?" Daphne exclaimed. "Why on earth—"

She was right. There were better choices—the Adolescent Unit or Affective Disorders Unit would have made more sense. I didn't want to admit that I hadn't considered any of them. Channing had asked me to take care of Olivia, and that was what I was going to do. "We couldn't admit her to the Drug and Alcohol Rehabilitation Unit," I said.

"Still. . . ."

Channing's voice came back to me. *I want another opinion.* She'd been adamant. In the midst of a crisis, Olivia had pulled away from Daphne. I was convinced I'd done the right thing. I just couldn't defend it.

"I know you've been working with her," I said gently. "Channing told me that when she asked me to evaluate Olivia."

"She never mentioned she'd asked you for an opinion." Daphne sounded surprised, hurt.

"To rule out Asperger's syndrome."

Daphne snorted. "Asperger's, my ass."

"I doubt if she's Asperger's," I agreed. "But I suspect she may have some less serious but related difficulty." There were plenty of indications that Olivia was having problems relating emotionally. The mood swings. The flat demeanor. The way she used her flamboyant appearance to keep people away. The friendships that were mediated by computer. "Judging from her actions, she *is* suicidal and needs to be watched. She had drugs in her pocket when she was admitted. Were you prescribing anything?"

"We were trying her on Ritalin," Daphne said.

"Drew said he didn't know she was taking Ritalin."

"Channing may not have told him. We just started trying it."

"Was it helping?"

"Yes. I think it helped her keep focused. That's one of Olivia's problems, you know. She's easily overwhelmed. She needs structure."

"I noticed she makes lists," I said.

Daphne smiled. "That's one of my interventions, a coping strategy to help her keep track of what she needs to do."

I wondered if Daphne had seen Olivia's long lists of items, where large and small activities, important and unimportant, daily and onetime tasks, were thrown together. It was a structure, yes. A linear structure. And if I were Olivia, even one of those lists would have made getting through the day seem even more daunting. I wondered if Daphne had the measure of her patient. Already I suspected she was trying to force-fit Olivia into a preconceived mold. But I didn't have enough information about Olivia yet to know for sure.

I said, "Of course, we'll consult you on her treatment—as soon as Olivia is conscious and I have permission to discuss her case with you."

Daphne's jaw dropped. Then her look hardened. "You'll let me know what I can do to help."

The last thing I wanted was to get into a tug-of-war over Olivia's treatment. "Of course. Right now, we're stabilizing her."

"And the police?" Daphne asked.

"We'll try to keep them away from her as long as we can."

"They think it's suicide. I told them the gun was on the floor by the chair when I got there. You'll say the same, won't you?" I didn't answer. "For Olivia's sake."

It made me uneasy. Given a choice between whether Olivia killed her own mother or Channing killed herself, I'd pick neither. But what did that leave?

• • •

After Daphne left, my phone rang. It was the hospital CFO, Arnold Destler. That wasn't so unusual. What surprised me was that he placed the call himself—usually his assistant called you and then left you hanging while Destler took his good, sweet time picking up. "Peter, I wanted to remind you of the protocol in these situations." These situations? He made it sound like the violent death of a psychiatrist was a routine event. "If the press contacts you, you're to redirect the call to Public Affairs."

I held the phone away from my ear. Where was the caring administrator calling to find out if I was all right? To inquire how Channing's daughter was doing? His number-one concern was predictable: how to spin the news so it wouldn't diminish the institute's reputation.

"Such a shame this had to happen on the hospital grounds," he said.

"I'm sure Channing's daughter and husband share your dismay."

"I don't mean to sound callous. Wherever it happens, it's a terrible tragedy, of course."

"Of course."

"No one will miss Dr. Temple's . . . insights . . . more than I will."

Like hell he would. Channing's so-called insights were a perennial pain in Destler's butt. She saw managed care as a Dante-esque hell, where administrators stood above, taking pleasure in tormenting the rest of us. Civil disobedience was the only response. She was known to lose paperwork, even misplace the occasional patient, just so she wouldn't have to discharge him or her when the need for care didn't conveniently stop when the insurance coverage ran out.

"Just wondering, you were there, weren't you?" he said.

"I found her."

"You spoke to the police."

"Of course."

"And did you get the impression that it was . . . "

"That it was what?"

He cleared his throat. "Suicide?"

From Destler's point of view, suicide was a better verdict than accident. No liability. No messy lawsuits. Far better than murder and all the endless speculation and nasty publicity that would accompany that.

"Beats me," I said, and hung up.

THAT NIGHT I had a restless sleep. At five I was awake, fumbling with the coffeemaker. I must have dozed off sitting at my kitchen table, because I was jolted awake by the sound of Channing's voice, urging me to "Run, run, run, run. . . ." Turned out to be the sound of the last of the water, steaming onto the spent grounds.

Run. That's what Channing always did when she needed clarity. When we met, she was a fitness nut, and I could have been a Charles Atlas "before" ad. But by the time we graduated college, I was running with her every dawn, and I could almost keep up and remain conversational.

After that, I kept running, every winter, whenever I couldn't get out on the river. And then, after Kate died, it became a compulsion. For an hour each day, my body was occupied.

I threw on some sweats, strapped on my portable CD player and let myself out. I was locking my door when my mother opened hers and peered out at me. My mother lives in the other half of the two-family side-by-side that Kate and I bought just after we were married. My parents moved in after my father got sick. He died about a year later.

My mother had on a pink quilted bathrobe, her white hair

wrapped in a gauzy scarf. She looked tired and concerned. I knew it wasn't just the early hour. We were both often up before the birds. "I saw the paper," she said. "Wasn't that doctor your friend?"

"I found her," I said. My mother gasped. "Her daughter was there, too."

"Daughter?"

"Seventeen years old."

My mother squeezed her eyes shut. "Such things shouldn't happen." Then she eyed me. "You're doing for that little girl?"

"I'm doing for her."

"Good," my mother said, and disappeared into her side of the house.

I jogged to the river. Soon I was running along Mem. Drive, watching one sneakered foot and then the other hit the pavement, a Richard Thompson CD playing in my ears. The river was slate gray, not a ripple on it. Nothing more than a shadowy outline suggested that the Hancock Tower was on the Boston side of the river. Mist coated my face.

I was barely a mile into my run, and already I felt steam rising off my body, stifling inside the heavy sweatshirt. Perspiration was dripping into my eyes. I wiped my arm across my forehead. Physical discomfort can be very reassuring, pinning you securely in the moment.

That's what I wanted. The physical present and nothing else. I tried to get there, to sync my strides to the beat of the music, to feel each foot hit the ground and the shock wave rise up my shin and then ripple from knee to hip. I pulled off my sweatshirt and tied it around my waist, yearning for even five minutes when all I could think about was my body and the effort it took to keep going. I could hear Channing's patient voice: "Talk to me. That way I'll know you're breathing."

But instead of anchoring me in the present, I found myself replaying the phone call I'd gotten last night from Drew. First, he'd asked about Olivia. His speech was slurred, one word slopping up against the next. He'd probably been drinking. I told him she was stable but still sedated.

He asked if I knew when Channing's body might be released, so they could make plans for cremation and a memorial service. I had no idea, but I offered to call and find out what I could. The logistics of death are a wonderful thing—they provide a rhythm, a driving force for getting you through those first few horrendous days. They move the body and the brain forward when the spirit wants to roll over and surrender.

"How did she look?" Drew had asked. "Her face. Did she look frightened?"

I didn't want to turn my mind back, to remember, but I closed my eyes and tried. "No," I could honestly say, "she seemed peaceful. At rest, even."

Drew gave an exhausted sigh. "Thank God for that at least."

I asked Drew if he'd eaten any dinner. He dismissed the question. The worst part, he said, was being alone. Even the housekeeper, overcome with grief, had gone home to her own family. "I'll be all right," Drew said. "I made up the bed in Channing's study. She's here, you know. Her books. Her papers. Her smell." I could picture him, curled up like a little kid in a blanket on the sofa bed. "It's my fault," he said, and noisily blew his nose. "I've been having an affair." He added quickly, "It meant nothing."

That was the problem with suicide. Everyone wanted to take credit. Shoulder the guilt. Daphne blamed herself for not paying attention. Olivia had said it was all her fault. Now Drew was doing the same. Survivors engage in an endless game of If-Only-I'd.

"You should see your doctor," I said. "Don't be stoic. Let him prescribe something to get you through the worst of this."

"I called. He can't see me until day after tomorrow."

"Take it easy on the booze," I said. "You're depressed. Alcohol only makes you more so."

"It's all I have," he said.

Many psychiatrists have a bathroom cabinet full of samples

dropped off by generous pharmaceutical salespeople. But Channing wouldn't. It was a side of medicine that infuriated her, another example of the incestuous relationship drug companies and physicians shared.

Then I remembered—Daphne said Channing was taking Ativan. I described what the pills looked like. "I'm not a physician," I said. "I can't tell you to take them. But I can tell you that one or two twenty-five–milligram tablets will probably help, and the side effects are minimal, but don't take one now. Wait until the morning, when you've slept it off."

This morning, I couldn't get Drew off my mind. I'd always thought he and Channing had had a good marriage. Perhaps no fireworks, but a solid partnership. Then I recalled the young, dark-haired woman in the pastel suit at Channing's party. Surely Channing hadn't known. She might not have been able to stop the affair, but she'd never have tolerated the woman's presence at her own birthday party.

By now, I was approaching the MIT Boathouse. My body felt like a mess of ill-fitting parts, the muscles dragging the bones, the joints complaining. I pulled the headphones down around my neck. My warm breath filled the hollow in my chest. Even without the music, Richard Thompson's words kept ringing in my ears. "The ghost of you walks right through my head. . . ."

I approached the Harvard Bridge and pushed past the ache in my legs, finally feeling the endorphins kicking in and starting to blow the pain away. I put the headphones back on and cranked up the volume, trying to fill my head with sound so my mind could empty. I crossed the bridge, building momentum, and effortlessly whipped around the downward spiral onto the Boston side.

When I'd asked Drew if Channing had been depressed by the *JAMA* article, he'd scoffed. "Depressed, bullshit! Pissed. Energized. She was planning to fight back. I told her she was tilting at windmills. She didn't care. She was going to go after the drug companies and anyone else who challenged her, and she was relishing the fight." That didn't sound suicidal to me.

When I got to work, I checked in with Gloria. "I can't tell," she said, when I asked her how Olivia was doing. "In shock. Or else she's shutting us out."

"Did she eat anything?"

"Not much."

I went to Olivia's room. The door was ajar. I knocked. "Hello?" I said. Then louder, "Olivia?"

No answer. I pushed the door open and put my head in. "Good morning."

A small suitcase sat on a table, open but not unpacked. The bathroom door was ajar. Olivia was nowhere to be seen.

I checked the common area. Matthew Farrell was sitting at the ebony grand piano, picking out a wooden-sounding version of "The Entertainer." Mr. Fleegle sat in a chair, tapping his toe and nodding to what little rhythm there was. The television in the far corner delivered its weather report to an otherwise empty room.

I returned to the nurses' station and announced, "She's not there."

Gloria gave me a pitying look. "Looked real hard, didn't you. She's there. I just checked on her a minute ago."

"Then she's invisible."

"Did you check the closet?"

"Of course. The closet. Now why didn't I think of that?"

"She's been in there since, well, since I got here."

I returned to Olivia's room. In the corner was a tall, narrow wardrobe. I tapped on the door and slowly pulled it open. Olivia was jammed inside, crouched down, hugging her knees to her chest. Her face was turned away from me.

I squatted beside her. Her forearm was bandaged. Her body was taut, every muscle straining to hold herself in a tight ball. Crumpled tissues were piled on the floor.

"Olivia," I said gently.

She didn't respond.

"I see your father brought you some clothes. Do you want help unpacking?"

Still nothing.

I knew ordering her out of the wardrobe would only cause her to shrink further into herself. I thought for a moment. "Does it work?" I asked.

Her head gave a little jerk.

"Does it work?" I repeated.

Slowly she lifted her head and turned her face to me. Her eyes were rimmed with red. Her skin looked white against the black hair. She looked at me as if I had two heads, but gave a dull shrug.

"Can I try it?" I asked.

A tiny smile tugged at the corner of her lips.

Encouraged, I continued, "I don't think there's room for both of us in there. Why don't you get out and let me have a go at it."

She was watching me, evaluating. Finally, she put out a tentative foot and then emerged from the wardrobe. She stood aside, arms crossed.

I wedged myself into the closet and, by flexing my knees, I could just get my head in. I felt like a size-fourteen foot in a size-nine sneaker.

"Does it work better with the door shut?" I croaked.

She nodded.

"Well, go ahead then. Let's give it a try."

She had to push hard against the door to get it to shut. I stood there, inhaling the dust of crumbling fiberboard, feeling the walls close around me, bands of light sliding in through the louvers in the door. Good thing I've never had a problem with tight quarters. Still, I was relieved when she pulled the door open and peered in at me.

"Thanks," I said, and extricated myself, being careful to unsnag my belt loop from the door latch. "I guess not much bad can happen in there."

Olivia went over to the bed and sat up against a pile of pillows.

She glanced around the room, from the gray window shade that spanned a large barred window to the small nondescript chest of drawers, to the heavyweight door with its curved aluminum handle. "Mom and I were going to go shopping," she said.

"Do you want to talk about what happened yesterday?"

"She promised me. We were going to Beadworks in the Square."

"Olivia, I can hold the police off for a couple of days. At least until you're back to some equilibrium. But there's a detective who's going to want to talk to you. It's not going to take him too long to figure out that your fingerprints are on the gun."

"You think I killed my mother?" The words floated in the air, emotionless.

"No, I don't," I said slowly.

Olivia twisted one of the rings on her thumb. She pulled it off, chewed on it, and put it back on. "We were going to get the cobalt beads, and the turquoise. . . ." she murmured.

"It would help if I knew what happened," I persisted.

A tear squeezed out of Olivia's eye. "I don't know what happened," she said. "I was supposed to meet her in her office. I was late. I'm always late. She hates that about me." A tear appeared at the corner of the other eye.

"Did you hear the gunshot?" I asked.

Olivia looked away. Then she squinted up at me. "No, I didn't. When I got there, she was . . ." She stopped, unable to form the next word.

"And where was the gun?"

"In her hand."

"Why did you take it?"

Olivia stared at her own hands. "We were going to go to the bead store," she whimpered. She turned away from me and curled up into a ball. "I want all different colors," she said in a monotone, "and I don't want to talk to cops. No cops." Olivia started humming under her breath.

"Olivia, I'd like to call Dr. Smythe-Gooding."

Olivia hummed louder and curled tighter.

"I need your permission to talk to Dr. Smythe-Gooding," I said, my voice clear and intense.

She mumbled something.

"What was that? I can't hear you."

She rolled back to face me, wide-eyed with anxiety. "No," the word exploded. "She's a sick bitch."

I tried to keep my face neutral. "If you're not going to talk to me, and you won't let me talk to Dr. Smythe-Gooding, then how am I going to figure out how to help you?"

Olivia contemplated me. I could feel the wheels turning, calculating. "It's hereditary, isn't it?"

"What?" I asked, though I was pretty sure I knew what the *it* was.

"Suicide."

I could have given her a canned response: No, suicide does not run in families. So definite and reassuring. But the research didn't support it. I hedged. "A lot of people would like to know the answer to that question. It's true, the risk of suicidal behavior is increased by a family history of suicide. But it's never the result of a single factor." I pulled up a chair to the bed and put my face close to hers. "That's a long way from saying that because someone's mother committed suicide, because their grandmother committed suicide, they're going to do it, too. There's nothing inevitable about it."

She stared at her bandaged arm. "I want to die," she whispered.

I ran the words I could not ignore forward and backward through my mind. I didn't think she meant it, but still I had to ask. "Do you mean that literally, or is this a feeling that things are overwhelming?"

She picked at the bandage and sniffled. "Everything seems so . . . so hopeless."

It wasn't enough to call off the suicide police. "Do you have a plan?"

She looked at me with a flicker of amusement. "You going to make me sign a contract?" she said. She must have heard her mother talk about going through this drill with patients. "You've already got them checking on me every two minutes."

I leaned back. "I can't take you off five-minute checks until I feel comfortable that you're not a danger to yourself. I don't think we need a written contract. But you have to promise me you won't try to kill yourself while you're here. And if you have any active thoughts of doing so, you'll tell me or one of the staff immediately."

She swallowed. "I promise," she said solemnly.

I looked at her appraisingly. "Olivia, I also want to know about the pills you've been taking. How long have you been taking Ritalin?"

"Maybe a couple of months," she said vaguely.

"And where did you get the pills?"

"Get? Uh . . . well, I . . ." she stammered, picking at the bedcovers. She stared at me. "Dr. Daffy." The disdainful tone took me aback. *Bad chemistry* was how Channing had described Olivia and Daphne's relationship.

"She started you on Ritalin?"

Olivia nodded. "To see if it would help."

"Help what?"

"My black mood, as Mother puts it." She squeezed her eyes shut and grimaced, as if her own words sucker punched her. It would take her a while to absorb the seismic shift her mother's death would make in the way she saw the world.

"Were you having trouble concentrating?" I asked.

Olivia shrugged. "I guess."

"How much Ritalin were you supposed to take?"

"A pill in the morning and another with dinner," she said, addressing her lap.

"And that's what you were taking?"

Olivia looked away. "Yes." It wasn't very convincing.

Her blood work showed higher levels of Ritalin than a therapeutic dosage. I wondered how long she'd been slipping herself extra pills. It can be a vicious cycle. Excessive doses over a period of time can produce habituation. Before you know it, you need two or three as much to achieve the same effect.

"Have you been taking anything else?"

"Just Ritalin."

"When they admitted you, they found other drugs in your pockets."

"*Just Ritalin,*" she said, glaring at me.

"So what were you doing with . . ." I tried to remember what else had been found on her.

"For my friends. Easy stuff to sell." She seemed unconcerned.

Channing would have been apoplectic. When it suited her goals, Channing had no problem flouting authority. She considered that civil disobedience. But this was breaking the law, another thing entirely. I wondered if Olivia saw it that way. Or was she using drugs as entrée to kids with whom she felt like an outsider?

"We're going to wean you off the Ritalin," I told her. Olivia looked frightened. "Gradually. We need to find out what you're like drug-free. Then we'll evaluate."

Her eyes went left and right, and back again. "Why can't I keep taking Ritalin? I need it."

"I know right now you feel you need it, but it's not at all clear that it's making you better. It could even be causing some of the problems you're having. Meanwhile, we're going to make sure that nothing bad happens to you. That's why you're here."

From the white-knuckled grip she had on the blankets, she didn't seem reassured.

MACRAE WAS leaving me phone messages, every hour on the hour. He wanted to interview Olivia, and he wanted me to come in and give a statement. I hoped he'd be happy with half a loaf. I canceled an afternoon meeting and drove to police headquarters in Central Square. MacRae fetched me from the busy front desk.

I followed him through a maze of corridors to the Investigations Division. His office was a surprisingly neat six-foot cubicle. One wall was covered with Post-it notes. On the desk a standing rack contained a tidy row of manila file folders, the tabs labeled in blue marker. The way a person keeps his office can be as revealing as the way he interprets an inkblot. He pulled in a wooden chair from a neighboring cubicle.

Solid and broad-shouldered, MacRae even sitting looked as if a touch in the right place would send him springing out of his chair. He turned on a tape recorder and asked me to say who I was and then to tell what happened. I told him everything, except the part about Olivia holding the gun. Then I asked him if they'd picked up any leads from the crime scene.

"Gunshot wound to the head," he said. "No bruising or other signs of force. It was her own gun. Powder residue on her hand."

He was laying out the case, watching my reaction. "So it looks like suicide."

"They're doing an autopsy?" I asked.

"It's been done. We'll have the results in a couple of days. Tomorrow, maybe."

"The body?"

"Already transferred to the mortuary."

My throat constricted. I tried to get my voice, to swallow. I pushed away the image of Channing, cold and still on a metal slab.

"I'm sorry," MacRae said. "I know she was a friend of yours."

I nodded, mute. I made a mental note to call Drew and check that he knew the body had been moved.

MacRae pivoted away from me, giving me a moment to collect myself. He picked up a folder from the top of his desk and pivoted back. He opened the folder and spread out some pictures. "I'd like you to look at the photos we took in Dr. Temple's office—just to be sure that everything is exactly as you remember it."

There were shots of various parts of the room, the desktop, and, of course, Channing herself. I stared at the eight-by-ten glossies and tried to shut down my insides.

"You noticed a coffee spill?" I asked, the detail floating out of nowhere.

"We analyzed the spill on the carpet and the traces left in the mug. Just coffee."

"Dr. Temple wasn't a coffee drinker."

"You think someone else was with her?"

"Maybe." The picture closest to me was of Channing. "She was sitting up when I got there," I said.

"Was she holding the gun?" he asked.

"No," I said. At least I could answer that question honestly.

He pointed to the next photograph. It was of the top of Channing's desk. There were the purple folders, the letter opener, the paperweight. "The computer was there, on the desk," I said, indicating the empty space. "And that's another thing. Channing was barely computer literate. I very much doubt that she'd know how to program a screen saver with a particular message."

"Screen saver?"

I glanced at MacRae's computer screen. "Like that," I said. His screen saver was hard at work—yellow scene-of-the-crime tape criss-crossing the screen. "Only on hers, there were words scrolling across the screen."

MacRae gave me a blank look.

"It was programmed to say something like 'I'm sorry. I can't live with myself,'" I explained. MacRae looked annoyed, scratched a note. "Sorry, I thought you knew."

"How about you just assume that I know nothing." He glared at me. "That shouldn't be too difficult."

Ouch. He was right. I'd underestimated him before. I'd try not to do it again.

"And another thing," I said. "As someone who knew the devastation suicide leaves behind, Channing Temple was the last person who'd assume that a one-liner was an adequate suicide note."

"That's your opinion?"

I just looked at him. He'd underestimated me, as well, during our last encounter. I hoped we weren't starting a replay.

"Anything else?" he asked.

I stared at the photograph. Something else was missing. I closed my eyes and tried to remember. "There was a cup on the desk," I said.

"It was on the floor when we got there. Maybe someone knocked it over when the coffee got spilled."

"No. The mug I saw was empty. And it was on the desk."

"What did it look like?"

"It was another Acu-Med mug, like this one."

MacRae looked skeptical. "And you don't think it's the one we found on the floor?"

He could be stubborn and myopic when he set his mind to it. "That one had traces of coffee in it. You told me that yourself." My voice was strident. "Channing didn't drink coffee."

MacRae blinked and wrote himself another note.

I stared at the next photograph, a close-up of a small, silver-handled handgun resting on the carpet alongside the chair.

"Anything you neglected to tell us?" he asked, his eyes drilling holes into me.

If I was going to tell him about Olivia holding the gun, this was the time to do it. "Why do you ask?"

He grunted and pressed his thumb down on the gun in the picture. "Just answer the question."

"I don't think so."

"Tampering with evidence is a serious offense," he said. "The gun is covered with fingerprints, and they're not all Dr. Temple's."

"I didn't touch the gun."

"Ri-ight," MacRae drew the word out. He narrowed his eyes at me. "You sure there's nothing else you want to tell me?"

I tried not to falter, but I probably responded too quickly. "I spoke with her husband last night. He thinks suicide is unlikely."

"In my experience, anyone can commit suicide," MacRae countered.

I shook my head. "In my experience, not."

He tented his fingers and leaned back in his chair.

I went on, "There are some people whose sense of self is too solid to allow them to kill themselves, and Dr. Temple was one of those people."

"That's not what I hear," MacRae said, raising his finger tent a few inches higher. "Sounds more like she was falling to pieces."

I felt anger rise out of my chest. "Who told you that?"

"People at the hospital. Didn't her mother commit suicide?"

"So what if she did?"

"Maybe you didn't know her as well as you think you did."

I wanted to shout, *And maybe you don't know her at all.* Instead, I clenched my teeth and told myself that he was just doing his job. This was nothing personal. "Anything else?" I asked.

He sat forward, put the photographs back in the folder and

shoved them into the top desk drawer. "You won't mind having your prints taken while you're here?"

"No problem."

"And Olivia Temple." He said it as if it were all caps and underlined. "We need to question her. As soon as possible."

"Give her a few more days. Please. Right now, she's too fragile. She's recovering from an overdose of Ritalin, and she's still in shock from her mother's death."

"Peter," MacRae said, his voice weary, "we could help one another here."

Or we could just keep butting horns. From our last encounter, I had reason to believe that underneath his policeman's badge beat the heart of a human being. "How about you come to the hospital next week," I said. "She should be stabilized by then. I expect the funeral will be over."

"Next week?" He made it sound as if that were a decade away.

"You'll get more out of her if you wait."

Reluctantly, he pulled out an appointment book and slapped it open on the desk. Just then the phone rang. MacRae answered it. He turned away from me, cupped the receiver, and talked quietly into the phone. Listened. Then he stood and took the receiver around to the opposite side of the cubicle wall, stretching the spiral phone cord taut.

The facing pages of his datebook were dense with scribbled appointments. But the writing that jumped out at me was in yesterday's slot: *Annie—8:00.* I told myself it wasn't *my* Annie, and if it was, it was probably business. She was a PI; he was a detective. And even if it was for pleasure, it was only once.

He was still on the phone. I quietly lifted the page and peeked at last week's calendar. There Annie's name was again, a week ago Saturday. Annie and MacRae? Had they become an item while I'd been messing around?

Sure, he and Annie had grown up together. Their families had once been close, but I thought in recent years they'd been estranged. I remembered Annie telling me how her father, a union activist, had been badly beaten while he was in jail after a demonstration. It broke his spirit as well as his body. MacRae's father was a cop. Annie thought he knew which cops had done it, but wouldn't say. Friendship took a backseat to loyalty to the force. The rift between the families had been permanent. Or had it? Perhaps there'd been a reconciliation after all these years. Why not?

I sat back and stared at the wall. There was picture of a boy, maybe ten years old. He was wearing shorts and a T-shirt, holding a soccer ball, and grinning at the camera. It had never occurred to me that MacRae actually might have a child. An ex-wife somewhere, too? I wondered if he was still dating that nurse from the rehab hospital. And what exactly was his relationship to Annie?

"Okay, I'll call you tomorrow," MacRae said as he came back into his cubicle. "Right, right."

He hung up the phone.

"So you'll come to the Pearce on Tuesday to interview Olivia Temple," I said, eyeing him warily.

"What's wrong with Monday?"

"Nothing's wrong with Monday. I'll make the arrangements."

As I was leaving, I paused to look more closely at the photograph of the young soccer player, as if I'd just noticed. "Your boy?" I asked.

He nodded proudly. "He's older now."

"Still playing soccer?"

"Yup."

"What position?"

"Sweeper. He's one tough hombre. Gets that from me. That's one of the few things my ex and I agree on."

"If you see that nurse from the rehab hospital, send her my regards." I tried to sound nonchalant, uninterested.

"Haven't seen her for months," he said. "But will do, if I run into her."

As I shook MacRae's hand, I tried to imagine Annie in the cubicle with us. I knew she was shorter than I was, but was she taller than MacRae? It was a close call. If his handshake was any indication, I sure as hell wouldn't want to arm wrestle him.

• • •

When I got home that night, there was a message from Annie on my machine. "Hey, Peter, it's me. I heard on the news. Just calling to see if you're okay. Is there anything I can do? Oh, hell, I know you. You're going to tell me you're fine. Everything's fine. I'll drop by tonight." There was a pause. "Don't eat before I get there."

I flipped on the porch light. A while later, the doorbell rang. It was Annie. I smelled the pizza before I saw the big, flat box from Il Panino, the best North End pizzeria, which now had an outpost in Cambridge. She had a six-pack of Sam Adams, too.

We sat at my kitchen table, and by the time I was chewing on the final crust, I'd brought Annie up-to-date on the latest.

Annie touched her hand to my face. "I wish there was something I could do or say that would help."

I covered her hand with mine. "Being here helps," I said. "Therapists like to say, 'Knowledge binds depression.' Talking to you helps me make sense of what's happened, so it doesn't feel so much like the world's spun out of control." I sighed. "Again."

After Kate was killed, I would have admitted no friends bearing pizza. Not even Channing. I'd wanted to be alone, where my conscience could eat at me from inside.

Annie pondered in silence. "You don't think Olivia killed her mother, do you?"

"I don't. But I don't much like the alternative."

"I barely knew her, but sometimes you can have a strong impression of someone. Channing didn't strike me as the kind of person who'd commit suicide."

"A senior psychiatrist, a woman who's been her mentor since her residency, told me she thought Channing had developed an unhealthy transference to a suicidal woman patient," I said.

"Transference?"

"Channing identified so strongly with her patient's feelings of despair that she experienced them herself."

"And that's why she killed herself?"

"That's what this person was suggesting as a partial explanation."

Annie hung there with her mouth open. "Wait a minute. Are you telling me that destructive feelings are just floating around and you can catch them?" Annie asked. "Like the flu?" I nodded. "Sounds like an X-File."

"I guess it sounds pretty out there. But it does happen. A good therapist has to be able to walk in another person's shoes. When you empathize too much, you can end up with feelings that aren't your own. Even acting on those feelings."

Annie put her hands on her hips. "Next thing, you'll be trying to sell me a bridge." When she saw I was serious, she downshifted. "Okay, so let's suppose for a minute you're right. Why didn't she leave a note? She's got a seventeen-year-old daughter and she doesn't leave an explanation? I mean, a few words on a computer screen explain nothing."

"I agree. It doesn't add up. Channing never got over her anger at her own mother for taking the easy way out, as she called it. She'd be furious if people thought she'd committed suicide, too."

"So you can't let them think that."

"But then they'll think Olivia did it."

"You can't let them think that either."

"Somehow, this has become my problem, hasn't it?"

"I think that's how you wanted it," Annie observed. She had the makings of a fine psychologist.

"But if Channing didn't kill herself," I said, "and Olivia didn't do it . . ."

"Then someone else did and engineered it to look like suicide. Did she have enemies?"

I barked a laugh. "A few. And I can't help wondering if all the rumors about her lack of clinical judgment, the drubbing she took in *JAMA*, if they're not all connected somehow."

"A plot," Annie said.

I knew she was pointing out how far-fetched this was starting to sound. But to me, it was just starting to make sense. "Dr. Smythe-Gooding suggested Channing was taking too much anxiety medication. In high doses, over a long enough period of time, that could have altered her judgment."

Annie said what I was thinking: "I wonder if they have the autopsy results back yet?"

"I was over talking to MacRae today. He said they might have the final results tomorrow."

Annie nodded. "I can get them. They probably have preliminary results now, even if they're not in final format."

I pictured Annie and MacRae cozy in his office, reading the preliminary report together. Before I could stop myself, I said, "I forgot. You have an in over there."

Immediately, I wished I could have reeled the words back in. As Gloria would have noted, I sounded like a bull elephant.

Annie recoiled. "And what's that supposed to mean?"

"I dunno," I mumbled. "Just that you and he seem to be finding a lot of opportunities to . . . collaborate."

Annie shook her head. "I haven't had anyone else monopolizing my time, exactly," she said pointedly.

I winced. Bad enough she was seeing someone else. But did it have to be MacRae? It wasn't just because he'd gotten the better of me in a fistfight—I'd ended up inhaling duck shit, my nose pressed into the boat dock and his foot grinding into my ass.

I said, "I thought you told me you two didn't have much in common, other than cops in the family."

"His father died awhile back," Annie said. "My mother and I went to the funeral. They got together, my mom and Mrs. MacRae, and it was like old times. They're both widows now. Getting back their friendship at this point in their lives is a gift."

"And what about you and MacRae?" I heard the words before I'd decided to say them.

Annie crossed her arms over her chest and gazed at me. "He

and I go way back," Annie said. "Though you know the question doesn't even deserve a response. And it's also none of your business." Her eyes flashed with anger.

I couldn't see it. How could she be attracted to me and be interested in him at the same time? "If you don't think it's any of my business, then I guess you're right. It isn't."

"What did you think I was going to do? Wait around, cooling my heels while you make up your mind whether you're ready for someone in your life?" I opened my mouth but nothing came out. Annie stood. "I'd better be going, before one of us says something we'll regret." She carried her glass to the sink. "Keep the beer."

Long after the front door shut, I sat there staring at the pair of unopened bottles of Sam Adams sitting forlorn on my kitchen table, my self-righteousness dissipating like a bad smell in the room. I felt like a jerk.

I WAS reviewing charts at the nurses' station Wednesday morning when Kwan appeared. Then, Jess hurried by, back straight, a tissue in her fist.

"Incompetence," Kwan growled. "Why is it that nothing gets done around here unless you do it yourself?"

Gloria stalked over to us. "Bully," she said to Kwan.

"Come on, Gloria, she's unreliable," he appealed. Gloria's mouth tightened, skepticism pulling it down at the corners. "Out of her depth."

"And what did she do?" I asked.

"It's what she didn't do," Kwan answered. "She was supposed to enroll Lydia Small in the Zercnidine trial," Kwan said. "Yesterday."

Grief-stricken over Channing's death, Jess had left Monday afternoon and called in sick Tuesday. She'd returned today, only to face Kwan's wrath.

"Can't she still do it?" I asked.

Gloria answered, "You haven't heard? Last night Mrs. Small fell and broke her hip. She's been transferred to the General. Painful for Mrs. Small. Inconvenient for someone who shall go unnamed."

If we'd been talking about anything else, Kwan would have had a snappy comeback that would have defused the tension. Instead, he lowered his voice. "If she's not going to do her job, she's not going to make a good psychiatrist. We can't allow our emotions to rule. People's lives are at stake here."

"People's lives or your research?" Gloria asked.

"Right now it's my research that's keeping this unit in the black." Kwan gave us both a hard look.

"That may be," Gloria retorted. "But I know for a fact it doesn't do squat for patient care. You're here the same amount of time you always are, only now you're juggling drug trials along with your patient load. You can't tell me one thing doesn't affect the other."

"It doesn't look good when we can't fulfill our study enrollment," Kwan huffed. "And *that* doesn't do squat for the hospital's reputation as a leading research institution."

He marched off, fuming.

"He can be such an asshole," Gloria muttered.

"I heard that," Kwan shot back over his shoulder.

I sighed. I hoped the old Kwan, the one with a sense of perspective, wasn't on permanent leave.

I started down the hall, intending to go up to my office. Protecting the hospital's reputation—it was the same excuse Liam Jensen trotted out to keep Channing from airing something in public. A death. I wondered whose. Perhaps an adverse event that Jensen was all too willing to overlook?

I paused outside an oversize closet we use as a shared office for the half-dozen or so temporary and part-time staff on the unit. Jess was sitting there, staring at a blank computer screen.

"His bark is worse than his bite," I said. I entered the room and sat down.

She lifted a trembling hand to her face. "He's right. I haven't been doing my job. I've been letting my personal feelings interfere."

"Grief is a legitimate emotion, even for a psychiatrist. Don't be so hard on yourself."

"I can't believe she's dead," Jess said, her voice raspy and quiet. She was weeping. Tears flowed freely down her face. "I can't eat.

I can't sleep. I can't focus on my patients. I haven't been able to think about anything else."

"Channing was more than a mentor to you."

Jess stared at the windowless wall. "Channing has been my anchor, my safe haven, all through my mother's illness."

"Your mother's been ill?" I asked.

"Early onset Alzheimer's. She was only fifty years old. A psychologist. She diagnosed herself, a year ago Thanksgiving, long before her doctors even admitted that she was sick."

I'd seen too many families try to cope with the incomprehensible brutality of Alzheimer's, watching a soul slip away while the body remained vital and strong. "I'm sorry," I said. "A terrible waste."

"I remember when she stopped practicing. It was the day she came home with a black eye. Blamed it on her own poor judgment. She'd gone in to evaluate an agitated patient and sat down with him between her and the door. When he exploded, she couldn't get out.

"My father and I tried to keep her home." Jess swiped the heel of her hand across one cheek, then the other. "But she was deteriorating fast. We hired caregivers during the day, but I never knew when there was going to be a crisis and I'd have to rush home. Seemed like every other minute I was dealing with someone flipping out.

"I could talk to Channing about how angry it made me, having to stretch myself thin, sacrifice any personal life, and at the same time how much I loved my mother. Putting her into an institution was one of the hardest things I've ever done."

Jess touched the old-fashioned gold locket she was wearing on a chain around her neck. She rubbed the engraved surface between her thumb and forefinger. "Channing helped me get past the guilt. She was a friend, and more."

Jess's bond with Channing sounded intense and personal. Jess idolized her. I wondered, what was Jess to Channing? A fledgling to be helped along? A daughter to be nurtured?

"I guess that's why this is hitting you so hard," I said. "You're grieving for a friend, but you're already emotionally raw from your mother's illness. It must feel like you're reliving that loss as well."

Jess put her hand over her eyes. "I keep wanting to pick up the phone"—her voice broke—"call her."

I touched her arm. "Do you feel up to working with patients?" I asked.

"I'm a psychiatrist," Jess said, her voice ragged. She put her head back and ran her hands through her hair, intertwining the fingers behind her neck. "I'm supposed to know how to control my emotions. That's one of the things I've learned from my mother and from Channing. How to behave like a professional." She straightened. "I need to work."

"That's good. Because we need you to work."

Jess gave me a weak smile.

• • •

I was on my way back to my office when Gloria and Kwan intercepted me. "Destler just called," Gloria said. "He wants to see the three of us in his office. Now."

"Shit," I said. I'd heard about unit heads and their staffs getting the Summons. It was never good news. Had punching holes in our conference-room walls been a prelude to something worse? I looked at my colleagues. I'd resign before I'd let them decimate our staff.

"His underground must be working overtime," Gloria said. "He's probably heard we're under census."

Kwan expanded his chest and tugged on the ends of his jacket. "It appears the barbarians are at the gates again. Time to rally the troops." That was the Kwan I knew and cherished.

• • •

The three of us trudged across the campus to the Administration Building, through the massive double doors and up the wide marble staircase to Destler's office. Virginia Hedgewick sat at her desk. She glanced up and pushed her wire-rimmed glasses to the bridge of her small, pointy nose. A fireplug of a woman who wore boxy suits and sturdy shoes, Virginia had been at the Pearce for more years than anyone could remember, though she hadn't aged a day since I'd first met her ten years ago. She was affectionately known as The Hedgehog, in part because she looked like one, and in part because she'd rolled herself into a ball, figuratively speaking, while the institution changed around her. How she'd ended up as administrative assistant to the CFO of the hospital was a source of wide speculation.

"Sorry about the last-minute summons," she said, glancing up at the wall clock. "I congratulate us all. You're practically on time. He's here, of course, but that's because he pulled another all-nighter. I know you folks always say that it's not healthy to be a workaholic, but if you ask me, Dr. Destler thrives on it."

She opened the door to the inner sanctum. Destler was standing as we trooped in, his hands behind his back. He reminded me of a fat, round white peach with his pale pink skin and blue eyes rimmed by reddish eyelids. The room was thick with his sweetish odor, as though he carried a pocketful of aging apple cores.

From a Sargent portrait hanging behind Destler's massive mahogany desk, Miss Wilhelmina Pearce, granddaughter of Silas Pearce, the benefactor of the institute, stared down at us. Long strands of pearls cascaded over her ample bosom.

We sat. Destler remained on his feet. He had a chart on a metal easel alongside his desk. "This is excellent," Destler enthused, not wasting a moment to acknowledge the tragedy that had occurred less than forty-eight hours earlier. "I'm glad you're all here. Sorry about the last-minute notice."

"Good news?" I said, hoping to smoke whatever it was out into the open.

"As you know, over the last four years we've come through a difficult period." That was an understatement. The average stay at the hospital had shrunk from a year to twenty days. Managed-care patients had replaced most of our wealthy clientele. "We're constantly fine-tuning."

He turned to his chart. The last column was labeled COST

EFFECTIVENESS, and it had red and black checks all the way down. I scanned quickly to find our unit. We were at the bottom with a red check-minus. I didn't need his M.B.A. to know that wasn't good.

Destler tapped an anemic-looking green bar on his chart. "I'm afraid throughput on the Neuropsychiatric Unit is lower than anywhere else in the hospital."

Throughput was The Number at senior staff meetings. It represented how many patients you could push through, given your resources, in a standard amount of time. If patients were the lifeblood of the unit—a turn of phrase popular with administrators like Destler—then improving throughput meant higher blood pressure for the unit as an organism. We could handle that only up to a point before the staff had a collective stroke.

"That doesn't surprise me," I said. "After all, our patients are neurologically impaired. You can't just pump a couple of pills into them and send them on their way."

"All patients need special care, Peter," Destler said, giving me his benign Buddha smile.

"And they need specially trained staff," Gloria added, rising partway out of her chair. "Remember what happened to Carol Tillingham." We all remembered the nurse who'd been floated onto our unit one day and tendered her resignation the next. "It wasn't her fault. Regular psych nurses get eaten alive with patients like ours."

"I know how you feel, Nurse Alspag," Destler said. I could feel Gloria twitching. She reacts to patronizing the way the rest of us do to poison ivy. Destler didn't notice. "That's why I asked you here to brainstorm with me. Better to stay ahead of the curve and avoid the kind of unpleasantness you all experienced before I came aboard."

That shut us up. When Destler had arrived at the Pearce, the place had been a war zone. Cost cutting hadn't kept pace as reimbursements shrank. There were ominous rumblings of impending bankruptcy, layoffs, mergers. The surrounding community was in a tizzy as the board considered selling off land to housing developers. It had been everything I could do to keep Gloria from accepting one of the job offers she had.

"And with all three of you," he beamed, "we should be able to come up with an excellent solution. So let's think on it."

There wasn't much to think on. To make his little bar creep up, we'd need to increase the number of beds, decrease the number of staff, or shorten the length of stay—preferably, all of the above.

Destler suggested, "We could broaden your mission, combine the Neuropsychiatric Unit with Geriatrics and—"

Kwan cut him off. "Just because many of our patients are older, that doesn't mean you can mix them in with the general geriatric patient." He was talking real slowly and leaving spaces between his words, the way he does when he tries to explain the fine points of men's fashions to me or baseball to Gloria. "Patients who have dementia don't mix with patients who don't."

Destler pursed his lips. "I can see your concern." Kwan started to say something, but Destler held up his hands. "Just for a moment, let's consider the benefits. With a larger, more diverse core population, we can probably eliminate a psychiatrist, maybe even two." There went Kwan's job. "Bring in a clinical nursing supervisor." So much for Gloria's. "And then, what role does a neuropsychologist play in all of this now, really?" He raised an eyebrow at me. "More and more, psychiatric hospitals are about *medicine* these days."

As opposed to what, I wondered.

Destler chuckled. "The one bright spot is the research you have going on."

Kwan shot me a triumphant look.

"I'm encouraging more units to get involved in clinical trials. That gives us additional resources to work with. And the pharmaceutical companies are excellent partners. Just this morning, in fact, I got a call from one of the VPs at Pharmacom. He was calling to say how pleased they are with the Zerenidine trial." He paused. I waited for the shoe to drop. "They did have one concern."

"I'm quite sure we'll fill our patient quota," Kwan said. "There's plenty of time yet."

"Actually, it was something else. Do you really think Pharmacom should be made to suffer because security on your unit fails to control a patient's access to liquor? The whole incident is quite embarrassing, to say the least."

They'd heard about Mr. Fleegle. Of course, they'd have been copied on the Adverse Event report. The three of us sat there dumbfounded.

"You categorized the event as 'severe,'" Destler went on. Here was the real point. "Since when is inebriation life threatening? The patient would have had to be in immediate risk of death from the reaction as it occurred—"

Kwan broke in, "If Mr. Fleegle had been driving. If he'd gotten himself a bigger bottle of booze. Yes, I'd say the reaction could have been life threatening."

"Could have been," Destler said, massaging his chin. "All I'm asking you to do is think about it." He gazed over at his chart. "Of course, I'd never suggest anything that goes against your clinical judgment. But I did need to pass along their concerns."

We stood on the steps of the Administration Building after the meeting. I was stunned. I couldn't see any other way of interpreting Destler's message—he wanted the report of Mr. Fleegle's drug reaction downgraded or suppressed entirely.

"Did what I think just happened happen?" Kwan asked.

"We just got hit by a bus," Gloria said.

"That's the good news," Kwan said. "The bad news is, we survived."

Gloria gazed up at the second-floor windows. "He wouldn't dare." She didn't sound at all sure of herself.

"That was no mild adverse event," Kwan sputtered. "If he thinks I'm going to change my report, Destler can take a flying . . ."

"Absolutely," I said.

• • •

When I got back to my office, Annie had left me a message. "Hey, Peter. I've got that information." I was relieved. She didn't sound as if she was going to stay pissed off, though she'd have had every right to be. "Let me know how you want it."

How I wanted it. . . . I smiled, imagining a few ways that would be nice. But I called back and left a tamer message: "How about over ice cream? Meet me at Toscanini's at nine? And Annie, thanks for the call . . . really."

When I hadn't heard back from her by eight-thirty, I went over anyway to the ice cream lovers' Mecca. I took over a corner table up against the plate-glass window and settled in to wait. Annie rolled in, literally, at twenty past.

"Waiting long?" she asked, all innocence, as she sat down and took off her sleek black helmet. She was wearing dark leggings, a T-shirt, a down vest with a sweatshirt tied at the waist, and in-line skates. Her cheeks were bright pink. "Took a little longer to get over here than I expected. I wasn't sure you'd wait."

She slipped off her wrist, knee, and elbow guards, and tucked them away in her backpack.

"Listen," I said, hoping my voice sounded sufficiently contrite, "I'm truly sorry about . . ."

She held up her hands. "No need to apologize. No offense taken."

Like hell. Then why wasn't she looking me in the eye?

"What would you like?" I asked. "Coffee?"

Annie eyed the four-foot-high brass Italian espresso machine with its spigots, valves, and pipes—whenever they turned it on, I half expected to hear an organ playing the Hallelujah Chorus.

"Ice cream?" I suggested.

She scanned the handwritten list of flavors. "Green-tea ice cream? Saffron? Khulfee? What's that?"

"It's good. Chocolate Sluggo's good too. So's the Belgian chocolate. Mandarin chocolate. White chocolate."

"I get the picture." Annie laughed. "A mochaccino, I think."

"No ice cream?"

"No thanks."

I brought back a frothy mochaccino for Annie; an espresso and a dish of burnt-caramel ice cream with hot fudge for me. I licked the hot fudge off the back of my spoon. "Want a taste?" I asked.

"Maybe later." She pulled a folder out of her backpack. "Preliminary autopsy results."

"Preliminary?" Let it go, asshole, I told myself, and hurried to add, "Thanks."

I took the folder and set it aside. I'd read it when I was alone.

"How's the mochaccino?" I asked.

"Delicious. Want a taste?"

"Actually, I do," I said.

She started to offer me her cup, but I put my hand on her arm. I leaned in and kissed her on the mouth, this time a gentle, lingering kiss. For a few moments, the noise of the ice cream parlor faded to nothing, leaving only the heady, sweet smell of vanilla and malt in the back of my nose, to mix with the bittersweet taste of the mochacchino and a little saltiness from Annie's skin.

"You're right," I said. "Delicious."

Annie leaned back against the brick wall, appraising me. "So, when are you going blading with me?"

I choked and put up my hands. "I don't think so. I'm not into broken bones."

"Come on. You'll love it."

"I hated ice-skating, the two times I tried it."

"It's not the same."

"I've got weak ankles."

"Not an issue. The boots support your ankles."

"What if I fall down?"

"You will. The first thing I'll teach you is how to fall. It's easy. Getting up is Lesson Two. That's harder."

Swell. The last thing I wanted to do was compete with MacRae, sprawled on the pavement like an overturned turtle. I mounted a counterattack. "Have you ever rowed?"

Annie screwed up her nose. "I hate boats. I get seasick, just looking at one."

"It's a little boat. And there aren't any waves."

"The water's so dirty in the Charles. A person could get dysentery. Body parts could dissolve. And it's too cold."

"It'll be warm enough in a couple of weeks."

"You can go blading now."

We sat there, grinning at each other. I suspected I was forgiven, but just to be certain, I asked, "Sure you don't want a taste of this?"

Annie didn't answer at once, knowing full well that she was torturing me. Then she wrinkled her nose and said, "Well, maybe just a taste."

I loaded up the spoon with the bittersweet ice cream and a dollop of hot fudge and fed it to her. She closed her eyes. "Mmm," she said. "You're right. That's delicious." She looked at me thoughtfully. "Some things are worth waiting for. Problem is, you never know for sure which ones."

Just then, a boisterous group of in-line skaters piled into the ice cream parlor. In the lead was a young black man with dreadlocks to his shoulders and a red, black, and green knit cap. He bellowed, "Yo, Annie!" Several others waved, including the petite redhead who held her back straight and head high like a ballet dancer. They were about as diverse a crowd as you'd ever see in Boston. From teen to middle-aged, male, female, all shades of skin color from blue-black to freckled Irish.

My spirits sank as I realized Annie was putting her protective armor back on. She must have sensed my disappointment, because she said, "Oh, I'm sorry, Peter. Didn't I mention? My skating group was making a pit stop here to pick me up. It's our weekly night-skate."

I watched as Annie put her skates back on. The place was starting to clear out as Annie strapped on her helmet.

She touched my shoulder. "Sorry. I should have said something earlier."

"Right," I said. Though I suspected this was part of my payback for being such a dope. Several of her cohorts whooped and whistled when Annie gave me a kiss. Then they left.

I finished the last of my ice cream, ditched our trash, and picked up the folder Annie had left for me. I wasn't looking forward to reading the autopsy results, and I no longer wanted to be alone when I did. I'd have to get into the driver's seat if I wanted bad luck and events to stop conspiring to keep Annie and me from going home together.

• • •

Back in my living room, I pulled out the typewritten sheets. As I read, I tried to shut down everything but my intellect. The technical jargon made it easier to remove myself from what this was — a minute analysis of Channing Temple's death.

According to the report, there was powder residue on the right hand. Bruising around the eyes. The back of the head was blown away, the hair soaked with blood. Except for a cut on the upper lip, there was no other external injury. Maybe the gun bucked when she pulled the trigger.

Injury: a single bullet wound. The entry wound was through the soft palette exiting six inches from the top of the head and just off the right midline. They found gunshot residue in the mouth. The bullet coursed through the right cerebellar hemisphere, nearly completely transecting the junction between the medulla and the upper-cervical spinal cord. Had she survived, she'd have been blind, vegetative, and partially paralyzed.

I turned to the toxicology report. The results were positive for lorazepam. That would be the Ativan.

Everything taken together, it certainly looked like suicide. Still, I couldn't help wondering. How much Ativan was there in her stomach? How much had been metabolized? I needed more information. MacRae's office could easily get the details. Maybe not if I asked, but . . . I swallowed my pride and called Annie, knowing she wouldn't be home yet. I left her a message, asking if she could prevail upon the kindness of MacRae and find out what I wanted to know.

As I hung up, I wondered, would any amount of Ativan and altered judgment be sufficient to make Channing's suicide comprehensible?

THE NEXT morning, I went to see Olivia. She hadn't been coming out of her room except for meals. She was curled up on the bed, facing the wall, but at least she wasn't hiding in the wardrobe.

I knocked on the open door. She didn't respond. "Olivia," I said. Still no response. I walked over to her. She had earphones on and a CD player on the bed. I touched her shoulder and she jumped, ripped the earphones from her ears and snarled, "I told you . . ." She stopped abruptly when she saw it was me. The anger that twisted her face evaporated.

She sat up. Her hair was damp, and she had on a plaid flannel pajama bottoms and a skinny black T-shirt with green letters slashed across it. PIT O' CHAOS. A pair of well-worn pink bunny slippers completed the outfit.

"You were expecting someone else?"

She narrowed her eyes at me, some of the anger creeping back. "No."

"How are you feeling today?" I asked.

"Like roadkill," she said, and started putting the headphones back on.

I smiled to myself and refrained from pointing out that this colorful term was one her mother had been fond of using, too. "That doesn't sound great. How about coming down to the dining room with me for a talk?"

She shrugged. I took it as a yes.

I stood to one side. She put the headset on the bed, slid off, and started out of the room. I was getting ready to follow her when I noticed three little balls of brown fuzz lying on the white bed cover. I picked one up and rolled it between my fingers.

As we left her room, Olivia gave a nervous glance toward Matthew Farrell. He was standing in the hall watching.

"He's always staring at me," Olivia said. "Creepy. What's wrong with that guy, anyway."

I waved at Matthew and got a wooden wave back. "Why don't you ask him that?"

"Can I do that?"

"Of course you can. Just be prepared for the same question in return."

When we got to the dining room, Olivia took a seat. I poured myself a cup of regular coffee and a cup of decaf for her. I shuddered as she shoveled in two heaping spoonfuls of sugar.

"So how does roadkill feel?" I asked.

"Shitty."

"Let me guess. You're feeling anxious. Like there's something important that you're forgetting to do. And kind of jet-lagged. Some people say they feel like they're underwater."

"Maybe if you gave me some Ritalin" — she took a sip of coffee — "or something other than this decaffeinated shit."

I wondered if the pent-up anger was the withdrawal talking, or if she'd been upset by whatever visitor had been in to talk to her earlier that morning.

"Hang in. You're halfway there. Another few days and your body will be weaned."

She gave a snort of disgust. "Yeah, right. In a few days, then what? What if I still can't concentrate?"

It was a good question. She might very well continue to crave the drug even after her body was free of it. That was exactly what Channing was testing a treatment for — the psychological addiction that lingers long after the physical need ceases. Kutril.

The voice in my head chided: Can't use it. Hasn't been approved yet for this use. Still, Channing called it effective and without side effects.

If only I could get my hands on Channing's research data. Kwan would know if it was safe to put Olivia on the stuff. Maybe there was a copy of the report in Channing's office. Or on her computer, if the hard drive could be salvaged. She'd said she'd given her report to someone to review. Daphne maybe?

I didn't want to say anything to Olivia to get her hopes up.

Olivia gave me a sour look. "It feels like I'm going crazy." She had her mouth clenched, her eyes wide as she tried to hold back tears.

"I work with plenty of people who are genuinely crazy, and you're not," I said. "Have you been thinking about what happened?"

She looked away. "It seems unreal."

"I know what you mean. That's part of what the mind docs when something unimaginable happens to you."

"It was just a few days ago, but it seems like years."

"Do you remember, did you take any Ritalin that morning?"

"I took some."

"How much?"

"Maybe two. Then I had a fight with my mother, and I took some more." She stared at me, like she meant to look defiant. But I had the sense that underneath, she was breaking apart.

"You drove here?" I hoped that by asking Olivia to focus on the mundane facts, we could pull away the emotions and she'd be better able to understand what had happened and begin to deal with it.

"I was so angry that she made me come in. And then I can't find the goddam car keys." Olivia's voice was raw. "And I get here and the elevator isn't working so I have to climb up three flights of stairs. Then I get up there and her door is open, like she's in there waiting for me. And I know I'm late and she's going to be pissed. And I'm thinking, I'll tell her how I couldn't find my keys, and the fucking elevator isn't working. And I don't even know until I come in . . ." She sobbed. "And she's sitting there in the chair. Her eyes are closed. The gun—" Olivia stopped, her hand rose, palm up and hung in midair. "And I go over to her. I want to take the gun away. But there's something weird, a smell. And then a sound, something moving. I must have jumped, because I knocked over a cup." Her words were coming faster now. "And now the room smells like coffee. And it's making me sick. Like I want to throw up." Olivia's face twisted, and she began to heave, the tears coursing down her cheeks. "And she's holding the gun . . ."

She gasped for air.

"Olivia," I broke in, "relax."

She took gulps of air but couldn't seem to exhale.

"Breathe out, Olivia."

Olivia gripped the table with both hands.

"Out through the mouth."

Olivia's eyes were open, startled. Finally, she blew air out.

"That's right." I lowered my voice. "Just slow everything down." I said the words slowly, deliberately. "Nice and easy. Just breathe. In . . . and out. That's good." Redness ebbed from her face. "Keep breathing."

Olivia's breathing slowed.

"You okay?" I asked.

Olivia nodded. She pressed a hand to her chest.

"You can feel your heart pounding?"

She nodded again.

"Just keep breathing, no need to rush." Her shoulders unhunched themselves. "You'll feel your heart slowing down, slowing down." I singsonged.

She leaned back. Gradually her hands lowered themselves to her lap.

"And I'm thinking," she went on, her voice quiet and calm now, "it's just like my grandmother. Only this time, it's my fault."

"Olivia, your mother loved you very much. She was concerned about you, yes. But if she did kill herself, it wasn't because of anything you did or didn't do. It wasn't because of anything you said. You have to believe me. I knew your mother pretty well."

Olivia stared down into her lap, her jaw clenching and unclenching.

"Do you remember going back into your mother's office after the security officer arrived? Why did you go back?"

Olivia's eyes darted back and forth. "She was alone. I didn't want her to be alone."

"Why did you throw the computer?"

"I don't know."

"And then you cut yourself."

She stared straight ahead. "It was my fault," she said, her voice flat. She seemed so small, and the burden she was carrying was oppressive.

"I know you probably won't believe me," I said, "but I understand what you're going through." Olivia looked at me, her mouth pulled taut at the edges. "When my wife was killed . . ."

"Kate," Olivia whispered.

"Kate. She showed you how to make a pot, didn't she?"

Olivia nodded, staring down into her lap. "She was nice to me."

"She was a very nice person," I said. "And she loved having you over, showing you how to work with the clay, use the wheel."

I'd watched from the doorway of Kate's sun-drenched studio on our top floor. Kate had sat on her stool with Olivia perched between her legs. Kate had guided Olivia's hands. Together they'd made a pot grow up from a shapeless mound of clay. Kate had seen me and smiled. Later, she told me how nice it felt to have the little girl there, fitting into the contours of her own body. Olivia's head smelled of baby shampoo, she said.

"Well, after she was killed, I felt terribly guilty. Like you're feeling now. But I kept going, like you'll keep going, because you don't have a choice. And because each day it's going to get a little easier. I know it's hard to believe that, but it will."

Olivia exhaled shakily. "Know what I said as I walked into her office? I go, 'I hope you're satisfied.' And she's sitting there, her eyes half-closed. I'm looking at her like, so what's your problem? And I say it again, louder." Olivia sobbed.

"She was dead by then, Olivia."

"Grandma died like that," Olivia said in a tiny voice. "Mommy found her."

"You took the gun away from her?" I asked.

Olivia's eyes beseeched me. "I couldn't let them find her that way. She'd have hated it."

"Did you hear the gunshot?" I ask.

A guarded look came into Olivia's eyes, like a pair of transparent membranes slid down over her eyes. "No."

"You told me there was a funny smell."

Olivia's nose wrinkled. "Smoky," she said.

Sounded like what I'd smelled. Probably gunpowder. That meant we'd both gotten there soon after the gun went off.

"You told me you heard something move. Can you describe the sound?"

She picked at a pimple on the side of her face. "I don't know. . . ."

"Was it the sound of something in the room with you?"

She closed her eyes. "Maybe. Or maybe it was out in the hall."

I wondered if it was me that she'd heard. "Were you holding the gun when you heard the sound?"

"I'm not sure. I don't think so."

"And then you spilled the coffee."

"I backed up and knocked it over with my foot."

"The cup was on the floor?"

She hugged herself. "Why do I have to keep talking about it? Why do I have to keep thinking about it?"

"I know talking about this is painful, but in the long run, it will help you stop remembering what happened all the time, the way you probably are now."

Olivia stared at her hands, kneading them together. It was as if someone had turned on a tap — tears were suddenly streaming down her face. I reached into my pocket and pulled out my handkerchief. I brushed away the brown ball of fuzz I'd found on Olivia's bed and handed the handkerchief to her. Sweater lint? Daphne had a nervous habit of picking the pills on her sweater sleeve, and she'd been wearing a brown cardigan when I last saw her.

"Was anyone here to see you this morning, before I came?" I asked.

Olivia looked down in her lap. Then raised her eyes to me. I could feel the wheels turning. "My father," she said at last. "He brought me some clothes."

"Anyone else?"

"No," she answered quickly and looked away.

"The police want to talk to you," I said. She chewed on her bottom lip and held the handkerchief tightly in a clenched fist. "They're coming Monday morning. They'll probably take your fingerprints."

"Monday," she whispered. It was only three days away.

I SENSED that Olivia was hiding something. Someone had been in to see her earlier that morning, probably Daphne. And there was more. Why sneak back into Channing's office, pick up the computer, and pitch it through the window? It didn't make sense. If she wanted to break the window and cut herself, the paperweight would have worked just as well.

Olivia had become agitated when the police officer emerged from the shrubbery with the laptop. Was she upset because he'd retrieved the computer? Or was she anxious about something else the police might find if they continued to look? Perhaps the second Acu-Med mug, the one that disappeared from the murder scene, had followed the laptop out the window.

For all the unanswered questions, it was still clear to me that Olivia's grief was genuine. The cuts on her arms were very real, and far from superficial. On top of everything else, she was having a very rough time without her daily doses of Ritalin.

I called Daphne and left a message. Even if I couldn't talk to her about Olivia, I could at least ask her about Channing's research. She was probably familiar with the Kutril regimen. When I checked my messages a few hours later, Daphne had left word that she had time late in the day.

I headed over to the Drug and Alcohol Rehabilitation Unit just before five. I brought along a flashlight. I ignored the stares of curious passersby as I foraged in the bushes below Channing's window. I found the broken branches in the surrounding yews, where the laptop had probably landed. I crouched and looked underneath. I flashed the light between the branches. The grounds at the Pearce are kept meticulous, so I wasn't surprised there·was no trash, no empty coffee cups strewn where no one could see. I searched systematically, in widening circles. I found nothing but some shards of broken window glass.

It had been four days since the murder. Plenty of time for someone, innocently or otherwise, to have found the mug or collected the pieces. The only thing I knew for sure was that someone wasn't Olivia. If she'd gotten off the unit, I'd have known about it.

I gave up and went inside. I took the elevator up to the fourth floor. There was a metal wastebasket against the wall, probably the one that had been used to prop the elevator door open when I'd last been here and found Channing dead.

I glanced up and down the hall. I could hear the elevator groan as it descended, and the hum of the overhead fluorescent lights. The carpet seemed radioactive green. My heart was pounding and my breathing shallow. I pushed myself down the hall.

The door to Channing's office was padlocked. All that was left of the yellow crime-scene tape was a pair of raw marks where the varnish had been pulled from the doorjamb. I touched one of the abrasions.

I looked up and saw Daphne, standing outside her office. She looked haggard, her face drawn and pinched as if she'd aged a decade in the last few days.

I went into her office and sat. A blue-and-white ginger-jar lamp cast a warm glow over the papers and file folders stacked on the desk. On the windowsill, the flowers of an African violet were turning brown. Colorful chintz cushions that would have softened the institutional chairs and sofa were scattered about on the floor.

There was a laptop in a sleek, purple plastic case on her desk. The coffeemaker burbled in the corner, filling the room with the comforting smell of fresh coffee. I scanned the walls. There were diplomas and plaques, along with an array of photographs.

Daphne walked over to a photo of her husband. "I took this when we were in London. Just last year, before Robert . . ." She shuddered. "Robert says . . ." She gave a self-conscious laugh. "I imagine myself talking to him. It helps."

With her finger, she traced around his face. "Robert was a great fan of Channing's. She was there for us at the end, you know."

I didn't know. I'd been to Robert Smythe-Gooding's funeral, but the standing-room–crowd of people — even the ones who'd spoken and shared their memories of the man — were a blur. Surely Channing had been among them, had spoken eloquently, but I didn't recall.

"How's Livvy managing?" Daphne asked, sitting at her desk.

"Hard to tell," I said. Daphne's brown sweater was over the back of her chair. "What did you think? You stopped by to see her this morning, didn't you?"

Daphne stroked her neck with one hand and helped herself to a few nuts from a bowl on the desk with the other. Her nails were stained yellow with nicotine.

"Can I get you some coffee?" she asked.

"Sure," I said. "Black."

She poured two cups. To hers she added a spoonful of sugar, then another. She handed me one cup, and took the other and sat at her desk. She settled back. "Actually, I did stop by. Channing asked me to come." I knew she meant Olivia. "You don't mind, do you?" Daphne asked.

"Mind? Why I . . ." As a practicing psychiatrist, never mind one of the top administrators, Daphne could pretty much go anywhere she wanted at the Pearce. I wondered what Olivia had needed to talk to her about, and why Olivia wouldn't tell me Daphne had been there? But I couldn't come right out and ask. After all, Daphne had every right to see her own patient, to talk to her privately. I only hoped she wasn't trying to continue seeing her regularly. With two of us, it would be confusing for Olivia, not to mention counterproductive. "Next time, would you just let me know? As a courtesy."

"So what can I do for you?"

"I'm trying to learn more about the treatment Channing was testing. It might be something we can use to help Olivia with her craving for Ritalin."

"Channing talked to you about her results?"

"Only that she was very pleased. She said someone was reviewing her analysis. I thought maybe you?"

"Her results are quite impressive," Daphne said. She opened up her top desk drawer and foraged around. She pulled out a floppy disk and offered it to me. "I wonder, what did you make of that row at the end of Channing's party?"

I tried to take the diskette from her, but she held onto her end. So this was going to be a barter. "I had the impression they were arguing about reporting a death," I said. Daphne's look turned grave. "Channing wanted to report it. Jensen didn't." Daphne let go of her end of the diskette. I went on, "Said it could hurt the hospital. I've been trying to make sense of it. Maybe one of the subjects in a drug trial died and no one filed an Adverse Event report."

"A death," Daphne said. "No, I hadn't heard anything about anyone dying during a clinical trial. Now that the Kutril trial is completed, there's only one other drug trial going on in the Drug and Alcohol Unit. Jensen's testing DX-200."

"You don't suppose . . ." I started.

"I was on the phone with Acu-Med this morning. They're delighted with the results, so far. There certainly hasn't been . . . I wonder . . ." Her hand hovered over her mouth, then dropped away. "I could dig a little. One of the benefits of being in charge of clinical trials for the hospital, it's just the kind of question I'm supposed to ask."

"Let me know what you find. And thanks for the report. This will be a big help." I stood. "Any idea where I'd find her raw data? The patient files? I'd like to understand what individual subjects experienced, just to be on the safe side before we try Olivia on it."

"Probably locked up in her office. I'd be very surprised if her research isn't in a file drawer, in tiptop order and neatly annotated. Just give me a minute to get my things together, and I'll let you in before I go. You're welcome to look about."

"Thank you," I said.

Daphne put on her sweater, then her coat. She picked up her briefcase. "She trusted us, Peter," Daphne said, grasping my arm. "Now we've got to help Livvy." Her voice shook with emotion, and tears pooled in her eyes.

I knew we were both trying to help Olivia. I just hoped we were pulling in the same direction.

• • •

Daphne let me into Channing's office and left for the night. The room smelled of disinfectant. I gagged and felt my coffee trying to make its way up my throat. The same smell had lingered in Kate's studio, insinuating its way into our bedroom and the downstairs, long after she was killed.

The telephone receiver was in its cradle. Even so, the three-tone screech replayed itself in my head. I forced myself to turn and face the corner where I'd found Channing. The leather chair was there. It had been cleaned.

I steeled myself and began to look for Channing's research. Someone had cleared her desktop. The drawers were locked. I checked under the blotter for a key. None. Then I tried in the mason jar she used to hold pencils on her desk. There I found a ring of small keys.

I opened the desk file drawer. There was an orderly array of neatly labeled hanging files holding purple file folders. It was a hodgepodge of stuff—her own health insurance, notes from talks she'd given, information about substance-abuse support groups.

I turned my attention to the tall gray file cabinet. A key was sitting in the lock. The top drawer was labeled RESEARCH. This was it—if the files were here, this is where they'd be. I pulled and the drawer flew towards me—empty.

I tried the second drawer. It was packed so tightly with files, it was hard to pull a folder out without tearing it. All patient files. The third and fourth drawers were packed with administrative reports and patient billing. Nothing on the Kutril trial.

I pulled the top drawer open again. The emptiness taunted me. Had she put all her research somewhere for safekeeping? Or had someone helped himself or herself, after her death?

I scanned the bookshelves. There were medical references, psychiatry texts, medical journals, a few standing boxes of scholarly papers. I took down a few and flipped through. Tucked in at the end of a shelf, I spotted a fat black datebook. I took it out. Weekdays were densely scribbled with appointments.

I turned to the day Channing was killed. In the eleven o'clock slot, she'd written down "P and O, caf.' At ten, she'd written "D." Who or what was D? Destler? Daphne? It could have been anyone—a patient, a staff person, a friend.

I put the datebook back. Then I scribbled a quick note to Daphne, saying I hadn't taken anything because there wasn't anything to take. I left the office, hooking the padlock back in place and squeezing it shut.

After I slipped the note under Daphne's door, I started to the elevator, passing by Liam Jensen's office. His door was ajar. I backed up and knocked.

"What is it?" Jensen barked, an edge of irritation to his voice. I went in. He looked up at me, surprised. "Yes? Peter?" He closed the file folder that he had open and slapped it facedown on the desk.

"I hope you don't mind," I said. "I was up here, talking with Daphne, and I saw your door open."

"Not at all, not at all." His lips stretched taut in what I think was supposed to pass for a smile. "What can I do for you?"

"Actually, I was hoping to track down Dr. Temple's research on the Kutril trial."

"I should think the files would all be in her office," Jensen said. He said it looking past me, his right hand twitching.

"I checked there. I thought perhaps she gave them to you."

Jensen gave a bitter laugh. "Me? I think not."

"Your research studies were in competition with one another, weren't they?"

My eyes drifted to the file cabinet alongside his desk. On top, a row of about two-dozen coffee mugs stood at attention. Lined up in alphabetical order from Acu-Med to Zoloft, he had quite a collection. I gazed down. A bottom file drawer was partly open. Jensen pushed it with his foot, but the tops of a few purple file folders kept the drawer from closing completely.

"I suppose you could say that," Jensen said. "Though it didn't have to be that way. After all, we're all working for the betterment of humanity."

He sounded so smug, I couldn't stop myself from saying, "Didn't I hear that there were some adverse events with the DX-200 trial? A death?"

"A death?" Jensen choked on the word. "Absolutely untrue. Who told you that?"

"Wasn't that what you and Channing were discussing at the end of her party?"

"What?" Jensen looked genuinely baffled. He seemed to think back. His brow cleared for an instant, then he looked even more guarded. "What we were discussing had nothing whatsoever to do with the DX-200 trial. Or any other drug trial for that matter. That was a private matter between Dr. Temple and myself."

"You don't think it had anything to do with her death, do you?"

"Her death?" Jensen's eyebrows raised in astonishment. "Well . . ." He considered this possibility. "No," he said slowly. "Not that." There was a pause. "I can't imagine—"

Whatever it was, he wasn't about to share the details with me. I said, "I was just in Dr. Temple's office. Her research file drawer is empty."

Jensen's waxy face colored slightly. "How odd. Perhaps the files have been moved to a more secure place, now that . . ."

"If the concern was confidentiality, I'd have thought patient records would have been moved as well. But they haven't been. Besides, the office is locked. Daphne let me in."

"As I say, I wouldn't know. But as director of the unit, it's my business to make sure all confidential files are kept confidential."

"Director of the unit?"

Jensen coughed. "Why, yes. Dr. Destler has appointed me to take over Channing's responsibilities."

"Acting director?"

"Uh, no. I believe the appointment is permanent."

Had this been in the works all along? "Sounds as if congratulations are in order," I said.

He waved away the remark. "I hardly think so, given the circumstances."

12

FRIDAY WAS my mother's birthday. I'd wanted to take her out to dinner, but she insisted on getting together for breakfast. It was the only time she could squeeze me in, as she put it. As usual, I was a little late. Also as usual, she wasn't waiting. At eight sharp, she rapped on my door. I opened it.

Her white, perfectly combed and curled head came barely up to my chin. She was wearing a purple running suit with pink flowers painted on the jacket and up the side of one leg.

"French toast?" she chirped, and immediately disappeared into the apartment in the other half of my two-family. I locked up and followed, down her dark entry hall into the kitchen, warm with light, redolent with the smell of brewing coffee.

"But I thought I was going to take *you* out," I complained. She already had a cup of coffee poured for me. "It's your birthday."

"So, happy birthday to me. Shouldn't I get what I want?"

I sighed. "And you want . . . ?"

"To stay here and make French toast for my handsome son." She beamed at me.

"You were afraid I was going to take you out for dim sum."

My mother looked aghast. When it comes to food, my mother

doesn't like surprises. She's afraid of what she'll find nestled in the warm Chinese dumplings that about a half-dozen Chinatown restaurants serve early in the day — my idea of heaven.

"Don't worry. I'm not sure we could even get dim sum during the week."

"Well, that's a relief."

"I was going to take you to the Spinnaker on top of the Hyatt. They're supposed to have a terrific breakfast."

"That's the one that goes around and around?"

"Great view."

My mother made a face as if she'd bitten into a very sour pickle. "Restaurants shouldn't twirl. They should stay in one place so you can properly digest your food. And so expensive. I'll bet three dollars, just for orange juice." My mother pulled a quart of Tropicana from the fridge, shook it, and poured me a glass.

"Don't you want any?" I asked.

"I've already eaten," she announced, and poked at the contents of a yellow mixing bowl. There was a fresh challah on the counter, its burnished crust gleaming, and in the bowl were two slices soaking in eggs and milk. Butter was melting in a frying pan. Real butter. My mother thought margarine was a plot — I'm not sure what kind, but a plot nevertheless.

There was no point trying to convince her to let me take her out. She'd taken charge. And to be honest, the prospect of her French toast weakened my resolve.

The pan sizzled as she dropped in the first soggy slice, then again as she dropped in the second one. Then the gentler sound of the bread sighing as it expanded, each slice turning into an airy pillow as it cooked. The rich smell filled my head, taking me back to our apartment in Brooklyn, to the kitchen that was bigger than any other room.

"How's that little girl doing?" my mother asked.

"She's . . . I don't know actually. She's been going through a difficult ordeal. Plus she's addicted to Ritalin. That's what they give . . ."

"Psssh," my mother exhaled. "Ritalin I know what is. How many times I wished we could have given your brother, Steven, a magic pill to calm him down."

"Not me?"

"Not you. You were easy. Except that you only ate Corn Toasties Breakfast for three years. That and a glass of milk."

The mention of Corn Toasties brought back the smell—something between cardboard and corn husks. Now I couldn't bear the sight of them. What my mother didn't know was that every day, on the way to school and on the way home, I was stopping in at the local candy store for chocolate egg creams, then at the bakery for a big black-and-white cookie, iced half with chocolate and half with vanilla. I've never found cookies to match, anywhere in Boston. And I've looked.

"Did you ever consider taking Steve to a psychiatrist?" I asked.

My mother smiled and shook her head. "Those days, if you couldn't see a problem, it didn't exist."

Maybe if they had, it might have saved my brother three unhappy marriages. Or maybe not.

I was halfway through my second helping when my mother said, "I've got to be down the senior center in forty minutes." *Down the* senior center? Sixty years in Brooklyn and five in Boston, and already she had a Boston accent. At least she didn't say *seen-yah cent-ah* like a native.

She disappeared, then came back a few minutes later wearing her parka and wheeling a black, zippered overnight bag. I stuffed a last piece of French toast into my mouth before she whisked the plate away. She gave the dishes a quick rinse, stacked them efficiently in the dishwasher, added some soap, and started it up.

"Ready?" she asked, and glanced at the clock on the stove. "Thirty-two minutes to departure."

"To where?"

"Windsor."

"Canada?"

"Too far to go by bus, if you ask me."

"Gambling?"

"And drugs," she said with a straight face. She waved away my surprise. "A person could go broke paying for pills in this wonderful country of ours. And I usually win. Blackjack," my mother added, well pleased with herself. "Can't win *bubkes* on slots, you know."

"I can easily help you pay for . . ."

"That's not the point. Do you know how much money those drug companies steal from us? *Gonifs,* all of them," she said, and wheeled her suitcase out the door.

• • •

Annie was out of town for the weekend. Saturday and Sunday passed in a blur of chores I'd agreed to look after in my mother's apartment. I replaced broken window ropes, rewired a light switch, put a new washer in a leaky faucet, patched some cracks in her bathroom ceiling, and painted. Between jobs, I called in to check on the unit.

I arrived at work Monday and stopped first at the nurses' station, as I always do. Gloria was sitting at the desk—very unusual for a woman who never sits down on the job. She raised her head when I came in and flicked her eyes in the direction of the waiting area. Sergeant MacRae was sitting there, reading a newspaper. Beside him was a uniformed female police officer. They were early.

When I asked how Olivia was, Gloria shook her head. "They caught her last night, trying to break in to the med room," she whispered.

"Damn. That's just great. Perfect timing."

"I already read her the riot act," Gloria said. "She's trying to pull herself together."

I went over to MacRae. He lowered the newspaper. "You're a little early," I told him. "Ms. Temple's father will be here at nine."

I expected him to complain, to say Olivia's father didn't need to be here since, after all, she wasn't a suspect. But he didn't. He just introduced me to his colleague, Officer Connor, a large, thick woman with a pleasant face.

"Coffee?" I offered. They declined. MacRae went back to his newspaper.

I poured myself another cup and carried it down the hall to Olivia's room. She was standing, staring out the window. Her elbows poked out from her T-shirt sleeves; her jeans rode low on her hips. Her face was scrubbed, her hair damp.

"They're here," I said. "You okay?"

She bit her lower lip and nodded. "Where's Daddy?" she asked. An eyelash lay curled on her cheek.

"We'll wait for him. He should be here soon."

She gave a ragged inhale. She was shivering.

"You're not feeling so good, are you?" I asked.

From her look, I knew she thought I had the IQ of a frog. "I can't concentrate. I ache all over. All I want to do is sleep. You took me off the Ritalin too fast."

"I heard you went looking for some yourself last night."

"I *need* it to help me think straight."

She clearly did need help. Even sugar pills. On the other hand, why settle for a placebo when we might have a bona fide treatment for her with Kutril? I felt in my pocket for the floppy disk Daphne had given me. "We might have something . . ." I started.

"What is it about 'I need it' that you don't get?" she demanded, cutting me off. The vehemence of the words made her head shake. The edginess, the raw mood, seemed excessive for withdrawal from a therapeutic dosage. Olivia had probably been taking a lot of Ritalin, and for a long period of time. She put her hand up to her temple and grimaced. Then her glance drifted down to the mug of coffee I was holding. "I'd like to see you give up coffee. You drink about a gazillion cups a day."

"No way," I said.

"Yo way," she shot back.

I looked at the coffee. It was my fourth cup that morning.

She folded her arms over her chest. "I'll bet you couldn't give it up."

Before I could think better of it, I said, "Sure I could."

"Bet you couldn't."

"Bet I could."

"Prove it."

I realized I was getting into a pissing contest with a kid. The problem was, she'd hit a nerve. I *was* drinking too much coffee. I needed it to maintain my equilibrium, as Gloria pointed out any time I arrived at work insufficiently precaffeinated. I didn't like to think of myself as dependent on any substance. The thought that I might not be able to cut back, never mind quit completely, rankled me.

I gave Olivia my X-ray look. "And in return?"

"Would you really?" Olivia asked, her eyes wide in disbelief.

"Depends on what you're offering."

"Wow," Olivia said. "Okay. I'll try."

"You won't sneak any more drugs?"

"Promise." She ran a finger across her chest one way, then back the other. "Cross my heart, hope to die, stick a needle in my eye." It was the kind of thing a charming six-year-old would say. Or was this an adolescent capable of murdering her mother?

I raised my cup. I took a deep inhale, then walked over to the sink. "Okay, then. Here goes."

Ready, set—I hesitated. It was like that moment when you're standing on the end of a diving board over an unheated pool. I held my breath and dumped the coffee down the sink. I immediately regretted it as I watched the rich brown liquid swirl down the drain.

Gloria appeared at the door with Drew. Gloria's face was tense, her mouth set in a thin line. Something was wrong, something more than our collective anxiety about Olivia's impending encounter with the police. When I saw Drew, I realized what it was. His button-down shirt looked as if he'd slept in it, and his tie was loose at the neck. He was clean-shaven, in a manner of speaking—but there was a bit of tissue paper stuck to one of the nicks on his face, and patches of grizzly gray shadow where he'd clearly missed. His face was pale, and his lips were overly pink.

He held his arms open to Olivia. In an instant, Olivia went from looking sick to looking frightened. "Now?" she whispered. She went over to him and buried her head in his chest. He stroked her hair, his jaw quivering.

"Drew," I said, "could I have a moment with you?"

"Daddy?" Olivia said.

"We'll be back in a minute," I said, and propelled Drew from the room. I continued down the hall, out of earshot.

I stood close to him and said in a low, intense voice, "What in the hell are you thinking of, coming in here drunk?"

Drew blinked at me, his mouth open. At least he smelled of toothpaste and aftershave, not liquor. He seemed stunned. The surprise rapidly turned to anger. "I'm . . . not . . . drunk," he said, the words slamming into the wall behind me.

"Shh," I said. "There's no need to shout."

He swallowed and looked around. "I'm not drunk." He ran his hand back and forth across his mouth.

"You don't think the police are going to get the same impression?"

He looked down at the floor "Last night. Maybe I had too much." He pulled a handkerchief from his pocket and blew his nose.

"Did you find the Ativan?"

"Couldn't find it."

"Is there anyone you can call? Are you seeing anyone?" I asked.

"Not anymore," he answered.

"I mean, are you seeing a therapist? Are you getting any treatment?"

"No." His eyes were rheumy.

"Seriously, Drew. You need to get help. And right now, you've got to pull yourself together. Olivia needs you. So help me God, if you screw this up, I'll get you banned from the hospital."

"You wouldn't—"

"I would."

He closed his eyes and seemed to find his center. "Just give me a minute," he said. He smoothed his hair.

"You've got some tissue . . ." I pointed to my chin.

He picked off the tissue paper stuck to his face. He tucked in his shirt. He undid his tie and tied it again, this time with the knot fastened smartly at the neck. Then, he took a deep inhale and squared his shoulders. "Okay. Let's go."

When we got back to Olivia, he took her under his arm. "Okay, kiddo. Let's get this over with."

I brought them to the dining room. Gloria escorted MacRae and Officer Connor in. MacRae set his leather briefcase on the floor, took out a tape recorder, and put it on the table. Connor lay a pad and a pen alongside.

I sat at the nurses' station, where I could keep an eye on what was going on through the glass panel. While I waited, I slid the floppy disk into the computer at the desk. There was a single file on it: REPORT-DRAFT. It was dated two weeks before Channing died.

In the dining room, MacRae was leaning back in his chair, his chin doubled into his chest, listening to Olivia. She seemed flat, emotionless.

I opened the file. There was Channing's thirty-page analysis of the Kutril-trial results. It was a draft with sections missing. But everything I needed to understand the treatment protocol was clearly spelled out. I scrolled through the tables and charts. Though I'm not an expert on clinical pharmacology, the results seemed impressive. I sat back and waited for the report to finish printing out.

Now MacRae was taking some pieces of paper out of his brief-case and showing them to Olivia. She grabbed them from him, crumpled them up and threw them into the corner. Then she broke down, weeping and shaking her head. Drew looked as if he wanted to vault over the table and strangle MacRae.

Then, suddenly it was over. MacRae put away the tape recorder. Officer Connor took Olivia's fingerprints. MacRae and Connor stood to leave. I went over and opened the dining-room door.

When MacRae saw me, his face went rigid. "You lied to me," he said through clenched teeth.

"I never lied," I said, keeping my voice calm and even.

"You . . . you . . ." he sputtered.

I held up my hands. "I didn't. Not once. I didn't tell you everything, but I answered your questions truthfully."

"You deliberately misled . . ."

Give it a rest, I wanted to say. I felt very tired. "I did what I needed to do to protect my patient. She needs to be under a doctor's care."

"Right now, that girl doesn't need a doctor. She needs a very smart lawyer." He waved me away and marched out with Officer Connor trailing after him.

I returned to the dining room. Drew and Olivia were still seated at the table. Drew looked ashen. Olivia was sitting very still, her head in her hands.

"Why are they treating her like a criminal?" Drew asked.

"Police don't like surprises," I said. "They don't like to be the last to find out that a witness handled the murder weapon."

"There's more," Olivia said quietly, raising her head and sitting erect.

I sat down. I knew I didn't want to hear what it was.

Drew retrieved the balled-up paper from the corner of the room. "They got this off Channing's computer. They were able to salvage the hard drive." He smoothed the three pieces of paper on the table.

I scanned them quickly, feeling sick. They were e-mail messages from Olivia to Channing. Paragraphs of vitriol. The last one dated the morning Channing died. It ended with:

> I hate you I hate you I hate you! I wish you would just
> die and then I won't have to deal with your shit.

Olivia sobbed, "See, it's my fault? I made her do it."

Now, I understood. This was why Olivia had freaked out, gone back into Channing's office and sent the computer through the window. She had to destroy the instrument she'd used to communicate her anger to her mother. Was it out of guilt and remorse? Or a deliberate attempt to hide evidence from the police?

"Olivia, when did your mother do anything in this world because someone told her to do it?" Drew asked. Olivia looked up at him, red-eyed. "Your mother could be the stubbornest, most bullheaded, contrary person in this world." Olivia giggled, in spite of herself. Drew put his hand under Olivia's chin and looked her in the eye. "If she killed herself, and notice I say *if*, because I don't believe for one minute that she did, you can be sure of one thing—it wasn't because any of us told her to do it."

As Drew was leaving, he and I talked privately for a few moments. I told him, "If the police decide that it wasn't suicide, they're going to be looking for someone to blame.

"I know that," Drew agreed, his look somber.

"Olivia had opportunity. Her prints are on the gun. The e-mails suggest motive. They could easily charge her with murder." I fished out my business card and wrote Chip Ferguson's name and phone number on the back. "She needs a good lawyer," I said. "And it wouldn't hurt if you talked to him sooner rather than later."

He hesitated. "We have a family attorney."

"You'll need someone who's experienced in criminal law. I've worked with Chip. He's been a public defender; now he's in private practice. He's excellent. A thoroughly nice man. And he's got a daughter, just a few years older than Olivia."

Reluctantly, Drew accepted the card.

13

WHEN I returned, Olivia was wrapped in a blanket and Gloria was making her a cup of cocoa. I took the report off the printer and went looking for Kwan. He was working in the conference room. He looked up and saw the report I was holding. "You've written a novella about a man who cuts off his nose to spite his face?"

Sometimes I think he's psychic. "How'd you hear?"

"About what?"

Of course he hadn't. But now I had to tell him. "I've given up coffee."

It was one of the few times I've ever seen Kwan at a loss for words.

"No big deal," I said. I wasn't about to admit that I'd struck a bargain with a seventeen-year-old. "Just felt like I was becoming overly dependent."

"I know there have been times before when I've thought you were losing your mind. But now I'm sure of it." Then with glee, "If this gets ugly, I hope I can watch."

"Don't worry. You'll have a front-row seat." I offered him the report. "Could you take a look at this for me?"

He glanced at the cover page and took the report from me. He opened it and started to read through the introductory summary. Then he paged through the rest of the report, pausing here and there to examine a table or chart.

"Looks interesting," he said. "I always knew Dr. Temple was a top-notch researcher. Tell me again, why exactly am I reading this?"

"I want us to consider putting Olivia Temple on Kutril. She's off Ritalin, but she's still craving it. She's dealing with her mother's death, various family problems, and on top of that, she might be charged with murder."

"It hasn't been approved for treating addiction, has it?"

"No. But it's not like it's the usual experimental drug. We know Trilafon is safe in small doses, as long as you don't stay on it for a long time. And kudzu has been used since the first century by the Chinese."

"Probably not concentrated in pill form," Kwan pointed out.

"Still, seems like there's not a huge risk."

"I have some time this afternoon," he said.

"As soon as you can. Last night she was caught breaking into the med room."

Kwan glanced at his watch. "Okay, okay. Give me an hour," he said.

• • •

It was almost lunchtime. I'd agreed to pick up my mother at the senior center, where the bus was dropping them off. I got there just in time.

"How was your trip?" I asked. I tossed her suitcase into the trunk of my car and opened the door for her. My mother had on a pink sweatshirt with the insignia Casino Magic.

She squinted at me through the shade of a clear, green plastic visor. "Not bad," she admitted as she sank into the seat. She pulled in her feet, settled back, and fastened her seat belt. "Made a few bucks."

I got in. As I pulled out onto the street, I laughed. "Score some drugs?"

She shrugged. "Actually . . ." She snapped open her pocketbook and pulled out one bottle of prescription pills and then another. She struggled to open one of them. "Child-safe, phooey. I don't know how they expect grown-ups to do this."

When we stopped at a light, I opened the bottles for her. She shook a pill from each. One was small and white, the other about twice as big and bright orange.

"I got these." She pointed to the white one.

I turned down our street. "And these are . . . ?"

"For my arthritis. It shouldn't cost me a buck and a half a day. If I wanted to spend that kind of money, I could have cable. These are supposed to be the same as these orange ones that I get from Walgreens."

I pulled the car into the driveway and glanced into her hand. "They sure don't look the same."

She dropped the two containers back into her bag and snapped it shut, giving me her patient smile. "We always said you could have been a rocket scientist."

"Don't get snippy."

"So how many of these" — she poked the white pill — "should I take, when I'm supposed to take one of these?" She poked the orange pill.

"You didn't get any instructions with it?"

"You don't ask a gift horse."

I took the two pills from her and examined them. The orange one was a large oval. The white one was nearly a figure eight and scored in the middle — it looked as if you were supposed to break it in half. "Well, don't take any of these until I find out what you've got," I said. With Kwan's help, I figured I'd be able to find out. The *Physicians' Desk Reference*, the doctors' drug Bible, has photographs of every medication being manufactured today. We'd be able to find a match and then equilibrate.

I'd pulled my mother's suitcase out of the trunk and was halfway up the walk when I realized she wasn't following me. The car door was open and my mother had her legs sticking straight out of the car. "Petey!" she called. I cringed. I've asked her a million times not to call me that.

I came back. "This car," my mother fumed. "The seats are so low, it's a wonder your tush doesn't scrape the road every time you hit a bump."

"Need a hand?" I asked, and helped her up.

"Aging, feh," she said, massaging her hip as she started up the walk.

• • •

When I got back to the Pearce, Kwan was up in his office. The research report was on his desk alongside a half-eaten Boston Cream doughnut—my favorite—with an oversize cup of Dunkin' Donuts coffee.

"You don't even like coffee!" I exclaimed.

"You've always extolled its virtues, so I thought I'd give it a try."

"You're just doing this to torment me."

"Is it working?"

This was something I'd have to get used to. "I need to ask another favor," I said.

"What will it be? Turn you into a handsome prince? We already tried that, and it didn't take."

"Some of us are just princely on the inside." I fished my mother's pills out of my pocket. "This orange pill is my mother's arthritis medication. The white one is supposedly the same thing. Problem is, she doesn't know how many of the white ones to take for each orange one her doctor prescribed."

Kwan looked leery. "Where'd she get this stuff, anyway, that she doesn't know how much to take?"

"Canada."

"Ah!" Kwan said, as if that explained everything.

He got up and took down a huge red volume from behind his

desk. He turned to the color photos of medications. He ran his finger across the rows of pictures, pausing on the occasional small white pill. "Close, but no cigar," he said at last. "Where did you say she got this?" Kwan asked, indicating the little white pill now sitting on his desk.

"In Canada."

"From a pharmacy?"

"That's my impression."

Kwan shook his head. "Well, if it's here, it's not obvious. Maybe it's something brand-new. . . ."

"I don't think so."

"Let me hang on to this for a day or two. I'll show it to someone I know. He may be able to figure out what she's got here."

"Thanks," I said. "So, you read the report?"

"Very impressive."

"Do you think Kutril could help Olivia?"

"Possibly," he said. "Only problem is, Dr. Temple was working with alcoholics and heroin abusers. It's never been tried with addiction to psychostimulants like Ritalin. And she was working with adults. Not eighty-seven–pound adolescents. On the other hand" — he shrugged — "I can't think of any other treatment that appears to be as overwhelmingly effective in reducing the psychological craving. And given that there are relatively few side effects, I'd say the potential benefits far outweigh the risks. But she should be closely monitored. We're talking large doses of a compound we don't know a whole lot about."

Then Kwan called the New Jersey company that had been making Kutril for Channing and arranged for them to ship us enough for a single course of treatment.

After Kwan got off the phone, he picked up the report and riffled through the pages. "Acu-Med is going to have a fit when this gets published. Aren't they trying to develop something that does basically the same thing?" He handed me back the report. "Be sure you put this in a safe place."

"I will. I had a helluva time getting my hands on it in the first place. But the raw data, test protocols, patient information — the rest is gone."

"You're kidding."

"I wish I were." Without the raw data to defend her conclusions, the research report wasn't publishable. And it could take years to duplicate the work. By then, Acu-Med's new drug would be established in the marketplace.

Kwan scratched his head. "You don't suppose she took the files home?"

I hadn't considered that possibility. "Maybe. Or maybe someone helped themselves. . . ."

Kwan liked that idea. "Those Acu-Med reps hang around here like flies on a rotting corpse."

"Or maybe someone from the Pearce, someone on retainer to Acu-Med . . ." I could see Liam Jensen's foot, shoving against that file-packed drawer. An oasis of disorder in an otherwise perfectly ordered landscape. I wish I'd gotten a closer look.

• • •

I called Drew at home that night. I told him we'd like to try an experimental treatment for the psychological aftereffects of drug addiction, the treatment Channing had been working on. I told him I wasn't certain it would help Olivia, but I thought it was worth a try. He agreed.

When the package arrived the next morning, I headed downstairs to see Olivia. At the nurses' station, I poured myself a cup of decaf. I took a sip. It wasn't too bad. I added milk and sugar. I could do this, I told myself.

I was afraid Olivia might have retreated to the closet again, but she hadn't. She was in the living room, curled up on the corner of a brown vinyl sofa. Matthew Farrell sat beside her. When I came over, Matthew left.

"You okay?" I asked. "The police gave you a rough time."

"How was I supposed to know they'd get my private e-mail messages?" she said, her voice shaking. "I never would have sent them if I thought that could happen."

Words on a page are so unforgiving. In black and white, they take on meaning that the writer is powerless to shade. Olivia's words could certainly make a jury think that she hated her mother, maybe enough to kill her.

I pulled over a chair. "Why did you send them?" I asked.

"She told me to!"

"She?"

"Dr. Daffy. I was so angry at my mother, she said I should write down my feelings, say all the things I couldn't say to her face." Olivia sobbed. "I was only doing what she said. I *hated* it. And now it makes it look like . . . look like . . ."

I'd heard of this therapeutic approach. It began with something called countertransference analysis, CTA, and Daphne had made herself a minor celebrity in the 1980s when she'd written a book about it as a technique to help therapists keep their perspective when working with troubled patients. She'd even been asked to testify in the high-profile trial of Dr. Margaret Bean-Bayog, a therapist whose psychotic young patient stole her personal journals filled with intense sexual fantasies about him. The doctor terminated treatment, but soon after that, the patient committed suicide. The doctor's personal journals became the basis for the family's malpractice lawsuit. There was an out-of-court settlement, and Dr. Bean-Bayog surrendered her medical license.

The case had sent a collective shudder through the therapeutic community—if your personal feelings and thoughts could be examined in court and used against you, then writing them down at all was committing professional suicide. Needless to say, it had a chilling effect on the use of CTA.

Following in her mentor's footsteps, Channing once told me she, too, kept a journal. She used it to work through her impulses and fantasies. That way, she said, she could confront her demons before they ambushed her.

Apparently Daphne hadn't abandoned the method. Working with Olivia, she'd pushed the approach, having a patient write down angry feelings. Maybe it helped. What I didn't get was, what's the point of communicating those angry feelings to the other person? Here was another one of those well-intentioned therapies I'd like to consign to the dung heap, along with encounter groups and primal scream.

"It doesn't work," Olivia said. "I told her it didn't, but she kept making me do it. Sometimes I made things up, just so she'd stop bugging me."

I bit my tongue. Daphne's own experience with CTA blinded her to how inappropriate it was for Olivia. Olivia's floundering, her tears, probably only convinced Daphne that she needed CTA. Just as she needed "structure." Rigid preconceptions are more than dangerous in therapy—they can be criminal. But as Daphne's colleague, I couldn't say any of that.

There were dark shadows under Olivia's eyes. "I never ever wanted to kill my mother." Then her voice turned strident. "She couldn't have just deleted them, could she? She had to save them. Like I'm one of her stupid patients. Or precious students. Leave it to her to screw things up."

Olivia's face had gone taut with rage. Anger at her mother for what she did, for what she didn't do, and especially for dying. Anger and grief—one the doorway to the other. It would be my job to help her pass through. Maybe it would help me deal with my own feelings of helplessness and rage at Channing's death.

"Your mother probably saved everything you did—your drawings, your stories—because it was all important to her."

Olivia's face softened.

"Dr. Smythe-Gooding can explain to the police that the e-mail messages were part of your treatment. And she can explain how you were taking Ritalin."

Olivia sniffled. "She promised . . ." She stopped abruptly. I had the distinct impression she'd just stubbed her toe on something she wasn't supposed to say.

"Has she been here to see you? Was that when she promised?" Olivia looked frightened.

"Dr. Smythe-Gooding told me she paid you a visit," I said.

Olivia's face relaxed. Then she spotted my mug. She peered into it. "You caving already?" Olivia's mood could turn on a dime.

"Decaf," I said. "I came down here to talk to you about a treatment we'd like to try. It should reduce your craving for Ritalin. It's called Kutril, and it's something your mother was working on. I talked to your dad and Dr. Liu about it, and we'd like to start you on it right away."

"It will make me feel better?" Olivia asked.

"It might."

"When?"

"I don't know for sure. A few days. A week."

Olivia groaned.

"Around the time this pounding headache stops," I added.

That got a smile out of her. It is, after all, one of the truest clichés in life that misery loves company.

14

WHEN I got home that night, I went down to my wine cellar. I pulled out a 1992 Caymus cabernet that I'd bought about five years earlier when Kate and I were in the Napa Valley. I brought the bottle upstairs, eased out the cork, and wiped a bit of mold from the rim. I poured a glass, walked it into the living room, and set it on the coffee table. The room was cozy, with its dark woodwork and Mission furniture. I turned on a reading lamp and sat down to the newspaper.

When I finished the sports section, I took a sip. The cabernet was rich and thick, with a smell of leather and a hint of cherry. It's amazing how a good wine can satisfy, like finally being able to reach an itch at the center of your back and giving it a good scratch. If only I had some cheese and crackers to go with it. I went to the cabinet and settled for a little package of peanuts that said American Airlines on it—I had no idea where I'd picked it up.

I was eating the last one when the phone rang. It was Chip Ferguson.

"I got a call from Drew Temple today," Chip said. There was a pause. "How much do you know about this guy?" I couldn't read Chip's tone.

"Known him a long time. Married someone I went to school with."

"So his wife was a close friend?"

"Um-hmm."

"I'm sorry, Peter. That's tough."

I grunted.

"And what does he do?" he said, getting back to business.

"He works . . ." I stopped. I didn't actually know exactly what Drew did. "He manages his family money, assets." That sounded pretty vague. "What gives?"

"Sounds like his wife was loaded. Her money's tied up in probate and won't be settled for a while."

"They live in this incredible house . . ." I started.

"Mortgaged to the hilt," Chip said.

"I'm surprised. I thought they had the kind of money that doesn't need borrowing."

"No one has that kind of money," Chip said. "But it sounds like he's been playing the market. Badly. Day trading, maybe. His wife's death came at a very inopportune time. He was over his head in margin calls, and now he can't dig himself out."

More reasons for Drew's despair, his drinking.

"I thought I was giving up charity cases when I left the public defender's office," Chip said, griping.

"Drew is under a lot of stress," I said. "And you'd be representing his daughter, not him. Chip, she's seventeen and they're probably going to arrest her for a murder she didn't commit."

"Sounds like they've got a strong case. The judge could easily deny bail and send her to one of the holding pens for violent young offenders."

"Not if you talk them into sending her to us for evaluation."

Chip didn't say anything. I waited. "I'm not real anxious to take this case," he said at last. "You know I'm not crazy about working with kids."

"No, I don't know that. Since when? Besides, she's not a kid."

"Okay. So she's an adolescent. Even worse."

"Just a few years younger than your daughter."

"Now you're hitting below the belt."

"Remember when you called me six months ago? Said you had a case and all you wanted to do was talk to me about it?"

"Yeah, yeah. I remember."

"And I ended up evaluating the memory of the surviving victim and nearly getting myself and Annie killed?"

Chip didn't answer. I thought I heard him shifting in his chair. Good. I hoped that made him uncomfortable as hell. "Now, *you* owe *me*," I said.

There were a few moments of dead air. Then, "You found the body?" His tone had turned businesslike, and I could hear his keyboard clicking.

"I had an appointment to talk with Channing and Olivia the morning Channing was killed. Channing wanted me to evaluate Olivia. . . ."

"Evaluate her for what?"

"To see if she had Asperger's syndrome."

More clicking. "Which is?"

"Actually, it's like a severe learning disability for emotions. And I don't think she's got it. Anyway, when they didn't show up at the cafeteria, I went over to her office. That's where I found her, dead. Olivia standing beside her, holding the gun." They were just words, like I was reading them from the newspaper, trying to get as much information across in the shortest amount of time. "I bent a few rules to get her admitted to my unit."

"Sounds like you're up to your neck in this, personally and professionally. I assume you're not going to be able to help me as an expert witness."

I gave a dry laugh. "I think not."

"But unofficially?"

"I'm at your disposal."

"Good. I'm going to need your expertise in planning for all contingencies. Are there other people with motive and opportunity?"

My fingers cramped on the receiver. Who would I point to? Colleagues? Friends? Drew?

"Peter?" Chip asked. "You still there?"

"Yes."

"You know, if they come up with enough evidence to arrest Olivia Temple, there's a good chance there's enough to convict."

"There are no eyewitnesses," I said.

"You saw her yourself, holding the gun!"

"I didn't see her pull the trigger. Besides which, if the gunshot wound was through the mouth, then how did she manage it? There was no sign of a struggle."

"Okay, okay." He gave an exasperated sigh. "Let's move on. Suppose something unexpected happens, like Olivia confesses. Or they dig up an eyewitness. As in, just suppose for a moment that Olivia Temple did kill her mother." He paused, letting that sink in. "Have we got any extenuating circumstances?"

I didn't like going down this path. It took some effort for me to give him a suggestion. "Olivia was taking Ritalin."

Chip guffawed. "Olivia Temple and half the kids in junior high."

"No joke. It's become a major problem."

He scoffed. "Get outa here."

"It's true. A good percentage of drug abuse among adolescents is Ritalin." I started to lay out the case. "Olivia's psychiatrist prescribed Ritalin, presumably to treat a brain dysfunction. The Ritalin helps her to keep focused and makes it easier for her to do her schoolwork. While taking Ritalin, the prescribed dosage —"

"The prescribed dosage," Chip whispered under his breath. I could hear his keyboard clicking furiously.

I slowed down. "She becomes addicted. She loses control over her cravings and takes more. The medication itself ultimately impairs her judgment, makes her hypomanic, impulsive."

"Hypomanic, impulsive," Chip repeated. The keyboard clicking stopped. "We're just talking Ritalin here, right?"

"That's all they found in her blood screen."

"Because you know, if it's something like cocaine or ecstasy, or even some other drug that she's using without a doctor's prescription, then it's a lot harder to make the case."

"As far as I know, just Ritalin."

"Diminished capacity," Chip said. "Always a stretch to prove. Requires someone to take the jury through a lot of torturous logic. I hate cases that hinge on legal technicalities. And without you in the witness box . . ."

"I can recommend someone."

"Can we demonstrate that she does, in fact, have diminished capacity—how did you describe her?"

"Impulsive. Hypomanic. See, she may not be either of those things any longer, now that we've weaned her from the drug. But we can certainly test her to establish that she has an organic disability for which she needed the Ritalin, which in turn is documented to have those harmful effects."

"When abused?"

"When abused," I admitted.

"She's at the Pearce now? In your care?"

"Yes. And we were planning to evaluate her anyway. Once she's tested, the tests become part of her medical record."

"We'll need her test results if we go to trial. Peter, I don't know how fast the police are going to move. Could you get started as soon as you can?"

"Sure. Right away."

"And who prescribed Ritalin?"

"Dr. Daphne Smythe-Gooding. A psychiatrist at the Pearce. Also a close friend of the deceased."

"Another friend. Great."

"Sorry, that's what happens when you're dealing with children of shrinks. It can get incestuous."

"Okay if I drop by tomorrow and talk with my client?"

"Make it in the afternoon. I'm going to start testing her in the morning. And thanks, Chip."

"Don't mention it," he muttered.

I hung up the phone, sat back, and tried to get into the newspaper again. But my brain wasn't ready to shift into neutral. I wondered, did Channing know Drew was hemorrhaging money? Was she aware of his affair? With her clear sense of right and wrong, black and white, wouldn't she have wanted to divorce him? And if she was planning to divorce him, then wasn't her death conveniently timed for Drew?

THE NEXT morning, I woke up in a foul mood. The world seemed
to move in slow motion, the air so thick I had to fight my way
through it. More than anything, I wanted a cup of coffee. Barring that, I was desperate for a run. But I'd overslept, and there
wasn't time.

I found some instant decaf at the back of a kitchen cabinet. The
jar was coated with dust and the expiration date was four years
earlier. I threw a handful into a mug of hot tap water and knocked
it back. It tasted god-awful. Then I managed to break my coffee
mug, tossing it into the sink. On my way to the car, I stepped in a
pile of dog shit, no doubt courtesy of some civic-minded dog
walker.

Scowling, I went back in to change my shoes. I was looking
for my car keys when my mother's knock sounded. I yanked open
the door.

"The tax collector gets a warmer hello," she said. She wrinkled
her nose. "What stinks?"

She has an infallible nose. I gave her a hug but didn't invite her
in. "It's exactly what it smells like," I said. "And now I'm late. Can't
find my keys."

"So? What did you find out?" she asked, up on the balls of her feet.

I must have looked baffled.

"The pills!"

"Oh, right! I gave them to Kwan, and he couldn't find them in the reference book. He said he'd ask someone else. Might have an answer today. That okay?"

"I should live so long," she said. "Are those what you're looking for?" she asked, indicating the set of car keys lying on the first stair step.

Before I could thank her, she'd disappeared into her own side of the house.

It took four tries for my car to start. But once I got it going, it didn't falter. I ran a hand across the dashboard and relaxed deep into the leather seat. I could feel the wheels hug the road as I turned into the street and accelerated into the flow of traffic. At least I could still enjoy driving. Traffic cooperated, and the ten-minute drive to the institute went without incident.

When I got there, Jess was already at work in the dining room, administering an intelligence test and a mental-status exam to Olivia. Jess had been pleased when I'd asked her to help.

An hour later, Jess and I huddled in the hall. She summarized for me: "Superior IQ. Verbal much higher than Performance."

That didn't surprise me. With a nonverbal learning disability, I'd expect Olivia to do better on language-mediated tasks.

Jess continued, "Problems with concentration. Irritability. Labile affect. She broke down when I asked her if she'd ever thought about killing herself. She's terrified that suicide is hereditary. And she's next."

It was succinct and to the point, though nothing I didn't already know.

I grabbed a leather case from a storage closet and went to the dining room. Olivia glared at me. "When is this Kutrid or whatever it is supposed to start working? I still feel completely gross."

I stood, rigid. Quit whining, I wanted to snap. Get past it. Think about something other than yourself for a change. But that would have been the caffeine withdrawal talking. I tried to relax the muscles in my back and shoulders, to release the tension from my neck and jaw.

"Do you need to take a break, or can we go on to another test?" I asked.

She shrugged. "You're not going to make me write things, are you?"

"Not this time," I said, putting the case on the table and unzipping it. Olivia watched as I pulled out an odd assortment of items. Forty-six in all. When I was done, they covered half the table. Olivia picked up the little brown-and-white plastic toy dog. I could see from her look that she didn't think much of my so-called test.

I took the dog from her and put it back on the table. "As you know, we have some concerns about how efficiently you're processing information," I said. "It's probably one of the reasons Dr. Smythe-Gooding started you on Ritalin." A small moth fluttered close to my head, and I brushed it away.

"What do you mean, 'processing information'?"

"It means how you make sense of the world and deal with it. Here's an example. You take a person with information-processing problems and plunk them down in the middle of Grand Central Station in rush hour and tell them they have to be on a certain train. They become overwhelmed by all the people racing around, the hullabaloo—so much so that they can't figure out how to get to where they're going. They become anxious and shut down.

"But, take that same person and plunk them in Grand Central Station at midnight. In the deserted station, they can figure out where they need to go, no problem."

Olivia still looked skeptical.

"In this test, the objects on the table are Grand Central Station. And the fact that I'm sitting here timing you makes it rush hour." Olivia tried to contain a smile, but it leaked out the edges. "The test gives me some idea how you take in and categorize the world around you."

"What do I have to do?" she asked.

"Just sort the items. Put the things together that go together. In any way you like."

"How much time do I get?"

"Five minutes," I said. Olivia eyes widened. "You'll see, that's actually quite a lot of time. Ready?"

Olivia nodded.

I started my stopwatch, and the second hand began its first sweep around the dial. Olivia tucked her feet up on the chair, hugged her knees, and rocked forward and back. She surveyed the table. She sighed, put her legs down, and propped her elbows on the table. She twiddled with her hair.

Abruptly, she stood up, knocking her chair over. "This is lame. Why do I have to do this?"

"Bear with me," I said. "I know this feels babyish."

She folded her arms and glared at the table. "There are too many things. And I'm probably already out of time."

"You're right, there are a lot of things. Sometimes people have trouble deciding where to begin. Why don't you just start with one or two things and see how it goes. If you need help, I'm here."

Reluctantly, Olivia sidled back into the chair. She put her elbows on the table, her head in her hands. Casually, she fingered the bicycle bell.

"That's a good one to start with. Now what goes with it?" I asked.

She picked up a red ball and gave me a sideways look before putting it down, alongside the bicycle bell.

"Very good," I said. As she worked, I took careful notes.

She added the sugar cube, the piece of candy, and the stick of gum to the grouping. Then she sat back.

"Great job," I said.

To most of us, this test is straightforward. But it went right to the core of the problems Olivia had, structuring her world. For someone who gave equal importance to tasks like brushing her teeth and writing a term paper, picking a starting point when faced with forty-six items was a risky act, opening herself up to the shame of making a foolish choice.

"How about another group?" I suggested. She had three minutes left.

Olivia pushed the chair away. She got up and walked around the table. Then she sat back down.

She pulled aside the plastic dog and held it in her hand while she stared at the remaining items. Her gaze shifted to the edge of the table, where the moth was now resting. Her head tilted to one side as she watched it sit there, and then fly off. After that, her attention drifted and she started rocking, stroking the ears of her bunny slippers.

"Any other groups?" I asked.

She looked at me as if she wasn't sure what it was she'd been doing. Remembered. And then concentrated once again on the remaining items.

Hesitantly, she touched the red picnic plate.

"Good," I said. "Is that the beginning of a new group?"

She set the plate to one side. On top of it, she placed the plastic cup, the napkin, the silverware, a package of saltines, a chocolate kiss, and a candy cigarette. As an afterthought, she pulled over a little toy fork and spoon as well.

"Super," I said.

Then she made another grouping with the hammer, matches, a jackknife, pliers, a screwdriver, nails, a padlock, and keys.

About a dozen items remained ungrouped. Olivia stared at them. Then she looked up at the ceiling. The moth now fluttering around the fluorescent light.

"Time's up," I said.

She was still holding the plastic dog.

"You did a great job. Let's look at this group." I pointed to the grouping with the bicycle bell, ball, and candy. "What would you call it?"

"Things that make you happy," she replied promptly.

"What about them makes you happy?"

She rolled her eyes. "Sugar is sweet. You play with the ball." She rang the bicycle bell and smiled. "I had one of these when I was little. On my purple bike. It had silvery streamers that came out of the handle." Her eyes glazed over. "My mom taught me to ride it." She brushed away a tear.

"And what about this," I asked, pointing to the grouping of utensils and plates.

Olivia gave me a pitying look. "Things for eating, I guess."

"What makes them things for eating?"

"Come on," she whined.

"Just humor me."

"Well, these are the things you put on the table, and you use them to eat your food. And these are toys. Like, you could pretend to eat your food with them. And these things, you eat."

"Good. What do you call this next group?"

She looked at me sideways. "These are things you can hurt people with," she said.

"Can you tell me more?"

"Well," she said slowly, picking up the jackknife and opening it up, "you can stab people with a knife. Or hit people with a hammer." She poked at the padlock. "You can lock people up, like I'm locked up, so they can't get out. And they can't go outside." She started to cry. "And they can't do anything but what you tell them to."

I took more notes and waited, hoping her frustration would dissipate itself. More than a dozen other items, mostly at the edges, remained untouched. It was odd that she had omitted the toy gun and the bullet from the things-you-can-hurt-people-with group.

"Any other groups?" I asked.

She opened her hand. The plastic dog was in her palm. She set it on the table. "This is by itself. It needs to be taken care of," she said.

I was reminded of the time I gave the same test to a patient who was a loner. He had great difficulty relating to other people. He divided everything into two groups. One group, he said, were objects that went with other objects. The other group consisted of items that stood alone. That, in a nutshell, was that young man's world—a place where he stood alone while other people were able to relate to one another.

Olivia's response was nowhere near that extreme. But that little dog that needed to be taken care of certainly reflected her own need for the same. The extent to which drives and emotions ruled the way in which she organized the items spoke to how she was still reeling from recent events. It was also evident that she had a hard time getting organized, deciding where to begin, and making good use of her time. The average person makes about ten groups, Olivia had made only four. Psychological tests never cease to amaze me—so simple and yet so insightful.

I asked her to sort the items again, in a different way. This time, she created only three groups, leaving more items unsorted. The things-you-can-hurt-people-with group reappeared, again without the toy gun or bullet.

When I asked her to sort the items a third time, she said she couldn't. There weren't any other ways.

I had more testing to do, but I could already hear clattering in the kitchen as the staff prepared for lunch. If a single moth was enough to distract Olivia, she'd never manage to concentrate with the anvil chorus going on.

I wondered if my results were consistent with Daphne's impressions. "Olivia, I'd like to call Dr. Smythe-Gooding," I said.

"I don't want—" Olivia started, her face hardening.

"Look, it will really help in determining the best long-term treatment for you if I can talk to her. She's been working with you for a year. She knows . . ."

"She doesn't know me at all," Olivia said. "She's always telling me that I have to stop being so stupid. I try. I make lists so I won't forget things. I write down my feelings, but it doesn't make them go away. None of it helps. *She* doesn't help. She just makes me feel like an idiot."

Olivia's inability to organize her world must have baffled Channing. It was a shame that she'd turned to Daphne for help. Olivia and Daphne were a mismatch. Instead of building Olivia's confidence and then teaching her new behaviors, Daphne had Olivia continually practice what she was weakest at doing. The wounds were picked raw, rather than bound and soothed. Self-confidence collapsed at a time in Olivia's development when she was most vulnerable.

"How about if I promise to restrict our discussion about you to these test results?"

Reluctantly, Olivia agreed.

"You'll be meeting with Mr. Ferguson this afternoon," I said.

Olivia looked at me, solemn.

"He's here to help you. Just be honest. Be yourself." It sounded obvious, but it was the best I advice I could give.

$$\cdots$$

I had bumper-to-bumper appointments all afternoon. I only had time to put my head in and say hello to Chip while he met with Olivia. Later, during a break, I was talking with Gloria when Kwan appeared.

"Sorry. I haven't been able to find out what this is," he said, holding out my mother's white pill. "I suppose we could have it analyzed."

Gloria picked the pill out of Kwan's open palm. "Looks like what Ginger takes for arthritis. I recognize the shape."

"It *is* for arthritis," I said. "But isn't Ginger your dog?"

"Dogs get arthritis," Gloria said defensively. I remembered the Christmas cards Gloria and Rachel sent out each year, photographs of their cocker spaniel in a red bow and felt antlers. "Ginger's getting on, poor thing," she added.

"It's probably got the same drug they give to humans," Kwan said. "Probably safe. We just have to figure out how much . . ."

"You'd advise *your* mother to take it?" I asked.

"My mother wouldn't go all the way to Canada and bring back mystery medicine. She's nutty in different ways from your mother. You know, acupuncture and ginseng."

I called my mother and told her why we hadn't been able to find her pill in the *Physicians' Desk Reference*. "It's a veterinary medicine."

My mother gasped. "You're kidding me. You mean, for cows and chickens?"

"More like dogs and cats. Cows and chickens usually get slaughtered long before they become arthritic."

"Is that what you think should happen to me now that I have a little arthritis?"

"Of course that's not what I think. What I think is that it's a crazy way to save money when you can afford to pay what drugs cost. And if you can't, I can."

"It just galls me . . ." my mother started, and was off on a tirade about how the drug companies were making their profits on the backs of the elderly poor. But I knew it was something else, too. My mother hates to pay full price for anything. I remembered the cold mornings my brother and I got schlepped to Union Square in Manhattan and stood on the sidewalk, huddled alongside her, jostled by the crowd of women waiting for S. Klein's to open its doors. We'd be steaming in too many layers of clothing, inhaling a miasma of wet wool, mothballs, and hair spray. Our reward was pants that we'd "grow into."

My mother had ended her rant. There was a silence. Then I heard footsteps. Then it sounded like a toilet flushing. "So much for their veterinary medicine! What do they think I am?" she asked, outraged. "A Siamese cat?"

• • •

Back in my office, my brain felt as if it had a fog machine going in it. I reached for my coffee mug. A reflex. I walked down the hall to the men's room and doused my face with cold water. That didn't help.

When I got back, my phone was blinking. I retrieved the message. It was Chip. "Can you come over and meet with Annie and me? The autopsy results show Channing Temple was comatose when she's supposed to have shot herself."

16

IT WAS nearly six by the time I made it over to Chip's office. By then, there were plenty of parking spaces in East Cambridge. The new office was in a brick building shaped like a miniature airplane hangar. Before renovations it had been an auto-repair shop, and long before that, probably a stable and blacksmith's. Double doors that would have swung open to admit a horse and buggy had been replaced by multipaned windows.

I climbed the stairs to the second floor. They had an old-fashioned oak door with a pebbled glass panel in the upper half and a brass doorknob that reminded me of the engraved ones on every door in P.S. 181. In black letters across the glass, it said FER-GUSON & ASSOCIATES. And in smaller letters beneath that: SQUIRES INVESTIGATIONS.

The door was locked. I rang the bell. A minute later, Annie pulled the door open. A roomy, skylighted central area opened up before me. The space dwarfed the meager furnishings—a half-dozen file cabinets and a few industrial-strength steel desks.

"Nice digs," I said, looking around at the beamed ceiling and exposed-brick wall. "Very nice." I gave her a quick kiss on the mouth.

Annie glowed with pleasure. Her hand lingered on my arm. "As soon as our receivables turn the corner, we'll have an assistant or two out here. In the meanwhile, I'm considering moving my futon in. This is a helluva lot nicer than my place."

She took me on a tour of the five-room suite. I was relieved that the coffeepot was turned off. Nothing to tempt me. Then we went into Chip's office. He was finishing up a phone call, his back to a huge arched window. In the distance, white cables supporting a new bridge were strung like a giant, inverted fan-shaped harp across the skyline at the northern edge of the Big Dig, Boston's Herculean effort to bury its primary north-south artery and let mere mortals reclaim the heart of the city and the waterfront.

I recognized the Grateful Dead poster on the wall, now in a chrome frame. Chip had had it tacked to the back of his office door in the public defender's office.

When he got off the phone, Chip got straight to the point. "The autopsy results turned up a fair amount of drugs in Channing Temple's stomach. But even more had been metabolized. She was probably unconscious when she was shot."

"Probably?"

"They always hedge. They're putting together an arrest warrant for Olivia."

"How soon?" I asked.

"MacRae wouldn't tell me that," Annie said. "But I think you can count on it by the end of the week."

"Have you told Drew?" I asked.

"That was him on the phone, just now," Chip said. "He's frantic."

I'd known this could happen—Olivia getting arrested for Channing's murder. But knowing something intellectually and then having it happen are two different things. How do you help a seventeen-year-old prepare to be charged with murder? All my training in psychology came up short.

"How was your meeting with Olivia this afternoon?" I asked Chip.

"She's terrified," he said.

"Seems like an appropriate response."

"The jury will want to like her. But she is off-putting. Not someone who gives you the warm fuzzies."

"I like her."

"That's because it's your job," Chip said.

I started to explain that it wasn't my job to *like* her, but I let it go.

Chip went on. "I wanted you here to help prepare for the arraignment. There are two ways we can go with this. Plead not guilty—someone else did it. Or not guilty and go with a Twinkie defense."

"Better if someone else did it," Annie said.

"Absolutely," Chip answered, "but I want to be ready to go either way, depending on what kind of evidence they dig up."

I wasn't surprised at their reluctance to embrace a Twinkie defense—a defense based on diminished capacity. The Twinkie part of it goes back to a trial for a double murder in San Francisco. A city supervisor shot and killed Mayor George Moscone and Harvey Milk, another city official. The press reported that the defense team blamed the killer's actions on Twinkies and other sugary junk food. Diminished his mental capacity.

As usual, the press got it wrong. What the defense actually argued was that the guy had a long-standing, untreated depression that diminished his capacity to distinguish right from wrong. He was incapable of the premeditation required for first-degree murder. How could you tell? Here was a guy who'd always eaten a healthy diet and suddenly, he's bingeing on junk food. Eating Twinkies didn't cause the depression, but it was *evidence* of it, like his lack of personal hygiene.

If the Twinkie defense was going to work for Olivia, Chip had to demonstrate she had an underlying problem that diminished her mental capacity.

"I'm about halfway through testing Olivia," I said. "There's already a basis for arguing that she needs to take a psychostimulant like Ritalin to help her focus. We know her doctor prescribed it. That should establish the foundation you need."

"What's the underlying condition?" Chip asked.

"A right-hemisphere learning disorder. Not nearly as powerful as depression," I admitted. "But excessive amounts of Ritalin can alter judgment. Still, it's a hard sell. Besides, I don't think she did it."

"You really don't?" Chip asked.

"They'll have a strong case," Annie said. "She's found holding the gun. She's got Ativan in her pocket. Hate-filled e-mail messages are in her mother's computer."

"She wrote those messages as part of her therapy," I said.

"You said Ritalin could have altered her judgment," Chip argued. "Could it have bent her to the point where she'd kill someone?"

I sighed. "People have this notion of the good Dr. Jekyll turning into the murderous Mr. Hyde, courtesy of a potion. But it's a lot of bunk. Listen, addiction doesn't bend the personality so much as subvert it. Loosen the screws. Drugs can disinhibit you, bring out latent personality traits. But they can't make you into a murderer if fundamentally you're not."

"And Olivia?" Chip asked.

"Not." I was pretty sure of that.

Chip cocked his head, pressed his lips together, and closed one eye at me. "Okay. So, let's say Olivia Temple didn't do it. And it's not suicide. Who else —?"

"Isn't it enough just to cast doubt?" I asked.

"Reasonable doubt. But a jury wants plausible alternatives. Let's see, there's her father," Chip said. "Financial problems. He have a girlfriend?" I didn't respond. "Know if Drew has an alibi?"

Chip and Annie looked at me. I swallowed. "I don't know," I said. "I tried to call him after I found Channing, and his assistant couldn't reach him for about thirty minutes."

Chip took notes. "Did Channing have any enemies?" he asked.

Channing had managed to piss off any number of people over the years. But I wasn't about to offer them up as sacrificial lambs. Finally, I said, "She had a few. Channing was a radical. She never lost her distrust of the establishment."

Chip looked up. "Sounds as if I would have liked her."

"You would have. Soul mates, in fact."

"People don't usually get killed over professional differences," Annie said.

She was right. There were other ways to handle those—tidier and almost as destructive. "No one had to kill Channing to discredit her work," I said. "It was already happening. There was a scathing review of her research in a medical journal a few weeks ago. Then there were rumors about improprieties. I don't know exactly what kind of boundary violations, or if the allegations have merit. No disciplinary hearing. She suspected that they were replacing her as head of the Drug and Alcohol Rehabilitation Unit, and I think she was right. On top of all that, the files documenting her research have gone missing."

Chip whistled. "Any idea who might have taken them?"

"No," I said. But I guess it didn't sound too convincing, because Annie responded, "Peter, come on."

"Liam Jensen. He claims he hasn't got them. But when I visited him in his office the other day, he had an overflowing file drawer he kept trying to push shut with his foot. Purple file folders were sticking out, and if you ask me, he's not the purple type."

"Isn't he the one who had a screaming fight with Channing at the end of her party?" Annie asked.

I nodded.

It was after six-thirty by the time we finished up. I called and left a message for Jess, asking her to give Olivia some more cognitive tests the next morning.

I said good-bye to Chip, and Annie walked me out. "It wouldn't be hard to get into Dr. Jensen's office." Annie said it nonchalantly, as if she was suggesting a stroll on the banks of the Charles.

"Break in?" I asked.

"Just to check what he's got in that file drawer. He'll never know anyone was there."

I wanted to help Olivia. I'd do just about anything to keep Channing's research from being consigned to oblivion. But breaking into a colleague's office was definitely over the line.

Annie pressed, "You searched Channing's office, didn't you?"

"It's not the same. Channing's dead. And one of the hospital administrators let me in. Going into Jensen's office without his permission, without anyone's permission—that would be another thing entirely," I said. I tried to sound outraged. But I was considering the possibility. If we just looked for the research data, avoided looking at confidential patient records . . .

Annie saw her opening. "It'll be easy."

I found myself asking, "How easy?"

"Real easy. Trust me." I always get worried when Annie says that. "Who knows, someone could be shredding the files right this moment, as we speak."

17

THE DA didn't waste any time. In the morning, I got a call from Security. The police were on their way over with an escort. I called Chip's office to leave word and asked them to alert Drew. Then I raced down to Olivia's room to give her at least a few minutes' warning.

The door was shut. I knocked. There was no answer. I knocked louder. "Olivia, it's Dr. Zak. Can I come in?" I called out.

Still nothing. I pushed the door open and looked inside. The room was empty. I checked the closet. No Olivia. The bathroom door was closed. I knocked. "Olivia, you in there?" I said.

The toilet flushed. Olivia, her head wrapped in a towel, pulled the bathroom door open and glared out at me. "Keep your shirt on," she grumbled. "Can't a person have five minutes peace in this place without someone wanting to know if I'm okay . . . ?" Her voice died out on the last word, when she finally looked me in the eye.

"Olivia, the police are on their way here."

She suddenly looked terror-stricken and about five years old. "Has something happened to Daddy?"

Of course—it's the first thing she'd think. Another tragedy.

When one unthinkable thing happens, life starts to feel like a walk along the edge of a crevasse where at any moment you or someone you love could fall in.

"No, your father is fine." I paused. I wished there were some way to put this gently. "The police are on their way over to arrest you."

Olivia stood there, momentarily at a loss for words. She backed up and sat on the bed. The towel uncoiled itself and fell onto the floor. Shocks of black hair with blond roots stood out from her head.

"They're going to take you to court. They'll put you in a holding cell. No one will hurt you. I called Mr. Ferguson. He'll get down there. There will be an arraignment."

"Will you be there?"

"I'll come as soon as I can." I had a full calendar so that would take a bit of doing.

"Arraignment," she echoed the word.

"You'll plead, guilty or not guilty."

"Not guilty," Olivia whispered.

"Of course."

"Then what?"

"They might release you on bail. Send you to a secure youth center. Or hold you for evaluation."

Olivia was trembling. There was a sharp knock at the door. We both jumped. Gloria came in carrying a little plastic cup. "It's that time again," she said briskly. Olivia blinked at her. "What's wrong?" Gloria looked at me. "What's happening?"

There were footsteps in the hall. Olivia ran over to Gloria and huddled against her. A Pearce security guard entered the room, followed by MacRae and two uniformed cops.

"Olivia Temple," MacRae announced, brandishing a pair of handcuffs. "I'm here to arrest you for the murder of Channing Temple."

"Handcuffs?" I said. "Give me a break."

"This time, we're doing it by the book, Dr. Zak," he said, and turned back to Olivia. "You have the right to remain silent. . . ."

Like a penitent, Olivia offered up her bone-thin wrists. I winced as MacRae snapped the cuffs around them.

He droned on. "Anything you say can and will be used against you in a court of law. You have the right to an attorney. . . ."

"She can't go anywhere," Gloria protested. "She needs to take *this* medication," she showed him the container, "every four hours."

I jumped on it. "It's an experimental treatment. We don't know what will happen if she misses a dose, or stops taking it suddenly. There's no way to know what kind of reaction she might have." I hoped the prospect sounded ominous.

"So gimme enough pills to get her through forty-eight hours," MacRae growled. "She looks like she can walk."

"But she needs to be monitored," Gloria said.

"We have a physician on call," MacRae countered.

I stepped into his face. "I'm going to hold you personally responsible if anything happens to Ms. Temple."

He blinked impassively. "If you cannot afford an attorney, one will be appointed for you free of charge. Do you understand each of these rights I have read to you?"

Olivia looked at me like, What's the right answer?

"Don't say anything," I told her. "If anyone asks you questions, don't answer. Tell them you want to speak to your attorney. Do you understand?" Olivia nodded, but I wasn't sure she was processing my words.

Gloria went over to her and took Olivia's face in her hands. "Olivia, do you understand what Dr. Zak is saying? Don't talk to anyone, right?" She smoothed Olivia's hair, first on one side, then the other. "Not even another prisoner, unless your lawyer is there with you."

MacRae glared at me.

"That's 'by the book,' too," I told him.

Impotent rage filled me as I watched Olivia being led away.

. . .

I kept checking my messages that morning. Finally, there was a message from Chip. The arraignment was scheduled for after lunch. I left the Pearce in plenty of time, but a few work crews, supervised by especially slow-witted cops, made getting across Cambridge a nightmare. I'd had to cut through Harvard Square, a route I normally avoid.

I sat at the light, grinding my teeth, resisting the urge to run down one of the pedestrians who consider the words DON'T WALK an invitation to charge across the street.

By the time I'd parked at a meter and walked over to the eighteen-story courthouse, my head felt as if it were going to explode. The building stood like a cinder-block embarrassment across the street from the stately, century-old probate court building. I waited in the line that snaked out the door, at what feels like a service entrance. That's because it was designed to be the service entrance, until the City of Cambridge denied a permit for the second-floor access bridge into what would have been an august lobby.

I passed quickly through the metal detector and into a warren of small, low-ceilinged spaces and interconnected corridors. The place was more jail than courthouse. A woman wearing a very long suit jacket and a very short skirt gave me a disdainful look as I banged on the elevator button. I got on with about a dozen other people, each of whom seemed to be holding a gallon-size cup of coffee.

I'd ridden these elevators dozens of times, on my way to weeks of jury selection and then more weeks of the trial of the man who killed Kate. I hadn't wanted the jury to forget the human dimensions of her loss. And I'd wanted Ralston Bridges to know I was there, making sure he got what was coming to him.

When the elevator opened on the third floor, more people got on. I stared at the back of a man's head, his blond hair grazing my nose. I felt a queasiness in the pit of my stomach. The man reminded me of Bridges.

As more people pressed into the elevator, I tried to inch back. The blond man trod on my toes and began to turn around. It was like the times when I entered that courtroom and Bridges seemed to sense it. He'd be sitting with his back to me at the defense table. His head would swivel around, as if it weren't connected to the rest of his body. He'd stare at me for a moment from dead eyes. Then turn back.

He'd give me no satisfaction, even with the jury watching. His look seemed to say, "Remember, if it weren't for you, we wouldn't be here." And it was true. If I'd never become an expert witness, if I'd never gotten into the business of evaluating murderers, then Bridges and I never would have met.

I found my way to the judge's chambers. Chip met me outside in the hallway. "Ready?" I asked.

"Sherman's here," he said. Montrose Sherman was the DA—a slick guy who'd just lost a run for attorney general by a slim margin. The last time I'd faced him on the stand, he'd gotten the better of me. "What I don't get is why," Chip asked.

"Why wouldn't he be?" I asked. "It's a murder case, isn't it?"

"It involves a juvenile. Normally, the assistant DA covers these kinds of cases."

"Maybe he's taking a personal interest," I suggested.

"Shit," Chip said.

My sentiments precisely. We went in together. The spacious office with windows, which overlooked the trophy-top of the Museum of Science, was lined with books. The fluorescent fixtures hummed overhead, casting a merciless light over the almost perfectly square room with its ersatz oak paneling and gray linoleum tile.

I took a seat at the large, oval-shaped conference table that filled the center of the space, opposite Sherman and the assistant DA. A court stenographer sat at attention, along with the judge's clerk. A pair of court officers flanked the door.

Olivia was brought in and took a seat beside Chip. She looked fragile as a twig. When Drew arrived, he squeezed in beside me.

Today Drew looked patrician and distinguished, his suit clean and pressed. The judge, an elderly fellow with layers of jowls connecting his head to the neck of his black robe, presided from the head of the table. He looked as if he'd already had an exhausting day.

Huddling with his colleague, DA Sherman reminded me of a 1950s ad for hair tonic — a briefcase-toting executive in a dark, pin-striped suit, his brown hair brilliantined in place. Alongside him, the assistant DA looked like a teenager trying out for a part in a play. The suit looked as if he'd borrowed it from someone slightly larger, slightly older.

The judge paged through some printed pages. Then he sat back and cleared his throat.

"I'm going to enter a plea of not guilty for you, Ms. Temple," the judge said, his voice gruff but not unkind. "Is there a question of bail?" he asked the assistant DA.

Chip jumped in. "The defense requests a civil commitment in lieu of bail and that Ms. Temple be returned to the Pearce Psychiatric Institute where she's undergoing evaluation and treatment."

"The Commonwealth . . ." the assistant DA started to respond, but Sherman leaned into him from the side.

The young man's voice died out, and Sherman took over. "The Commonwealth requests that the defendant be remanded to the Bechtel Center for Girls for evaluation. They have excellent psychiatrists who can attend to her there."

Olivia seemed to shudder on hearing this.

Bechtel was a secure, Department of Youth Services facility that specialized in violent adolescents. It had a good reputation, for what it was. But I hated to think what Olivia — or any kid for that matter — might have to learn there.

Chip countered, "The Bechtel Center doesn't have the medical expertise needed to treat my client."

Sherman raised his chin and looked down his nose at Olivia. "Your honor, the defendant is undergoing treatment for drug withdrawal. Her situation is hardly unique. The Bechtel handles similar cases every day of the week."

Olivia seemed dazed. I noticed a little twitch in her hand, like it was an insect caught between two window panes.

"If you'd let me explain—" Chip started, then stopped. The judge waved his hand for him to get on with it. "Ms. Temple is going through an experimental drug protocol. Her doctors at the Pearce know how to deal with this, should there be any unexpected reactions. She'll be on a locked unit, so there's no danger of her escaping. But if you send her to the Bechtel, where they have no experience with this use of the medication, there's a very real health risk." Chip paused and glanced at Olivia. She'd gone white. "Perhaps even a danger to her life."

The twitch that had begun in Olivia's hand had worked its way up her arm. Now her shoulder and her head were pulling to one side. I couldn't see her face. Were her eyes open or were they starting to roll back? I found myself pushing away from the table, ready to spring.

Sherman said, "Your honor, as long as the defendant remains at the Pearce, the Commonwealth's psychiatrist will be unable to evaluate her. I don't believe this delay is necessary."

"When did this experimental treatment begin?" the judge asked.

Chip glanced over at me. I held up two fingers. "Two weeks . . ." he started. I shook my head. "Two days ago, Your Honor." Chip didn't look pleased.

Sherman said, "That seems rather convenient. . . ." He stopped suddenly and stared across the table at Olivia. The tremor had now grown into a full-body shudder. She pitched forward and her chair went out from under her. Her chin whacked against the edge of the table as she went down.

I was up out of my seat before I'd even had time to think about what was happening. I rushed over to Olivia, but a court officer, a thick fellow with white hair and a toothbrush mustache, held me back while the other officer knelt by her side. Olivia had gone rigid. She was foaming at the mouth, the foam turning pink as it mixed with the bright red blood from where she'd bitten her lip.

"He's her doctor," Chip told the toothbrush mustache, and he let me go to her.

The second officer had turned Olivia over onto her back. I took off my jacket and folded it under her head. Then I pushed her head to one side so if she vomited she wouldn't choke. I pulled out my wallet and jammed it in between her teeth. Her heels beat on the floor, loudly at first. The second hand on the wall clock jerked ahead slowly as the drumbeat weakened.

When the sound stopped, the room was silent. The sharp smell of warm urine floated up. Drew was hovering behind me. Montrose Sherman was sitting right where he'd been, his arms folded across his chest, his pencil tapping against his yellow pad.

I eased my wallet from Olivia's mouth. She was sound asleep. I touched her shoulder. "Olivia," I said, pressing my hand gently against her. "Olivia, wake up."

Her eyelids fluttered open, the eyes unfocused. She seemed bewildered. Then her looked snagged on me. "Dr. Zak? I'm so tired," she whispered. She saw Drew behind me. "Daddy?"

She struggled to a seated position. Then her face twisted with surprise that turned to embarrassment as she put her hand between her legs. "What happened?" Then her glance shifted to the judge, who was peering down over the edge of the conference table.

"You had a seizure," I told her. "You lost control. It happens. Just stay here until you feel like you can get up." I gave her my handkerchief. "Here, you bit your lip." She pressed it up against her mouth, pulled it away, and grimaced at the sight of blood.

The judge called for a recess. I hurried out and called Kwan. I told him about Olivia's seizure.

"Probably a reaction to the Kutril," he said. "Could have been triggered by the stress. Sounds like the emergency is over. For now, just keep her calm."

When I got back to the judge's chambers, Olivia was anything but calm. "Get your grubby hands off me," she shrieked at one of the three EMTs who'd arrived.

Drew and I convinced them to back off. Drew pulled Olivia into his lap. She curled up against him. I was glad to see her color had returned. A few minutes later, she was asleep again.

When the hearing resumed, the judge said, "I'm going to allow Ms. Temple to return to the Pearce Psychiatric Institute to finish the treatment program."

"But Your Honor," Sherman started to protest.

The judge continued in a firm voice, "She's to remain in a locked unit. Two weeks from today, she goes to the Bechtel Center for Girls for evaluation."

Before the judge had finished talking, Sherman was shoving papers back into his briefcase. When the judge adjourned the hearing, Sherman was the first one out the door.

Two weeks didn't seem like much of a reprieve. But it would have to do.

THAT AFTERNOON, I called Daphne. I told her about the arrest and arraignment.

"Of course Livvy didn't do it," she said. "It's absurd."

"If she didn't, then someone else did," I said.

Daphne didn't say anything.

"Olivia said I could talk with you about her test results," I told Daphne.

Referring to my notes, I described the different ways Olivia grouped the objects. Then I summarized my initial findings. "She's impatient. Leaves a lot of items unsorted, especially those on the periphery, as if she doesn't see them. She's easily distracted, has difficulty maintaining her focus. And she's inflexible — she couldn't re-sort some of the items at all. It's as if she's overwhelmed by the sheer number of objects."

"Interesting," Daphne said. "Grouping things for eating, just for example. Her oral needs inform the way in which she interprets the world." The words of an analyst. "Typical adolescent, lets her emotions drive her. It's as I thought. She needs structure. Discipline. A firm hand."

I didn't say anything, though I'd have put it differently. Confronted by overwhelming information and limited time, Olivia's ability to cope shut down and her basic drives took a governing role. All the "structuring" in the world wasn't going to help. She needed a therapist who would be her partner, not a taskmaster or limit setter—someone whom Olivia trusted to step inside her psyche. She needed to hear, "Let's look at this together. Let me help." Instead, what she got from Daphne was, *That's not right. Do it this way.*

"That's why I used a modified form of CTA with her," Daphne said. "By writing down her feelings, they can't overwhelm her. She's better able to understand them and get control."

Again, I disagreed. I suspected the opposite was the case. When Olivia wrote her feelings down, they became even larger than life and more frightening. One more thing she had to feel ashamed about.

Despite Daphne's fine reputation as a clinician, she was out of her depth with Olivia. Here was a patient she didn't understand. Instead of treating her, Daphne was beating her up with her own weaknesses. If it had continued much longer, Daphne's treatment could easily have driven Olivia over a cliff.

"It's a bit spare to make a diagnosis, don't you think?" Daphne said.

"I'd say this is fairly typical of someone with a right-hemisphere learning disability, neither tuning in to environmental cues or categorizing efficiently. And it might also explain her social immaturity," I said. "Is that why you started her on Ritalin?"

There was a pause. It sounded like Daphne took a drag on a cigarette and exhaled. "Is that something Olivia authorized you to discuss with me?"

That stopped me dead.

"The Ritalin goes a bit beyond her test results, don't you think?"

I didn't have an answer. Strictly speaking, we'd already gone beyond test results. Why was Ritalin treatment off-limits, while CTA treatment was not?

"Good, then," she said briskly. "By the way, I did look into whether there have been any deaths, reported or unreported, in our drug trials. There haven't."

"You talked to Dr. Jensen?"

"I did. Among others."

"You asked him if any patients in his study died during the trial?"

"Right."

"Of causes related or unrelated to the drug treatment?"

"I said I did." She sounded annoyed. "Peter, that's all I can do. I haven't got mind reading abilities."

"If it wasn't a death in the DX-200 trial that Channing was threatening to report, then what were she and Liam arguing about?"

"You're sure they were arguing about reporting a death."

" 'A man is dead.' That's what Channing said. And she was going to make sure everyone knew what really happened." I heard the certainty in my voice, but in truth, my recollection was already fuzzy. "Maybe I'll talk to Liam about it again myself."

"But I've already told you—" Daphne stopped short.

"I wonder if he might have helped himself to Channing's research files."

"Peter . . ."

"Well, someone did. It wasn't you. And it wasn't me. And when I was in Jensen's office talking to him, there was a jumble of files stuffed into a file drawer. For such a tidy person, it seemed quite out of character. And it's conceivable that he'd prefer her research remain unpublished since he's working with Acu-Med on a competing treatment."

There was a long silence on the line.

"Peter, I think you should be extremely careful about these accusations you're making. An unreported death is a serious matter. It's one thing to confide your suspicions to me. It would be quite another thing to speak out when you're not sure." It was as if she'd flipped off the Person switch and flipped on Hospital Administrator. "My advice to you is keep out of it. There are plenty of nosey parkers and rumor mongers around here without you turning into one."

"Someone has stolen her research. . . ."

"You don't know that."

"She's got an empty file drawer that says so."

"There are plenty of other explanations for an empty . . ." There was a pause. "Hang on," Daphne said. "Yes? Who is it?" There were muffled sounds, as if she had her hand over the receiver.

I waited. If Jensen had Channing's research, if a subject in his clinical trial had died, then why was Daphne protecting him? Was she covering up something the hospital didn't want exposed? Or had I picked up some of Channing's paranoia?

Daphne came back on the line. "Sorry, Peter, I have to ring off. I've an appointment. We'll have to continue this another time."

The line went dead. I stared at the receiver.

The more I thought about it, the more I became convinced that harassing Jensen about the missing research files would backfire. I'd already asked him. Daphne had asked him. He insisted he didn't have them.

With me and Daphne breathing down his neck, Jensen could easily panic and destroy irreplaceable data, especially since Kutril was likely to beat DX-200 to market and cost a lot less. Jensen's patent would be worthless.

It wasn't long before I had myself convinced. I couldn't bring Channing back, but at least I could ensure that her legacy wasn't shredded. Breaking into Jensen's office was no longer unthinkable. It became inescapable, a responsibility I couldn't shirk. I called Annie and told her I'd changed my mind.

• • •

At two that night, we were at the back door of the Neuropsychiatric Unit, wind blowing sheets of rain in our faces. We went up to my office. I took off my coat and left my umbrella open to dry out. Per Annie's instructions, I was wearing dark pants, a dark shirt, and rubber-soled shoes. Annie dropped her backpack to the floor. She took off her rain slicker, shook it out, and draped it over a chair. She had on black leggings and a dark sweater.

I had a sudden urge to forget about sneaking over to Liam Jensen's office and, instead, spend some leisurely time peeling off the leggings and stroking those long legs that seemed to go on forever. For a start. But Annie was all business.

"Okay. Show me how those tunnels interconnect," she said.

I pulled a photocopied map from my drawer. It showed each of the buildings on the Pearce campus and the underground passageways that link them. The tunnels were original to the buildings. They'd been used for ferrying meals from a central kitchen to each of the units, and for moving patients to and from special treatment rooms. Still in constant use by day, at night the tunnels were pretty much deserted.

"Here's where we are, the Neuropsychiatric Unit" — I drew an X on a block that represented our building — "near the end of this main passageway." I ran my finger along the tunnel that stretches from one end of the Pearce to the other, interrupted only at the midway point by the doctors' office building, where the institute's maintenance and security headquarters were housed in the basement. Other tunnels fishboned off the main one. "And here's where we're going." I put an X on a building at the end of a branch at the opposite end of the campus.

"How far is it?" Annie asked.

"A half mile, maybe less."

"And security?"

"Once an hour, a security guard sweeps up and back through all the tunnels. He starts here" — I indicated the doctors' office building at the center of the map — "and goes this way through the tunnels, heading away from us. Then he comes back to home base and does the same going the other way. Takes about thirty minutes."

"Are all of these buildings in use?" Annie asked.

"Not all. Some are decommissioned." I wrote a D on the four buildings that had been mothballed. "Too expensive to maintain. Too controversial to tear down."

"Locked?" Annie asked.

"Everything's locked," I said. I fished my keys from my pocket and separated one out. "But this one opens all. Works on the elevators too."

Annie stared at the map as if she was trying to commit it to memory. She traced our path with her finger. "Very cool," she said. "When do we start?"

I checked my watch. It was twenty past. I looked out the window. I could see a dashed line of light at ground level, going from our building up and over the hill toward the next. Those were the lights from windows, high on the tunnel walls just above the ground. They were still on, which meant the guard hadn't completed his sweep back through, turning them off as he went. As I watched, one stretch of lights went out. A few minutes later, the rest went out.

"Now," I said.

Annie unzipped her backpack and lifted from it a smaller, black nylon pack, which she snapped around her waist. We slipped out into the hall. Only an emergency light glowed at the far end of the corridor. We moved quickly and ducked into the brightly lit stairwell. As we circled down, I ran my hand lightly along the cage of metal slats that surrounds the open central air shaft. Four flights down, we reached the basement and exited through a heavy steel door.

A tall, narrow tunnel stretched out in either direction, with horizontal windows running alongside the pipes and conduits that snaked along the ceiling. It smelled like a pile of wet leaves, and the air seemed alive with sounds—the bass beat of rainwater running off the roof of the tunnel, the clack of pipes pumping heat and hot water overhead. During the day, the tunnel was well lit. Now, there were only dim emergency lights.

We moved quickly down the first stretch of tunnel. The floor turned damp as rain leaked from the ceiling. In some places paint was peeling off the wall in sheets. Elsewhere, the old paint had disintegrated and turned granular, leaving little anthills of white powder.

At a bend, Annie paused and looked up. Above the asbestos-encased pipes were rotting wooden planks with insulation tucked into the corners. Dim light reflected off a skim of water that coated the floor.

We started a long downgrade. "Be careful, or you'll slip and fall on your ass," I whispered, "speaking from experience."

"Cool place to go blading," Annie whispered back.

Just then there was a new sound, like wind whistling through one of the conduits directly over our heads. "You pipe down, too," Annie said, shushing the ceiling. She shivered. "Let's get moving."

The stretch of tunnel ended in a door to the doctors' office building. This was the only tricky part. The security office was in the basement. So we took the stairs to the main floor and walked across to the stairs at the opposite end of the building. Halfway there, Annie put her hand on my shoulder. I heard it. Footsteps overhead. There were no doorways, no openings to duck into. My scalp prickled as the footsteps got closer and closer, and then passed over us.

I grabbed for Annie's hand and we hurried to the exit door, down the stairs, and out again into the tunnel. Already I was drenched in sweat.

At the end of the next stretch of tunnel, there were two doors. As I put my key in the door to the continuing passageway, Annie asked, "Where does the other one go?"

"To the basement of Albert House. Used to be the children's unit. And before that, it housed one of the institute's first patients, a wealthy dowager who'd lost her mind. Her family had an exact replica of her house built here. They spirited her from her home in the middle of the night, and she lived out her last days thinking she'd never left home."

"You made that up."

"Nope. It's the truth."

Like a little kid, unable to resist the temptation of a supposedly locked door, Annie reached for the knob. Then she pulled away. "Hey, little guy," she said, reaching out a cupped hand. There, dangling at eye level was a fat black spider. I looked up. The ceiling was festooned with cobwebs.

"Here you go," Annie said, pinching the thread from which the spider hung. She gently lowered the creature to the floor. It rolled itself up into a ball for a moment, then scuttled away.

Annie tried the knob. "Locked," she said. Then she paused, her ear to the door. "Listen," she whispered, stepping aside.

I pressed my ear up against the door. Rock music. I shrugged. "Sometimes patients find their way down here. We haven't got time to check it out. I'll call Security as soon as we're finished."

Annie took out a small flashlight, the size and shape of a pen. She flashed a surprisingly powerful beam along the edge of the door. "Still, it wouldn't be much of a job to jimmy this," she said.

I opened the other door, and we continued on our way. "I should have brought bread crumbs," Annie quipped after we turned one corner, then another.

"This is our in-house Alzheimer's test for the aging doctors," I said. "We're definitely not lost. In fact, we're here." The tunnel ended in a locked door. I inserted my key and the door to the Drug and Alcohol Rehabilitation Unit opened easily.

We found ourselves at the base of one of the two stairways at either end of the building. It was dark, the only light cast by the red EXIT signs. I groped my way forward until my foot came in contact with the riser of the first step. Annie turned on her flashlight. She shone the light up into the air shaft. I could just make out the skylight, all the way up at the roof.

I groped for a handrail but found, instead, the wall of closely set, turned wooden spindles running from steps to ceiling.

I listened. Nothing but silence.

"Let's go," Annie whispered, and started up.

The sound of our climbing, even with our rubber soles, seemed deafening. The stairs themselves resonated. I ran my hand lightly along the wooden spindles.

Four long flights up and we pushed our way out into a corridor.

There was emergency lighting at either end. Annie put away her flashlight.

The rain was beating hard on the roof. Wind howled through the eaves. We padded down the hall, past several offices until we got to the one with the sign LIAM JENSEN, M.D. outside the door.

Annie tried the knob. It was locked. I tried my key—it was worth a shot, though I knew it worked only on the doctors' offices on my unit. It wouldn't even fit in the lock.

Annie unzipped her bag and slipped out what looked like a leather pocket protector. She opened the flap and drew out one of the slender metal rods lined up neatly inside. She crouched and fiddled at the lock. Swore. Changed tools once, and again. "There we go," she said. She pulled the door open. Then she tried the inner door. It wasn't locked.

We slipped inside and closed both doors behind us. The room was pitch black with only a sliver of light between what must have been curtains over a window.

"Peter?" Annie whispered.

"Right here," I said, and took a step in the direction of her voice.

I felt her hand touch my shoulder, work its way down my arm, and hold my hand.

Annie turned on her flashlight. The beam lit up each corner of the room, in turn. There were chairs, a standing lamp, a potted plant. She ran the light over the top of Jensen's broad desk. It was cleared of all papers. The man was such an orderly soul. Even the pencils and pens on the desk blotter were lined up exactly perpendicular to the edge of the desk. The only element of disarray was a half-full Acu-Med mug. It still contained an inch of light coffee, the cream congealing at the edges in a tan circle.

Annie tugged at the curtains so they overlapped. Then she turned on a table lamp.

I went to Liam's desk chair, sat, and rolled myself closer to the file cabinet. It was unlocked. I reached for the drawer I'd seen open. In my mind's eye, I saw the jumble of purple file folders packed into the drawer and Liam's foot trying to push it shut. I said a little prayer: Please tell me he hasn't destroyed her work. I pulled. The drawer opened too easily. I knew before my eyes confirmed it that the overflow of files had been removed. The drawer was now three quarters full of neatly ordered, manila file folders, the tabs marching from left to right and back again. I pulled out one and read the typed label. "8.3641. DX-200 trial." It contained the records documenting the treatment of the DX-200 drug-trial participant who'd been assigned code number 8.3641. At the front of the drawer was a folder labeled "CRFs DX-200 Trial." I pulled it out.

"Find what you're looking for?" Annie asked.

"No. Those file folders I saw in here are gone. But hang on a minute. Here's something else. The reports of adverse drug reactions from the DX-200 trial."

God bless Liam's orderly little brain. There were about two dozen sheets of paper, each with a date, a patient number, and the description of an adverse event. Nausea. Dizziness. A depression with suicidal thoughts. Fatigue. I kept going. A minor heart attack was the closest thing to a death.

These were all subjects who'd completed the trial. What about the ones who hadn't? In the back of the drawer, I found the folder I was looking for. It contained the records of patients who'd dropped out of the trial. There were only three. Two had dropped out for "personal reasons." A third because of car trouble. I wondered if one of them was the dead man Channing was urging Jensen to report.

"Annie, is it hard to find out if somebody is dead?"

"Depends. With a Social Security number, takes about thirty seconds."

Two of the dropouts were female. Couldn't be either of them. The dropout with car trouble was a man. I read Annie his Social Security number, and she wrote it down in her little black book.

"How we doing for time?" she asked.

I checked my watch. It was 2:40. "We're fine. Security starts its sweep in twenty minutes."

I put the files away, straightened them, and closed the drawer. I checked that the room was the way we'd found it. The only thing out of place was that Acu-Med mug. There it was on the desk, when it needed to be washed and put back into the A position in the lineup of mugs on top of the file cabinet.

"Everything okay?" Annie asked.

"Just a little déjà vu. When I found Channing's body, there was an Acu-Med mug on her desk, too. The police claim there wasn't one when they examined the room."

"Is that unusual?" Annie asked.

"No," I admitted. After all, they give them to all the docs. "Still. I can't help wondering if this is the one that was on Channing's desk and then disappeared by the time the police took crime scene photos."

I was about to turn off the desk lamp when I noticed Jensen's briefcase, standing alongside the desk. It was open. Just like I keep my briefcase, open beside me while I'm working in my office. I might easily leave a dirty coffee cup on my desk or forget my briefcase if I left the office in a hurry. Liam Jensen seemed a lot less likely to do such a thing—unless he was only off to the men's room or checking on a patient.

Suddenly, I was anxious to get out of there. I turned off the desk lamp, and we left. I closed the office doors quietly behind us.

We hurried past Channing's office. The door was still padlocked. Now there was a square of pink paint on the wall where the plaque with her name on it had been removed.

Annie froze in front of Daphne's office. The door was open a crack. There was a light on inside. Was she working late? Maybe Jensen was here, working with her.

Instinct pushed me to get away quickly before one of them heard us. Then, common sense took over. Annie and I hadn't been that quiet. With the door open, anyone inside surely would have heard us by now.

I put my hand on the knob. If Channing had entrusted her research results to anyone, Daphne was the most likely person—if the files had, in fact, been entrusted to someone, as opposed to having been taken from Channing's office after her death. If Jensen had taken them, I could easily see Daphne confronting him, removing the files from his office, and putting them away safely in her own. Then, perhaps out of some misguided sense of loyalty to the institute, she wasn't letting on that she had them. It would take only a minute to check.

I pulled the outer door open and paused. I listened. I pushed the inner door open. The room exhaled stale cigarettes. The desk light was on.

"Peter?"

I jumped at the sound of Annie's voice. I told her, "This is the office of the woman who's now head of clinical trials for the institute. Daphne Smythe-Gooding. You met her at Channing's party. She was Channing's mentor and had Channing's research report. I wonder . . ."

"Well, if you're going in, you'd better make it snappy."

I was beyond caution. "Right. Just a quick look."

I stepped inside. The office seemed a bit more chaotic than it was the last time I'd been there. Yellow Post-its lined the wall above the desk. Only a single nut was left in the candy bowl, along with a pile of empty foil wrapping and miniature Hershey's Kisses streamers. The African violet looked tired, its leaves spread out and limp, the flowers curled and brown. There was no sweater on the back of her chair. No open briefcase alongside the desk.

On top of other papers on her desk was a scale drawing on blue paper. It was of an engraved tablet, over five feet tall. Along the side, on some lines labeled Inscription:, Daphne had written her husband's name, his dates of birth and death, "Revered scholar, beloved husband, brother, uncle," and the words "Called back before his time."

The monument was impressive, far more massive than most gravestones in modern cemeteries. With its fussy floral carving surrounding the inscription, it felt Victorian.

I hadn't had to pick out a gravestone for Kate. I knew she'd have been horrified at the thought of her bones taking up eternal space on a crowded earth. Instead, I made a pilgrimage to Martha's Vineyard and scattered her ashes from our favorite picnic spot, a bluff along the Moshup Trail overlooking the ocean.

I left the drawing where it was and quickly checked Daphne's four file cabinets. They were all unlocked. I was on the final drawer of the last one, having found nothing that resembled Channing's research, when Annie whistled. "Does everyone around here operate a little pharmacy out of their office?"

She was peering into an open bottom desk drawer. Inside were boxes of drug samples. Zoloft. Prozac. Valium.

"Pretty typical," I said. "The hospital has a policy that drug samples are supposed to be locked up, but it doesn't always happen." Then I spotted a blister pack of Ativan on the desk. Some of the pills were gone. That wasn't so typical. "Maybe she left in a hurry. After all, she left the light on."

The window rattled as a gust of wind pelted rain against it.

"We should get going," Annie said.

We had ten minutes. I closed up the file drawers and left the light on, the desk drawer open, and the doors ajar as we'd found them. We hurried to the nearest stairs—they were at the opposite end of the building from the ones we'd come up.

I followed Annie into the darkness. With all the amenities in this building, why the hell wasn't there any emergency lighting in the stairways?

"Annie, where are you?" I whispered.

"I'm here, just ahead of you," she answered, shushing me as the door shut to the hallway, making the dark even darker.

I groped for a something to hold onto. I connected with the wall of wooden spindles, like the one that ran up and down along the inside of the other staircase we'd come up.

I heard Annie starting down the stairs.

"Where's your flashlight," I said as I stumbled forward, pushing myself to move quickly, using the wooden spindles along the inside of the staircase to guide me along.

"I'm looking for it," Annie said. She unzipped her pack. We were almost down to the next landing. "Where the hell did I . . . Should be in here somewhere. . . . Aha!" The flashlight went on. Annie flashed it up at me, then on the floor in front of her. The beam reflected off the landing. It was coated with what looked like a light powder, streaked with scuff marks. "Looks like . . ." Annie said as she stepped forward. "Whoa!" Her foot slid. She skidded and landed with a thud. The flashlight somersaulted out of Annie's hand and bounced on the floor. I lunged for it.

"Watch out, Peter, don't," Annie cried out, but it was too late. The flashlight had rolled off the edge of the step and disappeared into the air shaft. I grabbed for the wooden spindles to keep from falling over. But where the wall of spindles was supposed to be, it wasn't. I bellowed as I fell forward, flailing, knowing that if I kept going, I'd follow the flashlight down to the basement.

Annie grabbed me from behind, just in time.

"Holy shit," I muttered, as I regained my footing.

I stood there on the stairs, gasping for breath. My heart felt as if it were trying to hammer its way out of my chest. My shirt was sticking to my back. My eyes had adjusted to the dark, and I could see that there was a wide gap in the wall of wooden spindles. I groped for where they should have been, swung my arm one way, then the other. "What in the hell?" I said. There was about a three-foot–wide gap in the spindles. I reached up. I touched what felt like jagged edges where the spindles had been broken off overhead.

Cautiously, I leaned out into the airshaft and looked down. It was dark and hard to see much of anything. But the beam of Annie's flashlight was visible, all the way down at the basement floor. Amazing that it was still working, after a four-story fall onto a concrete floor.

The sound of footsteps echoed up from below. We pulled back into the shadows and waited. The footsteps grew louder. It sounded like a door was being opened at the base of the stairwell. A man's voice echoed up, "Anybody in there? What the hell is wrong with the lights?"

A strong beam of light rushed up to fill the airshaft. An alarm blared, and red lights on each of the landings started flashing. The light confirmed what I'd surmised—about a dozen wooden spindles had been broken away, leaving a hole that the flashlight had fallen through, and through which I easily could have followed.

"They shouldn't find you here," I said to Annie.

Annie scrambled to her feet. "Don't worry about me. With any luck, I'll meet you later, somewhere near the tunnel entrance."

She brushed her hands on her dark pants, leaving light handprints. I touched the floor of the landing. The light particles that coated it were coarse. I sniffed. Sawdust. That's when I realized that though the wooden spindles were broken away at the top, at the bottom they'd been sawn through.

I crouched and leaned out over the airshaft. The flashing lights made the air pulsate. A man lay sprawled on the basement floor. Dark pants, jacket. His arms were splayed and his legs twisted grotesquely. A bald security guard was leaning over and picking up Annie's flashlight, which had landed on the man's back. Soft landing—that explained why the flashlight still worked. He examined it. Turned it off. Then he looked up.

"Don't move," the security guard barked up at me.

19

IT TOOK the security guard a few moments to turn off the alarm. My ears were still ringing, long into the silence. When I shut my eyes to clear my head, circles popped like flashbulbs behind my closed eyelids.

The guard hollered up at me again, and I identified myself. He told me to come down and wait with him. He'd called the security office, and the police were on their way. I descended to the bottom of the staircase and stepped into the base of the airshaft.

The guard hadn't turned the body over, but he didn't need to. I recognized the Brioni jacket. It was Liam Jensen. And I knew he was dead. His head and forearm lay in a pool of blood. In death, he seemed smaller. In some disconnected corner of my brain, I envisioned bones telescoping as a body lands on a concrete floor.

I turned away. I felt the emotional dam that had erected itself eroding. The last thing I wanted to do was close my eyes and be alone in my head with my memories. I felt drained and tired as I slumped against the wall. I stared down at my hands and twisted my wedding ring.

We waited. About ten minutes later, I heard footsteps clumping down the hall. Voices. I took a deep breath and turned my hands into fists, forcing energy into my arms. I straightened my back, squared my shoulders. By the time MacRae and his partner appeared, I was ready.

All MacRae said was, "You again."

He snapped on some latex gloves and quickly examined the body. "Who is he?"

"Dr. Liam Jensen," I said. "Head of the Drug and Alcohol Rehabilitation Unit. This building."

MacRae had his pad out. He flipped it open and started to write. "J?"

"J-E-N-S-E-N," I said. "Liam. L-I-A-M. MD."

MacRae wrote quickly, paused, added some more scribbles. "How the hell did he . . ." MacRae squinted up into the air shaft. "Jee-zus H. Christ. Fell from way up there. Accident?"

"Doubtful," I replied.

MacRae didn't look surprised. He was eyeing my sneakers, which were coated with sawdust. "You were up there?"

I nodded. "I almost fell through the hole myself. The lights weren't working."

MacRae glanced around the base of the stairs until his attention snagged on an empty light socket. "Is that the emergency lighting?" he asked.

"Looks like someone sawed through the wooden supports between the third and fourth floors," I said. "If Jensen was coming down and lost his balance or was pushed, it wouldn't have taken much pressure to break through."

MacRae looked at me speculatively. "You here alone or have you got company?" For a dumb guy, he was uncanny.

I brushed the sawdust off my pant leg. "I don't see anyone with me, do you?"

"How long have you been in the building?"

How long had Jensen been dead, I wondered. "I've been here for about an hour."

"And before that?"

"With a friend. Since ten."

"You don't work in this building, do you?"

"No," I admitted.

"Two suspicious deaths in as many weeks. And you're here both times." He eyed me up and down, registering the black pants, black shirt.

I stared back. I tried to remind myself that he was only doing his job, but all I could think was, what did Annie see in this asshole, anyway?

"So what are you doing here now, sneaking around in the middle of the night?" He looked at me, waiting for an explanation. I folded my arms and stared back at him. He planted his feet, hooked his fingers in his pant loops, and didn't blink.

There were footsteps overhead. We both looked up.

"Hullo? Who's there?" Arnold Destler was gazing down from the main floor, a flight up. "What in the name of God is going on?" he barked.

Destler thumped down the stairs. He arrived wearing gray sweats, looking like an overstuffed sock with a very pink head sticking out one end. I'd never seen him out of a suit, without his bow tie. "I came over as soon as Security notified me," he said.

He approached Jensen gingerly, up on the balls of his feet. "Poor devil," he said. He looked up into the airshaft, probably calculating the institute's liability. Then he took inventory of all of us crowded in at the base of the stairs. Security. Police. Me.

"Peter?"

"He was here when Security discovered the body," MacRae said. "He was just about to explain what he's doing here."

"Research," I said, the word popping out of nowhere.

"Research?" MacRae echoed in disbelief.

"Our staff are very dedicated, Detective," Destler said. I tried not to look surprised, but Destler was the last person I'd expect to leap to my defense. "It's not unusual to find us working into the wee hours of the morning. I was even working late myself." Destler was a renowned workaholic — known to hole up in his office long after the rest of us had gone home to our lives.

By now, additional officers had arrived, including a medical examiner. He asked us to give him some space so he could do his work. We shifted into the corridor.

"This isn't even your unit," MacRae pointed out.

I was about to answer when my beeper went off.

Destler said evenly, "Medical research crosses organizational boundaries. We try not to operate in individual stovepipes. Isn't that so, Dr. Zak?"

"We try not to," I said. The beeper was blinking the number of the nurses' station on my unit. I looked up. Destler and MacRae were waiting for me to say more. "There's some work being done here using Kutril, an extract of kudzu, to treat addiction. I was looking for the raw data." I needed to get to a phone.

"You should have come to me for that," Destler said.

"Pardon me?" I said, belatedly processing his words.

"Yes. Those files were given to me for safekeeping."

"You have them?"

MacRae looked like he was watching a tennis match. He could see two players, swinging their rackets, but he couldn't locate the ball.

Destler went on, "I know Dr. Temple didn't think we were as supportive of her work as we might have been, but she did have a sizable grant from the NIMH. And despite the questions that have been raised about her methods, her results are quite . . . interesting."

The medical examiner stepped into the corridor and pulled MacRae aside. They conferred. I took the opportunity to use the in-house phone in the hall to call my unit. "We noticed all the emergency vehicles," the night nurse said, "so we did an extra bed check. Olivia Temple isn't in her room. Neither is Matthew Farrell. We've searched everywhere. They're not here."

Immediately I thought: Albert House. "When were they last seen?"

"According to the charts, at eleven o'clock checks."

"I'll be back as soon as I can," I told her. "I think I know where they are."

When I got off the phone, MacRae finished talking to the medical examiner. Destler looked at him expectantly. "Apparently Dr. Jensen died at least several hours ago," MacRae told us. I was relieved. "And he probably died instantly." He turned to me, "You have someone who can vouch for your whereabouts this evening?"

After an instant's hesitation, I said, "Annie Squires."

He'd have made a great poker player. MacRae didn't even blink. He just nodded and took a note. All he said was, "You can go now. I'll be in touch."

Destler walked me partway down the hall. When we were out of earshot, he stopped. "Research?" It was a controlled explosion. "In the middle of the night?"

I swallowed. "We have a patient who's gone through physical withdrawal from Ritalin, and we're treating her with Kutril for the psychological dependence. There's nothing else that . . ."

Destler interrupted, "I know what Kutril is." He glared at me. "But it's an experimental treatment. Who is this patient you're treating for Ritalin addiction?"

"Olivia Temple."

"You're *still* treating Dr. Temples daughter, even after her arrest? Doesn't that seem just a bit inappropriate?"

"Dr. Liu is her doctor, and I believe the treatment is appropriate. I already have Dr. Temple's research analysis, her preliminary paper—"

"You do?" Destler's eyebrows rose to meet his nonexistent hairline.

"Yes. But Olivia has experienced some side effects, and I wanted to . . ."

"What side effects?"

"A seizure. We need to see if other patients experienced similar problems, and how they were treated for it."

"The data from the trial was given to me for safekeeping," Destler said, his voice cold. "Now I can see why. I think you and Dr. Liu had better be in my office, first thing in the morning."

He put both hands up to his collarbone. I had the impression he was reaching up to straighten the bow tie that wasn't there.

"Christ," he said, "when the press gets a hold of this, they're going to have a field day." Then he muttered, "Damage control," and started back.

• • •

I hurried to the opposite end of the building, to the door from the basement to the tunnel. My mind was churning. If Jensen fell to his death before midnight, then the wooden spindles had to have been sawn through within a few hours of that. Annie and I might have come across Jensen's body earlier if we'd come up that staircase. And why was Destler being so helpful? Was it just to protect the institute from more public tarnish?

I stood at the door to the tunnel and looked up into the dark stairway. I whispered, "Annie!" I listened to the silence. I called her name again, as loud as I dared.

I heard her light footsteps. In a minute, Annie was beside me. "You survived," she said.

"I had to tell MacRae I was with you tonight."

"Well you were," she said. She didn't miss a beat. "I'll bet you enjoyed that."

"Actually, I did." I couldn't hold back the grin. But I quickly turned serious. "I'm sure Jensen had to have been pushed off the staircase. But how? It wouldn't have been easy."

"Maybe he was drugged first. That coffee on his desk could have been spiked," Annie suggested. That would have explained why it was left there, unwashed. He never made it back to tidy up. "One way to find out. We take a sample of what's in that mug, and I get it analyzed."

Annie had already started up the stairs. I followed. I said, "Olivia Temple and another patient are AWOL."

Annie paused. "That music?"

"Probably. The idiots."

"This shouldn't take more than a couple of minutes," Annie said, continuing up.

This time, Annie took a minute to get Jensen's door open. We knew we didn't have much time before the police showed. I groped for the lamp and turned it on. I stared at the desktop. The only suggestion that someone might have been in there after us was that the pencils and pens alongside the blotter weren't parallel with the edge of the desk. I was sure I'd left them perfectly aligned. That, and the fact that the Acu-Med mug had vanished.

On top of the file cabinet, leading the mug lineup, an Acu-Med mug now stood. I examined it. It had been rinsed out, but it was still damp.

There were footsteps in the hall. We both froze. It sounded as if someone had put a key into the outer office door. A moment later, the knob to the inner door turned. Was it the police or someone coming back to erase any other clues to Jensen's murder? We waited. The doorknob returned to neutral.

I yanked the door open. No one was there. I rushed out. The door to the stairway at the far end of the hall was closing. And there were footsteps clomping up the opposite staircase. Probably the police and security guards. Annie and I ran the other way.

It felt as if I didn't take another breath until we'd reached the basement and were out in the tunnel. There was no sign of whoever had preceded us. The rain had stopped pounding, but the ceiling still dripped, and the walls exuded the smell of decaying concrete.

When we got to Albert House, Annie put her hands in front of her face as she advanced on the door. She took a credit card out of her wallet, crouched, and started working on the lock.

"Hold on a minute," I said, and inserted my master key. It worked.

"Show-off," she said.

Annie pushed the door open. The basement corridor of Albert House was dimly lit. Mildew and dust thickened the air. Some old furniture lined the hall—a battered metal desk, a stack of mattresses, iron headboards. I pressed a finger under my nose to keep from sneezing.

The music wasn't too far away. Annie tried the first door. It opened into a closet. Inside was a deep white porcelain sink with a galvanized metal bucket in it. The next door was another closet, this one with shelves. It had old linens that no one had bothered to remove, neatly folded inside. The smell of mildew was over-powering.

We approached the next door. The music was louder. I turned the knob. A moment later, the music shut off. I pressed, and the door started to open, then stopped and stuck. Something was holding it in place.

"Olivia, are you in there?" I said, hoping my voice wasn't carry-ing into the tunnel.

There were scuffling sounds.

"Open the door."

There was a high-pitched giggle.

Now I was pissed. "I'm not playing around. Open up."

I waited. Nothing but some intense whispering. Then, the squeal of furniture being moved. The door pulled open to reveal Olivia, bug-eyed, staring back at me, wearing a light-blue terry-cloth bath-robe. Her once pink slippers were soiled and wet.

Matthew stared at us from a mattress in the corner. About a dozen candles flickered at his feet, alongside a bottle of water. He was making a feeble attempt to push something under the bedding.

As I followed Annie inside, something crunched underfoot. I reached down and picked up a white tablet. There were two more on the floor along with a half-full blister pack. I picked it up. Ri-talin, ten-milligram tablets.

I retrieved what Matthew had shoved under the mattress. It was a paper plate with a residue of crushed pills on it, and a length of plastic soda straw. Snorting Ritalin? That was a new one on me.

Matthew was sweaty, pupils dilated. Olivia was panting, like an overheated terrier. If she'd been any other patient, I'd have been evaluating the course of treatment, racking my brain for additional support systems, reviewing our security procedures. Instead, anger boiled up inside of me. Olivia shrank away, cowering.

"What in the hell is the matter with you?" I cried.

She flinched. "I didn't do any," she squeaked.

I felt like a parent, staring down my nose at an ungrateful child. I'd lost my professional distance, but at least I knew it.

I lowered my voice. "I don't think you realize how much you have at stake here. The only reason the judge let you come back to the Pearce instead of carting you off to jail is because you're in a secure unit. If the police find out you're getting out, taking drugs—"

Now, Olivia's fear turned to petulance. She planted her feet and faced me. "So what?"

"They're not going to take you to reform school, you know. If you're lucky, it will be a detention center. Maybe even jail."

"This *is* jail," she retorted.

"Have you ever been to a real jail?" Annie asked her. Olivia stared down at the bedraggled ears of her bunny slippers. "Well, I have."

Olivia gave her a sideways look. "What's the big deal?" Olivia folded her arms across her chest, but the sullen tone was tinged with curiosity.

Annie went on. "You won't like it."

Olivia wiped her nose with her sleeve.

Annie asked, "How old are you? Fifteen?"

Olivia gave an indignant snort. "Seventeen."

"That's how old I was." Annie and I exchanged a look. "I didn't do drugs. But I did drink. A lot. I thought I could handle it.

"One night, I was out late with my friends, hanging out behind the high school. I'm driving home, like about the time it is now, when a cop pulls me over. Turns out it's my uncle Jack. He shines a flashlight in my face and growls, have I been drinking? I tell him no. I figure, all I've had is a few beers and over four or five hours. He'll never know. So he asks me to recite the alphabet."

Olivia was hanging on Annie's words.

"Got up to G. Or maybe H. Then the letters got all mixed up. Surprised the hell out of me. So I say to him, 'You gotta let me sing it.' I *know* I can do it that way. I was so shit-faced, I couldn't even sing it."

Olivia suppressed a giggle.

"He says, driving around like that, I could get myself killed. Besides, I'm underage. So I said to him, 'What are you going to do? Arrest me?' And he says, 'Exactly!' I laughed. I thought he was kidding. But he was dead serious.

"He takes me in, books me, puts me in a cell with this other woman who's drunk, dirty. Puking her guts out. As the night goes on, they put more and more people in with us. The cell across from ours is full of men—drunks and perverts. One guy is screaming and banging on the bars. Another one is exposing himself. The place stinks. Urine. Vomit. BO. The worst part is, there wasn't anywhere to go. Just a couple of cots and the floor. There I was, locked into this little space. I couldn't get away. I felt violated, just being there." Olivia gaped at Annie. "It felt like anything could happen to me. I'd have died if I'd had to stay in that jail for another night."

Olivia took a few moments to digest Annie's words. "What happened—" she started, when Matthew Farrell staggered to his feet. He pressed himself against the wall and started banging on it with the back of his head.

Olivia went over to him, examined his face, then raised her arm and pressed the inside of her wrist to his forehead. It was tender, caring gesture—the kind of thing a mother does with a feverish child. "Is Mattie okay?" she asked me.

Mattie? He sank down to the ground. He was scratching at his arms. Now, he was rubbing his legs with jerky movements and swearing under his breath.

I squatted beside him. He pulled away, holding his hands up in front of his face. His forearms were covered with an angry rash. "Looks like an allergic reaction to too much Ritalin," I said. Not surprising. We'd started him on Adderall, also a psychostimulant. The combination could make a Ritalin overdose worse.

I took Matthew's arm. He tried to pull away. "I just want to take your pulse," I explained.

"Pulse?" he gasped.

"Um-hmm," I said holding his wrist. His pulse was racing.

"You want to abduct me," he said, the words staccato.

Olivia crouched beside him. "No one wants to abduct you, Mattie."

"X-ray me with infrared beams," he continued.

Common reactions to Ritalin overdose were psychosis and paranoia. "I'm Dr. Zak, Matthew," I said. "All I want to do is get you stabilized."

"In-fra-red." Matthew repeated the word, rocking on the syllables.

"We should get them back to the unit," I said, hauling Matthew to his feet and dragging him out into the hall. Olivia tried to help support him on the other side.

Annie pulled the door to the tunnel open and stuck her head out. "All clear," she called back to us.

We held onto Matthew and started back. The dripping from the ceiling had slowed. Our trip through the tunnel was quick and uninterrupted.

When we got to the unit, Annie left through a basement exit and the rest of us took the elevator to the first floor. A nurse who'd worked nights on the unit, on and off for years, greeted us. Her gray hair was disheveled and her uniform was rumpled, as if she'd been in bed for the last four hours but not sleeping. It's amazing how anxiety can wrinkle clothing. "Thank God you found them," she said.

I sent Olivia to the common room to wait for me. I watched her walk off, struck once again by how waiflike she seemed, her clothes hanging on her thin frame. But something seemed off. Her gait was stiff-legged. I knew she was probably tired, but this wasn't a tired walk. It was the walk of an old person with the beginnings of Parkinson's disease.

I passed Matthew Farrell over to the nurse. She clucked under her breath.

"Can you be sure he gets back to his room?" I asked. "Put him on five-minute checks. I don't care if he sleeps—he probably won't be able to for a couple of hours—but I want him in his room. I'll beep Dr. Liu and ask him to come in and examine him. Oh, and one other thing. Once he's settled, can you have Ms. Temple's room searched? We're looking for drugs. Probably sample packs."

Then I joined Olivia. She was curled up on the sofa. I turned on a light and brought a chair to sit opposite her. She blinked, put her arm up across her eyes, and turned away from me.

"Olivia, please sit up for a moment. I need to check something."

"Turn off the light," she whined.

I turned it off. Gray dawn barely made a dent in the gloom. But I could easily see her.

She sat up. "What?" The belligerence was back.

"Put your arm out," I said.

She made a sour face but put her arm out anyway. I took her hand in mine and put my other hand around her biceps. Slowly I raised her hand, bending the arm at the elbow. The muscle ratcheted instead of contracting smoothly, jerking from one position to the next, like when you try to pedal but your bicycle chain has missing teeth.

Olivia sat up straight. "What the hell is that?" she asked, staring at her arm.

"Cogwheeling," I said, giving her the medical term.

Olivia held out her arm and slowly flexed and bent it. "No shit."

I watched her for almost a minute, looking to see whether she was also smacking her lips, drooling, or if her tongue was protruding from her mouth. Fortunately not.

"Can you make it stop?" she asked.

"Dr. Liu is going to come in and have a look at you. I hope so."

She lay back down. I got a blanket and covered her. Then I called Kwan.

"This better be good. You've interrupted my beauty sleep," he grumbled.

I told him about finding Jensen dead, and Olivia and Matthew in Albert House. When he asked what I'd been doing, roaming around in the middle of the night in the first place, I told him I'd been looking for Channing's research files in Jensen's office. "There wasn't any other way to find out what I needed to help Olivia. And I'm worried that if I don't find Channing's work, someone's going to destroy it to keep it from being published. I was stunned when Destler told me he has the data."

"Unbelievable," he muttered.

Then I told him about Matthew's rash and Olivia's tremors.

He agreed, that it sounded as if Matthew was having a reaction to a Ritalin overdose. Of Olivia, he said, "I don't like the sound of that. If she weren't so young I'd be worried about something like tardive dyskinesia."

It wasn't a pleasant prospect, a teenager with her tongue going in and out, arms shaking, doing the Thorazine shuffle. "I'm hoping it's only temporary," I said.

"You're right about one thing. We really do need to see Dr. Temple's research notes. There's nothing about this kind of side effect in her report. If we keep Olivia on Kutril, I want some assurance that these symptoms are only temporary."

"This is your lucky day. Destler says we can see Channing's research notes first thing this morning. Right after he talks to us about the novel approach we're using to treat Olivia's drug craving with Kutril."

"Does this story have a happy ending, or should I bring my resume to Xerox?"

"Wouldn't hurt," I said.

20

WHILE I was waiting for Kwan to come in, the night nurse brought me the incident report she'd completed on Matthew's and Olivia's disappearance. The "Resolved" box was checked. I signed it.

I looked in on the orderly and nurse who were methodically disassembling Olivia's room. They'd stripped the bed, turned over the mattress. The nurse was taking Olivia's clothes out of the drawers and wardrobe and checking the pockets. The orderly was on a stepladder, looking behind each ceiling tile. When he saw me, he climbed down and handed me a half-dozen sample drug packets. Then he went back to his work.

After that, I paced the unit, trying to stay awake. First to one end, then back to the other. As I passed the nurses' station, I smelled coffee that was warming on a burner behind the desk. How good a cup would have tasted. My passes up and back were getting shorter. I *needed* a cup of coffee. I found myself standing over the pot, inhaling the aroma. I looked one way, then the other. There was nobody about.

Just an inch, I told myself. What harm would it do? I poured myself a half a cup. I was about to take a sip when I heard footsteps coming down the hall. I downed the coffee in a single, scorching gulp. I was coughing and clutching the collapsed paper coffee cup when Kwan rounded the corner.

"This is a pathetic thing. A grown man." He clucked and shook his head. "You've done stupid things before, my friend. But giving up coffee on a dare — that takes the cake." He pounded me on the back.

I threw away the cup. It was one of the few times I willingly admitted that he was right.

We went to check on Matthew Farrell. He was in his room. He'd shoved his bed against the wall and was counting linoleum floor tiles. While Kwan examined him, Matthew began on the ceiling tiles. When Kwan had finished, Matthew cataloged his results in microscopic printing on the back of the day's menu. Then he started on the holes in each ceiling tile.

Kwan quickly confirmed a Ritalin overdose, the effects of which were beginning to wear off. Eventually, he'd sleep.

• • •

I caught a few hours of restless sleep on the couch in my office. When I came back down, Gloria was there.

"I've got something for you," she said.

She handed me a brass key. I turned it over. I fished my keys out of my pocket. It matched the master key on my ring. "Where'd you get this?"

"From Olivia's bathrobe. When we moved her to bed, we checked her pockets."

"Probably her mother's key," I said.

Gloria looked somber. "And I'll bet you anything that last night wasn't the first night they've gotten out."

I agreed. "Just the first time they got caught."

At least that explained how a pair of kids had effortlessly breached security on our unit without even tripping an alarm. I started for Olivia's room.

Gloria stopped me. "She's still asleep, Peter."

I leaned against the desk. I was tired. I could feel the veins banging in my head like noisy heating pipes. I wanted to go home, get into bed, and forget all about Olivia Temple. She was a royal pain in the ass.

. . .

Kwan and I met at Destler's office at nine. Kwan came bearing a small Starbucks coffee. "It's half decaf, half caf," he told me. A peace offering. I took it gratefully.

I sipped slowly, contemplating how abstinence makes the heart grow fonder. At twenty past, Virginia Hedgewick backed into the office. Her arms were loaded with a stack of newspapers and a box of doughnuts, which she set on a seven-foot–long teak credenza. She looked grim-faced when she turned to us. "Doctors aren't supposed to die here. What next, I wonder?"

"Was it on the radio?" I asked.

"Dr. Destler called me with the news. Good thing he was doing one of his twenty-four–hour sleep overs."

Just then, Destler popped out of his office, looking as if he'd just stepped out of an ad for successful portly men. Blue suit, red bow tie, gleaming head. He looked clean and rested. I remembered. There'd been a fuss over how much money was spent renovating his office when he came to the Pearce—looked like the rumor that they'd installed a shower in the connecting bathroom was correct.

With him was a well-dressed business type. I thought I recognized the man—a pharmaceutical-company executive or sales rep. But I couldn't remember which or where from. They shook hands, and the visitor left.

Destler gave me a disapproving frown. I hadn't slept much, and I knew I looked it. At least Kwan balanced the equation.

We followed Destler into his office. We sat across the desk from him in chrome and leather sling chairs, under the watchful eye of Wilhelmina Pearce. Destler had his seat pumped up high so he could look down on us.

"A nasty business," he said. "And you up there, rifling through your colleague's files. I could take you before the board on this." Destler stroked his chin thoughtfully. "You've both demonstrated questionable judgment, not to mention performed illegal acts —" Kwan started to protest. "I mean, some of you," Destler amended. "It would be entirely appropriate to initiate an investigation, to relieve you of your duties, suspend your privileges."

The words were ominous, but his tone wasn't making me squirm.

"But I've decided against doing that for a number of reasons." There was a long pause. He pressed his lips together until they disappeared. Apparently he wasn't going to share his reasons with us.

Destler's eyes rested on a magazine lying open on his desk. It was an issue of *JAMA*, and it was open to the clinical note on Channing's Kutril research. Parts of it were highlighted.

I looked up at Destler. He was staring at me. His soft face had turned hard. "Dr. Temple's Kutril study is complete," he said. "The institute has met the requirements of the grant."

"You'll see that her research gets submitted for publication?" I asked.

"As you know, her methodology has been questioned."

That's when I remembered who the man was that we'd seen leaving Destler's office. It was an Acu-Med executive. A senior VP, in fact.

"And Dr. Jensen's research?" I asked. "I don't believe he was as far along as Dr. Temple in completing the clinical phase."

"I've assured Acu-Med that the work will be completed. And submitted. The institute will meet its obligations. DX-200 is a very promising therapy."

"Promising and expensive," I said.

"Peter —" Kwan started.

I wasn't about to shut up. "Dr. Temple's research should be published. If Kutril offers a cheap, effective treatment for psychological addiction . . ."

Destler crossed his arms. "That's a big 'if?'"

"You're going to bury it, aren't you?"

"I'm not going to bury it," Destler said, enunciating each word as if he were reading fine print off a cue card, "and I'm not going to suspend either of you. The Kutril study is . . . well, it's over. Completed, as far as the Pearce is concerned. The work is well-intentioned but flawed." The only thing keeping me in my chair was Kwan's hand locked on my arm. "Ill-conceived. Poorly executed." Kwan pressed hard. "And Dr. Temple must have realized as much. She must have been disappointed. Perhaps even distraught. Quite distraught. She had high standards. She must have seen this as a failure." He closed the issue of *JAMA*.

"Channing Temple did not kill herself," I said, trying to keep control.

"Whether she did or not is immaterial to this discussion," Destler said dryly. "You are to back off the Kutril study. Do you understand? It's in the best interest of all concerned." Destler's voice was quiet and firm. "The last thing I need right now is another brouhaha. The violent deaths of two physicians is a public-relations disaster. People will think we're running a fly-by-night for the criminally insane. And you harboring a murderer isn't helping the situation."

I rose to my feet, sending my chair crashing over behind me. "She's not a murderer!" It was a good thing his desk was the width of a Buick.

Destler stood up also. "She was out and about last night, too, wasn't she?" he asked, his chin disappearing into his neck as he pressed himself back, his head nestling up against Wilhelmina Pearce's ample lap.

Kwan righted my chair, and I eased back into it. I wondered how in the hell that news had reached Destler so quickly. Incident reports usually take at least a few hours to make their way through channels.

"Dr. Destler," I said, keeping my voice stony calm, "Olivia Temple is a patient at the Pearce, and our number-one obligation, public relations aside, is the well-being of patients."

Destler inched back to his chair and sat.

I went on, "I need to see Dr. Temple's research notes. Last night Olivia had another severe adverse reaction."

His expression shifted, became speculative. "Of course you can see her data. But I want you to see something else, too. Take as much time as you like. The only thing I ask is that you look at the documents here, in my office. And leave them here when you go."

I felt a wary uneasiness, certain that we were about to step into a very attractively baited trap.

He continued, "I'll ask Virginia to bring you the documents. Read them carefully, and think about the implications."

Destler picked up his phone, punched in three numbers, and waited. "Virginia . . ." he started, and gave her instructions. He listened for a few moments, then hung up.

"I've just been reminded," he said, pulling a black appointment book out of his top desk drawer and opening it, "I have another appointment to get to."

He swept the appointment book and the issue of *JAMA* into the drawer, closed and locked it. "I'll leave you gentlemen to your work," he said, standing and straightening his bow tie. Then he left the room.

Kwan pronounced the appropriate verdict: "Bizarre. Truly bizarre." Then he looked around warily and lowered his voice, "You don't suppose this place is bugged, do you?" The same thought had occurred to me.

Virginia Hedgewick staggered in carrying a storage box with a manila folder balanced on the top. Kwan leaped up and took them from her, consummate gentleman that he is.

"A bit early for calisthenics, if you ask me," Virginia said, smoothing her midcalf length skirt across her thick legs. She clucked disapproval as she gazed at the storage box. "This business of impounding files—in all my years, I can't remember another time when we had anything like this. The only thing that comes close was that business with Robert Smythe-Gooding."

"You worked for him back then, didn't you?" Kwan asked.

"I was his secretary — that's what they called us in the old days, before everyone got so damned politically correct. Very unfair, if you ask me. Heart wrenching. To see him brought down by that pipsqueak."

"What pipsqueak?" I asked.

"Fellow's long gone. He was a resident. Came in to assist Dr. Smythe-Gooding in his research. Ended up accusing him of plagiarism. Utter nonsense, if you ask my opinion. He'd copied a few sentences, maybe. But still, they shunted him aside. Didn't want the accusations to become public. Too much at stake. Hospital reputation and all that."

Virginia eyed the file box she'd brought in, as if she didn't like its smell. "Of course that's all ancient history now," she said, and left us to our work.

Kwan opened the box, heaved out the files, and started going through them. I helped myself to the folder from the top of the box.

"What on earth?" I muttered, as I leafed through. It looked like pages photocopied from a smaller journal. The handwriting was compact, precise, backward-slanting. I recognized it right away as Channing's. The date on top of the first page was six months ago. The final entry was about a month later.

Destler had a reason for wanting me to see this. It seemed very unlikely that these were pages Channing Xeroxed and gave him herself. Reluctantly, I started the first entry.

Indian summer today. Hot and close. With the A/C off, this place is like an oven.

I see you lying on the couch and I'm in my chair, pen ready. You're upset. Ready to chuck it all. You're letting it get to you. Letting yourself absorb the dark sadness. You are so vulnerable. So unsure of how to proceed. I want to make you strong.

You are talking about your experiences now. I am half listening, half not, mesmerized by the beads of sweat on your upper lip. I want to lick away the salty sweetness.

I let my hand drift off the edge of the armrest, as if I don't realize I'm touching your leg. Your skin is soft, smooth, pale and iridescent. My fingers stroke your bare skin. You are feeling it too. You let your legs fall apart. I let my fingers wander to the insides of your thighs. Your legs part further, your skirt pushes up. I can see you're wearing nothing underneath. Surely you know. You agree, it is inevitable. I tell you, I want to make love to you. You act like you don't hear, but your back arches, your body tells me you want it too.

I kneel. You have a dragonfly, just here in the hollow between your legs. It matches the other one. I touch it with my tongue. You moan, but not in protest.

There was more, but I couldn't keep reading. I felt queasy—violator and violated at the same time. Was this diary or fantasy? One thing was clear. It was personal, and I had no business reading it. If this were to fall into the wrong hands . . . it already *had* fallen into the wrong hands. I shuddered to think who else had pawed over Channing's private thoughts. So this was the basis of those accusations of inappropriate behavior, boundary violations. Of course there had been no formal hearing. No charges brought. These were only words on paper. Never intended to be read by anyone but Channing herself.

"What is it?" Kwan asked.

I hesitated. The last thing I wanted to do was expose Channing's intimate thoughts to yet another person who barely knew her. "Destler somehow got his hands on some pages from Channing's personal journal. Remember those rumors of impropriety? Wouldn't surprise me if they're based on this."

"Diaries?"

"I think she was recording what she thought, not what she did. I know she's been writing a daily journal since she started working with Daphne. It's basically the same thing Olivia was doing when she wrote those e-mails to her mother—working through thoughts and feelings that disturbed her. Still, it makes it look like . . ." I didn't want to say what it looked like. Others had already done plenty of that. "If the press got hold of this—" I started. The thought was terrifying. Reporters crawling all over the place, interviewing former patients, crucifying a dead psychiatrist who conveniently wasn't there to defend herself. It occurred to me, this was exactly what Destler intended me to think.

I made a mental note to tell Drew to gather up the rest of Channing's journals and put them somewhere secure or destroy them. I put the journal pages back into the folder. I hated leaving them there for Destler and his cronies. But I had no choice. There were probably other photocopies and the journal itself was some-where, too.

"No fair, you took the easy job," Kwan complained. "Are you going to help me go through these?"

I turned my attention to the purple file folders Kwan had taken from the storage box—they looked a lot like the files I'd seen in Jensen's open file drawer. It took the better part of an hour to go through them all. Most of the adverse events reported were minor. Nausea, blurred vision, drowsiness. We did find two subjects who'd experienced seizures. Channing had given them Neurontin to raise their seizure threshold, and continued treatment without any further problems.

Then Kwan found a subject who'd had tremors. "But this guy's fifty-three years old," Kwan said, offering me the file. "At that age, tremors may not be an adverse event. They could be a sign of aging. At any rate, he dropped out of the study, it says, for personal rea-sons." The file hung in midair, Kwan not letting go, me not pulling it away. "Damn," Kwan said. "Isn't her trial supposed to be targeting younger addicts?"

I rummaged in the box and found the file containing the ads

they'd run to recruit subjects. "Between twenty and forty," I read. "A fifty-three-year-old shouldn't be in this study at all."

Was this something else that Destler wanted us to see? That in her zeal to complete the study on time, to get the results she wanted, Channing had accepted subjects who should have been out of bounds?

"I wonder if there are others," I wondered aloud. Kwan was already leafing through the files. Within minutes, he'd assembled three additional file folders, all subjects over forty.

If she was including overage subjects, I wondered if there were more irregularities? No doubt, this was precisely the line of inquiry Destler hoped I'd get sucked into.

I contemplated the pile of file folders. Four inappropriate subjects were sufficient to cast doubt on any study. I told Kwan, "It doesn't make sense. It shouldn't have been that hard to recruit people who fit the protocol—why stray?"

"Maybe she thought she was just bending the rules."

"Kwan, you know she wasn't a rule bender."

"Maybe she was stressed out. Was she drinking? Or taking something to help her deal with the pressure?" Kwan asked.

"Ativan."

"A lot or a little?"

"Don't know."

I felt as if I had the good Channing perched on one shoulder, the bad Channing on the other. One was straitlaced, too good to be human. The other was unethical, drug addicted, and power hungry. Somewhere between lay the truth.

"If she was going to cheat, why not go all the way and alter the ages?" Kwan said.

Why not indeed, I thought. "You know, it would be easy for someone who wanted to discredit the Kutril trials to take a legitimate subject record and change the date of birth. It's not something that can be easily checked. And with Channing out of the way, who would know? If that's what happened, a cheap, effective treatment for psychological addiction goes up in smoke along with Channing's reputation."

"I'd say you're being paranoid. But there's a lot at stake," Kwan said. "I've got a friend, a cancer researcher — did a study that didn't find the kind of whizbang results that the drug company funding the research was hoping for. He finally had to sue them in order to publish."

"Suppressing results is one thing. Cooking her data, that goes quite a bit further," I observed. Where was the line between self-serving and criminal behavior? If someone had altered patient data, they'd crossed it.

I opened the top file in the stack of overage subjects. A man. Forty-six years of age. But was he really that old? There was no name in the file. Only a number code assigned to the subject. In another file, probably in the box somewhere, there'd be a master list with the actual names associated with each code number.

I pulled a pen out of my pocket, but there wasn't a scrap of paper on Destler's desk to write on. I rummaged in the garbage can, pulled out an envelope, and began to copy information onto the back of it.

In crabbed handwriting that would have done Matthew Farrell proud, I wrote the case number of each overage subject, plus the age and gender. I asked Kwan to look for the file containing the master list of patients.

"Just tell me I'm not on *Candid Camera*," Kwan said, but he started searching anyway.

I had a rationalization ready. "It's perfectly okay. Destler's the senior administrator. Right now, he's the one with oversight for this research data. By showing us the files, he gave us permission to look at private information."

"And I suppose you believe there's a sanity clause, too?"

"What matters is that we don't disclose this information to anyone else."

"Found it," Kwan announced, just as Virginia stuck her head into the room.

"You boys about finished?" she asked. "I'm just going to down-stairs to drop off some mail."

"When is Dr. Destler due back?" I asked.

"Now," she answered, and disappeared.

Kwan had the master file open. "Gimme the numbers."

I read off the numbers, one at a time, and copied down the names he read back. We were closing the storage box when Destler returned.

"I hope you've seen what you needed to see," Destler said.

I hoped we had.

21

As we walked back to the unit, Kwan was pensive. "It's an easy line to cross," he said finally. "There's a lot of pressure to get the right"—he drew quotation marks in the air—"results. To meet your quota. You find yourself tempted to take shortcuts and . . ."

"Getting all self-righteous about it," I added, helpfully.

"I suppose I may have been a bit overzealous," he admitted. "Lucky me. I have you handy to keep me honest. I just hope the next suit we fit you out for isn't horizontal stripes with a ball and chain."

"Horizontal stripes. So unflattering."

As we entered the unit, I asked, "What do you think about continuing Olivia on Kutril?"

"We don't know much more than we did before we looked at the research data," Kwan observed. "Only one patient with similar symptoms, and he was over fifty and dropped out of the study. Not very helpful."

"I hate to take her off it. I think it's working."

"How much can it be reducing the craving? Wasn't she snorting Ritalin just last night?"

"She says she wasn't. And actually, I'm not sure," I admitted. "She looked like she could have been."

"But?"

I paused to sort out my thoughts. "If she was taking any, it was a choice she actively made. I have this strong feeling that she's just a hair away from choosing not to. I hate to yank her off with just a week to go."

"Suppose you finish the treatment and the tremors and cogwheeling don't disappear?"

"Couldn't we slow down the treatment?"

"I suppose we could reduce the dosage. Continue for a couple of days longer. If the tremors continue, we stop. She'd need to continue treatment for some additional days. But doesn't she go to prison at the end of the week?"

"Maybe Chip can use this to give us another week with her."

Kwan slowed and stopped. "Peter, if Destler knows Olivia was out and about last night, you can bet the police will find out, too. And suppose we get another week? Isn't it just delaying the inevitable?"

"The drug treatment could buy a little time," I said. "Unless someone pulls the real killer out of a hat, there's not much more I can do."

• • •

I called Chip and told him about our plan to extend Olivia's treatment regimen for another week. He said he'd file a motion the next day and asked if Kwan could be at the hearing, in case the judge needed to hear from her physician. "And maybe we should have Olivia's psychiatrist testify, too. Those threatening e-mail messages speak to whether she's dangerous. We might need someone who can explain how they were part of the therapy."

"I'm sure Daphne will be there if we ask her to. I'll talk to Olivia and see if she'll agree to it," I said.

It was midmorning by the time I got to Olivia's room. I was beyond exhaustion. My head felt like the inside of a recently used cannon. The coffee I'd had only increased the craving.

Olivia wasn't there. A chair was pulled up to the window, and the curtains were pushed aside. It might have been my imagination, but I thought there was a dent in the protective screening over the dirty window, at about where Olivia's forehead would have been.

I checked the closet. Empty. The bathroom door was open. She wasn't in there either. I checked the dining room and the common area and continued on to the nurses' station.

"I put her to work, helping Mr. Fleegle pack up," Gloria told me. "He's off to a nursing home." As I stood there with my mouth open, she added, "Something must have snapped last night. It's like she's got religion. Good religion."

I walked down to Mr. Fleegle's room. Jess was in the doorway. I came up behind her and watched over her shoulder.

Olivia was folding one shirt, then another, and laying them in a beaten-up plaid cloth suitcase. Mr. Fleegle was sitting, one elbow on the chair arm, gesturing with outstretched fingers as if he were conducting an orchestra with a cigarette held aloft.

"Are you going to perform during your stay here?" Mr. Fleegle asked Olivia. "The place could use a pick-me-up. I'd be enchanted to hear you sing again."

Olivia smiled at him and gave a little curtsy. "Why, thank you so much, Mr. Fleegle."

"We've been friends too long. Please, call me Sam." He glanced up and saw me and Jess in the doorway. "Celeste, you have visitors."

Olivia glanced over at us. She folded the last shirt and came over to the door.

"Got a minute?" I asked.

She looked back at Mr. Fleegle, who was nodding lightly, like there was a jazz beat going on in his head. "Gloria wanted me to . . ."

"I know. But this is important. Why don't you go tell Gloria that I pulled you away?"

Olivia hurried off. "Definitely not Asperger's," I said to Jess. "She's far too empathic."

"Mr. Fleegle thinks she's someone he knows."

"Reduplicative paramnesia," I said, putting a name to the symptom. "We see it in patients with Alzheimer's or with schizophrenia. All forms of dementia. And Olivia is doing by instinct something that, as a psychologist, I had to be trained to do. Enter into the delusion with the patient. To deny, to try to argue, only backfires. Reality never mediates delusions. It's too unsettling."

I watched Olivia walk back toward us. She seemed to be moving easily, not shuffling. We went into the dining room.

"What's the Coconut Grove?" she asked as she took a seat.

"It's an old Boston nightclub. Why?"

"Mr. Fleegle says he's a waiter there. And he thinks I'm a singer who works there, too. I played along. I didn't want to upset him."

I laughed. "The Coconut Grove burned to the ground about fifty years ago."

"Fifty years ago?" Olivia gasped. "Was anyone hurt?"

"A lot of people were killed. Four hundred something is the figure that sticks in my mind. Psychologists studied the effects on survivors."

"I guess you could get pretty bent seeing that," she said.

"Sleep disturbances, nervousness and anxiety, paranoia, guilt," I said. "It was the beginning of our understanding of what we now call post-traumatic stress."

"Is that what's happening to me?" she asked. "And this?" she said, holding her upper arm and bending the lower half. The movement was smoother, but there was still a jerkiness.

"We think that's because of the Kutril. But we don't know for sure. It could be a drug interaction. Ritalin on top of Kutril."

"I told you," she grumbled, "I didn't do any." I was glad the old Olivia hadn't completely disappeared — overnight cures make me nervous. "Is this going to get worse?"

"We don't think so. To be on the safe side, we're reducing your Kutril dose. If that doesn't work, we'll stop the treatment completely."

I took the master key out of my pocket and slid it across the table. Olivia stared at it, then up at me. "You want to tell me about this?"

Olivia didn't answer.

"It's your mother's master key, isn't it?"

She nodded.

"And last night isn't the only night you and Matthew escaped, is it?"

Olivia stared down into her lap. She twisted off her thumb ring, put it back on again.

"How long have you two been getting out?"

"About a week," she mumbled.

"Where did you get the drugs?"

"From Dr. Smythe-Gooding's office."

Not "Dr. Daffy"? Maybe Olivia was starting to realize she was in over her head. "This key doesn't open her office. How'd you get in?" I asked.

"She never locks."

Of course. That was how Olivia kept herself supplied with enough Ritalin and God knows what else—courtesy of Dr. Daffy's open door, open drawer, and the generosity of the drug reps.

"So you helped yourself. To what?"

"Ritalin." She looked at me. "For Matthew. I showed him how to snort it, but that's all."

"What else?"

"Valium. Prozac. The usual shit." She was so matter-of-fact about it.

"You took the drugs and then what?"

"We went to one of the buildings no one uses anymore."

"Last night, did you hear anything while you and Matthew were in Dr. Smythe-Gooding's office?"

Olivia didn't blink. She looked at me as if my face had some puzzle in it and if she stared long enough, the pieces would fall into place. "No, I didn't."

"Which staircase did you go down? The one closest to Dr. Smythe-Gooding's office?"

"I . . . I don't remember."

"A man fell to his death last night, around the time you and Matthew were in that office. He fell off a staircase in the Drug and Alcohol Unit." Olivia's face grew long. Her hands tightened into fists. "It was Dr. Liam Jensen. He worked with your mother." The name didn't spark a flicker of recognition. "Remember, they had an argument at the end of her party."

Olivia's face hardened. "He wanted to hurt her." She stared down at her hands. She spread the fingers. "I know what you're thinking. I mean, I'm not where I'm supposed to be. It looks like I'm doing drugs. But I didn't kill anyone." Channing's eyes stared out at me from Olivia's face, daring me not to believe her.

"I know you didn't," I said.

"Are they going to think I did?" Olivia asked. "Are they? Why is this happening? I wish Mommy was here."

"You miss her."

"I want to lean up against her. She used to run her fingers through my hair, right here." Olivia touched her head, closed her eyes, and stroked her own forehead gently. Her breathing slowed, and her body relaxed. Olivia folded her hands in her lap. "Only she's not here. And I can't forget." She exhaled a shaky sigh.

"There are lots of things people do to help them move on. I row. Fix my car. Work long hours."

"Does it help?"

"All of it helps. It lets you get on with the day-to-day. But you don't forget. And you don't really *want* to forget. It never stops hurting. The pain comes back at you when you least expect it. When your guard is down. That's why so many people try to keep their senses occupied. They smoke. Eat all the time."

"Drink too much coffee. Do drugs," Olivia added.

"I don't think that's why you've been doing drugs."

Olivia didn't say anything.

"You're more than a little bit like your mom, you know. You deal with fear by running headlong into whatever it is that frightens you. By acting like you're not afraid, it makes you feel like you're in control."

We sat in silence. Olivia tucked her feet up under her and rested her head against my shoulder. I put my arm around her. I touched her face. She was crying. It was a gentle crying, a letting go.

Finally, Olivia sat up. "Am I going to prison?" she asked.

"We're trying to do everything that we can to prevent that," I said. "Mr. Ferguson is working to get your stay here extended by another week. That will give us time to complete your treatment and give your body a few more days to regain control."

"I don't want to go to jail," Olivia said. "It all feels so out of control. Like nothing I do makes a difference. Like I'm tied down and they're making me watch a terrible movie. Only it's not a movie. It's my life."

That was a pretty melodramatic image. Still, I knew what life as a bad movie felt like. "You can't control whether they send you to prison. Or that your mother died. But you'll feel less helpless if you put yourself in charge of what you can control. For one thing, you can say it's okay for Dr. Smythe-Gooding to testify on your behalf if we get a hearing scheduled. She can explain to the court why you were taking Ritalin, and that writing e-mail to your mother was part of your therapy. That might help convince the judge to let you stay here."

Olivia bit her lower lip. "And if she doesn't testify?"

"Then, I don't know what," I said. Olivia's eyes widened with dread. "Is there something that you haven't told us? Because once your attorney questions Dr. Smythe-Gooding, the prosecutor can ask questions, too."

Olivia looked down into her lap. She picked at her pant leg and shook her head.

"You sure about that?" I asked.

"Sure I'm sure," Olivia said, her old defiance in place.

Olivia and I walked back to the nurses' station. I smelled it before I saw it. A fresh pot of coffee was burbling in the little glassed-off office behind the desk. I held back a groan.

"Go ahead, have a cup," Olivia said. "Bet's over. You won."

"I didn't win," I admitted. "You were right. I was drinking too much coffee. I was having a few before I got in here. Then I couldn't get through morning meeting without more."

"Gloria says that you're a grouchy pain in the ass when you haven't had your coffee. And she says lately you have the attention span of a gnat."

I laughed. Sounded like Gloria. "She's a fine one to talk."

"She drinks decaf in the afternoon," Olivia offered.

"She does?"

"Moderation." Olivia said the word solemnly.

"Do you think that's what you need?" I asked her seriously.

"No. If I started to take Ritalin again, I'd probably take too much. And I don't want to feel like that, ever again." I hoped Channing was somewhere listening. "Dr. Zak, it's okay with me if you want to go back to drinking your coffee. Maybe I'll try it, too."

Moments like this were the reason I'd gotten into doing therapy in the first place. Here was classic transference — Olivia identifying with me. I felt a surge of satisfaction.

• • •

Later that afternoon, I met Daphne in front of the Drug and Alcohol Rehabilitation Unit. We were strolling down the path toward the cafeteria. The air smelled loamy. The forsythia was budding, and one bright yellow witch-hazel bush was in bloom. Daphne lit a cigarette.

"I don't know," she said, when I told her she might be needed to testify at the hearing.

"Olivia has given her permission," I said.

Daphne didn't answer at first. "What kinds of questions are they going to ask?" she said finally.

"They may ask what you know about how Olivia became addicted to Ritalin. How she abused it. And they may ask your opinion about the messages she wrote to her mother."

Daphne squinted into the low sun. "Has Olivia told you she's been stealing Ritalin?"

"She has."

"And you're sure my testimony will help her? You could be opening up a tin of . . ." Daphne waved her hand as she tried to come up with the expression.

"A can of worms?" I suggested.

Daphne nodded.

"You're right, it could backfire. Especially since the DA can ask you anything he likes once you're on the stand. Is there anything that he could ask that would be a problem?"

Daphne paused, midstep. "I don't think so. But lawyers can twist your words. It's what they do."

She was right. And Monty Sherman was a gifted word twister. "Her lawyer will call you only if it's necessary," I said.

"You know I'll do whatever I can to help. Olivia is innocent."

Despite our differences, that was one thing we agreed on. "I'll let them know," I said. We resumed our walk. "By the way, I've seen the raw data from Channing's Kutril study."

"How did you manage that?" Daphne asked. She sounded surprised.

"Destler showed me the files."

"Ah," Daphne said, as if that explained something. "So they had it all along." I couldn't read her look.

"Did you know she included subjects that should have been out-of-bounds? Too old. I can't help wondering if other improprieties are buried in the data."

Daphne stopped, momentarily at a loss for words. Then, "You aren't seriously suggesting that Channing deliberately included subjects who didn't meet the study protocol? Bloody hell's bells!" Daphne said, her eyes flashing. Then, more quietly, "I wonder what they're up to."

"They?"

"It's the same thing that happened to Robert. Plagiarism? Bloody unlikely. But that's how it works. They bring in a young resident, keen as mustard, supposedly helping you organize your papers. And before you know it, he's saying your research is corrupt, you've copied passages whole from other people's work. Not the conclusions, mind you. No one has ever suggested that Robert's work was anything but original and brilliant. He managed to get past it, but the ordeal weakened him. If you ask me, gave the cancer a place to grow." She paused, her face animated. "If he were with us, he'd be there for her. Telling her how to survive."

Sadly, I thought, survival was beyond any help even Robert could offer. "You don't think we've overestimated her, do you?" I asked.

"Channing?" Daphne asked. She shivered. "That's what they want you to think." There was that *they* again. She gave a wry smile. "That incorruptible Channing, *sans peur et sans reproche*, who always colored inside the lines, suddenly smudged the rules because she'd do anything to reach her goal." Daphne sniffed. "Not even remotely possible."

She smoothed strands of silver hair on one side of her face, then the other. "I'll grant you, she was quite obsessed with her research. Worked nights, weekends, like it was all that mattered. That's because she had a passion for truth. About that, she was steadfast. Perhaps a bit too steadfast for her own good."

"*Veritas*," I said.

"Pardon me?"

"Just something Channing once told me. Truth. Sometimes it can devour you."

22

THAT WEEKEND Annie and I met on Memorial Drive near Harvard Square. It was a gorgeous day with only the occasional white cotton-ball cloud suspended in a clear field of blue. The street was closed to traffic, and bicyclists, runners, and in-line skaters competed aggressively for the right of way, treating ordinary pedestrians like obstacles in a slalom.

The grassy riverbank was still sparsely populated, the occasional couple sitting on a blanket and admiring the sparkling water, the Boston skyline, and the hardy varsity rowers gliding under the arched brick bridges of the Charles.

I waited for Annie in front of a yellow tent set up on the grass by Roll-Our-Own Rentals. I was working on a large coffee from Peet's. Annie rolled up and screeched to a halt in front of me — if she'd been on ice, she'd have kicked up a spray of shavings.

She had on a bright blue down vest and purple leggings. She pulled off her helmet and shook her hair loose.

"I thought you gave up coffee," she said.

"I got a reprieve. Actually, I'm trying to go easy. This is just my second cup today. I'm savoring it to the last drop."

"Good plan," she said, and gave me a light kiss on the cheek. We went inside to find a pair of skates that fit my size-twelve feet.

"Trust me, you'll love it," Annie told me, as we found an empty bench. I unfastened the Velcro and started to loosen the lace on one skate. "Here, I'll do that for you," Annie said. "You should put on your safety gear first."

"Just in case I fall off the bench?" I said.

"Don't laugh. It's been known to happen."

I eyed the pile of padded armor with something less than enthusiasm. Helmet, wrist guards, knee- and elbow pads—the black plastic was already scraped and scuffed from earlier encounters with paved surfaces.

When I'd put it all on except for the helmet, Annie handed me the skates. I put one on, then the other. Annie knelt in front of me and pressed the buckles in place. "Comfy?" she asked.

"Just ducky," I replied, and started to get up.

"Whoa. Helmet next."

I put on my helmet, fastened the strap, and pulled it taut.

"Okay. Now set your feet so your toes are pointing out, just a bit. Now, up we go."

I held onto Annie and stood.

"Now we take a little walk on the grass. Keep your toes pointed slightly out."

I did. With every step, I felt more like a dancing ostrich from *Fantasia*, the skates my oversize toe shoes.

"Now, stop and balance on one foot," Annie instructed when we got outside the tent. I obeyed—an ostrich doing a flamingo imitation. "That's terrific. Now the other foot." She watched me perform. "You sure you haven't done this before?" It was dumb, but I grinned anyway.

"Okay. Now let's practice finding your balance." Annie faced me and held palms up to mine, our arms bent at the elbow. "Flex your knees, and lean forward on the balls of your feet."

For a minute it felt as if my knees wouldn't bend. But then they did, and I leaned forward.

"A little more," she coaxed. I did. "That's good. Weight in the toes, knees bent. Perfect."

It felt perfectly idiotic, standing there with my butt hanging out. "This feels ridiculous," I said.

"That's because you're doing it right. If you go too far forward — go ahead, try it." I leaned forward some more until it was only because Annie was holding me up that I didn't fall to my hands and knees. "Right. That's just what you want to do. Fall forward."

"Only you won't be here to catch me."

"Right. Now here's the deal about falling. It's going to happen. And when you fall down, you're going to need to get up."

"Fall down. Get up," I said. In-line skating. How the hell had I gotten myself into this? Not only was it dangerous, it was complicated.

"Okay, give it a try. With your arms out in front of you, fall forward onto your knees. And keep your knees together because the kneepads have a tendency to slide apart."

"Arms in front, fall forward," I said. I did it, feeling extremely undignified. It seemed like every little kid in Cambridge was whizzing by, backward, on in-line skates.

"See that hard plate on your wrist guard? It's designed to slide on the pavement, not slam straight down. Try to use your body like a shock absorber — crumple into the fall."

"Uh-huh," I grunted. "Now, how the hell do I get up."

"Okay, first one knee up." I did it. "Now put your hands on the ground on either side and push up slowly." It was working. I was almost up. Annie was saying, "Don't forget to put your feet in a V position, then you won't fall. . . ." But before I realized what was happening, I was flapping my arms like a pair of propellers. I landed with a crash on my ass.

"Shit," I said.

Annie had a hand over her mouth. She lowered the hand and said, "The one piece of protective gear you haven't got is a pillow bungeed to your butt."

"I knew we forgot something."

"So rule number one of in-line skating: Always always always fall forward. That's where you've got all your protection. If you start to feel yourself falling backward, do *not* flap your arms."

"Right," I said, still on my back staring at Annie's knees. She had very nice knees and firm thighs, and a nice round behind encased in those shiny Lycra leggings. "No flapping."

At last, we were ready to launch. I'd gotten to my feet without a hitch. I took a tentative step out onto the pavement. I took a breath, counted to ten, focusing on feeling my own center of gravity. Then I pushed out. One step, two, three. Then I rolled to a stop on the grass.

Sweat was already dripping from my eyebrows. I longed to take off the helmet and wipe it away. Clever Annie was wearing a sweatband under her helmet.

We skated up the sidewalk, over the Anderson Bridge, and started down the path on the Boston side. Annie skated backward as I lumbered along—one, two, three, roll. "Don't forget to bend at the knees and the ankles. And try to relax," she instructed.

We rolled past the tidy brick buildings of the Harvard Business School. Annie was right about one thing. The stiff boots meant my ankles weren't hurting at all. It was the balls of my feet that felt like red-hot pokers were sticking into them.

The pleasantly cool air in the shadows of overhanging trees turned chilly as we passed in front of the Acu-Med Building. The redbrick monster, topped by a tower, loomed like a processing center for refugees entering a Brave New World. Through its massive windows, the only things visible were machinery, cabling, and pipes.

Once we were out in the sun again, Annie rolled up to a railing and stopped. I crashed into her and stayed there, my body pressed up against hers.

"Stopping," we said simultaneously.

"You haven't taught me that," I observed.

"Next time."

"Maybe we can skip that lesson. I kind of like doing it this way."

Annie gazed at the Acu-Med Building. "That place gives me the willies. One day lightning will hit the steeple and a huge guy with a bolt through his neck will come stomping out."

I laughed. "Acu-Med. They fund a lot of the research at the institute. Liam Jensen's research, just for example."

"Which reminds me," Annie said. "That Social Security number you asked me to check on—the guy who dropped out of Jensen's study. He's not dead."

"Not dead," I murmured. "So, we still don't know what Liam and Channing were arguing about. And with Liam dead, he can't tell us. By the way, turns out the CFO at the institute had Channing Temple's research files."

"So they're not missing after all."

"Apparently not. He says he was given them for safekeeping. I assume he got them from Jensen, who I can only assume helped himself. Destler let me look through them. I think he wanted me to see that Channing included some subjects in the trial who were too old."

"Is that a big deal?"

"Major league. It's really got me agonizing. I can't conceive of Channing doing that. She was compulsive about details, about ethics."

"And you're sure they're too old."

"That's what I'm wondering. It doesn't make any sense. There's a lot of things about this that don't make any sense at all."

Annie stared at me. "So, what does your gut say?"

Go with what you *know* about people. Ignore reality. It was what I was paid to do. Day in and day out, working with patients, my gut worked overtime. Sometimes I let it guide me, sometimes I acknowledged the feelings and consciously set them aside. Outside the therapy room, I wore lenses to filter out all that extraneous noise.

"Okay," I said, "my gut says Channing wouldn't include overage subjects."

"Therefore . . ." Annie urged me on.

"Maybe someone doctored the records to make her subjects look as if they're older than they are. To discredit her work."

"Or maybe someone inserted records, after the fact, of people who weren't in her trial at all, to make it look like she was behaving unethically," Annie suggested. "It's easy enough to find out. I can track down these people and ask them if they participated in the Kutril trial and how old they are. Just give me the names."

That stopped me. "No can do," I said. "Patient confidentiality. It's bad enough that I've got them written down."

Annie rested her chin in her hand and pondered. "Okay. So we're looking for—how many?"

"Four."

"Four addicts, or former addicts. Who may or may not be how old?"

"Over forty."

"And who may or may not have participated in the Kutril trial." It sounded impossible, but Annie didn't seem at all dismayed. "I'd start with AA meetings," Annie said, a gleam in her eye.

She was right. The protocol required that they go to AA for support.

"And addicts getting treatment at the Pearce tend to go to the same AA meeting," Annie added.

"You're right. But how do you . . . ?"

"That story I told Olivia about how I used to binge drink and ended up in jail? I fudged the truth a bit—all that really happened to my sister. But I figured Olivia would take it more seriously if I was speaking from firsthand experience. Valerie finally stopped drinking a few years ago. I'm the one who got her into AA. She still goes regularly, and I go with her from time to time. It won't raise an eyebrow if I show up. Then I can nose around after the meeting and see what I can find out."

I didn't like the sound of that. The last thing I wanted to do was subvert treatment that substance abusers were voluntarily seeking. Reading my concerns, Annie said, "Don't worry. I won't do anything to upset the meeting. I'll just hang around after. Then I'll bring *you* names of over-forty folks who've participated in a drug trial at the Pearce. Maybe we'll come up with a match, maybe not. In any event, you won't have given me any names, and no one's privacy gets mangled without their consent."

I thought about it and couldn't come up with an objection, though it still seemed as if what Annie proposed was just barely on the side of the angels.

We started back. Pushing off was easier this time. I was actually starting to enjoy myself. We skated across the Western Avenue Bridge and started up Memorial Drive on the Cambridge side.

Still, when we got back to the tent, I was relieved to sit, ease my feet out of the skates, and return them to the Roll-Our-Own folks.

We walked up onto the bridge and gazed down the river toward downtown.

"I'd have thought it would be impossible to find out. You're amazing," I said.

"It's what I do," Annie said, "and I'm good at it."

"I've noticed."

"And in this case, I care."

The sun was low in the sky, and the temperature was dropping fast. "Hey," Annie said, "isn't that the courthouse?" She pointed to a tall, red-and-gray building in the distance with red lights blinking on top. "Which reminds me. I knew there was something else I was supposed to tell you. The hearing. It's Wednesday afternoon at three."

"Wednesday. I'll tell Kwan and Daphne. I hope this works."

"A delay isn't an acquittal," Annie observed.

She was right. The only way to save Olivia from an extended stay in purgatory was for the police to find someone else to arrest, and time was running out.

The traffic pulsed across the bridge behind us. Before us the river gleamed, smooth and peaceful. A sleek boat with a crew of eight sliced toward us and slid under the bridge into the dark shadows, leaving behind only their puddles and a rapidly fading, silvery wake.

I put my arm around Annie and pulled her close to me. "Soon," I said. I put my face into her neck and inhaled.

"Soon what?" Annie asked, laughing.

"Soon"—I nipped her earlobe—"it will be warm enough for me to get back to rowing. Turnabout is fair play. You tortured me. Now I get to torture you."

"Mmm. Maybe."

"Good. Doing anything for dinner?"

Annie put her arms around me. I could feel her breasts pressing against me. I ran my hands down into the small of her back.

"I have some bad news," she said.

"You're not hungry? That's not such bad news," I said.

"If only that were it. Actually, I'm ravenous. But it's Sunday— that's the night patients from the Pearce usually go to AA." I groaned. "Used to be anyway."

I knew we couldn't afford to wait. "It's not fair," I said, pulling Annie's hips into mine.

Annie looked up at me, her face golden in the setting sun. "Tell me about it."

23

THE HEARING was on a blustery day. I watched Gloria and Olivia get into a taxi that would take them to the courthouse. Olivia seemed subdued. Under a navy pea coat and a plaid muffler, she had on a skirt and a white blouse that buttoned down the front. Her black hair with an inch of blond roots made an odd contrast to the schoolgirl outfit.

Kwan and I drove over together and parked. We ran into Daphne on our way to the courthouse. She was walking, full tilt into the wind, protecting her eyes with one hand from the bits of street sand being kicked up by gusts and holding a cigarette in the other. She took a puff and exhaled, looking like a determined steam locomotive pushing uphill.

By the time we got to the courthouse, Daphne's face was pink and her hair was in tangles. After we got through security, she excused herself and went to find the ladies room. Kwan and I went upstairs to the judge's chambers. Daphne joined us a few minutes later. I took an empty chair between Drew and Kwan. DA Montrose Sherman was there again with the assistant DA. At just two minutes past eleven, the hearing was under way.

"The doctors at the Pearce Psychiatric Institute have recommended that Miss Temple continue her treatment there for another two weeks," Chip said. Olivia was sitting at the table next to him. "She's been experiencing some serious side effects that have required the doctors to slow down the drug regimen she's been undergoing."

"More than the seizure she had during her arraignment?" the judge asked.

"Yes. Tremors. Parkinson's-like movement disorders."

Sherman scowled. The assistant DA just leaned back and let his boss take over. "The Commonwealth has already agreed to a two-week delay for this experimental treatment. How do we know that after this extension, there won't be another, and then another? I'm sure I don't need to remind Mr. Ferguson of the seriousness of the charges facing his client."

"And I'm sure I don't need to remind Mr. Sherman of the risks of prematurely terminating treatment," Chip countered. "The Commonwealth loses nothing by a short delay. Dr. Liu is here and can explain the medical reasons."

"Olivia Temple can get the treatment she needs in jail," Sherman intoned. "With all due respect to the security procedures at the Pearce" — he paused and tapped his pencil against his pad of paper — "she presents a danger to the community and should be locked up. The e-mail messages she sent suggest planning, deliberation."

"That's for the court to decide," Chip countered.

The judge intervened. "We're all well aware that this is a hearing, not a trial."

Chip said, "Those messages she sent to her mother were part of her therapy. That was . . ."

Sherman interrupted, "Miss Temple sends a message saying she wishes her mother was dead. The next day, her mother is killed. That's not therapy. That's premeditated murder."

"I'm inclined to agree with Mr. Sherman," the judge said. "I think I'd be remiss if I allowed her to stay at the Pearce. Especially with this second murder."

"E-mail therapy," Sherman sneered.

Drew was starting to rise out of his seat. I put my hand on his shoulder, and he sank back.

"Your Honor, Ms. Temple is not accused of committing a second murder," Chip said. "Her psychiatrist, Dr. Smythe-Gooding, is here. She can explain the e-mail messages. She can also give her professional opinion as to whether or not Ms. Temple presents a danger to society."

Sherman gave Chip a surprised look. Then he gazed at me without blinking. I tried to keep my expression even, but I could feel my face grow hot. The last time we'd met in court, Sherman was supposedly cross-examining me regarding the memory of a victim who'd suffered traumatic brain damage from a gunshot wound to the head, but he'd laced his questions with subtle innuendo about my wife's murder. He'd baited me, and I'd nearly snapped. I knew lawyers played down and dirty, but Sherman could do it without creating even a ripple of suspicion.

"Mr. Sherman?" the judge said.

"I have no objection."

All eyes turned to Daphne. She looked like someone who was about to give a speech and was unprepared.

She was sworn in. Chip asked her to identify herself and walked her through her credentials. Then, "Doctor, would you please tell the court, what is your relationship to Miss Temple?"

"For the past year . . ." Daphne cleared her throat. "For the last year, Olivia Temple has been my patient. She's been in therapy."

"What were you treating her for?"

"She was having difficulty concentrating in school. Problems at home." These answers came with polish and authority.

"And what was your treatment?"

"I, uh . . ." Daphne shifted in her seat. Chip waited. Daphne glanced quickly at Olivia and back at Chip. "I gave her Ritalin"—I didn't like the uncertainty in her voice—"to help her focus." She sounded as if she were picking her words carefully. Sherman leaned forward to write on a yellow legal pad. Then he leaned back and folded his arms across his chest.

"Thank you, Doctor," Chip said. "And was it part of your therapeutic approach to have Olivia Temple write down her feelings about her mother?"

"I object," Sherman barked. "Leading question."

Chip looked surprised. Hearings for juvenile offenders tended to be a bit more relaxed than for adults. "I'll rephrase. What was your therapeutic approach?"

"We met once a week. Talked. And I had her do some writing."

"What kind of writing."

"It's based on a technique called countertransference analysis." Now the self-assurance returned. Daphne gestured with both hands. "Writing down unsettling thoughts and feelings helps people regain a healthy perspective. It's an approach I developed to help therapists . . ." She caught Chip's look and stopped.

It reminded me of the many times Chip had prepped me to testify. He always ended with the warning, "Just answer the questions, Peter. Elaborate, and you may be giving the DA rope to hang us with."

"Thank you, Doctor," Chip said. "In your opinion, does writing down a feeling indicate that the person is going to act on that feeling?"

"Mr. Ferguson is leading the witness," Monty said. "Again."

"Mr. Ferguson . . ." the judge started.

"I'll rephrase," Chip said, sounding annoyed. "Is there a relationship between what people write and how they act?"

"We think about doing all kinds of things we would never, ever actually do," Daphne answered.

"Do you recognize this piece of writing?" Chip asked, offering Daphne a printed page.

She glanced over it. "It's one of the letters Olivia Temple wrote to her mother," Daphne said. There was a pause. Chip leaned toward Daphne. She seemed momentarily flustered. She added quickly, "As part of her therapy."

Chip sat back. "Olivia Temple wrote that she wished her mother was dead. Is it your opinion that Olivia Temple was planning to hurt her mother."

There was no hesitation. "Absolutely not."

"And was it part of the therapy to put her thoughts and feelings into e-mail messages and send them to her mother?"

"I object," Sherman barked again. He wasn't going to make this easy.

"Sustained," the judge said.

Chip sighed. "And did you have Ms. Temple do anything with this message that she wrote to her mother?"

Daphne said, "I had her show the message to her mother. Olivia used e-mail to do so. Her mother was herself experienced with CTA. I felt it would be beneficial to them both."

"Thank you, Doctor."

Daphne sank back, evidently relieved.

Sherman said, "Excuse me, Doctor. I have just a few questions." Daphne looked startled. "You said you gave Ms. Temple Ritalin. When you give medication to a patient, Doctor, do you typically write a prescription?"

"Do I write a . . . well, of course I do."

"And so, when the patient gets the prescription filled, there's a record that the pharmacy keeps. If insurance is involved, they are notified."

"I would assume so."

"Then perhaps you can explain to me how you prescribed Ritalin for Miss Temple when none of the pharmacies in the Commonwealth have any record of one having been filled?"

Daphne pulled back, blinked. "Well, that's because —"

Olivia strained forward in her seat.

"Did you or did you not, write a prescription for Miss Temple?" There was a pause. "I'm sure I don't need to remind you that you are under oath."

Daphne glared at Sherman. "When a patient is starting a new therapy, psychiatrists often supply them with sample packages to get started. To give it a try before we write a prescription."

"Did you, or did you not *prescribe* Ritalin for Miss Temple?" Sherman asked again.

"If you mean, did I write a prescription, the answer is no. But she was taking it under my guidance." Daphne's voice was icy with disdain.

"For how long, Doctor?"

"Four, maybe five months. I'd have to check my notes to be certain."

"Is that an unusually long time for someone to be taking sample packets of medication?"

"No. It's not unusual."

"Hmm," Sherman said. "And about four months ago, do you recall reporting to hospital security that your office had been broken into and medication stolen?" Sherman held out a piece of paper. "One of the drugs missing was Ritalin."

"I don't see what that has to do with—" Daphne started.

"Did you file this report?" Sherman offered her the piece of paper.

Reluctantly, Daphne took it. She eyed what looked like a photocopy of a form. "Yes. Apparently, I did." She handed the paper back to Sherman.

"Thank you, Doctor. I have just a few more questions. Just a few nights ago, did you file a report to security that drugs were once again missing from your office?"

Her answer was inaudible.

"Could you speak up, please?"

"Yes," Daphne said. "Yes I did. But how was I supposed to know that Olivia was out and about—" Daphne's mouth snapped shut. She looked stunned. It reminded me of how Sherman had ambushed me the last time he'd cross-examined me.

"Exactly," Sherman said. "How were you supposed to know that Olivia Temple had escaped from a supposedly secure unit that same evening and was roaming freely among the hospital buildings—a night when, coincidentally, another doctor was killed." He paused for effect. "Just one more thing, Doctor. Did you, or did you not, *prescribe* a course of therapy in which Miss Temple was to send electronic messages to her mother."

Daphne drew herself up. "Of course, that's part of the approach."

"And it's a part you specifically prescribed, as opposed to being something that your patient did on her own, just like she helped herself to Ritalin. . . ."

"Objection!" Chip said. "Mr. Sherman is using suggestion and innuendo. . . ."

The judge cut him off. "I think I've heard all I need to. I'm denying the motion."

"But Ms. Temple needs medical treatment that she can only get at the Pearce," Chip argued.

"Mr. Ferguson, you are trying the patience of this court," the judge said. He took off his glasses and rubbed the bridge of his nose. "There is nothing to distinguish your request, other than the fact that Ms. Temple comes from a privileged home. The setting she's in has been demonstrated to be insufficiently secure. And I have to agree with Mr. Sherman. This *is* a murder case, and there is evidence that the defendant may be dangerous, even a flight risk. I will give the doctors at Pearce until Friday to terminate their treatment, at which point Ms. Temple will be taken to the Bechtel Center for Girls. This hearing is over."

Sherman and his colleague left. I stood and waited for Chip to finish packing up his papers. Drew had his arm around Olivia. We all filed out.

In the hall, Chip muttered under his breath, "Holy shit. Two days."

Olivia was agitated. "Lying bitch. Lying bitch . . ." She said it over and over, as if she were turning the key in her own ignition, again and again.

Daphne came over to her. "Livvy . . ."

Olivia hunched her shoulders and blew air out—it was like the hiss of a feral cat. "My mother never should have trusted you."

"Livvy, you don't know what you're saying! I was under oath. . . ."

"Doctor Smythe-Gooding," Chip said sharply. "I wonder if you have a few minutes to meet? There's a conference room just across the hall that we can use."

Daphne gave Olivia a pleading look. Olivia wouldn't even look at her. Finally, Daphne gave a mute nod and walked over to the conference-room door.

"Would you mind just waiting for us inside?" Chip asked.

Daphne went in. Then Olivia lost it. She stood and spat after her. She shrieked, "You crazy bitch! You promised you'd protect me."

Kwan was at Olivia's side, talking to her quietly. But the soothing words had no effect. Olivia got louder. "Bitch! You promised you'd help." Kwan pressed his hands on Olivia's arm, Drew held her on the other side. "Liar!" she screamed and strained to break away. "I never should have trusted you," she shrieked and sent Drew staggering back into the wall. A pair of uniformed court officers came out of a nearby courtroom and hovered, trying to assess whether the situation was under control.

Gloria came up to Olivia and put her hand on her face. She spoke quietly as Olivia shook her head, back and forth. Kwan squinted at me, his look one of concern. "Olivia should return to the hospital," he said, adding after a brief pause, "right now. She's quite agitated. She needs something to calm her."

Chip said, "There's no reason for her to stay."

"Bitch! Liar!" Olivia screamed as Kwan and Gloria led her away.

I felt as torn as Drew looked, as we watched Kwan and Gloria lead Olivia away, agitated and muttering. I wanted to go with them, to help get Olivia calmed down. To ensure that she didn't hurt herself. But I also needed to stay here, to do what I could to help with her defense. And I knew Olivia was in good hands.

Chip herded Drew and me into the conference room. The small, windowless room had a table and some chairs. Daphne was standing, staring at the blank wall. She looked pale, spent. We all sat.

Chip leaned back, tilted his head to one side, and gave Daphne an appraising look. "You surprised us," he told her.

Daphne's face was pinched. Her hands were shaking.

"If we'd known that you didn't actually write a prescription for

Ritalin, we wouldn't have asked you to testify," Chip said, putting it bluntly.

"I thought you knew. When I talked with Peter . . . I must have misunderstood. I have made rather a cock-up of things. I only wanted to help. I don't know why I said anything about Olivia roaming about. It slipped out."

Slipped out? As a therapist, Daphne knew as well as anyone that nothing just "slips out."

Chip said, "Surely you must have realized that saying what you did could affect the judge's decision."

"It was an accident!" Daphne insisted, gripping the edge of the table with both hands. "How can you even suggest that I'd deliberately sabotage my patient? The daughter of my dearest friend?"

"What a mess," Drew said, putting his head in his hands.

Daphne touched his shoulder, "I'm so sorry, Drew," she said.

Drew pushed her away. "Isn't there anything you can do?" he asked Chip.

"I think we're out of options," Chip replied. "Day after tomorrow, she goes." He looked at me pointedly. "And I don't think any more suicide attempts or drug reactions are going to make any difference."

24

I DROVE back to the Pearce, my jaw clenching and unclenching as I replayed the hearing in my head. I thought about Daphne, how unsure she'd seemed on the stand. Had it been a misunderstanding? Had she tried to tell me that she hadn't written a prescription? Was it usual or unusual to treat a patient for months with a drug without writing a prescription? Borderline, I thought. Getting nailed by Monty—well, so had I, the last time he cross-examined me. Still, I wonder if the slip was altogether innocent. Then it occurred to me. Perhaps Daphne hadn't given Olivia Ritalin at all. Maybe she was saying so to protect Olivia from a harsher reality—that Olivia had been stealing the drug all along and self-medicating.

On Mem. Drive, I slowed down and pulled the car over into the turnout in front of an office building. A driver passed me, his horn blaring. *Go with your gut.* That's what Annie had urged me to do. What did my gut say? I shoved the car into neutral, pulled the emergency brake, and closed my eyes.

I saw a kaleidoscope of images. Olivia at the top of the stairs at the party. Holding the gun by the barrel and looking dazed in her mother's office. Cutting her arm. Hiding in her closet. Staring at me bug-eyed from the mattress in the basement of Albert House. Folding Mr. Fleegle's shirts.

I opened my eyes and gazed out the window. A tree, planted on the shoulder of the road, snagged my attention. The trunk of a tree was snakelike and sinuous, like the one in the Annie Brigman photograph on Olivia's wall — a wall of school-age killers and teenage girls in Cinderella prom dresses. Which was it?

Carefully, I pulled the car back out into traffic and continued to the Pearce.

Gloria was at the nurses' station. Her short hair was standing up on end. She was holding a patient's chart as if she were reading it, but her glasses were on the counter. I knew she was actually communing with space.

"Earth to Alspag," I said.

Gloria gave me a tired smile. "We've got her calmed down. Finally. She'd worked herself up into quite a state by the time we got back. Then she broke down and couldn't stop crying. Kwan gave her some Klonopin. That didn't do much, so he gave her more. Even that hasn't knocked her out."

I started toward Olivia's room.

"Not there," Gloria said. "She's in the quiet room."

The quiet room is a cell-like space we use with agitated patients. It's got a simple bed in it with slots for restraints, white walls, low light. No hard edges or other furnishings. We keep the door open and someone posted on a chair outside until the patient is stabilized.

Jess was sitting on the chair outside the quiet room. She had a portable computer balanced in her lap, her black pumps on tiptoe to make a flat surface.

"Since when do psychiatrists do one-on-ones?" I asked.

"I volunteered," Jess said. "I'm just spelling Joe while he takes a break. He'll be back in a minute."

"I can take over for you," I said.

She turned off the computer, bent down, and stowed it in her backpack, which was under the chair.

"At least she's quieted down now," she said.

Jess stood and dropped her pen. As I stooped over to retrieve it for her, I caught a glimpse of the tattoo on her ankle. It was a dragonfly. I stood slowly. Something was familiar, but it took me a minute to make the connection to the page from Channing's journal—the patient had a dragonfly tattoo. Or I'd assumed it was a patient. It could as easily have been a devoted disciple.

Slowly, I handed Jess her pen. Was Jess the suicidal woman whom Daphne said Channing was working with—the one who was causing Channing to lose her clinical perspective? Surely, Jess was the subject of Channing's intense sexual fantasy.

Jess dropped the pen into her backpack.

"You carry that around a lot don't you?" I asked, trying to sound nonchalant.

Jess glanced down at the bag with some surprise. "I guess I do."

"You even had it with you at Channing's birthday party. It seemed a little odd at the time. You were so dressed up. And still, you were carrying your backpack."

"I guess it's a habit."

"When I met you up on the second-floor landing during the party, you were coming out of Channing's study carrying it."

"Joe promised he'd be right back." Jess looked at her watch.

"You were zipping it up."

"I've got to go see a patient." Jess took a step back from me.

"Do you remember what you said you were doing? You said you were using the bathroom."

"Did I?"

"Only there isn't any bathroom adjoining the study. If there had been, then Channing would have sent me there instead of down the hall to get cold water for the stain on Jensen's jacket."

Jess was frozen, her mouth open, the backpack clutched to her chest.

"Why were you in Dr. Temple's study the night of her party?"

"It's not what you think," she said.

"What do I think?"

"I was trying to put it back."

"Trying to put what back?"

Just then, Joe came ambling up the hall carrying a can of Diet Dr Pepper. A thick man with a soft, kind face, he checked into the quiet room. Then he lowered himself into the chair outside the door and opened up his newspaper.

From inside the room came Olivia's weak voice, "Dr. Zak?"

"I can explain everything," Jess said, her voice urgent. "Just give me a chance to explain."

"Dr. Zak?" Olivia called out again. "Is that you?

I put my head into the room. "Olivia, I'm here. Be there in a sec."

I turned back to Jess. Her eyes were bright, the way they'd been when she emerged from Channing's study. Had she been putting something back or taking something?

"It's not what you think," Jess repeated, her voice pleading.

"I have to go in and see Olivia," I said. "After that you and I need to talk."

"I'll be in the dining room working. Come get me when you're finished," she said. Then she hurried off.

I told Joe he could take another five-minute break while I borrowed his chair. I dragged it into the quiet room and sat alongside Olivia.

She was lying on her back, her eyes barely open, the lids drifting shut and then jerking open. Spittle was dried at the corner of her mouth.

"Olivia," I said, pulling my chair close, "why don't you let yourself relax. Sleep."

"Can't shleep," Olivia said, her tongue thick with sedative. "Mustn't sleep."

"Shh," I said. "We can talk later, you know. I'm not going anywhere."

"Talk . . . now." She rolled over on her side and held a finger to her mouth. I leaned close. "She promised she wouldn't tell."

"Who promised? To tell what?"

"About the Ritalin."

"Dr. Smythe-Gooding?"

"Mommy didn't want me to take it."

"Dr. Smythe-Gooding gave you the drugs?"

Olivia nodded. "She said Mommy wouldn't understand."

"Was she lying about you stealing Ritalin?"

Olivia closed her eyes.

I pressed, "She wasn't lying about that, was she?"

"I needed more. She wouldn't give me more. She promised she wouldn't tell."

A bell went off in my head. "Were you in Dr. Smythe-Gooding's office stealing drugs when your mother died?"

A tear squeezed out of Olivia's eye and made a damp spot on the mattress.

"Mommy," she whispered.

"You heard the gunshot, didn't you?"

"I promised I wouldn't tell."

"Who did you promise you wouldn't tell?"

"Lying bitch," Olivia said, her eyes closing.

"You promised Daphne you wouldn't tell?"

Olivia's eyes drifted shut.

"Dr. Dyer was a friend of your mom's, too, wasn't she?"

"Special friend," Olivia said, slurring over the words.

"Like Daphne was a special friend?"

"Lying bitch," Olivia said again. This time the words made a gentle sound.

I sat there for a few minutes, listening as her breathing deepened. Her clenched hand fell open. I smoothed the hair away from her face. She looked very young and vulnerable.

Special friend? Was that all it was, friendship? Or did Jess and Channing's relationship go beyond?

I found a blanket, and as I was putting it over Olivia, I noticed her necklace. It was an old-fashioned, engraved gold locket. Where had I seen it before? The locket was open a crack. I reached over, meaning to snap it shut, but instead I found myself opening it. A black-and-white photograph of a little girl, maybe ten years old, stared back at me. She resembled Olivia, her hair still blond and soft around her face. I'd seen that little girl before. It was Channing, the way she looked in the pictures in her family photo album.

Now I pressed the locket shut and rubbed it between my thumb and forefinger. This was the locket Jess had around her neck just a week earlier. Was this what Jess was trying to return?

When Joe came back, I told him I was going to write an order restricting Olivia's visitors. "So, please, don't let anyone in except me, Nurse Alspag, and Dr. Liu. Okay?"

Joe nodded. "Just you three."

"Right."

"What if . . . ?" he started.

"If anyone else wants to see Ms. Temple, and I mean anyone at all, I want you to beep me to get permission first."

• • •

I checked in with Gloria and Kwan, told them I was restricting Olivia's visitors to the three of us. Good thing that neither of them questioned it, because I'm not sure I could explain, even to myself, what—or whom—I was protecting Olivia from.

Jess was working in the dining room. I caught her attention through the glass and pointed up, to indicate I was heading up to my office. She nodded, held her hand up and spread her fingers. Five minutes.

I took the elevator and let myself into my office. I leaned back in my chair, took off my glasses, and stared up at the ceiling. So Olivia had been right there, a few feet away, when Channing was killed. She'd heard the gunshot. What had Daphne made her promise not to tell? Had she seen anyone? Someone Daphne didn't want named?

Which brought me back to wondering what Jess was doing in

Channing's study the night of the party. If she was returning something, then why lie and say she'd been in the bathroom? Unless she was returning something she'd stolen. Something like a locket. Or maybe she was taking a gun.

Channing had written *D* in her datebook on the morning she was killed. Dyer? *J* would have been a more likely shorthand for a woman Olivia termed her mother's *special friend*.

The phone rang. I checked my watch. It had been more than five minutes since I'd left Jess on the unit. Maybe she was calling to say she'd been delayed. I picked up.

"Hey, Peter!"

It was Annie. I felt a rush of pleasure. "Hey, yourself," I said.

"I heard things didn't go so well this morning. How's Olivia?" Her voice sounded echoey, as if she was calling from her cell phone.

"Sedated. Sleeping." As an afterthought, I added, "Feeling betrayed."

"Friday she goes to the Bechtel."

"Two more days."

Annie didn't say anything for a few moments. "Well, I guess there's nothing for it but to keep going," she said. "I went to those AA meetings and schmoozed with anyone who looked over forty. Told them I'd been thinking of signing up for one of those drug trials at the Pearce and wondered if anyone else had gone that route. People can be so helpful. I've got a couple of names."

"Amazing," I said. I pulled out the envelope I'd scrounged from Destler's trash. There was the list of overage subjects. "Shoot."

Annie gave me three names and ages. One of them was a match.

"I can't believe it. Shit. Looks like Channing really did recruit participants who didn't meet the Kutril trial criteria."

"Whoa. Slow down. Did I say they participated in the Kutril trial? These folks were in the DX-200 trial."

"Jensen's . . ." I murmured as I traced and retraced a circle around the name. "So how did a subject from the DX-200 trial find his way into the Kutril research?"

"Good question," Annie said.

I considered the alternatives. Desperate to increase the number of participants in her trial, Channing "borrowed" a record from Jensen's work without realizing the person was too old for her study. I doodled on the envelope's return address, turning an A into a pyramid and drawing a little flag on top. No, she was too ethical. And even if she were tempted, with her head for detail, I couldn't imagine Channing overlooking something as obvious as a patient's age. Maybe someone had inserted the patient record in among hers, a cuckoo's egg that could be used to discredit her work. Would Jensen stoop to that? Wouldn't anyone be willing to slip a few pieces of paper into a file if the alternative was watching a patent worth millions of dollars turn to dust? After all, what doctor would prescribe DX-200 when an effective treatment at a fraction of the cost was available with Kutril? But if it had been Jensen, was he in this alone?

I stopped doodling, my attention snagged by the text printed on the envelope: Notice: Stockholders' Meeting. The envelope was addressed to a Francine Bentsen in Weston. Destler's wife's name was Fran, and he lived in Weston.

My scalp prickled as I realized the implications. Of course. Destler wouldn't have dared purchase Acu-Med stock in his own name, or have stockholder material addressed to the Pearce.

"You still there?" Annie said.

"You know that piece of paper I scrounged out of Destler's trash? It's a notice of an Acu-Med stockholders' meeting."

"And?"

"I think it's addressed to Destler's wife. He must have brought his mail in from home and then discarded the envelope, never dreaming I'd be rummaging around in his trash."

"So? Am I missing something?"

"The ethics of medical research are pretty clear. If what you do as part of your job could affect the value of a stock, then you can't own it. A promising new drug, especially with no competition, could make a company's stock price go through the roof. It's almost certainly not okay for Destler, as a senior administrator, to own Acu-Med stock. Just for example, he might be tempted to sabotage competing research."

"Or at the very least," Annie said, "turn a blind eye."

"At the very least."

"Well, that certainly is food for thought," Annie. "Speaking of which, about tonight. Weren't we going to have dinner together?"

"Why, you trying to wriggle out of it?"

"Hardly. But here's the thing. I'll be in your neighborhood in about an hour anyway. And I didn't have any lunch. Can I talk you into early?"

"You can probably talk me into just about anything. But early sounds great."

After I hung up, I tried to start on the mountain of paperwork that was threatening to take over my desk, but I couldn't focus. I needed to think. At least those competing images of Channing Temple were starting to converge. Someone was trying to discredit her, to paint her capable of all kinds of professional and personal improprieties. And suddenly I was a few steps closer to figuring out who.

I checked my watch. It was thirty minutes since Jess had said she'd be up in five. I called down to the nurses' station and asked Gloria where Jess was.

"I'd like to know that myself," Gloria said. "She's scheduled to be at neuro rounds starting five minutes ago. And she's not there."

"She was in the dining room . . ." I started.

"With a patient. I know. Then she makes a call and takes off. I just beeped her."

"Have you checked on Olivia lately?" I asked.

"Joe is outside the quiet room sitting there cool as a cucumber, if that's any indication."

"I'm coming down," I said.

I left my office and hurried to the elevator, punched the button, waited a couple of seconds, and heard it creak into action. It felt as if someone was poking me in the back with a stick—probably Channing. I took the stairs. The metal bars enclosing the inside of the staircase clanged as I ran down.

I was past Joe and in the quiet room when Joe looked up from his paper and issued an automatic "No visitors" command. "Oh, it's you," he said, and went back to reading.

Olivia was sleeping soundly. She stirred when I touched her forehead and then sank back into a deep sleep.

I found Gloria. "Did Jess return the page?" I asked.

"Not yet."

"Any idea who she was talking to on the phone?"

Gloria looked insulted. "Now how would I know that?"

"Beats me. But you do seem to know most everything that goes on around here."

Now Gloria smiled. "Usually, I guess I do."

"She didn't say anything when she left?"

"I didn't even realize she'd gone," Gloria said. I glanced past Gloria into the dining room. Jess's things were still on the table. The kitchen staff had set the table around them. Gloria followed my look. "Like I said, she thought she'd be right back."

I went in to gather up Jess's things and set them aside for her. I opened the backpack to shove her books and papers inside. Vibrating in the bag was her beeper. What the hell good was a beeper if you were going to leave it behind? Jess needed more than a little centering. She needed a healthy dose of common sense.

Something else caught my eye. One of the books was a fabric-covered journal, the kind that contains blank or lined pages. Of course. Countertransference analysis. Jess probably was following in the footsteps of her mentor, keeping a journal of her thoughts and feelings. I'd have to warn her against the dangers of carrying it around with her. It wasn't the kind of thing you wanted someone else to read and misinterpret.

As I shoved the journal into the backpack, I took in the words written neatly on the cover: *Feelings and Fantasies — Volume 11*. Eleven? Jess had hardly been at this long enough to fill that many notebooks. My stomach turned over. The handwriting was Channing's.

Was that what Jess was doing in Channing's study during the party? Taking, or maybe as she said, trying to put back Channing's journal? Was she the one who'd shown it to Destler, giving him more ammunition? Rumors of inappropriate behavior, questionable research methods — all of that could have been orchestrated to make suicide believable.

I opened the journal. The first pages were dated June, the last ones December. I couldn't remember the dates on the pages Destler had, but she'd written something about the Indian summer. I flipped to September and turned the pages, scanning. Near the end of the month, there was the entry: *Indian summer today. Hot and close. . . .* I didn't need to read it again. I remembered it well enough.

I took the backpack to the nurses' station and left it on a shelf under the counter. I kept the journal. It felt hot in my hand as I waited for the elevator up to my office. I didn't like having it. It had never been meant for anyone's eyes but Channing's own. But she was dead. Meanwhile, her murderer was getting off while her reputation was getting destroyed. I realized I probably should be giving the journal to MacRae to examine. But I couldn't do it. That would have compounded the insult, violated her privacy even further.

I let myself into my office and started to leaf through the notebook. Channing's real and fantasy life seemed to mingle on the pages. Daphne's husband's obituary was tucked into an early page. Robert Smythe-Gooding's illness dominated July. It seemed as if Channing had been a constant visitor. She'd been very fond of him, and she'd agonized over him, watching him fade from his own body.

After Robert's death, Channing seemed to turn inward.

> *I can intellectualize—I know she felt it was the only choice. Still, "suicide" re-writes the past. Afterwards, it's as if that's all there was. No laughter. No day-to-day. No life.*

Was she meditating on her mother's suicide? I wasn't so sure. Her point was certainly valid. Suicide. Murder. The effect was the same. Now it was happening to Channing herself. The way she died was swamping all other memories of how she lived.

I flipped through October. The entries turned to feelings about her patients, her work. It was as if Channing took her own darkness—her lust, envy, greed—siphoned it away like some bitter poison and spread it across the pages of her journal.

Then, in November, an entry caught my eye.

> *subtle changes*
> *-more rigid and inflexible*
> *-forgetful*
> *-insecure*
> *-more distant*
> *-blows hot and cold*
> *Overwhelmed?*
> *Benzos?*
> *Guilt?*
> *Olivia ok?*

I puzzled over the list. Were these observations about Olivia? About Channing herself? I paged ahead. There was another list, six weeks later. Before I had a chance to read it, the phone rang.

It was Gloria. "Jess just called in."

"Where the hell is she?"

"She's over at Drug and Alcohol. Said she'll be back in an hour."

"Did she say what the hell she's doing over there?"

"She said Dr. Smythe-Gooding asked her to help go through what's left in Dr. Temple's office, to be sure they don't throw out anything important. Administration wants that office cleaned out by morning."

25

I WAS determined that, in an hour, I'd be somewhere quiet, having a glass of wine, and ordering a meal with Annie. But Olivia's arrest loomed. I couldn't wait a day to find out how pages from Channing's notebook had found their way to Destler. I had to talk to Jess.

I called Channing's office. The phone went immediately to voice mail. It was unnerving to hear Channing's voice, telling me to leave a message and she'd get right back to me. It was pointless to beep Jess. I called Daphne's office, but no answer there either. I'd have to go over myself if I wanted an answer.

I checked my watch. "I've got Annie meeting me here at five," I told Gloria. I started to leave. "If she gets here before I'm back, tell her I'm sorry and make her wait."

Gloria grinned. "*Make* her wait?"

"You may need to let the air out of her tires."

"By the way, Admitting called," Gloria said. "They've been contacted by the police to arrange for Olivia's transfer to the Bechtel. Day after tomorrow."

I didn't need to be reminded.

Halfway to the Drug and Alcohol Rehabilitation Unit, I ran into

Destler returning to his office. He was red-faced from the uphill walk. I seized the moment.

"I've been meaning to ask your advice on something," I said, trying to sound ingenuous.

"My advice." His face turned wary, and he checked his watch.

"Won't take a minute. You see, I've been offered an opportunity. One of the reps from Pharmacom was telling me about some promising new drug therapies they're investigating. It's not secret information or anything—there have been news stories and all, I just hadn't read them. Anyway, I'd like to invest in the company. And then I thought, I'd better run that by somebody, just to be sure it's kosher."

He tilted his head and gave me an appraising look. "Pharmacom. Isn't that the company that's sponsoring Dr. Liu's research?"

I tried to look surprised. "Why, yes, I guess so."

He sniffed. "Both the institute and the med school have clear guidelines. The research is going on, on your unit. Under your watch, as it were. Not kosher."

"That's a shame," I said, checking into my pocket to be sure I had Destler's envelope announcing an Acu-Med stockholders meeting. "I hate to pass up such a good opportunity. Well . . . I guess that answers that." I paused. "Unless, of course, you'd consider investing for me?"

He looked surprised. Then wary. "Surely you're not serious. It would be as much a violation of ethical standards for me as it would be for you. If not more so."

"If . . . not . . . more so," I repeated the words. "And here I thought you owned stock in Acu-Med."

"I . . ." Destler turned pink and stammered. "Well that's different."

"How is that different?"

He narrowed his eyes, checked his watch again. "I really have to be somewhere," he said, turning to go. "Why don't you call Virginia and make an appointment so we can discuss this when I have more time."

I pulled the Acu-Med envelope out of my pocket and unfolded it. "I believe you have to own stock in order for them to send you one of these. Stockholders' meeting. Addressed to your wife."

"How the hell . . . ?" Destler snarled. He snatched the envelope out of my hand and crumpled it in his fist. "Son of a—"

"Isn't owning stock in these companies discouraged, prohibited even, because it can cloud clinical judgment?" I asked. "For example, just suppose two physicians at the institute are working on therapies to treat the same condition. And suppose an administrator has a stake in the company sponsoring one of the studies. Mightn't that person be tempted to behave in a way that encourages one line of research and discourages the other. After all, there could be a considerable amount of money at stake."

Destler stuffed the envelope in his coat pocket, rocked back on his heels, and gave me an appraising look.

"Of course," I continued, "the bias might be subtle. More resources made available to one researcher. When there were efforts to discredit the other researcher, the administrator might suddenly develop tunnel vision. When a little investigation would have shown the evidence was suspect"—my voice rose—"trumped up."

He laced his fingers over his midsection and pulsed them against one another. "You're improvising," he said.

"You showed me Dr. Temple's research because you wanted me to see that she included subjects that were too old for the Kutril protocol. Did you know that those overage patients weren't even in her study?"

"That's absurd," Destler barked.

"Someone took patient records that belong in Dr. Jensen's DX-200 trial and planted them in Channing's Kutril trial data."

He gawped at me. It was possible that he was hearing this for the first time. "What are you saying? That Dr. Temple poached patient records from Dr. Jensen's research and put them into her own, to make her numbers look better?"

"Even you can't seriously think that. Dr. Temple was meticulous, and she was smart. If she were going to cheat, why not pick patients that fit her protocol? No. I think someone doctored those records and inserted them into her research."

Destler had turned ashen.

"And the diary. Evidence of a psychiatrist gone around the bend, having a sexual relationship with her patient? The only thing it demonstrates, for sure, is that Dr. Temple had sexual thoughts. We *all* have sexual thoughts. It comes with the turf. What matters is what we do with them. Dr. Temple wrote hers down. There's no evidence here, no evidence at all that she acted on them. Did you check? Or did it just suit your purposes to set the rumor mill in motion? So much neater and tidier when pesky radicals resign. Or kill themselves."

"Now hold on a minute," he blustered. A pair of nurses walked by. Destler lowered his voice and glanced behind him. "Surely you're not suggesting that I had anything to do with Dr. Temple's death."

"I'm not suggesting anything. Yet. But I would like to know how you got the journal pages. Did you steal them? Or did you get someone to steal them for you? I'm quite certain Channing didn't offer them up as a birthday gift."

"Of course I didn't steal . . ." Destler sputtered. "I've had quite enough of this . . . this inquisition," he said, his voice stony with rage. "How dare you suggest that I've been tampering with research, sneaking around in a colleague's office." He felt in his pocket. "Though I can see why you'd think so, since you seem quite capable of doing so yourself.

"And now, I have a meeting to go to." He turned on his heel and left.

• • •

I hurried over to the Drug and Alcohol Rehabilitation Unit, convinced that I'd blown it with Destler. I still didn't know who'd tampered with Channing's research or how Destler had gotten his hands on her diary. All I'd managed to do was piss him off, and warn him so he could engage in his favorite activity—damage control. I rode the elevator up to the fourth floor.

The doors to Channing's office were open. As I approached, I got a wave of fresh-paint smell. I looked in. Spattered drop cloths covered a formless mound of furniture, pushed to the center of the room.

The door to the rest room at the end of the hall swung open. Daphne came out. She was carrying a glass coffeepot filled with water.

"Peter!" She sounded surprised, guarded. "What brings you up here?"

One side of her sweater was hanging lower than the other — she'd mismatched the buttons and the buttonholes.

"I was looking for Dr. Dyer," I said. "Is she up here somewhere?"

"She's about," Daphne said vaguely. "Popped over to sort through what's left in Channing's office." Daphne peered into the empty office. "You checked under the shroud?" She backtracked to her own office, leaving a wake of flowery perfume.

I stared after her. The comment was bizarre. Out of character and out of place. And she appeared a bit disheveled. I followed her, intending to ask if she was feeling all right. But she went into her office and closed her door behind her. I took it as clear indication that she wasn't interested in my solicitude.

I returned to Channing's office. The painters could have at least left a window open a crack to dissipate the smell. I went around to the double-hung window and opened the latch. The woodwork was still tacky. I tried to raise the window, but it was painted shut. I took my keys out of my pocket and ran a key tip up the window edge on one side and down the other, slicing through the paint. Then I set my palms under the top edge of the bottom window and pushed. At first it wouldn't budge. I pressed as hard as I could, feeling the strain first in my arms and shoulders and then down into my torso and legs. The window gave way and flew up, letting cool air into the room and sending me ricocheting back into the pile of furniture.

I tried to regain my balance, expecting to feel the hard edges of a desk or bookcases or file cabinets beneath the drop cloth. Instead,

I felt something firm but softer. I jerked away. I pictured Jess, crumpled beneath what now had taken on the sinister aspect of a shroud. It was absurd—the power of suggestion. I took hold of the edge of the cloth. It was heavy with stiffened paint spatters. I started to raise it.

"Dr. Zak?" The sound of Jess's voice wasn't coming from under the tarp.

Jess peered into the room. She was carrying a stack of file folders. "You all right? You look like you've seen a ghost," she said.

"Aren't you supposed to be at neuro rounds?" I snapped.

"Am I? What's today? Oh, my gosh, you're right. I completely forgot about it."

"It might help if you had your beeper with you."

She touched her jacket pocket. "I don't?"

"No. It's back on the unit, in your backpack, which you left sitting open on the table." I paused to let that sink in. "And you said you were going to come up and see me in five minutes."

She blinked at me. One of the file folders slid from the top of the stack. I retrieved it for her.

"I'm not usually like this," she said.

"I can believe that. If you were half as unreliable as you've been lately, Dr. Temple never would have trusted you to coordinate her research. You wouldn't have lasted five minutes."

"She did trust me. That's why Dr. Smythe-Gooding asked me to come over and help archive her research."

"I hope that trust wasn't misplaced," I said.

Jess put the pile of folders down on a chair. There was a skim of perspiration on her upper lip.

"Are you ready to tell me what you were you doing in Dr. Temple's study during her party?"

"I was putting back her journal."

"Putting it back? Did she know you'd taken it?"

"No. I . . . I borrowed it." She hurried on. "And I was trying to put it back. Only I wanted to be sure I put it in the right place.

And then I heard you, outside on the landing, so I ran out. And then . . ." Her voice trailed off.

"And then Channing got murdered," I said, "and you couldn't return it."

Jess's face convulsed, and a tear started down one cheek.

"Why on earth did you take it in the first place?"

"I know I shouldn't have"—her words came out in a rush—"I guess I was just curious. Wondering what kind of things she wrote in it. When I read what she wrote about me, I wished I hadn't. She wrote about things . . ."

I wanted to shake her, but I kept my voice calm. "Things that you knew had never happened." Jess nodded miserably. "Didn't you understand what she was doing?"

"I know. Countertransference analysis. It's fine in the abstract. Or when it's me writing about my own patient. But this was *about* me. It was so"—she searched for the words—"raw. Sexually explicit. Even though I knew it was pure fantasy, I felt like I'd been violated."

"Haven't you had sexual thoughts about a patient? About your own therapist even."

Jess blushed. "Everyone does."

"Of course. It's what transference is founded on—it's libidinal. You can't avoid it. And as therapists, it's necessary to fully understand the transference so that it doesn't affect the relationship. Channing used CTA to push those thoughts and feelings to their logical conclusion, to the extreme. By writing them down, she was robbing them of their power to distract her. That's all."

Jess twisted her hands together. "I know, I know. But when I read them . . ."

"So let me get this straight. You steal Dr. Temple's private journal." I was trying not to yell, but I could hear my voice rising. "Then you show so little regard for her privacy that this afternoon you leave it lying in your open backpack."

"I didn't mean to!" Jess said, cowering.

"You know Dr. Destler has copies of pages from that journal. He's been showing it around. Using them to make it look as if Channing had sexual relations with a patient."

"I never showed it to . . ." The words died out.

"You never showed it to Dr. Destler. But you did show it to someone."

"He promised it would be confidential."

"Who?"

"Oh, God," Jess moaned. "I brought it to Dr. Jensen because I trusted him. And because I couldn't bring myself to ask Channing about it. I should have realized. Why would he offer me a job? How pathetically naive . . ."

"He offered you a position when you've finished your residency?"

"Said I could work with him, managing outpatient services in the new Research Institute."

"What new Research Institute?"

"You know, the Albert House renovations."

"Huh?"

"You didn't know? It's going to have outpatient offices, new research facilities. And when Dr. Smythe-Gooding retires . . ."

"Retires?"

"How long can she continue? Everyone knows, she's barely holding it together. I've heard now it's even worse. They're saying that without her husband, she's ineffective. Flaky, and then some."

"But she's still getting the work done, isn't she?"

Jess shrugged. "The research programs she's supposed to be running were pretty much running themselves. When there was a problem, Channing covered for her."

Items from the list in Channing's journal seemed to float above me. *More rigid and inflexible. Forgetful. Insecure.* That's why Channing came to me. She saw her friend, her mentor, changing, she found herself questioning the judgment of someone she'd always trusted—and she was worried about her continuing to work with Olivia.

I remembered the half-full sample pack of Ativan on Daphne's desk. It wasn't Channing but Daphne herself who was taking anxiety medication. Too much Ativan could explain what Jess wrote off as flakiness. But I had a feeling more was going on. Something beyond grief, compounded now by more grief.

"No one's said anything to Daphne about it?" I asked.

"And get your head bitten off?" Jess picked up one of the folders she'd been carrying. "It's a shame there's no one to continue Channing's work. I imagine they'll just throw these in storage somewhere."

"Research files?" I asked.

"Yes. Patient data. From a research study she published few years ago. At least I'll make sure it's properly archived."

"I wonder. You coordinated her research. Were you aware of documentation on additional subjects getting added to the Kutril data, after the fact?"

"I'm not sure I know what you mean."

"Well, wasn't there a usual way for a patient file to get created, and for information to get entered into it?"

"Of course. We had standard procedures. She always gave me the forms. I entered them into the system, then filed the hard copy."

"And did any patient records come in any other way? Maybe someone other than Dr. Temple gave you patient records to be included in the study?"

"Oh yes, but that was after she died."

"What was after she died?"

"Dr. Jensen. He gave me, maybe three or four records. You don't think . . ."

"And you entered them into the database and put them in the file."

"Of course."

I wondered in how many other ways Jess's superiors had taken advantage of her. "I think Jensen may have used you," I said. "I believe he had you add those files to make it look like Channing included patients that were too old for her study."

"No. She was meticulous about selecting participants."

"I know that. But Jensen wanted to make it look as if she would stoop to anything to achieve her goals."

"He used me—" Jess froze, like a cat suddenly alert to an alien sound. We both looked at the open office door. With a crash, the outer door slammed shut. Before I could spring to my feet, I heard the scrape of metal against metal and a click. Someone had padlocked us in.

26

I TRIED the door. The knob turned, and the door opened a crack, then held fast. I pressed my shoulder into it, pulled back, and rammed it. I pulled back and rammed it again. Pulled back a third time—and thought better of it. I was going to break my shoulder before I broke the hasp. It already felt as if I'd hit myself with a sledgehammer.

I rubbed my shoulder and cast about for something to pry the opening. I pushed the tarp from the pile of furniture I'd fallen against. There was Channing's leather chair, loaded not with a dead body but with a pile of books topped by a crocheted afghan and a piece of scarlet and gold silk.

I picked up the shimmering cloth. I remembered—it was a scarf Channing had brought back with her from Thailand. She'd worn it around her shoulders on the evening she gave me the bad news, that she'd met someone while she was away, she was going to get married. I rubbed the stiff silk. The sharp citrus scent made my eyes prickle.

I heard Jess's rapid breathing. She was staring at me, wild-eyed, her nostrils flaring. She went over and tried the door. "We're trapped," she said. "How are we going to get out of here?"

I pushed the other drop cloth off the top of the desk. There was a phone, a cord coiled neatly around it. I tracked along the baseboard until I found a phone jack. I plugged the phone into the wall and picked up the receiver. Nothing.

"Kaput," I said.

Jess's voice rose. "Someone's got to get us out." She threw herself against the door and banged with both fists against the solid oak. "Help!" she screamed. "We're trapped in here!"

She turned around and pressed her back against the door. Her eyes darted around the room. "I have a problem," she gasped, her hand to her throat. "Being locked in. Knowing I can't get out. . . ." Her breath was coming in quick pants. Her face was starting to flush.

"You're hyperventilating," I told her. I scooped the books off the leather chair. "Sit." I took her hand and helped her over to the chair. "Easy does it."

"I know, I know," she gasped again. "It's not like it's the middle of the night." She gripped the chair arms.

I put my hand on her shoulder. "Don't talk. Breathe."

"There's all kinds of people around, right?"

"Right, right, plenty of people," I said.

"Do you . . ."

I shushed her. "Don't talk. Breathe."

She put her hand over her mouth and closed her eyes. Her breathing slowed.

"Take it easy." Her color was returning to normal. "That's right, nice and easy. Inhale. Exhale."

Jess leaned back in the chair, put her hands in her lap, and took a deep inhale.

"That's good. Did you see who was out in the hall?"

Jess licked her lips. "Only Dr. Smythe-Gooding. She went back and forth a couple of times," Jess said. "Do you think she heard what I said? About her being incompetent? I shouldn't have been talking so loud. I wasn't thinking."

Of course, Daphne must have heard. But why lock us in?

I was about ready to try hollering out the window when there was a knock. "Peter, you in there?" It was Annie.

Jess threw herself against the door. "We're trapped in here!" she cried.

"Annie?" I called. "Boy am I glad to hear your voice. How'd you find us?"

"Gloria. When you didn't come back . . ."

Thank God for Gloria. "Can you get us out of here?"

There was a pause. "Sure. Looks trivial." She jiggled the padlock. "Need some tools, though. Hang on, I've got them out in the car."

"Hurry back!" I said.

"Who's that?" Jess asked.

"A friend of mine who can get us out of here."

"Soon, I hope," Jess said.

"She's probably parked up by the Neuropsychiatric Unit." I could picture the distance—down three flights of stairs, about a quarter mile uphill and back down, up three flights. I leaned against the wall, slid down to a squat, and settled in to wait. Jess seemed calm, now that she knew we were going to be sprung.

"Where's that necklace you were wearing?" I asked.

She touched her fingers to her neck. "My necklace?"

"Yours?"

"I gave it to Olivia," Jess whispered.

"Do you want to tell me about the necklace?"

Her face turned pinched. "It was Channing's. It belonged to her mother."

"Channing gave it to you?"

"It was in her study. When I took the diary . . ." She sobbed. "I was only borrowing it. But I never had a chance to put it back."

"You gave it to Olivia?"

"Yes."

"How did you explain . . ."

"I lied. I told her Channing had let me borrow it and I hadn't had a chance to give it back. I said I was her mother's friend."

"Special friend?" I asked.

"Special friend," she echoed.

"Was that a lie, too?"

Jess didn't answer. She reached for Channing's red silk scarf and held it up to her face.

I stood and stared out the window. After a few minutes, Annie appeared, running down the hill toward the building. "Here she comes," I said.

"Thank God," Jess said quietly.

A few minutes later, there was a tap at the door. "I'm back," Annie called.

Jess sprang up and pressed her body against the door. "You're going to get us out of here?"

"I'm working on it," Annie said.

There was silence. Then the sound of metal on metal. "Shit," she said. More scraping. It felt like being at the dentist, wishing that he'd stop gouging away at a particularly sensitive spot, feeling the seconds tick, waiting to be liberated from the chair.

"Goddamnit. . . ." Annie said. There was a minute of silence. Then, "Here goes," followed by a few scrapes, a grunt, and the sound of wood splintering.

The door pulled open. Annie was standing there holding a crowbar. An assortment of metal picks were scattered at her feet.

Jess fled into the hall.

"Am I glad to see you," I said. I eyed the crowbar, the hasp now wrenched out of shape. I touched the woodwork, which was split where the screws had been ripped away. "I guess when finesse doesn't work, there's something to be said for brute force."

"My sentiments, precisely," Annie replied. "How'd you get locked in?"

"I think it was Daphne Smythe-Gooding," I said.

"It's my fault," Jess said. "I was blabbing away about how Dr.

Smythe-Gooding wasn't—" Her mouth snapped shut, and she glanced anxiously toward Daphne's office.

In a few strides, I was there. The door was open, but the room was empty. There was a pall of cigarette smell. What I remembered as orderly piles of paper on her desk had turned into drifts, and an Acu-Med mug served as a paperweight. The African violet on the windowsill was now beyond help. The pot of water she'd brought back from the bathroom stood forgotten in the seat of a chair.

Alongside the window, a square on the wall seemed to glow whiter than the wall around it. There was a picture hook in the middle of the space. Daphne had taken down the photograph of her husband. Below was a dark, wide bookcase with glass doors. One of the shelves held about two dozen journals, each with a number hand-lettered on the spine. Years.

I pulled one of the doors to the bookcase open. I was about to reach for a journal when I hesitated. Annie and Jess were out in the hall. I went out to them. "Just give me a minute," I said, and shut the door. I'd run out of ways to rationalize looking through other people's personal property. At least I could do it without implicating everyone else.

I took out the last journal. I flipped through. The pages were dated, each one in a dense, neat hand. I turned to the days surrounding Channing's death. The day after Channing's party, the entry began:

My own special child. Brilliant. Beautiful. Now she turns on me, like a viper. Like her own daughter turned on her. Like her own mother, her shame. Shame. Suicide. Shame. Suicide.

Robert and I. We will do it together.

Quickly I scanned the pages that followed, the days leading up to Jensen's death. They were filled with the pain of loss. Daphne wrote her memories of Channing, her protégé. The words *brilliant, insightful, honest, scrupulous,* peppered the pages as she turned Channing into a saint. Then:

It's begun. Her papers are missing. I can only imagine what they are up to.

There was a knock at the door. "Peter?" It was Annie.
"Give me a minute more," I said.
I pulled out the book from the previous year. Robert had died in early August. There I found what I was looking for.

Saturday

I am home. I sit alongside, listening to the shallow breathing. The sour smell of urine and decay seems to cling to the wallpaper, to the drapes. I can't bear to look. So much substance—personality, brilliance, strength, wasted away. His face stretched thin across the skull, a membrane crisscrossed with blue veins. Eyes recede.

I try to read but I am nodding off. So I write instead, listening, rocked by the quiet inhale, exhale. Then for a few moments, nothing. My heart stops. Is it over? A snort, a weak cough. And I am angry at the relief that floods me. What am I without you? And yet, that's what must be.

He stirs. Eyelids flutter. Holes of darkness stare back at me. This person who cannot walk, can barely sit, still can struggle upwards on stick-thin arms, head wobbling on a slender stalk.

He stares at me. The voice I once loved and now can barely hear. Taunting me for being weak. I know, we agreed. I will, I tell him. Soon. Still his look scorns me.

I touch his hand, trying not to apply even a small amount of pressure for fear of bruising, of tearing. Eyes close. Is that a grimace of pain or the edge of a smile? Then, the spirit goes under again.

It must be now. Last night, I dismissed the night nurse. Cancelled the day shift. Why do I sit here, doing nothing? Why do I still wait, counting breaths, writing instead of taking action, hoping God will do what I promised? It is up to me now.

I open the drawer alongside the bed. There lies the gun. A gift, "borrowed" from a disapproving friend. Cold and hard, how neatly it fits the hand. A single squeeze and it's done, God willing.

Or perhaps the feather pillow. I see myself, pressing gently. But no, gentle will never do. How long will it take and can I last? Last.

Pills? How easy to wash them down. Neat and tidy. I take a pill myself. I wait. I cannot stand the waiting. I take another.

Sunday

Thank God, it is over. Now, what am I?

Of course, this was what everyone knew without asking. Robert Smythe-Gooding had died before he was ready. Not the slow wasting away of cancer. But not by his own hand either, as many suspected. Daphne had killed him.

It was starting to come clear—why I kept seeing a tangle, no matter how I examined what was going on: Assisted suicide. Unreported death. Channing's murder. Stolen diary pages. Jensen's murder. Research tampering.

Tease apart the pieces. It was like one of my psychological tests. Put together the things that go together. Then name the groups. I came up with two: murder and character assassination.

Two crimes. Different criminals? Of course. And if I didn't hurry, there would be another killing.

I picked up the phone and called Destler's office. I prayed that Virginia would still be there. When she answered, I barked, "Is he there?"

"Hello, Peter. Sorry, no he's not. He seems to be very much in demand this afternoon."

"Was Dr. Smythe-Gooding looking for him?"

"As a matter of fact . . ."

I cut her off with, "Did you tell her where he is?" I knew I was being rude, but Virginia was a very forgiving soul.

"Of course."

"And where is that?"

"Well, let's see, he was at a meeting that should have ended at five-thirty. Then he usually goes over and . . ."

Much as I like Virginia, if she'd been in the room with me I'd have strangled her then and there. I interrupted the stream of consciousness. "Where do you think he is right now. Please, it's quite important."

"Oh, my. He's probably over at Albert House. He took the plans for the renovation with him, and he was going to check up—"

"Is there any way to reach him?"

"I could beep him. But there aren't phones over there—"

"I'll find him," I said, and hung up.

I burst out into the hall. Annie had packed away her tools and was carrying the crowbar. "We've got to get over to Albert House. Destler's over there, and Daphne's gone looking for him."

"I'm coming with you," Jess announced, as Annie and I started for the stairway.

"I don't think that's such a good idea," I said.

"Please? I've screwed everything up. Trusting Dr. Jensen. Shooting my mouth off here."

We hurried down the stairs, past the spot where Jensen had fallen to his death. A piece of plywood had been fastened across the broken spindles. Jess struggled to keep up. Her high heels and straight skirt weren't designed for speed. She was still carrying Channing's scarf.

"It could be dangerous," I said.

"There has to be a way I can make up for the mess I've made," Jess insisted.

We were outside now, on the steps of the Drug and Alcohol Rehabilitation Unit. "We should get security to meet us over at Albert House," I said.

Jess said, "I'll do it. I'll get them and meet you there." She hurried back inside.

27

ANNIE AND I cut across aboveground to Albert House. It was faster than taking the tunnels — straight instead of zigzag. And it was all downhill. I ran flat out, Annie matching me step for step.

Despite the spotlights at the upper corners, Albert House looked derelict. The circular drive was sprouting thigh-high weeds. At one side of the building was a Dumpster. Some of the trademark windows were covered with plywood. A NO TRESPASSING sign was hanging crooked, and the massive oak door was padlocked shut. I borrowed Annie's crowbar, wedged it in, and leaned into it. Wood splintered as the screws pulled away, until the hasp was hanging, the padlock dangling from its ring.

The door swung open. Annie flashed her light around the entryway. We peered into the gloomy interior. There were wide steps up into the lobby. The embossed ceiling was etched with cracks, some so deep that you could see up into the dark space between the ceiling and the floorboards above.

We started in, past a large rubbish bin loaded with old lath and plasterboard. The sharp smell of turpentine rose from some rags lying on the top. Alongside were crates of miscellaneous pipe.

There was a pile of broken two-by-fours, along with a giant wooden spool of electrical wire.

Annie flashed the beam across the main lobby and up into the ceiling. The two-story space had once been imposing. There was a wide staircase going up, and overhead hung a huge brass chandelier, dull with dust.

"Feels more like a mausoleum than a mansion," Annie said.

The place smelled of dry rot, and the floor felt spongy in places. I wondered how much they'd be able to salvage. Annie was making her way over to a panel of light switches.

"Be careful," I said. "The floor's not . . ." Just then a floorboard cracked under Annie. She pulled away to solid footing and advanced more slowly toward the wall panel.

"Dr. Destler!" I called out. I stared up into the darkness. I expected my voice to echo, but it didn't. The pulpy walls and rotting floorboards seemed to absorb sound.

There was a click, and the chandelier flickered to life. Then two or three bulbs popped, sending off a shower of sparks. A bulb fell to the floor and shattered. The room descended into gloom again.

"Must've blown a fuse," Annie said. "We could look for the box."

"Forget about it," I said as my eyes adjusted. "There's no time. We've got to find them."

Annie pulled something from the edge of the central staircase. "Looks like someone's here."

She handed me the tall roll of paper. I sniffed at it. No dust or mildew smell. I opened it while Annie held up the light. There were several sheets, rolled into one other.

I examined the top sheet. Architectural plans. The legend said "Albert House"—it was the main floor. The grand entrance hall remained, but it was no longer at the center of a harmonious symmetric layout. A new wing was getting added off to the east side, with its own entrance. It looked like the kind of space that could be used for outpatient therapy—a lobby, and medium-size interior spaces leading to smaller ones that could be offices or examining rooms. Most of the original building was to be gutted. The offices at one end of the first floor were being replaced by a lecture hall with a semicircular stage and stadium seating. In careful calligraphy the room was labeled *Destler Hall.*

I whistled. We were talking major capital campaign to pay for plans this grandiose. But as far as I knew, there wasn't one under way. There had to be a donor — one with very deep pockets.

"Which way?" Annie asked.

She flashed the beam down the hall one way, then the other, then up the stairs, then in my face. I blinked away the light. She turned the beam aside. From somewhere upstairs, there were footsteps, scuffling sounds.

I dropped the plans, and we rushed up the curving stairs. We stood on the second-floor landing and listened.

"What's that?" Annie asked, indicating down one of the stretches of hallway leading off the landing. A light flashed back at us from floor level near the end of the corridor. Annie got to it first and picked up a yellow hard hat with a light mounted to it. With a metallic ting, the filament in the bulb snapped. I ran my hand across a deep dent in the yellow dome. I hoped the head wearing it had fared better.

There were voices from farther down the hall. We ran. One of the office doors was open. In the gloomy twilight, Destler was backed up against the window. His face was in shadow. "Get away from me," he growled at Daphne, who had a length of two-by-four aimed at his gut.

"Channing was right about you," Daphne said, her voice disdainful. "You'll do anything to get what you want. You had to keep your pals over at Acu-Med happy, or else what would happen to this brilliant monument to your hubris?"

"I didn't kill her," Destler said.

I stepped into the room. "Daphne," I said.

Daphne jerked her head toward me, but the battering ram remained pointed at Destler.

"Keep her away from me," Destler demanded. "She's out of her mind."

"Go away, Peter. This doesn't concern you," Daphne said.

"If it's about settling accounts, then it does," I said. "He didn't kill her."

Daphne laughed. "Of course, he didn't. He doesn't have the balls to kill."

"But he had no compunction about screwing her after she was dead," I said.

Daphne took a step closer to Destler, her sweater sliding off one sloping shoulder.

"Keep away." Destler bleated. "I have a gun."

"You?" she scoffed. "That's a load of rubbish. You're nothing but a sodding coward." Destler could have grabbed the end of the piece of wood. But he didn't. He pressed himself against the window.

Daphne lunged at him. Destler reached into his pocket and pulled something out. He waved it around. I could just make out a small handgun.

"Destler, put that away," I said. "You'll get someone killed. . . ."

Daphne swung the two-by-four. Destler ducked, and it crashed into the window, breaking the glass. Then, with a thud, it connected with Destler's hand. Destler howled as the gun skittered across the floor and into a corner. Daphne threw herself across the room and grabbed it. Destler ran past me and out of the room.

Daphne turned and confronted me. "Get out of my way," she said. "He's not going to get away with it."

"You don't have to kill him," I said, raising my hands, the palms facing her. "I know what he did. He was willing to destroy Channing's reputation, let the accusations of improper behavior and dishonest research stand. Even though he knew better. Soon everyone else will know, too. He'll be out on his ear, and there won't be another hospital in the world that will touch him. Without his job, without his title, without Acu-Med to bankroll him, you'll have your revenge."

"It's not enough," she rasped. "He disgraced her." She gave a weak, dry cough. "Her reputation. All her brilliance, her goodness . . ."

"He only finished what you started. So much easier to destroy her reputation after you killed her and tried to make it look like suicide."

Daphne backed away. Glass from the broken window crunched under her feet. "Kill her? How could I? I loved her. She was like my child."

"And Robert was your husband. Wasn't that the beginning? Killing him and making it look as if . . ."

"Robert wanted to die. He forced me to do it when he couldn't," Daphne said, sobbing. "I loved Robert. I couldn't shoot him." Her voice turned to quiet crooning. "Couldn't shoot him."

"But you could shoot Channing. Doesn't that tell you something about what's happened to you?" Daphne stared at me, her mouth open, her eyes shadowy. "Making it look like suicide—you played right into their hands. Jensen could make it look as if all of Channing's work was corrupt, her relationships with the people she loved most were twisted. And Destler was happy to go along. After all, she committed suicide. How else to explain it?"

Daphne wrapped her arms around herself. "I had to stop her. How else could I stop her?"

"She wanted you to resign. She thought you weren't yourself. When you killed Robert—maybe it was assisted suicide, maybe he wasn't quite ready to die, only you know that—that's when Channing realized something wasn't right. That's what she and Jensen were arguing about at her party. She was willing to go public with what she knew if you wouldn't resign."

Daphne's eyes widened. "Dangerous incompetence. How dare she? What did she know? I was the one who taught her everything. Molded her. Made her who she was." The words ended in wrenching sobs.

"So you kill her. And then you turn into her avenging angel. Did you kill Jensen because he realized you killed Channing, too? Now you're ready to murder Destler. All in the name of protecting Channing's reputation. I wonder what Channing would make of all this."

There were heavy footsteps in the hall. Destler's voice. "They're down here. Careful, she has a gun."

Daphne backed up, nearing the broken window. Beams of light danced in the hall as the footsteps came closer. Two burly security guards appeared in the doorway.

"Keep back!" Daphne screamed.

She glanced behind her into the darkness, then turned back to face the guards. A gust blew through the broken window. She raised a hand to her face. With her hair now standing out around her head, she looked like Medusa. "No!" she screamed, and turned, as if she was about to climb onto the windowsill, but Annie had slipped behind her.

Daphne raised the gun she was still holding.

"Don't!" I shouted.

Daphne turned back to me. She steadied the gun, pointed it at her own head, then placed it in her open mouth.

"No!" I screamed.

Before I could lunge for her, she'd squeezed her eyes shut and pulled the trigger. But there was only a click. She took the gun out of her mouth and gaped at it. Another click.

"You bloody coward," she said, staring at the gun. She threw the gun, narrowly missing my head. "Bloody, stinking cowards, the lot of you," she cried, and sank down in a heap.

Annie and I closed in on Daphne from either side.

"Doctor Smythe-Gooding?" It was Jess. She'd come in behind the security guards.

Daphne looked up, hesitant. In an instant, her face turned radiant, smiling, as if she'd experienced an ecstasy of revelation. "Oh, Channing! Thank God it's you!"

Jess looked at me in confusion. "Of course, I'm here," Jess said, the uncertainty in her voice contradicting her words.

Daphne rose to her feet. She drifted past me, past the security guards, until she'd reached Jess. "Such a lovely shawl," Daphne said. "It was always my favorite." Daphne touched the scarf Jess had taken with her from Channing's office.

Jess held out the red and gold scarf. She opened it up and spread it across Daphne's shoulders. As she did it, Jess seemed to find her center. "Yes. It is a lovely shawl, and now you're wearing it."

Daphne pressed her face into the scarlet silk and inhaled deeply. Then she grasped Jess's arm. "You have to defend yourself!" Daphne said. "Your work. They're trying to destroy you. Just like they did Robert."

"Robert . . ." Jess turned the word over slowly.

Daphne straightened herself. She held the ends of the scarf together in one hand and with the other hand tried to smooth her hair. "Plagiarism. Utter nonsense. His work was entirely original, his hypotheses brilliant. He was pushed out of the way, just like you're being pushed out of the way. And they get away with it because it's all"—Daphne put her finger to her lips—"hush-hush. Never mind that it's . . . it's patently inconceivable."

Daphne sniffed. "Phonying up your research? Having an affair with a resident you were supervising?" She snorted a laugh. "You couldn't even let me help Robert die. You with your moralizing, your rules"—she concentrated on the floor and began pacing up and back, her voice strident—"the arbiter of right and wrong. You made me so angry, I wanted to kill you." She paused. "I dreamed about doing it."

"You're not well . . ." Jess started.

"Why do you keep telling me that? I'm perfectly fine." Daphne coughed. "Just a few things I need to do. I have to make them stop. Destler. Jensen . . ."

"Dr. Smythe-Gooding, Dr. Jensen is . . ." Jess said gently.

"Oh, dear," Daphne murmured. Then with mock seriousness: "*Doctor* Smythe-Gooding. You haven't called me that, not since we first worked together. I remember how bright you were. How eager to learn. How tireless, vital . . ." She choked on the last word.

In the silence I could hear sirens. "I remember, too," Jess said. "Those were good times. But right now, you have an appointment. And they're waiting for you." Jess checked her watch. "Have been for about twenty minutes." Jess put a hand on Daphne's shoulder.

"Get your hands off me," Daphne snarled. But she didn't push Jess away. She embraced her. "What the hell do you think you're doing? You with your high and mighty . . ." She gave a racking sob. "Think you know what's right for everyone else. Fucking judgmental bitch. Sometimes—" She started to laugh, but it turned to a dry croaking. "Sometimes I want to kill you."

"I know, I know," Jess said. "Your appointment is waiting. Shall we go?"

Daphne stood back and gently pushed a strand of hair from Jess's face. "You always were so beautiful," she said.

28

THREE WEEKS later the forsythia was in full bloom. The slender branches of the weeping willows along the riverbank had turned chartreuse. When the sun rose, a layer of steam coated the water as it warmed to keep pace with the air. The renovation of Albert House was on hold, though Acu-Med was reportedly still keen to foot the bill. Apparently, saving face was worth any price.

In an ironic twist, Chip had been asked to consult on Daphne Smythe-Gooding's defense. He'd called me to ask if I thought she was competent to stand trial. I told him I didn't.

"But she's been a practicing psychiatrist, a member of the hospital administration right up to the day she was arrested," he'd said.

"As long as Robert was there, she seemed to be effective. But with his death, and especially the way she had to help him die, she lost her center. She began sliding, clinging to routine, to her job. But she wasn't able to pull herself together. Channing urged her to resign. She refused. So Channing threatened to expose her, to publicly accuse her of killing Robert. Channing backed her into a corner."

"So the murder was an act of self-preservation."

"I suppose. But I think there was more. I believe Daphne was also taking large doses of Ativan. It's for anxiety."

"Antianxiety? Isn't that what they found in Channing Temple's autopsy results?"

"Daphne wanted us to think Channing was taking Ativan. But she wasn't. Daphne put an overdose of Ativan in Channing's tea." That's what had confused me. The coffee that Olivia knocked over onto the floor had been Daphne's. It was the tea that was laced with Ativan. Daphne must have managed to remove the cup before the police got there.

"Problem is," I went on, "Daphne overdid it. Used too much, then waited too long to shoot her. It was probably a replay of what she'd done to kill Robert. It was one thing to set her mind to murder—quite another thing to do it. Then Olivia shows up and complicates matters further."

"Okay, so we have drug abuse and psychological illness. Is there a case for diminished capacity?"

Sounded good to me. "Daphne feels guilty, depressed over helping her husband commit suicide. She takes more and more benzos, and they suppress REM sleep, suppress dreams. She increases the dosage, becomes more and more disinhibited."

"Disinhibited. Are you suggesting that she wanted to kill Channing Temple all along?"

"In a sense, yes. Mentoring relationships are complicated to begin with. Daphne loses Robert and with him, their partnership, her way of defining herself in the world. Then who is she in relation to Channing, now that her protégée, is poised to make a real contribution to medicine with her research and succeed in ways that Daphne never could? Feelings of jealousy are inevitable. Then Channing sees her mentor failing, tries to get her to resign. She threatens the only way of life that Daphne has left.

"What we're seeing here is the psychic collapse of an individual. Between the guilt over killing her husband and chronic benzodiazepine use, she becomes nervous, insecure. To compensate, she becomes rigid and inflexible. A formerly tidy person, her office slides into disarray."

"Sounds like the drugs she was taking were the opposite of what she needed," Chip said.

"Exactly. Daphne did a U-turn after she killed Channing and turned her into a saint. Psychologists call it reaction formation. It's a defense mechanism. For example, we take something and turn it into its opposite. We don't get a promotion at work, and we tell ourselves we didn't want all that extra work anyway. This is more extreme. Daphne fears Channing overtaking her, kills her, and then puts her on the pedestal, making Channing exactly what Daphne feared she would become."

"Why kill Jensen?" Chip asked.

"Daphne realized how Destler and Jensen were using Channing's diary to destroy her reputation. She knew Jensen had taken Channing's research. It was one thing to kill her protégée, another thing to destroy her good name. Jensen and Destler seemed intent on doing just that."

I recommended a psychologist to help the defense.

Things had returned to normal at the Pearce. As I swung by the nurses' station to get my mail, Gloria was grinning at me. She waved a sheet of pink paper like a victory flag. "Check your mail," she said.

I'd gotten the same pink paper. It was a memo from our CEO, "RE: Reorganization." It read like a press release, because that's what it was. "In order to improve operations efficiency, Finance has been reorganized. . . ." Bottom line: Destler's operations would report to a new controller. Finance's responsibilities were being redefined. Hopefully, less independence and more oversight. At the bottom, tacked on like a P.S.: "Arnold O. Destler, M.D., has decided to shift his focus in the hospital and will be managing special projects."

Special projects and the door were usually about a half inch apart at the Pearce. No one ever just got fired. Though I suspected that in this case there wouldn't be the usual round of good-bye parties.

"The psychopath," Gloria said. "See, someone finally put him out of his misery." She high-fived me.

"Do you know what's happening to Virginia?" I asked.

"She's staying where she is, reporting to the new controller."

"She's pretty amazing," I said. "Every time there's a tsunami around here, she manages to sail through unscathed."

I glanced through the rest of my mail. A yellow flyer announced a new Program of Education on Medical Ethics for all staff. It was the first initiative undertaken by a new committee to review ethical standards for doctors. The CEO had called me with an invitation to serve on the committee, but I politely declined. "We're quite determined that this is never going to happen again," he'd said.

Maybe so. Nevertheless, if the rest of what was in my mailbox was any measure of what he was up against, it would take more than a committee and some training. There was a packet advertising a new medication for hyperactivity, formulated specifically for children under five. Along with it came twenty-five refrigerator magnets of giraffes emblazoned with the name of the drug.

Beneath that were two envelopes that had to have been delivered by hand—no stamp, only a handwritten *Dr. Zak* on the envelopes. They were invitations to a harbor cruise and to a dinner at the Ritz, sponsored by pharmaceutical companies eager for a little mind share to deliver their message.

Last, there was an ivory envelope containing an engraved announcement. The first annual Channing Temple Lecture on Psychiatry and Ethics would take place in a few months. It was the perfect memorial. Jess Dyer would be one of the speakers. She was staying on after her residency as a research fellow, to prepare Channing's Kutril study for publication.

I checked my watch. I was expecting a patient in about five minutes. "I'll be up in my office," I told Gloria.

"No you won't. Some folks are here to see you."

I turned around. There was Matthew Farrell with a young

woman I almost didn't recognize. Olivia's hair was back to its natural blond. She was wearing a short skirt, a sweater, and a pair of clunky green combat boots. A blond, green-booted Olive Oyl.

She came forward and gave me a hug. She felt pretty solid for a skinny little thing. She was wearing Channing's locket on a choker of thin red velvet.

I extended a hand to Matthew Farrell. He gave me a limp shake.

"How's your dad doing?" I asked Olivia. I knew Drew had been drying out at a rehab center in the Berkshires.

"He's home again. Says he's going to ninety AA meetings in ninety days. He's up to five."

"And what about you?" I asked.

"Clean," Olivia said. "I'm not even craving it."

"Excellent." I paused to examine her more closely. She looked as if she was getting enough sleep. "And the rest of it?"

She shrugged. "Okay."

I knew she wasn't really. "You will be," I said.

"It would be worse if I thought she'd killed herself."

"Not your mom."

"I'm seeing the therapist you referred me to. It helps. She says I'm prone to depression."

"And?"

"I need to monitor myself."

"Sound right to you?"

She thought about that. "Yeah, I guess. What do you think?"

"I think each one of us is different. The testing we did showed that you do have this difficulty processing the world around you. That means that when you get into a complicated situation, you may feel out of your depth, not sure what to do. The bad part is that the confusion can make you feel anxious and bad about yourself. Your therapist is right. Depression is something you need to be on guard against—at least until you find what you're passionate about in life."

I went on. "Don't forget, it's also compounded by your age. Your body is changing, your brain is being constantly barraged by hormones. It's natural for teenagers to experiment with different personas. But I suspect, when the dust settles, you'll be someone of substance."

Olivia stared down at her feet. She looked as if she wasn't sure how to handle the compliment. Finally, she said, "I brought you something."

She elbowed Matthew. He produced a small, flat package wrapped in blue paper with a yellow ribbon. He gave it to me.

"You shouldn't have . . ." I started.

Matthew snatched the packet back. "Shouldn't . . . have . . ."

Olivia put her hand on his shoulder. "Dr. Zak doesn't mean that, really. See his face? The mouth?"

"Smiling," Matthew said, and hesitantly offered the package to me again.

"Thank you very much," I said, taking it this time.

I was impressed with the way Olivia was helping Matthew, acting as interpreter, while at the same time teaching him how to interpret on his own.

"Aren't you going to open it?" Olivia asked.

I slid off the ribbon and tore away the paper. It was a framed picture. I turned it over. A black-and-white photograph — two women in diaphanous dresses, arranged in the crevices of a rock formation. A third one was intertwined in the limbs of a windswept cypress that grew up out of the rocks. It was erotic, disturbing. It was signed in the lower right corner: Annie Brigman, '08.

"I can't possibly . . ."

"You have to. Daddy got it for me for my birthday. And to tell you the truth" — Olivia screwed up her face — "I don't much like her work anymore. And I know you do."

I stared at the photograph, the young women merging into nature and disappearing. "Olivia, this isn't you," I said.

"I know." Olivia sounded surprised and pleased. "I made Daddy get me a digital camera. I'm a lot more interested in making my own pictures than I am in collecting them."

I said good-bye to Olivia and Matthew, and carried the photograph up to my office. I propped it up on my bookcase.

There were a couple of voice messages waiting. One was from my mother. An invitation to join her and Mr. Kuppel, her friend who worked part-time at our local video store. The two of them were going to a Bette Davis retrospective at the Brattle Theater. The movie was *All About Eve*, a rich melodrama in which a back-stabbing starlet destroys her older mentor. Mentoring is such a complicated dance, made more so when the leader weakens, when the follower strengthens. Missteps, hurt feelings, jealously, seem inevitable. In real life the drama had played itself out as double tragedy.

I called back and told my mother thanks, but I had another engagement—and I hung up before she could ask what. I opened up my calendar. I twisted my wedding ring as I glanced over the page filled with today's meetings and appointments. It was the evening and dinner with Annie that I was looking forward to. Tonight I'd unplug the phone, turn off my beeper. I savored the anticipation.

As I thought about that grilled steak and the special cabernet I'd been saving, I found I'd taken off my ring. I gazed down at it. I remembered when Kate slipped it on my finger during our marriage vows. She'd looked radiant, with flowers in her hair and a simple dress of white lace with a brilliant pink sash. I smiled at the memory. Even a few months ago, remembering brought only pain.

I kissed the ring and dropped it into my pocket.